Convergent Architecture

Building Model-Driven J2EE Systems with UML

Richard Hubert

Wiley Computer Publishing

John Wiley & Sons, Inc.

NEW YORK • CHICHESTER • WEINHEIM • BRISBANE • SINGAPORE • TORONTO

Publisher: Robert Ipsen
Editor: Robert Elliott
Assistant Editor: Emilie Herman
Managing Editor: John Atkins
Associate New Media Editor: Brian Snapp
Text Design & Composition: MacAllister Publishing Services, LLC

Designations used by companies to distinguish their products are often claimed as trademarks. In all instances where John Wiley & Sons, Inc., is aware of a claim, the product names appear in initial capital or ALL CAPITAL LETTERS. Readers, however, should contact the appropriate companies for more complete information regarding trademarks and registration.

This book is printed on acid-free paper. ∞

Published by John Wiley & Sons, Inc.

Published simultaneously in Canada.

This publication is designed to provide accurate and authoritative information in regard to the subject matter covered. It is sold with the understanding that the publisher is not engaged in professional services. If professional advice or other expert assistance is required, the services of a competent professional person should be sought.

Library of Congress Cataloging-in-Publication Data

Hubert, Richard
    Convertent architecture: building model-driven J2EE systems with UML
/ Richard Hubert.
      p. cm.
    "Wiley Computer Publishing."
    Includes bibliographical references and index.
    ISBN: 0-471-10560-0 (pbk.: alk. paper)
    1. Computer architecture. 2. System design. 3. Information technology.
I. Title.

QA76.9.A73 A82 2001
658.4'038'011--dc21   2001046537

Printed in the United States of America.

10 9 8 7 6 5 4 3 2 1

Advance Praise for *Convergent Architecture: Building Model-Driven J2EE Systems with UML*

"Software engineering is a well established discipline by now. However, the role and importance of a proper underlying architecture is very often not yet recognized by the software community. This book-with its positioning of architectural styles in general and the Convergent Architecture specifically-provides another major step towards the ultimate goal of architecture-driven software engineering. This is critical for companies that wish to meet the specific challenges of today's e-business world-flexibility and adaptability, time-to-market, and quality of software solutions. The author not only describes the fundamental principles of Convergent Architecture and the integration of system design with business and project design, but also covers the methodology, organizational structure, and support necessary to effectively translate the conceptual framework into action."

Jürgen Henn
Principal and Practice Leader, e-business Architecture Consulting
IBM Business Innovation Services

"Bridges generally work reliably. Large software systems generally don't. The essential difference is in design complexity, and in our inability to tame it. Ironically the management of this complexity has precedents in the architecture of buildings, and in this book Richard Hubert identifies the concept of Architectural Styles as the missing ingredient in large software initiatives. Architectural Styles and the Convergent Architecture are about systematic reuse and progressive refinement of collective software design wisdom. Anyone involved in complex software projects should read this book cover to cover."

Barry Morris
Chief Executive, Total Business Integration

"Engineers dream of a tool-supported design process for transforming high-level models of system requirements into robust systems. In software engineering there are many partial answers, but a comprehensive approach has been lacking until now. This book gives a lucid account of a full life-cycle approach to designing large-scale, Internet-oriented business systems where Model Driven Architecture, combined with a mature architectural style, is the key. Readers-whether managers, designers, or programmers-will profit from this and incorporate architecture-centric design in their own practice."

Dr. David Basin
Professor for Software Engineering
University of Freiburg, Germany

To Stephanie

OMG Press Books in Print

(For complete information about current and upcoming titles, go to www.wiley.com/compbooks/omg/)

- *Building Business Objects* by Peter Eeles and Oliver Sims, ISBN: 0-471-19176-0.

- *Business Component Factory: A Comprehensive Overview of Component-Based Development for the Enterprise* by Peter Herzum and Oliver Sims, ISBN: 0-471-32760-3.

- *Business Modeling with UML: Business Patterns at Work* by Hans-Erik Eriksson and Magnus Penker, ISBN: 0-471-29551-5.

- *CORBA 3 Fundamentals and Programming, 2nd Edition* by Jon Siegel, ISBN: 0-471-29518-3.

- *CORBA Design Patterns* by Thomas J. Mowbray and Raphael C. Malveau, ISBN: 0-471-15882-8.

- *Enterprise Application Integration with CORBA: Component and Web-Based Solutions* by Ron Zahavi, ISBN: 0-471-32720-4.

- *Enterprise Java with UML* by CT Arrington, ISBN: 0-471-38680-4

- *Enterprise Security with EJB and CORBA* by Bret Hartman, Donald J. Flinn and Konstantin Beznosov, ISBN: 0-471-15076-2.

- *The Essential CORBA: Systems Integration Using Distributed Objects* by Thomas J. Mowbray and Ron Zahavi, ISBN: 0-471-10611-9.

- *Instant CORBA* by Robert Orfali, Dan Harkey and Jeri Edwards, ISBN: 0-471-18333-4.

- *Integrating CORBA and COM Applications* by Michael Rosen and David Curtis, ISBN: 0-471-19827-7.

- *Java Programming with CORBA, Third Edition* by Gerald Brose, Andreas Vogel and Keith Duddy, ISBN: 0-471-24765-0.

- *The Object Technology Casebook: Lessons from Award-Winning Business Applications* by Paul Harmon and William Morrisey, ISBN: 0-471-14717-6.

- *The Object Technology Revolution* by Michael Guttman and Jason Matthews, ISBN: 0-471-60679-0.

- *Programming with Enterprise JavaBeans, JTS and OTS: Building Distributed Transactions with Java and C++* by Andreas Vogel and Madhavan Rangarao, ISBN: 0-471-31972-4.

- *Programming with Java IDL* by Geoffrey Lewis, Steven Barber and Ellen Siegel, ISBN: 0-471-24797-9.

- *Quick CORBA 3* by Jon Siegel, ISBN: 0-471-38935-8.

- *UML Toolkit* by Hans-Erik Eriksson and Magnus Penker, ISBN: 0-471-19161-2.

About the OMG

The Object Management Group (OMG) was chartered to create and foster a component-based software marketplace through the standardization and promotion of object-oriented software. To achieve this goal, the OMG specifies open standards for every aspect of distributed object computing from analysis and design, through infrastructure, to application objects and components.

The well-established Common Object Request Broker Architecture (CORBA) standardizes a platform- and programming-language-independent distributed object computing environment. It is based on OMG/ISO Interface Definition Language (OMG IDL) and the Internet Inter-ORB Protocol (IIOP). Now recognized as a mature technology, CORBA is represented on the marketplace by well over 70 Object Request Brokers (ORBs) plus hundreds of other products. Although most of these ORBs are tuned for general use, others are specialized for real-time or embedded applications, or built into transaction processing systems where they provide scalability, high throughput, and reliability. Of the thousands of live, mission-critical CORBA applications in use today around the world, over 300 are documented on the OMG's success-story Web pages at www.corba.org.

CORBA 3, the OMG's latest release, adds a Component Model, quality-of-service control, a messaging invocation model, and tightened integration with the Internet, Enterprise Java Beans, and the Java programming language. Widely anticipated by the industry, CORBA 3 keeps this established architecture in the forefront of distributed computing, as will a new OMG specification integrating CORBA with XML. Well-known for its ability to integrate legacy systems into your network, along with the wide variety of heterogeneous hardware and software on the market today, CORBA enters the new millennium prepared to integrate the technologies on the horizon.

Augmenting this core infrastructure are the CORBA services, which standardize naming and directory services, event handling, transaction processing, security, and other functions. Building on this firm foundation, OMG Domain Facilities standardize common objects throughout the supply and service chains in industries such as Telecommunications, Healthcare, Manufacturing, Transportation, Finance/Insurance, Electronic Commerce, Life Science, and Utilities.

The OMG standards extend beyond programming. OMG Specifications for analysis and design include the Unified Modeling Language (UML), the repository standard Meta-Object Facility (MOF), and XML-based Metadata Interchange (XMI). The UML is a result of fusing the concepts of the world's most prominent methodologists. Adopted as an OMG specification in 1997, it represents a collection of best engineering practices that have proven successful in the modeling of large and complex systems and is a well-defined, widely accepted response to these business needs. The MOF is OMG's standard for metamodeling and meta data repositories. Fully integrated with UML, it uses the UML notation to describe repository metamodels. Extending this work, the XMI standard enables the exchange of objects defined using UML and the MOF. XMI can generate XML Data Type Definitions for any service specification that includes a normative, MOF-based metamodel.

In summary, the OMG provides the computing industry with an open, vendor-neutral, proven process for establishing and promoting standards. OMG makes all of its specifications available without charge from its Web site, www.omg.org. With over a decade of standard-making and consensus-building experience, OMG now counts about 800 companies as members. Delegates from these companies convene at week-long meetings held five times each year at varying sites around the world, to advance OMG technologies. The OMG welcomes guests to their meetings; for an invitation, send your email request to info@omg.org.

Membership in the OMG is open to end users, government organizations, academia, and technology vendors. For more information on the OMG, contact OMG headquarters by phone at 1-508-820-4300, by fax at 1-508-820-4303, by email at info@omg.org, or on the Web at www.omg.org.

2001 OMG Press Advisory Board

Karen D. Boucher
Executive Vice President
The Standish Group

Carol C. Burt
President and Chief Executive Officer
2AB, Inc.

Sridhar Iyengar
Unisys Fellow
Unisys Corporation

Cris Kobryn
Chief Technologist
Telelogic

Nilo Mitra, Ph.D.
Principal System Engineer
Ericsson

Jon Siegel, Ph.D.
Director, Technology Transfer
Object Management Group, Inc.

Richard Mark Soley, Ph.D.
Chairman and Chief Executive Officer
Object Management Group, Inc.

Sheldon C. Sutton
Principal Information Systems Engineer
The MITRE Corporation

Ron Zahavi
Chief Technology Officer
MedContrax, Inc.

Contents

Acknowledgments

I would like to thank and at the same time congratulate the many convergent engineers and information technology (IT) consultants who have helped evolve, test, and refine the concepts of the Convergent Architecture throughout numerous projects. This includes, of course, the consultants and developers at Interactive Objects Software GmbH, who continue to serve as sparring partners and codevelopers of the Convergent Architecture. The contents of this book bear clear witness to the value of our long-term team effort.

Although this book builds on the accomplished works of many experts, particular recognition goes to my friend and mentor, Dr. David A. Taylor, who not only helped the IT industry explain object technology to the masses but also back in 1995, with his book on convergent engineering, helped us discern the critical path of IT architecture through the next decades of the Internet age. Without David's contribution, the "Convergent" in Convergent Architecture would not exist.

Last but not least, I would like to thank my reviewers, in particular Dr. Jan Vester from Simulacrum GmbH and Axel Uhl from iO GmbH, whose relentless constructive feedback and attention to detail helped improve this book in many aspects.

Foreword

Imagine if every office building was designed and engineered from scratch. I mean truly from scratch, with each architect working from first principles to solve the problems of fabricating raw materials, achieving structural integrity, providing protection from the elements, putting out fires, moving people among the floors, and delivering air, light, power, and water to the occupants. It would be a disaster. The costs would be astronomical; each building would be an isolated tower of one-off systems, and maintenance would be an engineering nightmare. Worse, catastrophic failures would be so routine that they wouldn't even make the morning paper.

Does this sound familiar? It should; it's a fair portrayal of how business software is designed and constructed today. The results are no better than we have a right to expect.

Someday, application development will outgrow its painful adolescence and gain the kind of maturity that building architecture now enjoys. As with modern office buildings, business applications will be assembled out of proven components that offer standard solutions to recurring problems. Each will be a unique construction, but—like buildings—they will share compatible subsystems, be easily maintained, and deliver reliable service.

This book is a seminal contribution to that goal. It offers, both through its content and by the example it sets, the possibility of coherent architectures for business software. The particular architecture it describes, the Convergent Architecture, may well be the most comprehensive, detailed framework ever proposed for large-scale business applications. Although many parts of the architecture are new, it incorporates the best of current practices, such as Model Driven Architecture (MDA), Responsibility Driven Design (RDD), and the Unified Modeling Language (UML).

The inspiration for this architecture is a discipline called convergent engineering—a discipline my colleagues and I developed a decade ago to facilitate the design of scalable, maintainable business systems. The founding premise of convergent engineering is that the design of a business and its supporting software should be one and the same. For each key element of the business, there is a corresponding software object

xvii

that acts on its behalf. These objects come in many forms, but they fall into three broad categories: organizations, processes, and resources. Rules govern how these three kinds of objects can be combined and how they interact. For example, processes consume and generate resources, and can take place only in the context of an owning organization. These rules bring useful order to the difficult task of re-engineering a business, and they do so in a way that directly specifies the software to support that business.

Richard Hubert learned convergent engineering in May 1996, when he took my week-long certification course at the Convergent Engineering Institute (CEI). Within a year, Richard had gone on to receive his master's certificate, entitling him to certify others, and had opened the second international branch of CEI in Freiburg, Germany. He and his staff of consultants at Interactive Objects Software (iO) were soon using convergent engineering in large-scale development projects throughout Germany, combining it with other techniques to expand it into a more comprehensive architectural style.

Frustrated by the lack of adequate tools, Richard and his team began developing software to better capture the results of their design efforts and to automate the generation of code. The end result was the release of iO's award-winning ArcStyler product, a suite of tools that models a business in terms of organizations, processes, and resources, and then drives that model into an executable system that can be deployed on any of the major Java application servers. Remarkably, the business model remains visible throughout the development lifecycle. If a process is improved or an organization restructured, the necessary changes are made to the corresponding business objects using high-level design tools, not by altering the low-level code. The tool is a compelling demonstration of Convergent Architecture, and it gives the architecture a solid grounding in the hard realities of software development.

The architecture described in this book is a significant contribution to the software industry on two distinct levels. At the most evident level, it provides a detailed prescription for application development, one that can be adopted as is or adapted as desired. At a deeper level, it illustrates the kind of effort that will be necessary to impel the industry out of its prolonged adolescence and into a mature engineering discipline. For the first time, we have a coherent, compelling vision for application architecture combined with precise instructions for implementing that vision, including all the necessary tools to go from concept to code. It is a combination that is certain to raise the bar for the application-development community.

—**David Taylor, Author,** *Business Engineering with Object Technology*

Introduction

But what's the point of having everything measured by poles? Why not build everything higgedy piggedy, like a house?

First, because it's cheaper this way. All the arches of the arcade are identical, so we can re-use the falsework arches. The fewer different sizes and shapes of stone we need, the fewer templates I have to make. And so on.

Second, it simplifies every aspect of what we're doing, from the original laying-out — everything is based on a pole square-to painting the walls — it's easier to estimate how much whitewash we'll need. And when things are simple, fewer mistakes are made. The most expensive part of building is the mistakes.

Third, when everything is based on a pole measure, the church just looks right. Proportion is the heart of beauty.

Ken Follett, The Pillars of the Earth

Would any serious engineer design a jet airplane with a helicopter propeller on top of it? Common sense would tell any decision maker that such an aircraft would hardly be able to take off. And the approaches and methods used in mature engineering disciplines, such as aeronautics, simply prohibit such a development.

Yet, irrespective of your position in the information technology (IT) industry, you will almost definitely have come across a software system or an IT organization that very much looks like a jet airplane with a helicopter propeller on top of it. Even though as members of the IT industry we are aware of the problems of poor design, inefficient organizations, and ad-hoc solutions, most of us have been asked to buy, design, or participate in the development of such a thing. What is it that distinguishes mature engineering disciplines from our industry? The answer is *architectural style*—the main topic of this book.

Have you ever wondered why system development is still so complex despite the rich array of products, techniques, and tools available today? Certainly, modern development aids such as design methodologies, patterns, computer-aided systems engineering (CASE) tools, Web application servers, and packaged solutions—just to name a few examples—can serve as useful parts of an IT strategy. However, just having these diverse parts is not enough. To be effective, all these pieces must be positioned within the context of an IT architecture. Few would dispute this statement, but repeatedly achieving good IT architecture in diverse situations has long been an elusive task. This is mostly because trying to nail down the key aspects of IT architecture leads to some other fundamental questions:

- What role does IT architecture play in our overall IT strategy, and what does this look like?

- How can we repeatedly achieve the advantages of solid IT architecture across multiple teams and even across globally distributed organizations?

- How can our existing IT organization evolve to new levels of architectural quality in realistic increments?

- Can we define and implement an architectural big picture that realistically simplifies all our diverse IT constellations from a single project to a global IT landscape?

These are some of the questions answered by this book, which defines IT architectural style and demonstrates its advantages using a mature architectural style called the Convergent Architecture.

The qualities of good IT architecture have always been difficult to define and even more difficult to reproduce consistently in practice. In fact, many of the qualities of good IT architecture have been so elusive as to remain undefined and unnamed on the whole. This book is about capturing these qualities and making them systematically attainable in practice.

First and foremost, this book explains and applies IT architectural style. It defines IT architectural style and gives a vague and amorphous set of key architectural qualities both a name and a number of tangible features. Then the major portion of the book proceeds to show how these features are applied in the Convergent Architecture. The Convergent Architecture not only clearly demonstrates how architectural qualities are captured in IT architectural style, but also proves that they can be consistently applied, taught, and effectively automated using available technologies. It explains how the Convergent Architecture resolves many of today's complex IT-related problems at the source instead of just dealing with their symptoms. By addressing the sources of error and complexity, it revolutionizes the effectiveness of IT teams and, more significantly, of whole IT organizations—with the returns increasing in proportion to the size of the organization. In short, this book demonstrates how to achieve a new level of quality in IT systems. And this quality now has a name: Convergent Architecture.

Second, this book can be seen as the applied sequel to Dr. David A. Taylor's book entitled, *Convergent Engineering: Business Engineering with Object Technology* (Wiley 1995). The Convergent Architecture was born out of applying the concepts of Convergent Engineering in diverse corporate environments. One of its principal goals is to transport the vision of Convergent Engineering into the field of applied architecture. In doing this, it shows, for example, how to apply the Rational Unified Process and the concepts of the OMG Model Driven Architecture (MDA) to achieve Convergent Engineering using state-of-the-art tools and technology.

Third, this book is for practitioners. It is written not only for IT strategists and chief architects, but also for project managers and developers in the field. Although beginning with the important conceptual underpinnings of IT architectural style, it quickly moves into the nuts-and-bolts usage of Convergent Architecture. The concepts, techniques, and tools employed in this book have been tried and tested in practice. They are the result of hands-on experience in diverse environments. Based on this experience, the Convergent Architecture has defined how to optimize the application of the Unified Modeling Language (UML), the Rational Unified Process (RUP), and J2EE/EJB to achieve new levels of architectural integrity. It demonstrates how all these parts work together in an integrated tool environment, the architectural IDE. In this sense, the Convergent Architecture is an architectural style for MDA as currently envisioned by the OMG. As long-time members of the OMG, we are actively participating in the MDA initiative in order to ensure alignment of the Convergent Architecture and to help drive progress in this very promising area of standardization.

Lastly, this book presents an IT architectural style to the public. It puts a stake in the ground by defining something concrete that can be used, discussed, and improved on by many parties over time. We are convinced that the Convergent Architecture constitutes a reasonable and logical step in the ongoing evolution of the Information Age. In other words, we do not think that it is a question of whether many of the concepts demonstrated in this book become widely used in the software industry; rather, it is just a question of when and under what name or designation.

We also believe that after reading the first few chapters of this book, strategic decision makers will feel at home with our approach to continuous long-term improvement. One of the primary goals of the Convergent Architecture is to help strategic IT managers at the corporate level to instill a sense of overall direction and purpose into their IT strategy. It should help them remove numerous sources of complexity and stress across their entire organization and help them put an end to the frustrating cycles of reactive symptom control. By introducing the era of corporate architectural style, the Convergent Architecture will help IT managers open new doors to otherwise unachievable returns at all levels of a business.

How This Book Is Organized

This book proceeds with increasing levels of detail. It begins with the design and justification of IT architectural style in general and moves on to explain each part of the Convergent Architecture in a logical manner. The coverage of the Convergent Architecture begins with an outline, or roadmap, and then drills down into the specific features of the roadmap. Each subsequent chapter then describes the design and justification of one of these features. It also explains how to apply this feature beginning at the level of individual projects on up to the level of corporate IT organization.

Chapter 1 introduces the concept of architectural style in general and its potential in the IT field. Analogies and examples are used from other industries to explain the significant advantages attainable through an IT architectural style. It also defines IT architectural style and its design—its structure, models, principles, and relationships—and the application of a style in reality-scale situations.

Chapter 2 provides an overview and roadmap of the Convergent Architecture as an IT architectural style. It describes how the concepts and design from Chapter 1 are applied in the Convergent Architecture. It also presents the anatomy and the big picture of the Convergent Architecture, introducing each stylistic feature and its advantages in real-world projects. Each feature is then detailed in the remaining chapters of the book.

Chapter 3 justifies and defines the Convergent Architecture metamodel. This top-level feature of the Convergent Architecture composes the long-term vision and fundamental design principles of the architectural style.

Chapter 4 presents the Convergent Component metamodel as a prime vehicle of the architecture. This is the first of three design models that visibly transport the principles from Chapter 3 into real-world modeling styles, techniques, tools, and automated infrastructure mappings. It defines the application of MDA and an architectural tool suite (the architectural IDE) in the context of an architectural style.

Chapter 5 outlines the IT organization model and its application of the RUP. This model constitutes a concrete reference frame for the business of building IT systems in the context of an architectural style. It defines the organization, workers, roles, tools, and interactions of all stakeholders in the Convergent Architecture.

Chapter 6 presents the Development-Process model, which complements the IT organization model. This detailed development process constitutes an applied instance of the RUP and its architectural tool support in the context of the architectural style.

Chapter 7 illustrates the integrated architectural tool suite and how it supports the architectural style as defined in Chapters 1 through 6—how it supports the component, organization, and process models of the Convergent Architecture. The tool suite, known as an architectural IDE, is described in detail. The chapter exhibits how the concepts of MDA and the Convergent Architecture are applied using an available architectural IDE (ArcStyler) that embeds and drives best-of-breed component tools such as Rational Rose, JBuilder, and diverse J2EE/EJB application servers in the context of the architectural style.

Chapter 8 is a tutorial that applies the concepts of the Convergent Architecture in an end-to-end example using the architectural IDE. It exhibits each step of the model-driven development process from the initial business design through to the generation, deployment, and testing of J2EE/EJB components, including their Web services and Web front-ends. It shows how MDA is supported by the architectural IDE to develop and manage all four tiers of the J2EE blueprints (J2EE Blueprints 2001) in the context of a comprehensive architectural style.

In addition, a bonus chapter in Microsoft Word format can be found on our companion Web site (www.ConvergentArchitecture.com), which constitutes a reference manual and user's guide containing the design and usage details of the MDA modeling styles and the J2EE/EJB technology mappings that were introduced in Chapter 4 and applied throughout the book. It also shows how these features are explicitly supported by the architectural IDE. This detailed reference material is available on the Web so that it may be easily maintained, thus providing the reader with an up-to-date version at all times. However, the material in this chapter can only be properly understood and applied when read in conjunction with this book because the chapter makes extensive reference to the architectural concepts, terms, processes and tools covered in Chapters 1 through 8.

Who Should Read This Book

A variety of readers will be interested in the subject matter covered in this book, each from a different perspective. The following reading sequence is recommended for each respective audience:

- CEOs/CIOs and business consultants will find the message regarding IT-architectural style and Convergent Architecture in Chapters 1 through 3 of particular relevance. For the next level of detail, they should proceed to the introductions in Chapter 5, "The IT Organization Model," and Chapter 6, "The Development-Process Model."

- Chief architects, IT consultants, project managers, lead developers, and those interested in the OMG Model-Driven Architecture Initiative are the prime audience for the entire book.

- J2EE/EJB developers and Web service developers may want to first read the tutorial example (Chapter 8) to get a hands-on feeling for the development process and environment, and then move to the chapters explaining the development process (Chapter 6), the architectural IDE (Chapter 7), and the details on the Modeling Style and Technology Projections (the bonus Web site chapter). At some point, Chapter 2 should be read in order to better understand the big picture and roadmap of the architectural style.

Tools You Will Need

The examples in the first seven chapters of this book, as well as the hands-on tutorial in Chapter 8, use the following tools to demonstrate the model-driven approach and the integrated architectural environment:

- **A J2EE/EJB application server.** Borland Application Server, BAS 4.5 or higher, available from www.Borland.com, or the WebLogic Server 6.1 or higher, available from www.BEA.com.

- **Java IDE.** JBuilder or JBuilder Enterprise version 5 or higher, which includes the BAS application server, available from www.Borland.com.

- **UML Modeling Tool.** Rose 2001 or 2001A Modeler Edition or higher, available from www.Rational.com.

- **Architectural IDE.** The latest release of the ArcStyler Architectural IDE for MDA, available from www.ArcStyler.com.

The Convergent Architecture Web Site

Of course, it is impossible to put everything concerning the Convergent Architecture into a concise book outlining the entire architectural style. Extensive material pertaining to the Convergent Architecture is available in addition to this book. Also, the Convergent Architecture continues to evolve, so new material and updates will emerge. Thus, a Web site has been created to accompany this book with new and complementary material in a readily accessible forum at www.ConvergentArchitecture.com.

The basic contents of the site are as follows:

- Tutorial and sample material applying the Convergent Architecture including its MDA/RUP features and tools

- References, case studies, presentations, papers, and demonstrations

- Extended specifications and user guidelines

- Reusable assets ranging from open-source, reusable projectware to extension modules for the architectural IDE

- Updates to the architectural IDE and related product information

- Contacts, community, and event information

From Here

The concepts, techniques, and tools presented in this book have been applied in numerous IT environments, both large and small, to achieve significantly higher levels of IT effectiveness. The purpose is to enable corporate architects, CIOs, project managers, and individual project team members to immediately leverage MDA in the context of a holistic architectural approach by applying a well-defined IT architectural style.

We hope that the definitions and examples in the initial chapters convince you of the far-reaching advantages of IT architectural style as we define it. Above all, we hope to convey the advantages of a tried and tested IT architectural style, the Convergent Architecture, as a lasting remedy to significant problems experienced by almost every IT organization today.

The bottom line is that the Convergent Architecture was developed by practicing IT architects to help any IT endeavor achieve higher goals. It is about making the sum of our efforts much greater than the individual parts. It is about defining how we approach business design, project design, and system design at all levels of an organization in a cumulatively synergistic manner. It is about putting diverse pieces together in a holistic big picture to provide IT organizations with a long-term vision and lasting improvements. It is about achieving a consistent cycle of simplification and optimization across the entire landscape of IT development and throughout its long-term evolution. And it's about the positive energies that we all share when we do things with style.

IT-Architectural Style

Professional engineering disciplines use architectural styles.

In many industries, engineers repeatedly improve on large, complex systems and achieve impressive levels of productivity and quality. What enables industrial architects and airplane and automobile engineers to deliver solid improvements year after year? Why is the software industry still a far cry away from such engineering maturity? A key answer to both these questions is architectural style.

This chapter introduces architectural style as a crucial element of mature engineering disciplines and suggests how it may be applied to obtain the same levels of maturity in the information technology (IT) industry. First, this chapter looks at how architectural style has been used for centuries to ensure the success of major engineering efforts. History reveals architectural style as the most important means of efficient, high-level communication among developers. Without it, we would not have many of the masterworks of architecture and engineering that we now take for granted. After the short historical outline, I define modern IT-architectural style and explain how it may be applied to improve software development significantly across the board.

This chapter focuses on the definition of architectural style, its elements, and its principles in the context of software engineering. These concepts form the design foundation for the *Convergent Architecture*, an IT-architectural style. You should read this chapter if you want to understand the concepts of IT-architectural style above and beyond their specific application in the Convergent Architecture. Above all, this chapter is important if you want to create your own IT-architectural style or contribute to the further development of the Convergent Architecture.

Discovering the Source of High Returns

In the mid- and late 1990s, I was involved as chief architect in several large projects. The requirements in these projects were all quite similar and are common to almost every large institution: An established IT organization with a complex, heterogeneous landscape of mission-critical systems needed to modernize and Internet-enable its corporate IT infrastructure. My mission in each case was to establish architecture-driven design in the existing IT organization and to return the internal IT team to the point of self-sufficiency using modern architecture, tools, and technologies. I did not want to leave the team with a short-term solution; to the contrary, the biggest problem was the existing ad hoc landscape of short-term solutions. In each project I was continually confronted with one central problem: How to effectively instill architectural concepts into the entire organization? How to get everybody working constructively and in concert toward the common goal? How to make this a permanent process of optimization, in every discussion, at every level, without requiring an experienced architect to be omnipresent in each instance? In other words, how to establish IT architecture as a culture, a school of thought across the entire organization, and not just as another short-term solution?

These are not easy questions to answer as any lead developer or project manager can confirm, although they are by no means unusual. Consultants are paid to deal with just these types of problems. However, there was something else bothering me. I had a feeling that we—the IT field at large—were still missing out on some approach, some technique, something, whatever it was, that other industries use in such situations. It just appeared to me that other industries have reached a level of architectural competence and expression that we had not yet reached. I could not put my finger on it, but the feeling grew with each day. Maybe this nagging feeling came from my background first as a chemical engineer and then as an IT architect. In any case, I wanted to figure it out and to see if I could apply it to solve my problem.

My search intensified. I was reading everything about project management, process methodologies, and IT design that I could get my hands on. As early as 1994, this search took me to Austin, Texas, to hear Jim Coplein (1995), a father of the pattern movement, speak about IT design patterns. Indeed, patterns were helpful, as they still are, but neither patterns nor any other available IT knowledge allayed my suspicion that we were still missing something, that there was more to this than meets the eye. Thus, I broadened my search to include more and more cross-industry sources on product design, civil architecture, and project management.

I am not sure exactly when, but with time, the answer began to evolve, and one day, a form began to appear in the fog. However, I do know when I became certain that I had the answer and, at the same time, that I also knew its name: *architectural style*. I had picked up a book in Atlanta, Georgia, in 1997 in a bookstore specializing in civil architecture. The book was a compilation of German manuscripts that had been translated into English. The original texts had been written by a group of architects in a period from 1828 to 1847 at the University of Karlsruhe, Germany. The book was titled, *In What Style Should We Build? The German Debate on Architectural Style* (Herrmann 1992). While I was reading about these disputes, everything started to fall into place. These architects were debating contemporary architectural style, but it was clear from the discussion that the Greeks had started this debate thousands of years ago. It turns out that this thing called architectural style is a powerful design and communication tool that the entire IT field has been missing out on. It was clear to me that we had not yet reached the level of design communication already in use many years ago in other industries. Finally, I had found an effective and lasting way to solve my problem. I had seen proof that it works, and I even knew its name. I knew where I needed to go. Now I determined to get there.

That was 1997. Since then, a lot has happened. Over time, I used my observations on architectural style to define a form tailored for use in the IT field, which I call *IT-architectural style*. My colleagues and I also developed a particular IT-architectural style, the *Convergent Architecture*, which has evolved and has been refined through intensive use over the years. The Convergent Architecture is a concrete application of IT-architectural style that makes up the lion's share of this book. First, however, I would like to share with you some of the observations and analogies that helped me not only comprehend architectural style in general, but also understand how it can be applied to achieve manifold benefits across the field of IT design and system development.

Before I get started, it is important to note that the concept of IT-architectural style appears to be a logical and natural evolution in the field of IT architecture—it is in the air. My early start elaborating, developing, and practicing IT-architectural style has been encouraged by increasing evidence from respected sources that I am on the right track. In recent years I have seen the term *architectural style* mentioned repeatedly in the IT context, albeit briefly and at a contemplative level. One notable reference here is the "Introduction" to the *Rational Unified Process* (Kruchten 1998), which I can recommend for its concise introduction to IT architecture in general. In his book, Mr. Kruchten briefly mentions the relevance of architectural style as a viable IT-architectural concept. I agree, of course, that an IT-architectural style increases both the uniformity and understandability of designs. Kruchten and I are also in vehement agreement that an IT-architectural style achieves this, for example, by optimally combining patterns, tools, descriptions, and frameworks to better support IT architects. It is now time to take a more in-depth look at IT-architectural style both in theory and at work.

A Long History of Success

At a first glance, it is difficult to recognize the use of architectural styles in some industries. This is because no industry uses architectural style exactly as another industry. Each has its own terminology, its own unique, customary way of doing things. This means that architectural style appears in various shapes and forms, making it sometimes difficult to see parallels between industries. However, these parallels—the use of some form of identifiable architectural style—do exist. We will look at a few of these parallels in the rest of this section to better understand what architectural style is and how it can significantly improve the way we work in the IT industry.

Architectural styles have been around for thousands of years. For example, Greek architects spent hundreds of years perfecting an architectural style: the Ionic temple architecture. Civil architects consider the Parthenon in Athens to be the epitome of the Ionic temple—meaning that it is the exemplary instance of an architectural style. Over the years, hundreds of architects built hundreds of temples according to this style, each making his or her own contribution to its perfection over time. Each of these contributions was to the clear advantage of the next generation of architects as well as the benefactors of each individual temple. In modern terms, we would call this a win-win situation.

Ionic temple architecture is not an isolated example. Gothic[1] architecture was perfected in the same manner over hundreds of years. Each Gothic cathedral, for example, is an instance of the Gothic architectural style. The architect of each cathedral based his or her complex design on the proven achievements of other professional architects who had used the Gothic style to build other cathedrals. In turn, many of these architects made contributions to the Gothic style to the benefit of the next generation. The architectural style evolved, step by step, through generations of highly skilled designers. No single designer, no matter how skilled, could have achieved this feat alone. If you ever have the chance to travel in Europe, it is fascinating to visit and observe the churches and cathedrals bearing clear evidence of the evolution of several distinct architectural styles. For example, early Gothic churches consisted of basic pointed arches with thick walls, small windows, and low ceilings. They were pretty dark and dreary. This was so because the architects of that period did not yet know how to effectively combine high ceilings and large windows. Hundreds of years and hundreds of churches later, the same style had evolved to manifest magnificent vaulted ceilings, large windows, and thin walls supported by flying buttresses on the outside. Notre Dame de Paris, the Koelner Dom in Cologne, Germany, and the Strasbourg Munster in France are prime examples of highly evolved Gothic architecture. Engineers still marvel at these masterworks. None of this would have happened without the cooperative culture of architects contributing to incrementally improve the architectural style. Each instance of the style, each Gothic structure, consists of contributions accumulated and refined over hundreds of years, all adding up to significant engineering progress.

From a more modern perspective, the similar use of architectural style can be observed in every mature engineering discipline, from boat design to city planning, from airplane design to automobile production. Prime examples of architectural style in the automobile industry are the roadster, the pickup truck, or the Formula One racing car. In the aerospace industry, we can easily distinguish jets, helicopters, or even Zeppelins as clear representatives of architectural style analogous to the Gothic architecture just described.

A Higher Level of Communication

Not only does the architectural style define how things look—cathedrals, cars, airplanes, and so on—it also often defines other critical design properties such as aerodynamic features, tolerances, and capacities. In addition, it defines how these properties may be achieved dependably with particular materials, tools, and forms (or patterns). Whether it needs to define these aspects, and how it precisely defines them, depends on the particular field. Moreover, where easily distinguishable styles turn up depends on the field. In the automotive industry, for example, we recognize several distinct styles of motor design (Otto, Diesel, or Wankel), each manifesting an intense focus on the intricate performance and thermodynamic properties of internal combustion engines (compression ratios, combustion chambers, fuel mixtures). The consistent evolution of motor performance over the past decades, with little change in their external form, emphasizes that styles also convey hard-to-see design optimizations, not just the definition of external form.

An architectural style expresses the language and design culture that helps stakeholders at all levels to communicate at a higher, more effective level. All mature schools of art, engineering, and science have their own special languages that have evolved over years to help experts express themselves more accurately. If you listen to a group of surgeons conversing during an operation, you probably would not understand much, but they are communicating in a highly effective manner. They are versed in the language of their trade. Such languages are more highly developed, meaning more expressive or more formalized, in some fields than in others. Civil architects have most actively addressed their special language, as indicated by such titles as "The Classical Language of Architecture," "Classical Architecture: The Poetics of Order," or "A Pattern Language" (Alexander 1977), where the grammar and vocabulary of various architectural styles are discussed. For example, terms accurately describing structures such as arches (archivolt, architrave) and columns (Ionic, Doric, Corinthian) are the words of an architectural language. Correspondingly, the organization of structures with respect to one another forms the grammar of the language: The rose window of a Gothic cathedral is always round and is placed above the portal. These words and the grammar are then used to express complete styles—Gothic, Romanesque, Ionic—just as styles of writing, theater, and poetry exist in literature.[2] The style is the next higher level of design expression.

In an IT-architectural style, this translates to, for example, the use of accurate terms for component structures and their relationships to express something the architect considers to be of higher value. In the Convergent Architecture, such structures are its *convergent*[3] *organizations, processes,* and *resources* (OPRs) and their relationships. Processes and resources are managed by an organization; a process consumes and produces resources, and so on. Together, and only together, these characteristics lead to the high-level property of convergence in a system based on the Convergent (style) Architecture.

Clearly, there is still much progress to be made concerning the language of IT architecture. Today the common language used by IT designers is very weak. Even though they often use the same words, they are not communicating well. All too often, we experience IT design situations in which people have to explain the terms they use from ground zero. Such meetings can go on forever while making little progress, and everyone has to explain their basic words and grammar to each other every time a new group convenes. Viewpoints then change from one meeting to the other, so the whole frustrating process starts again. It is not just the rare or special term being discussed, but very fundamental concepts such as basic component designs or role definitions. It is as if each designer had entered the meeting having defined his or her own private time system. First, the whole group must discuss and agree on the time system before a simple time plan can be made. Inevitably, each individual will define terms differently. It is no wonder that IT projects are so expensive and high-risk.

The agreement on a language, on a particular style, is often more important than the language itself. No architectural style claims to be the only way to build something, nor does it claim to have found some absolute truth. An architectural style is always a proposition. It is putting a stake in the ground. It is saying that people can build something successfully if they agree to work this way. In other words, there is more than one way to skin a cat, and there will always be several ways to define an architecture. However, this did not keep civil architects from agreeing on architectural styles, whether Gothic, Romanesque, or Renaissance, and then using and refining these styles for hundreds of years. They understood that the major benefits are attained as soon as an organization agrees on an architectural style, not beforehand. By the same token, what large IT organizations need is less philosophical discussion regarding absolute truths and more agreement on an architectural style.

Thus, to improve the present situation immediately, designers can start by agreeing on a common basis; they can begin at the level of an existing architectural style. This provides a common reference frame in which words and other critical design features are defined accurately. Designers then begin communicating at an effective level and can work from there. In addition, using an architectural style as the basis for definitions means that the developers do not have to convince the whole world that their definition is the correct one. Establishing a worldwide standard, that is, a worldwide definition, for the many aspects of architecture is not something that most designers have time to do. Besides, it may be an impossible task anyway. This is one reason architectural styles exist in most fields. The architectural style lets large communities of designers work more effectively without having to wait for the whole world to agree on something. In other words, the style complements worldwide standards with stylewide standards. It defines the common dictionary of a specific architectural language. The language can be used across time, persons, and projects to communicate better. Needless to say, the design patterns movement and standardization work on component models, such as J2EE/EJB, have been a very significant step in the right direction. However, someone still has to define exactly what forms of the patterns or components are being used and how they will work together to add relevant advantages. As you will see, an IT-architectural style does exactly this by incorporating tools, techniques, patterns, and component standards as part of its language. It then goes on to refine the language in additional important areas. These additions enable, for example, a more accurate expression of such things as architectural principles, development life cycles, tool integration, or the relationships among project, business, and system design.

Once an organization has agreed on an architectural style as its language of IT architecture, it can move beyond improved communication in the development organization to improved communication between all levels of the business. For example, the Convergent Architecture formalizes the expression of business-IT convergence by defining convergent organizations, processes, and resources as parts of its language. These elements form a sort of architectural grammar that has both business and technical significance. This means that business specialists can use these elements to communicate with technical specialists, and vice versa. Misunderstandings and culture clashes are avoided from the outset. For example, when a designer and a business strategist discuss a billing process, both of them know exactly what is meant by a billing process. Once this level has been achieved, the next level is possible. This is where the IT system graduates from being a tool for implementing business strategies to an effective business optimization tool. In 1995, Dr. David A. Taylor explained how this works in his book entitled, *Convergent Engineering*. The Convergent Architecture is the IT-architectural style that then transports these concepts into applied system design. Introducing an IT-architectural style therefore is one of the best investments an organization can make toward business optimization in the Information Age.

More than a Macro Pattern

Why don't we just call the IT-architectural style a macro pattern or meta pattern? The simple answer to this question is: for the same reason we do not call a component a macro-object. The best reason to introduce a new word is to denote important differences. The word component was defined in the IT field to distinguish it from an object or a macro-object. Although components leverage object technology, they add significant design aspects such as composition and deployment on top. To use the word object to refer to both objects and components would simply confuse two important concepts. By the same token, an IT-architectural style is more than a pattern. It uses and consolidates specific patterns, but not all patterns. In addition, it comprises other development aspects such as component standards, modeling languages, business design concepts, and technology mappings. It even includes its own streamlined development process. Thus, just as components accompany and complement object technology, IT-architectural styles leverage and complement patterns.

The Next Level of Design

An architectural style constitutes the next level above applied architectures. This level is the place where design knowledge of all sorts is packaged to be reused by many individual architecture projects. It is the level where proactive design preparation takes place that enables design projects to get off to a better start. This means that we now recognize the following three levels of development, beginning with the architectural style at the top and ending with the finished system or construction.

The architectural style.   Examples of this would be, Gothic (civil) architecture, the Diesel (motor) architecture, and the Convergent (IT) Architecture. This level is developed and maintained outside a particular production project.

The architecture.   This is an instance of the architectural style,[4] the application of the style for a particular situation. For example, the architecture of Notre Dame de Paris is an instance of the Gothic architectural style, the architecture of the CAT900 series diesel motor is an instance of the Diesel style motor architecture, and the architecture of the Travel Exchange portal is an instance of the Convergent Architecture style. Normally, the chief architect or the corporate architecture team leverages an architectural style to develop many compliant instances over long periods of time or across many projects in parallel.

The system or construction.   This is the end result, the system or construction itself. There may be any number of systems or constructions, each being an individual instance (or incarnation) of the architecture. Examples are the Notre Dame de Paris cathedral itself, each and every CAT900 series motor built, and release 2.0 of the Travel Exchange portal. Each of these is the result of an individual production project to construct something according to the architecture.

An Everybody-Wins Approach to Quality

One of the most important aspects of an architectural style is its built-in quality controls. The style will only survive if it offers tangible, long-term engineering value. Its contributors are a diverse group of practicing developers who carry out their day-to-day business using the architectural style. It is critical to their success in real-world situations. The use of new concepts and technologies in the style will not be accepted without first completing ample due diligence. The temptation of quick fixes or marketing-driven technology trends[5] is reduced because the designs must stand up to maximum scrutiny by quality-conscious peers. Developers gladly participate in a perpetual cycle of reuse, evaluation, and improvement because it is an everybody-wins situation. This is because everyone benefits from improvements in the style, and every repeated application of the style contributes to higher quality. This process of nonpartisan evolution helps ensure that the architectural style remains a high-quality engineering instrument.

One way the architectural style ensures an increasing level of repeatable quality is by prescribing properties of design. In addition to properties, it also may prescribe procedural aspects of development. It is the repeated use of these properties that distinguishes an architectural style from ad hoc approaches in terms of both recognition and quality. For example, Gothic cathedral architecture strictly requires the building to be cruciform. It also prescribes numerous form characteristics of its portals and windows. These mandatory characteristics constitute key elements of the architectural style. This does not mean that the style is a straightjacket for the designer or that it dictates every last detail. However, the mandatory elements, even when subtle, exist for good reasons: They increase quality for all users of the style. Whether this quality is measured on an engineering, aesthetic, or even a theological scale depends on the target group of the style. An architect recognizes the value of these mandatory elements and makes creative adaptations only within the degrees of freedom they allow. This is why the architects of Gothic cathedrals did not randomly mix in stylistic elements from Romanesque architecture. If they had, they would have taken unnecessary risks. In this respect, an architectural style is also like a good recipe. You can make creative alterations in many areas, but to arrive at the intended dish, you had better pay attention to the advice in the recipe, even if it appears to be minor at first glance. If the recipe says to add a pinch of salt and you decide to dump in the whole box of salt, then you have missed the point.

The consequences of disregarding the advice of a recipe are obvious to us all. However, complex systems—buildings, motors, airplanes, IT systems—all possess subtle design elements that are far from obvious. Often, these elements must act in concert with others across the entire design to produce the desired effect, no single one of these elements being visibly critical in its own right. For example, it took several decades, numerous companies, and hundreds of engineers to figure out how to build motors that did not knock and rattle. The changes made were hardly visible in each new generation of motor. This is because they consisted of hundreds of small changes at many places in the motor, which made a big difference only when they worked together. Lastly, it is important to note that these consolidated efforts to constantly improve quality did not happen in single projects, in single companies, or in standards organizations; they happened at the everybody-wins level—at the level of architectural style.

Evolution without Revolution

An architectural style evolves continuously to take advantage of the best available techniques and technologies. Entire communities of developers repeatedly create instances of the style. Over time, situations arise within this community in which a developer is able to make an improvement to the style itself. Normally, an improvement is first made in a particular project, for whatever reason. After proving itself in the field, the improvement may be added to the style as a whole. This happens on a regular basis. If it did not, then the style would not be in use for very long. This is so because the users of the style expect it to leverage the best technologies available. Depending on the field, this evolution can be very rapid. Formula One motors, for example, evolve at an extremely rapid pace. A corresponding example from the Convergent Architecture consists of the many improvements to leverage new Internet and component standards such as J2EE/EJB or CORBA components.

Often, the variations made to a specific architecture, an instance of a style, are not general enough to be candidates for the style itself. Instead, they are adaptations made by the designer to meet the special requirements of the particular situation. No one Gothic church, for instance, is exactly the same as another. This is because every town in which one was built had special requirements and constraints, such as the availability of building materials, machines, and labor. The wishes of the church community or bishop to create something special and unique also played an important role. It is important to note that changes were not made to the style itself. In fact, the style supported such efforts by freeing the architect from the standard engineering problems and allowing him or her to be creative in completely new areas. The architectural style did not hinder creative design modifications to meet these needs. It simply defined a standard reference frame—not a normative standard—by which both developers and users of the enhancement orient themselves. This brings us to another point regarding standards and architectural styles.

An architectural style is never finished until the community of designers stops finding improvements for it or until it just goes out of style. The Ionic temple is an example of both these situations. First, its architectural style went out with the dispersal of ancient Greek culture. The religious reasons to build such temples became a remnant of history. However, the Parthenon is still considered to be the epitome of an Ionic temple. Constructions based on its architecture were built hundreds of years later in Rome, Paris, and even Thomas Jefferson's Virginia.[6] Each of these reproductions bears witness to the relevance and value of an accomplished architectural style, which is reused as is, perfectly fulfilling its purpose each time.

There are also cases of architectural styles experiencing a renaissance by being reactivated into the active engineering mainstream. Often, it is sufficient for just a few parameters to change within the paradigm, such as the availability of certain materials, a new processing technology, or a shift in the economic settings in order to give the style completely new potential. The crash of the *Hindenburg* in 1937, for example, put an abrupt end to the first era of Zeppelin-style airships. The Zeppelin style, however, has now been revived and further evolved. Modern cargo airships are now being designed by several large consortiums to transport certain goods much more economically than airplanes. These are continuations of the Zeppelin architecture—a clearly distinguishable architectural style.

If so many persons are using and contributing to the architectural style, then who defines and maintains it? I refer here to the current owner of the style. This is the person or group of persons who are both respected practitioners in the field and are willing to manage the process of consolidating diverse inputs, publishing new reference documents, and informing all interested parties. This can be a tricky situation because, conceivably, two parties could claim concurrent ownership to a particular style or two diverging branches of the style. Such branches are a healthy and natural consequence of evolution. To prevail over time, an architectural style clearly must have an active owner or an owning group and contributors who continuously use and add value to the style.

Adding Innovation while Hedging Risks

An architectural style defines how standards are best applied, as does any good architecture. However, it hedges risks by providing an additional level of verified innovation above and beyond standards. Risk is always associated with development projects. This is because designers must break new ground to add value or to build unique solutions. Widely accepted standards do not provide complete systems; they are, at best, parts of a complete solution. The cost and risks due to necessary innovation above and beyond standards are usually extremely high. This is especially true in the IT industry, where intrepid optimism often leads to the fiery death of projects. An architectural style hedges these risks by providing a level of innovation that has been developed and evaluated by many experts. In other words, it lowers the amount of experimentation necessary. It also ensures that the innovations preserve architectural integrity and do not lead to the long-term problems of ad hoc design.

Consider the following scenario: The Triple-A Motor Company wants to develop the most modern diesel motor on the market and has a few innovative ideas for technical improvements on currently available diesel motors. Now, the current normative standard for fuel injection in diesel motors specifies the use of mechanical injection, whereas modern diesel motors all use electronic injection to achieve superior performance. In other words, the standard says to use mechanical injection, whereas the architectural style has already evolved to electronic injection. If the Triple-A Motor Company remains at the level of the standard, it is no longer competitive, and if it reinvents electronic injection, it has added no value. Thus, instead of developing the electronic injection, Triple-A uses the design, tools, and instructions of others who have added this (nonstandard) innovation successfully to the diesel motor. Achieving this level of innovation, often referred to as the *industry standard*, is provided by the architectural style, not by the standard. At this point, Triple-A can better afford to add its own unique innovation, such as a new cylinder geometry, without taking on unnecessary risk. If things are not working out with the new, experimental cylinder geometry,

Triple-A can fall back immediately to an industry standard electronic injection motor. By doing this, Triple-A has hedged its risk. If things go well, the new motor sets a new level of industry standard. Some day, this feature may even become part of an official international standard. In other words, if the experiments fail, then Triple-A still has a marketable fallback, ensuring that it can deliver and that it will live to try again another day. This scenario emphasizes the important role architectural styles play in helping developers use standards effectively to manage risk and maintain a future-safe architecture.

There is an additional advantage: Since Triple-A will build many generations of diesel motors in the future involving many different design projects, it defines and maintains its own corporate architectural style. The style provides stipulations regarding critical design and process features, such as its new cylinder geometry. By using the corporate style, projects are less likely to diverge from the path of architectural integrity. In addition, each project can better reuse not only design know-how, but also parts, tools, infrastructure, and procedures. This reduces both risks and cost by improving the overall quality of design information.

The Importance of Style in IT Architecture

Thus, why is it that architectural styles are not yet widely used in the IT industry? This is most likely due to the relative youth and fledgling status of the IT industry as compared with others—we just have not gotten to it yet. Certainly, technologies and techniques are being handed down across generations of IT engineers. This happens today in the form of patterns, frameworks, methodologies, and blueprints. However, this is not happening at the level it could—not at a level commensurate with the architectural styles found in other industries and not at the level distinctly possible today in the IT industry.

There is a second reason of equal importance: You cannot see the 90 percent of the design (or lack thereof) of IT systems without tools. In contrast to every other type of system or construction, you cannot stand in front of a running IT system and see how it was designed. Humans do not have sense organs for the virtual worlds of IT. The only thing a human can easily judge is the human interface of an IT system. This is the tip of the iceberg. Many a system has been delivered with adequate (or inadequate) user interfaces but with a design and implementation more characteristic of a time bomb than anything else. The problem is that you cannot walk into an IT system like you can walk into a house or a cathedral and experience, with eyes and ears, aesthetic pleasure or easily observe many parts of its structure. This is also the reason poor design often goes unnoticed in the traditional IT industry. This is particularly disconcerting because IT systems are almost pure design. Aside from the hardware, few raw materials are required to produce and run IT systems. Even more unusual, there is virtually no raw material cost to reproduce software. Essentially, design work dominates the cost of building and maintaining software systems.

The fact that IT systems are design-intensive virtual worlds means that models and tools take on a particular importance. IT development tools are the *only* means for a human to see and manipulate the IT architecture effectively. There is a lot of room for improvement here not only in the use of tools, but also in the tools themselves. To ensure the effective visualization and manipulation of its specific virtual world, an IT-architectural style must address the area of tools and their use. The tools will evolve with the style that makes them more effective with each generation. Ironically, other industries have been more aggressive in their move to computer-aided design (CAD) tools than the IT industry itself. This situation is especially baffling because before the advent of CAD tools, these industries could at least physically see and feel their prototypes and constructions. This is not the case with the IT industry. Without the proper design tools, a developer of large-scale systems is practically blind. The result of this blindness is easy to see in the problematic ad hoc architectures that plague large organizations today. Sooner or later, the increasingly critical role of IT will force these organizations to move to an IT-architectural style that defines tools to visualize and manipulate effectively all levels of design. Only with such tools will an organization finally be able to view and verify its IT-architectural style and thus its architectural integrity.

To date, the open-source UNIX and Linux community has achieved the most significant step in the direction of architectural style in the IT world. The evolutionary development approach to Linux offers undisputed proof of the benefit and productivity of the everybody-wins situations I associate with architectural style. However, in the IT world, there is much more potential in architectural style than anything currently available. This is why I am reluctant to call UNIX or Linux an architectural style despite their success. I could live with calling them a strong forbearer and a case in point of many advantages promised by IT-architectural styles. In the following chapters I will define what I consider to be the features and the potential of a modern IT-architectural style.

My colleagues and I consider IT-architectural style to constitute a natural and inevitable step in the evolution in the IT industry. I will not just leave you with this assertion and some historical analogies; I will back this up in later chapters with a concrete IT-architectural style, the Convergent Architecture, as proof of my conviction. Having said this, I reiterate that I certainly have not perfected the universal definition of IT-architectural style or even arrived at the epitome of a single IT-architectural style. However, I am convinced that we are on the right track and continue gaining experience with an ever-increasing number of talented designers. Exciting progress is already being made with the Convergent Architecture, which makes up the lion's share of this book. My intention in this book is, in fact, not at all a debate on IT-architectural style in general. My primary goal is to explain how pragmatic advantages can be achieved today with the Convergent Architecture. With it, I hope to convince you of the virtues of IT-architectural style and win you as a fellow designer in a rewarding cultural experience along the road to the next generation of IT systems.

Designing an IT-Architectural Style

Thus far I have introduced architectural style in general, mostly from a historical perspective. It is now time to move to the present-day situation and concentrate on IT-architectural style from the perspective of software design. In this section I outline a design for *any* IT-architectural style. The Convergent Architecture constitutes a particular IT-architectural style. However, any other IT-architectural style may be formulated or enhanced according to the design presented here.

First, since everyone likes short, one-sentence summaries, no matter how broad the field, I will begin with a condensed phrase for the concept of architectural style that includes IT-architectural style:

> *An architectural style conveys the principles and the means to most effectively achieve a design vision.*

The basic concept of an IT-architectural style also can be derived from the widely accepted definition of IT architecture established by the IEEE Computer Society (IEEE 2000): "Architecture is the fundamental organization of a system embodied in its components, their relationships to each other and to the environment, and the principles guiding its design and evolution." Based on this definition, it can be said that

> *An architectural style is a family of architectures related by common principles and attributes.*

An IT-architectural style is both a holistic and a specific approach to IT architecture. It is holistic in that it covers the entire software life cycle, including project design and tool design aspects. It is specific in that it consolidates and integrates the many structural, procedural, and descriptive aspects that have been addressed as separate entities in traditional methodologies. Every experienced developer or project manager has at some point suffered through the integration and coordination of such critical elements as tools, patterns, component technologies, and methodologies, just to name a few. These things are intimately related to each other, and to work well together, they must be considered together, as pieces of a whole—holistically. Once this has been achieved, the structure, relationships, and application of each of the pieces must be simplified by being as specific as possible about its nature and its use.

In other words, the IT-architectural style addresses both breadth and depth. It tackles the problem of the "big picture" while being specific about the parts of the big picture. This is important in today's complex world of specialists: Somebody has to specialize in the relationships between all the specialties—somebody must specialize in the big picture. This role can be compared with that of a composer. The composer focuses on creating a (whole) concerto to be played by musicians using (specific) instruments. Every experienced developer knows how difficult it is to make all the parts of an IT development work together in concert. Defining and implementing such aspects as the right process in conjunction with the effective use of component standards, patterns, tools, and implementation technologies are daunting tasks even for experts. Many a project has met its demise by attempting to make all these things work together while at the same time trying to develop a system—like trying to compose a concerto before understanding the musical instruments. The proactive definition of the big picture and instructions on how it is applied specifically across many projects are not just desirable; they are critical for large software organizations.

The breadth and depth covered by an IT-architectural style enable even the best IT organizations to achieve higher levels of effectiveness and returns. For example, consider the long-awaited breakthroughs due to object technology, many of which have eluded the entire industry for years. Contrary to what is often written in the IT tabloids, it is not the fault of object technology that many of these breakthroughs have not yet been realized; rather, object technology has been a victim of ad hoc architecture. In other words, the failure is due to a reluctance on the part of companies to address tough IT architectural issues. Just as an apple tree will not bear fruit if it is planted in the desert, the advantages of object technology cannot be cultivated without the proper IT environment. An IT-architectural style defines this environment. It defines how reuse is to be handled in the entire development life cycle across all projects in an enterprise. The high-level returns due to reuse, just to name one advantage of object technology, can now occur realistically in the context of the IT-architectural style discussed in this book.

This brings me to the inevitable question of whether the breadth-and-depth approach of an IT-architectural style is realistic. This question often arises because breadth, or holistic, is often confused with generality. Breadth does not mean that the IT-architectural style is completely general in nature and thus of limited use in practice. This would conflict with the requirement that it be specific. Breadth means that it coordinates a wide spectrum of activities and structures. Specific means that it does this down to a level that is detailed enough to be applied effectively and rapidly. Can this be achieved while still being useful for diverse systems across entire organizations or domains? Yes, it can. In fact, this is what good architects achieve in all industries. It requires one of the most important skills of an IT architect: the skill of abstraction. Over time, the designers of the style recognize simple, widely applicable solutions that can be used to solve specific problems. Design patterns are one example of such useful design abstraction. Carefully selected design abstractions are then coordinated as a whole to form an IT-architectural style. This continuous process of abstraction, selection, and specific coordination is paramount. More formally, it can be said that *an IT-architectural style provides a useful set of reasonable alternatives—not all alternatives—and coordinates them to work well together.*

This can be achieved at a level that meets the needs of entire domains and entire organizations. The Convergent Architecture is my proof. An example scenario from a mature industry should make this point more obvious. Suppose an airplane manufacturer wants to build the next generation of planes. It is clear that an architectural style exists for each of the broad areas of propeller planes, jet planes, and helicopters. Each of these architectural styles supports an entire industry. A single manufacturer uses one of these styles, not all three at once. Our particular manufacturer envisions building the best jet planes on the market. Even though a new generation or new model of plane is being built, the manufacturer will start with the existing jet-plane style. The designers do not start by considering all alternatives; instead, they start more effectively by considering the reasonable alternatives offered by the style. For example, the style does not offer them the alternative of a helicopter propeller on top of a jet plane. Sure, this is imaginable, but it has obvious drawbacks. The reason a jet-plane style omits this as a viable alternative is evident. However, thousands of more subtle design decisions, each expressed by the reasonable alternatives in the style, are far from obvious. Such things as material choices, thrust requirements, and the intimately related guidelines for shape and weight distribution are the result of millions of dollars of research and experimentation over many decades. The jet-plane style helps the designers proceed with a high return on investment to build the next generation of jet aircraft. However, this style will not help them build a helicopter—that is a completely different animal, even though both of them fly. More important, if the jet-plane designers want to use liquid hydrogen as a fuel instead of standard aviation fuel, they will have to make modifications to the style. The style helps them with all the rest of the decisions, but it does base its design on the reasonable assumption that the standard fuel will be used. In contrast, it does not prevent the designers from making alterations for liquid hydrogen in a specific instance of the style.

By comparison, if one looks at the IT industry today, one observes a whole lot of jet planes with helicopter propellers on top. This is so because designers are not yet working at the level of architectural style. Instead, they reinvent, beginning at an extremely low level each time. It does not help if they can buy expensive components from the marketplace—the propellers and turbines of the IT world—if these are not applied properly. Without an IT-architectural style, the developers cannot leverage the millions invested by others in experimentation and research. They are unaware of the extremely subtle but decisive design decisions made in previous, very similar designs. They are bound to repeat a lot of costly mistakes. The bottom line is that most production IT systems in large enterprises will remain at the level of initial experimentation—the experimental prototype—until an IT-architectural style is introduced. Nobody ever built a modern jet plane without using an existing architectural style as a stepping stone. The same logic will apply for IT systems in the future.

The IT-architectural style explicitly targets the problem of unnecessary complexity in IT architecture. It simplifies the design as well as development work by showing why things are done and how things work together in the overall big picture. It achieves this by starting from its basic principles. From these principles, it derives, justifies, and explains each level and part of an architecture, including process and tool aspects. This means that the concepts of IT architecture can be taught, or at least clearly explained, to key individuals at all levels of an enterprise—starting with top-level management. These concepts are then applicable to not just one, but all systems and designs using the architecture, such as the entire IT of a major organization. Based on their common knowledge of why things are done, the proper persons can be actively involved at each level of design. This means that better decisions are made, systems become more effective, and risks are removed from development.

This also means that IT-architectural style is most valuable when used as the basis for entire IT infrastructures. Although it can be used for individual projects, the most compelling reason to introduce an IT-architectural style is its ability to support architectural integrity across many projects. This is so because it replaces many ad-hoc designs with a single, well-understood style. Its holistic approach to the software life cycle enables IT managers and developers to base entire IT landscapes on the style and to evolve such landscapes in a controlled manner over long periods of time.

Getting down to detail, the remaining sections of this chapter define the features and principles of *any* IT-architectural style. This sets the stage for the remaining chapters of this book, which detail a concrete architectural style, the Convergent Architecture. Chapter 8 then shows, step by step, how an actual instance of the style is created and used in a concrete development situation.

The Four Features of an IT-Architectural Style

An IT-architectural style comprises four high-level features, or layers. These features have been distilled out of observations from diverse IT architecture projects over the last decade. They have been identified as critical to the success of an IT-architectural style. In addition, several principles are deemed particularly important to the designer of any IT-architectural style. These are also covered in this section. Needless to say, the process of analysis and evolution of these concepts continues.

An IT-architectural style fulfills its purpose by implementing these four features.

1. **An architectural metamodel**

2. **A full-life-cycle development model**

3. **A full-coverage tool suite**

4. **Formal technology projections**

The Architectural Metamodel

The architectural metamodel is the top-level model. It is a metamodel, meaning that when applied, it produces or influences another model as its result. In this particular case, the architectural metamodel influences practically every decision made in the entire architecture. It does this by defining the vision and principles of the architecture. It sets the fundamental judgment criteria for every design decision, analogous in many ways to a constitution, which sets the judgment criteria for legal decisions. The metamodel justifies why we do things the way we do throughout the architecture and provides the basis for individuals to make the proper decisions at all levels. It is the reference frame in which the architecture is refined and evolved over time. It also defines under which constraints such refinement and evolution take place.

The principles in the architectural metamodel can be seen as the basis for the laws of the architecture. These principles describe the important high-level vision and goals of the style, and they do this in a way that can be understood by a large, diverse audience. This is important from the perspective of architectural integrity because only persons who understand where laws come from normally will follow them or even change them in a coordinated manner. In other words, it permits people to start communicating in terms of the vision and the principles that determine its design character—the elements characteristic to the particular style. This level of communication is key to achieving a set of common goals. For example, the long-term vision of convergence in the Convergent Architecture has a significant impact on all levels of its design, its development process, and its use of tools and technology. Once the concept of convergence has been understood, stakeholders can see and comprehend more easily how the other layers of the style achieve this vision. By understanding the principles driving design decisions, people are put in control of technology instead of technology controlling them. They begin to understand and see how technology is being applied in the context of a style to realize its principles across any number of projects. They begin to perceive the important role they play and become more involved in the creative improvement of the design. This is the first important step toward creating a design culture of people who share a common sense of style. Having a shared culture and a shared sense of style is the best way, if not the only way, to achieve long-term architectural integrity.

A few analogies may serve to illustrate the significance of the architectural metamodel. Good examples of this metalevel are the Bible, the Koran, the Communist Manifesto, or the United States Constitution. Each of these defines specific visions, principles, and identifiable elements of style for religion or for government. The mere success of these pillars of religion and government is evidence enough that this level of formal communication is necessary in many cases and at least advantageous in others. The fact that we start at this level in an IT-architectural style may rub some persons the wrong way at first sight; however, we are just dealing with reality. Beliefs, whether they be religious, political, or architectural, are the only way to bind persons into a strong culture over long periods of time—in this case into a culture of solid IT architecture. People get emotionally involved in their beliefs, not in their knowledge. The IT industry is no exception to human nature. For example, the commonly cited "IBM culture" and the "Microsoft way" bind people by the beliefs and principles they share. They are not bound by their technical knowledge, which could be applied at either company. In civil architecture, a prime example of a large group sharing common principles is the Bauhaus school of architects. Bauhaus began in Europe around 1919 (Droste 1998) and remained active in the United States through the 1950s, where it gave rise to the International Style of civil architecture (Heyer 1993). Bauhaus produced astonishing works of architectural and product design, most of which are still in mainstream use. The shared set of identifiable principles helped these groups of individuals work together, over long periods of time, to achieve a common goal. The architectural metamodel serves this purpose in IT architecture.

A precise example at the level of an architectural metamodel from the Bauhaus school was their vision to harmoniously unite form and function in their designs. In other words, they believed that an aesthetically pleasing form should not be something added after the structural engineering is finished. Their slogan was "Art and technology, the new unity." Essentially, this meant that every design element could be structurally functional while at the same time contributing to a pleasing form. This was a real challenge, but the Bauhaus school of designers *believed* that it should be done, and they succeeded. Their achievement of this vision and their contribution to architecture and product design remain undisputed to this day.

A corresponding example from the architectural metamodel of the Convergent Architecture is its long-term vision of convergence. Essentially, convergence says that business and IT models can be united into one common model. This vision, which also can be formulated as a set of principles, motivates and justifies many decisions throughout all levels of the Convergent Architecture, and it is responsible for many of its most recognizable elements of style.

The architectural metamodel helps avoid risk by clearing up potential misunderstandings and disagreements early. Using the architectural metamodel, the chief architect puts a stake in the ground and defines a clear, long-term direction—the architectural vision—for an entire organization, not just for one project. This extremely important step is carried out by any professional civil architect at the outset of a major undertaking. It is important for two reasons. First, the chief architect must have a long-term strategy and communicate it clearly at all levels of an organization. Without such a long-term strategy, the proliferation of ad hoc architecture, both at business and IT levels, cannot be avoided. Second, if the stakeholders are not clearly informed and in agreement regarding the strategy, big problems will arise later. The later these problems arise, the worse they are. Take a look at cities around the world to see clear proof of this point. To cite a couple of positive examples, both Paris and Washington, D.C., owe much of their lasting beauty first to a chief architect with a clear, long-term vision and second to stakeholders who joined in and supported this vision over many years. Without the clear architectural vision, neither of these impressive, lasting achievements in civil architecture would have occurred. A clear architectural vision is particularly important with respect to IT systems. This is so because, contrary to civil architecture, the soundness of an IT system is not clearly visible to anyone who cares to look. The state of today's IT systems bears ample evidence of the problems that creep up behind the scenes due to an unwatched architecture. The architectural metamodel is the most important step toward resolving this problem: It tells the stakeholders first that there is something to look for and then, in principle, what it should look like. The rest of the architectural style picks up at this point and provides the necessary detail.

It is clear that if an organization cannot agree on the general principles of the architectural metamodel, then agreeing at every other level will be an even bigger problem. This means that the only way to avoid the problems of ad hoc architecture is to agree on an architectural style, beginning with the basic principles in the architectural metamodel.

The Full-Life-Cycle Development Model

The second-level model is the *development model*, and it defines how we achieve the vision and fulfill the principles expressed in the *architectural metamodel*. It formulates and transports principles into concrete structures, such as components and development organizations, as well as procedures, such as the development process. These structures and procedures are the vehicle of the architectural style.

Only with the existence of the architectural metamodel is it possible to define appropriate development structures. Let's return to the example from the preceding subsection, where we saw that the U.S. Constitution is at the level of the architectural metamodel. At that level, it expresses principles such as equality and the presumption of innocence. The vehicle of these principles, corresponding to the development model, is the judicial branch of the U.S. government. The concrete structure and the procedures of the entire judicial system are derived from the principles in the U.S. Constitution. Essentially, it would be impossible to set up an effective judicial system without the Constitution. By the same token, it is impossible to set up a highly effective development model without the architectural metamodel.

Similarly, referring again to the Convergent Architecture as an example in the IT field, the development model defines the specific structural features, such as *Convergent Components* for OPRs, within the architecture. In addition, a specific project organization and development process are defined at this level to effectively meet the particular requirements of the architectural metamodel. For example, a specific instance of the Rational Unified Process (RUP) is defined to most effectively prepare and erect convergent systems. Together, the specific structures and procedures are the prerequisite for a specific, highly effective tool environment, the job of the next layer of an IT-architectural style.

The managed evolution of an IT infrastructure would be very difficult without the development model. What, for instance, would happen if developers unilaterally changed fundamental design and development structures in individual projects? When things such as component models, techniques, and tools are defined unilaterally in individual projects, ad hoc architecture is the inevitable result. Without the development model, such changes occur automatically and unintentionally. There is no effective way for project managers or developers to synchronize themselves across projects without a common development model. The only way ad hoc dilution of an architecture can be avoided is to provide the lead designers of projects with a development model. If fundamental structural changes do need to be made, for instance, then they are made relative to the common model as used by all projects. Experts can then properly assess the impact on all designs, systems, and organizations, both present and future. At this point, a solid basis for a decision founded on dependable information exists. In addition, once decisions to modify the architecture are made, the migration of every aspect of the architectural style can be planned and coordinated properly. Above all, such decisions are not made in an ad hoc manner by, perhaps, the wrong persons. This is the most important step toward managed system evolution.

The development model is very different from generalized design methodologies in that it is concerned only with aspects specific to the particular IT-architectural style, not with generalized advice. For example, it should not present a discourse comparing various pattern approaches, development process alternatives, or component models. It should be as specific as possible, telling the developers which processes, patterns, and components to use and, concisely, why this choice was made. Whenever design options are provided, then precise decision criteria should be available as to when a given option applies. This is so because the probability of ad hoc and incompatible constellations increases with the number of unclear or competing alternatives.

To ensure adequate coverage (depth and breadth), the following three fundamental themes should be addressed by the development model:

The development structures theme.   This describes the concrete resources used to design, implement, and deliver the system. The focus here is on describing the structures to be built and the structures required along the design and development path. These include such things as layers of the architecture, component stereotypes with their models and their diagrams, and other artifacts used to construct and deploy systems. The ownership of these structures and how they are derived are described in the IT organization and development process, respectively. The full-coverage tool suite layer, presented in this chapter, outlines how these structures are manipulated and managed with the help of specific tools as part of the process.

The development process theme.   This describes the specific development tasks. These tasks focus on the creation and evolution of the development artifacts and are specifically supported by the tools and organization of the style. Its process should at least cover the entire critical development path, which must be defined by the style, including the repeat cycles necessary to address the change and evolution of the system properly. However, defining the process is not enough; it must be coordinated properly by an IT organization.

The IT-organization structure theme. This defines how responsibilities, roles, and persons are best coordinated to simplify and support the specific development process. Often, methodologies neglect the intimate relationship between the process and organization, assuming that the process is complete. However, no matter how complete and well-thought out the process is, there is no way to cover everything that can possibly occur during a development effort. An organization must be prepared to handle everything that happens in between and around well-defined tasks, both the everyday things and the surprises. In addition, not everything can or should be defined as a specific task. For example, attempting to define the activities of an IT architect as a series of tasks would be fruitless. The tasks are too complex and intertwined to be able to be described in an appropriate way. On the other hand, establishing an architecture organization with specific responsibilities and tools is extremely useful. Thus, the IT-organization structure both complements and supports the development process.

How each of these themes is presented is left up to the IT-architectural style itself. In any case, this entire development model will evolve with time, just as any other layer in the style. Things will be added, removed, modified, and refined in the spirit of an evolutionary approach.

The Full-Coverage Tool Suite

Based on the specific requirements set forth by the preceding features of the IT-architectural style, the third feature of a style defines effective tools to support architecture-driven development. Due to the coverage and specificity of the development model, tools can be designed, integrated, or implemented to actively assist style-conforming development. They can be tuned specifically to intelligently support development according to the development model. Without the previous definition of the features of the style, a comparable range of coverage, intelligent support, and tuning would be impossible. How else is the tool developer to know, specifically, what the developer requires?

Since specific requirements for tools are set in the models of the IT-architectural style, experts can be used to develop and tune the tools in one place to support all projects using the style. This means that the time, costs, and risks associated with tool development are reduced. Moreover, the tools are more effective. A project starting with the tools can get started faster, at lower risk, with fewer persons and deliver better results. This sounds like a marketing ploy. However, it is simply the result of sitting down and thinking about a shared IT-architectural style, including its tool suite, *before* projects are started. The situation is comparable in many aspects with the use of specialized CAD tools by manufacturing industries. First, the designers of the tool sit down and think about the specific requirements for their tool in a given industry context—not in all industry contexts. The specific CAD tool then can be applied to improve efficiency in many development projects within the particular industry. It is used to design various models and to support production, for example, in the special context of helicopters. Similarly, in the IT industry, we use the architectural tool suite to produce various models and to support production in the special context of a particular IT-architectural style.

The IT-architectural style improves the effectiveness of the development environment by raising its level of coverage and precision. The specific information regarding procedures and structures along the entire development life cycle permits tools to be developed that more specifically reflect the developer's intent and needs than can generalized tools. The level of assistance and intelligence of each tool can be increased. For example, a design model can be checked for its proper use of structural features such as patterns because the style defines which patterns are applicable. The tool also can actively clean and improve the model. It becomes a development environment in which the designer can add creative value rapidly instead of being confronted continually with the problems of tool integration and the poor performance of lowest-denominator tool support.

The Formal Technology Projections

As pointed out earlier, tools can be defined to support many more development tasks in the context of an IT-architectural style than would be possible without a well-defined style. Above all, significant new levels of automation are possible. Today the accepted level of automatic construction is the compiler. The compiler translates source code, such as Java or C++, into executable byte code or machine code. The compiler is a code generator that every developer takes for granted in everyday practice. Nobody in his or her right mind would consider producing machine code by hand. Instead, we program in a higher-level language, which is read by a generator—the compiler in this case. This generator gives us immediate feedback regarding many errors while allowing us to describe a program precisely at the level of source code. At this level, the source code can be seen as the model, which is interpreted by the compiler. The compiler produces a predictable result in every situation; it is a formal mapping of source code to machine code. Suppose now that we move our source code to a completely different type of hardware, where the machine code is different. Today's compilers take care of such tasks. The compiler on the new system generates the proper machine code with formally predictable behavior. In other words, the compiler, as a generator, formally projects the source-code model onto any number of different target platforms. We call this a *formal technology projection*.

In a modern IT-architectural style, the level and effectiveness of such formal technology projection are raised several levels above the compiler. This next level of technology projection is simply a natural evolution of the scenario presented in the preceding paragraph. In this scenario, the value of source-code-driven projection is very clear. There is no reason why this process cannot evolve to the level of model-driven projections to entire server platforms. Examples of such platforms would be middleware infrastructures, application server infrastructures, or even mainframe infrastructures. Model-driven technology projection simply means that we translate high-level models to entire IT infrastructures instead of just translating source code to machine code. Such higher-level generators cover much more ground than the source-code-based compilers while delivering comparable dependability and quality. There is no downside to this scenario if it is positioned properly as part of an overall IT-architectural style. However, if not used in the context of an IT-architectural style, such generators just become a faster way to produce ad hoc architecture.

Code generation from models is starting to catch on in the IT marketplace. However, generating code from just any model is the best way to produce a software landscape that practically nobody understands, nobody can reuse, and nobody can maintain. The models and tools of an IT-architectural style provide the only sound basis for high returns from the technology projection of models to diverse implementation technologies—not just to source code. Within the context of the IT-architectural style, the development model provides guidelines as to what models and their resulting systems should look like. The architectural tool suite then supports these design guidelines to help designers produce consistent models according to the organization's IT-architectural style. The tools can actively check models before generation, based on the guidelines for modeling and technology projection. This level of model checking is analogous to the immediate feedback provided by a compiler, only at a higher level. This is a best-of-both-worlds situation. The effectiveness of the generator is increased because a model contains more information about the entire infrastructure than just source code. The quality of the model is increased, which means that it is of more value as documentation and as a basis for design reuse. Lastly, the developer is more effective because much of the development work can now be completed, and verified, in a high-level model.

Technology projections are, as required by an IT-architectural style, as complete as possible. All the information a model can provide should be used to generate as much of the technology infrastructure as possible—reducing programming, configuration, and build environment development to a minimum. This is important because completing these tasks by hand adds virtually no value to the information already available in the model. To the contrary, these are the areas where, currently, much of the risk is incurred in projects. In contemporary development organizations, most of the time is spent coding by hand from poorly elaborated models. This is also where the most expensive mistakes are made—from both the short- and long-term perspectives. By raising the coverage and level of automatic technology projection, an IT-architectural style immediately increases quality and speed in individual projects while at the same time attaining the long-term cross-organization benefits of IT architecture.

Technology projections should be as formal as possible while not losing sight of usability; there is always a pragmatic tradeoff between usability and formal specification that must be made in each IT-architectural style. Although compiled programming languages are formal descriptions, most every level of abstraction above them is, at best, semiformal today.[7] For example, the widely accepted modeling language UML is semiformal and will remain so for some time. This does not mean that UML is not useful—to the contrary. However, the long search for the best possible mix of formal rigor and ease of use continues. This mix is not localized to one particular area of design. It stretches across the whole development process, from business model representations to technical model representations to technology projections of the models. This is why the entire process is covered by the IT-architectural style. It is a prerequisite platform for improving the interaction between design models and technology projection, an area where much progress will be made in years to come.

The technology projection must separate two life cycles that do not belong together: the life cycle of the business-relevant architecture models from the completely different life cycle of implementation technologies. Implementation technologies change at a breakneck pace. The market and vendors dictate these changes, not the system architect. Instead of evolving, implementation technologies often are simply replaced by alternative technologies. This pace of change is one of the most significant problems in today's IT systems. Contemporary design models, if they exist at all, are tailored to the underlying technology. They are more or less images of the implementation technology. In these cases, when the implementation technology changes or is replaced, the design model breaks with it. This is a big problem because it means that the life cycle of our business is disrupted by the life cycle of external software and the decisions of software vendors. For this reason, most design models seldom live longer than one system generation. Unfortunately so, because this means that the model never gets past the level of a prototype. Little or no incremental improvement takes place.

The bottom line is that the business and design models must live and evolve over time as independent as possible of technology life cycles. This is what the technology projection guarantees. It reads a design model and translates it to the current best implementation technology. It is a useful level of abstraction that cleanly separates the concerns of business and system modeling from their mapping to highly volatile, rapidly changing technologies. This enables the business and design models to improve over time in a natural, evolutionary manner.

The benefits of technology projection stem from a forward, architecture-driven approach.[8] As pointed out in the preceding paragraph, the clean separation of design from variants and the volatility of technology platforms can, with rare exceptions, only be achieved via forward technology projection. Normally, attempting to derive a model from the technology platform recouples the model with the life cycle and volatility of the platform or with the requirements of one particular platform. A good analogy to illustrate this point is the translation of human languages. Written language in the form of text is analogous to design models in that the text is a written, structured expression of ideas, in many ways similar to a modeling language. Now, suppose that we have an English text. We want to effectively improve and extend this text over time, analogous to the way we need to refine and extend a business model at our own pace, with many iterations. Forward-translating the English text to several different languages is relatively simple. This is comparable with forward-translating a design model to an IT infrastructure. Western languages are the simplest targets because they have Latin alphabets and similar grammar, but I can translate my English sentence to more exotic Asian and Arabic languages as well. I can repeat this forward-translation as often as I like, for every edition of my text and to any languages I want. Each new translation improves with the quality of my text. However, the reverse direction poses a major problem. If I try to recreate my text from any of these translations, it will be different. Not only the structure but often the precise meaning of my text will have changed and usually will differ from the ideas I originally wanted to convey. In addition, the recreated text is different for each language, even for the similar Western languages. Is this the same text? Are any of them better than my original? Can I ever get my original, which I understand best, back? The obvious answer is no.

From this scenario it is clear that the reverse derivation of nontrivial models from implementation technology, for whatever reason, does not meet our requirement. In other words, forward technology projection has every advantage, but reversing the process causes the exact problem that we are trying to avoid. A forward technology projection to, for example, various application servers on various operating systems or even to mainframe infrastructures is quite useful, even though each of these requires significantly different artifacts and code structures to represent the same model. In summary, a forward technology projection is the only long-term means to benefit from the positive aspects of new technology while protecting the business from its negative aspects.

Aspects Affecting Any IT-Architectural Style

A few general aspects or principles are of particular importance when creating an IT-architectural style. These aspects affect the refinement and use of each of the top-level features listed previously. If they are not taken into account when defining the style, then it will most certainly be more difficult to apply than it should be. Since this is not an introduction to IT design, I will not cover adjectives describing self-evident features of any good design, such as pragmatic, understandable, useful, adequate, and so on. This does not mean that these aspects should be ignored. It means that they are so basic to overall design that I consider them to be self-evident and omnipresent in every design decision of a skilled designer.

Specificity

Designers are paid to build systems and prefer to spend their time completing this task, not on preparatory work such as the invention or definition of an IT organization, the refinement of the development process, or tool integration—to name just a few. Sadly, most contemporary methodologies are collections of generalized best practices that are too nonspecific to be applied directly in a project. They require considerable tailoring, refinement, and experimentation before they can be used in a particular instance. In addition, they often contain many overlapping alternatives, obscuring any clear guidelines for their specific use to get the job done.

The closer we can come to a cookbook, the better, as long as our recipes are still valid for the situations at hand. In other words, the more specific an architectural style is, the better. Of course, the degree of specificity in any given area depends on the amount of flexibility required. This is where the architectural style can add significant value. The designers of the architecture preselect the most effective set of tradeoffs to best meet the goals of the architecture. The specific mixture of tradeoffs is precisely what differentiates one IT-architectural style from another. Referring once more to the analogy from the automobile industry, it is obvious that a roadster-style automobile addresses simply a different set of design priorities or tradeoffs than a pickup-truck-style automobile.

For another example nearer to home, the developers of the Convergent Architecture have taken volumes of generalized methodologies such as the Object-Oriented Process Environment and Notation (OPEN 1997) and the Rational Unified Process (RUP 1998) and filtered out the best set of *specific* practices for its style of design. It tightly integrates these specific practices and defines exactly how they fit together. The designer no longer has to deal with a sack full of alternatives and options. Instead, more specific roles, procedures, and techniques are applied using tools designed to support these specific features. The definition of specific techniques and procedures is clearly a prerequisite to defining high-productivity tools to support specific techniques.

Specific guidelines reduce ambiguity—a major source of error, risk, and cost. Without specific guidelines, it becomes next to impossible to build things to be compatible. Consider, for example, a scenario where several groups are given the task of building something as simple as a chair. If instructions are not given as to the height, size, and basic structure of the chair, every group will produce something different. However, since everyone knows from experience what a chair looks like, all the chairs probably will work. Now extrapolate this situation to something as complex as an automobile and as invisible as an IT system. It is clear that every bit of specific information, together with the quality of the tools, will help avoid frustrating problems, particularly when diverse groups build pieces of systems that should work together.

Specificity is not limited to low-level detail. It pays off at every level of abstraction. A high level of clarity and effective communication can begin just by naming the particular IT-architectural style. Compare this, for example, with the specification of cultural cooking preferences used by most of us quite frequently. A whole lot is communicated simply by specifying a French restaurant, in contrast to a Chinese or fast-food restaurant. Once the style of cooking has been named, many details are automatically clear to all parties involved.

Specificity, when done properly, is not synonymous with aggravating constraints. To the contrary, it means highlighting the best path to success in a complex constellation of alternatives. This is not something that happens as a by-product of day-to-day development projects. It is only achievable through a concerted effort by people who have enough experience and an ample portion of constructive foresight—the owner (or owners) of the IT-architectural style.

The Force of Entropy

Even in the field of software design, some laws of physics or, more precisely, laws of thermodynamics apply. To make progress, any engineer must recognize the fundamental laws of physics and act accordingly. Otherwise, bridges fall and software systems fail dramatically—sooner or later. Virtually all software systems today suffer to an unnecessary degree from the force of entropy.[9] The larger the system or set of systems, the worse the problem tends to be. An IT-architectural style is the best place to counter this trend.

Simply put, the force of entropy means that uniform disorder is the only thing that happens automatically and by itself. In other words, if you want to create a completely ad hoc IT architecture, you do not have to lift a finger. It will happen automatically as a result of day-to-day IT activity. Everybody has seen entropy at work. Most of us have worked hard cleaning out the attic or the garage. Who worked on creating the mess? Nobody, the mess happened by itself. The only way to prevent it is to work against it up front, by installing shelves, for example, or otherwise investing energy to better organize the attic or garage. In large software systems, the word architecture is synonymous with work invested at the proper level to organize the system. IT architecture defines the organization of a system. However, most IT architectures today are done within single projects or small groups of projects. This is like letting one person define the order and shelving in one portion of the garage and allowing others to determine it in other parts of the garage without thinking about the organization of the entire garage first. In this case, the entropy simply takes its toll at another level, namely, in between the projects and systems, which is not much better than no architecture at all. This is precisely the reason many companies have started addressing *Enterprise Application Integration* (EAI). EAI devotes itself to the problems caused by the lack of a holistic, overall architectural strategy. Unfortunately, EAI usually only deals with the symptoms of entropy, not the source. It only patches the problems caused by entropy. If EAI is not applied in the context of an overall IT-architectural strategy, it itself becomes subject to the force of entropy. This means that, over time, *EAI becomes part of the very problem it is attempting to solve.* The holistic approach taken by an IT-architectural style handles this problem at the proper level, across any number of projects and systems comprising an overall IT landscape, that is, across the whole attic or garage. It curbs the force of entropy not only within projects, but also across projects. This sounds like a lot of work, and it is, both for the owner of the IT-architectural style and for the chief architect in a large organization. However, the payoffs more than remunerate for the effort.

In summary, design levels that are left to chance will result in ad hoc, creeping entropy that significantly increases complexity—the source of most IT-related problems. In contrast, explicitly accounting for the intrinsic force of entropy (software entropy) will be the single most significant contribution to overall simplification an IT-architectural style can make.

The Designer's Paradox

Be aware of what some see as a paradoxical relationship between design flexibility and design coverage, known as the *designer's paradox.* There is a tendency to believe that to keep a design and its resulting system flexible and independent of change in a particular area such as technology, tools, or organizational structures, it is best to ignore this particular area in the design. In other words, if you leave it out of the equation, then you are free to change it at will. The contrary is true: If you want to be flexible and independent of something, it must be *explicitly* covered in the design; otherwise, you risk an *implicit* coupling that resists change.

For example, I once worked on a large project where the support of major organizational changes was of utmost priority. When I entered the project, I was confronted with a design that showed no trace of an organizational unit, although the current organization clearly had been used to partition the design. When I inquired how the team intended to repartition the system to fit new organizational structures, the answer was: We left the organizational structure out of the design to remain independent of it. The paradox was that this omission had the opposite effect. The current design was completely bound to the current organization—its partitioning of work, its access control, its profit centers. There was no clear way to reconfigure the system to compensate for significant organizational changes. To enable such flexibility, the design team had to introduce the concept of organizational structure into the models.

The apparent paradox here is that we are dependent on our design models and techniques to attain independence in our system. Our designs must explicitly focus on things that we want to flexibly change. This means *that to increase business flexibility, the business must be visible in the IT model.* If a business process needs to be changed, then it had better be visible in the design. Otherwise, time and effort will be wasted as well as risk increased just figuring out where the process is and how it can be changed. By the same token, *to achieve independence from the constraints of technologies, these constraints must be dealt with explicitly in the design style and in the tools we use.*[10]

There are two important messages here for the developer of an IT-architectural style. First, the style must try to cover all areas where independence and flexibility are required in the business of building IT systems. Second, the style and its tools should avoid constraints that would inhibit them in their capability to achieve flexibility through design. To the contrary, the style should increase design expressiveness while at the same time simplifying the design and development process as a whole. This principle alone rules out most, if not all, fourth-generation language concepts and tools as candidates for IT-architectural style. Although such tools may simplify some particular situations, they also severely constrain the designer.

Organic Order

Many observations of the Bauhaus school of architecture and modern architectural icons such as Christopher Alexander directly apply to the field of IT architecture. An aspiring IT architect can learn a great deal from such observations, which are not limited to the domain of civil architecture.

Of these observations, the principle of organic order as formulated at length by Christopher Alexander (Alexander 1975) is particularly important when developing an IT-architectural style. In short, he states that "[A rigid master plan] . . . creates an entirely new set of problems, more devastating in human terms than the chaos it is meant to govern." This principle emphasizes that properties of complex systems cannot be predicted over long periods of time no matter how gifted the designer. For this reason, these properties cannot be determined or governed by a rigid master plan. The principle of organic order also confirms that the long-term success of large system designs is as much a factor of the people involved and their motivations as of the techniques and technology used.

This is another way of saying that waterfall-like development efforts do not work in the area of complex system design. Thus, a good IT-architectural style will consider the human-organizational requirements of IT development in addition to the development structures and the development process. It also will foresee an iterative, incremental approach and the distribution of responsibilities required to achieve healthy organic order.

Organizational Evolution

Large IT projects place significant requirements on both the IT organization and other organizations of the business. To achieve positive change, these organizations will have to adapt. Sadly, the capability to adapt also must evolve; most organizations resist change. They too can only evolve incrementally. Alexander (1975) refers to this as "piecemeal growth." The bottom line is that the architect must view business organizations as living systems, not formally designed machines. Thus, a successful IT-architectural style will assist the architect in achieving incremental evolution at the organizational level in addition to the technological level.

Correspondingly, Dr. David A. Taylor (Taylor 1997) observed that the long-term goal of any business must be to reduce the impedance to positive change. It must strive to evolve organizations from reactive to creative adaptivity: "Move organizations from a reactive to pro-active adaptivity and then from pro-active to creative adaptivity." How well this human factor can be supported actively by an IT-architectural style is questionable. However, the owner of the style certainly can recognize this goal to ensure that its features and tools, as well as the systems produced using the style, do not constitute an additional barrier to creative adaptivity.

Describing the Style Using Standards

The holistic breadth and specific depth of an IT-architectural style require the expert integration of diverse notational and description standards. No one modeling or notational standard could be expected to effectively cover the entire development life cycle at so many levels of abstraction. For example, even the most comprehensive standards for architectural description, such as IEEE 1471-2000 (IEEE 2000), or contemporary proposals for design reuse, such as Rational's Reusable Assets Specification, are quite correctly defined to cover certain design elements at specific levels of abstraction, not all elements at all levels. For example, these standards leave the definition of modeling languages and notations such as UML and XML up to the respective experts. They complement and add value to these standards; they do not replace and compete with them. The role of the IT-architectural style is complementary in a similar way. It uses a combination of architectural description standards, modeling standards, and other standards to describe the holistic and specific aspects unique to the style. It adds value by applying these standards in concert at all levels of the big picture. It does this in a particular fashion to best meet specific principles—the essence of a style.

The scope of an IT-architectural style requires extensive know-how to define an effective and synergistic constellation of standards. The complexity of this task is already visible at the highest levels of an architecture. The four top-level features of an IT-architectural style traverse many design domains, each of them having its own best means of representation. As you will see in the Convergent Architecture, representations exist for such diverse aspects as business design, the IT organization and process design, large-scale and detailed component system design, tool and repository design, deployment and reuse design, code generation, and build environment design.

According to the principle of specificity, this does not mean to use all standards and all views available. The developer of an IT-architectural style must select among many standards and views to best represent the big picture at every level. This means that a specific constellation should be defined to best support learning and use of the style. Such a constellation, for example, would optimally represent each design level with minimal overlap and without translation loss. Not many developers possess the broad experience, nor do they have enough time, to properly complete this task. Nonetheless, it is a prerequisite for effective development of large systems. Thus, once completed by an expert and packaged in the context of an IT-architectural style, all users of the style immediately reap considerable benefits.

Summary

This first chapter described the origin of architectural style and its potential advantages when these concepts are applied in the field of IT architecture in the form of an *IT-architectural style*. It then defined the design of any IT-architectural style. This will enable readers to better understand the fundamental concepts behind the Convergent Architecture, a specific IT-architectural style presented in the remainder of this book. In addition, the definition in this chapter will help readers describe, enhance, or even create their own IT-architectural style.

A historical perspective compared various forms of architectural style as found in civil architecture and many mature industries. Examples showed the rationale for architectural style, and analogies were used to convey its potential benefits in the IT industry. Scenarios from today's most significant problems in enterprise IT systems and software design were used to show how an IT-architectural style can provide permanent solutions. The scenarios explain why many of the current-day approaches only doctor up the most visible symptoms of a more fundamental architectural neglect. They demonstrate how an IT-architectural style goes further to actually remedy the fundamental source of the problems—the only long-term solution. The chapter reveals IT-architectural style as a significant, evolutionary advance in IT system development, not just another workaround or quick fix.

In this chapter, an IT-architectural style was defined as consisting of four major features:

- The architectural metamodel
- The full-life-cycle development model
- The full-coverage tool suite
- Formal technology projections

In addition to justifying and explaining each of these four features, the chapter also covered several important aspects that should be considered when creating any IT-architectural style:

- Specificity
- The force of entropy
- The designer's paradox

- Organic order
- Organizational evolution

Now that the advantages of the IT-architectural style are clear, it is time to show how these concepts manifest themselves in a particular IT-architectural style, the Convergent Architecture. The next six chapters of this book provide a complete description of the Convergent Architecture. Chapter 8 then gives a pragmatic hands-on example to get projects off to a fast start. It is important to note that the rest of the book is not just an example of IT-architectural style; rather, it is a complete style that is in active use today in many projects. Chapter 2 starts the journey through the Convergent Architecture by providing the top-level roadmap. This is the big picture, the bird's-eye view. It introduces the four features of IT-architectural style as realized in the Convergent Architecture and explains how they complement each other. The subsequent chapters provide detail on each of the features and their relationships. This roadmap approach should help designers and project managers orient themselves at any time within the big picture while exploring the details of the Convergent Architecture.

CHAPTER
2

The Convergent
Architecture Roadmap

Defining and managing the big picture.

A roadmap is key to communicating information technology (IT) architecture effectively. The first thing that an experienced planner does in any field is to orient his or her team according to a common scheme or roadmap. Whether it is an expedition, a military event, a construction plan, or an IT strategy, the roadmap helps visualize and coordinate common goals and, more important, indicates the best path to take. It is the single most important form of information management. The larger and more complex the endeavor, the more important it is to start with a roadmap. Even small IT projects are complex enough to require a roadmap. A map is essential to any IT organization that must coordinate persons, projects, and ever-changing technology effectively over large periods of time.

In fact, most IT organizations will require several levels and types of roadmaps to guide themselves properly along the precarious journey to effective systems. First, a high-level roadmap is required to show the path between major milestones of the journey. This level corresponds, for example, to a highway map between Paris and Berlin. Once the organization is moving in the proper general direction, more detailed maps can be used. However, if the general direction is wrong, detailed maps will not help much. Buying a detailed map of Rome will not help much if we are on our way from Paris to Berlin. In other words, the maps do not just help us find the best route somewhere, they also help us figure out where we are at any given time, where we have come from, and how we get back home. Above all, they help us explain to others where we are, how to find us, and even better, how to get there alone, without requiring an experienced guide at every turn in the road. There will never be enough experienced guides—experienced IT architects—to go around. Nobody would expect an automobile driver to know a route automatically without having looked at a map. By the same token, it is obvious that not every driver can have an experienced taxi dispatcher in the passenger seat. However, this does not seem to be so obvious in the IT industry. Many organizations do expect each and every one of their developers to somehow know the route and, although they often have never met each other, to even agree on the destination and a common route. These are clearly unreasonable expectations that inevitably lead to major problems. To be successful, organizations must get accustomed to using the destinations and roadmaps for system design published by IT architects. This chapter presents the roadmap of the Convergent Architecture.

It is hard to understand how modern organizations even manage to get along without an easily understandable IT roadmap. Actually, they usually have no IT roadmap at all. As a result, most IT organizations are just barely surviving, driven from one problem to the next, always teetering on the edge of a breakdown. They spend so much time finding detours and correcting dead ends that their backlog of unfulfilled requirements is bursting at the seams. How do these IT organizations know where they are going? The honest answer is that they usually do not really know, not past the next generation of systems anyway. They cannot know where they are going because they have never set a long-term destination. It is as if everyone were under the impression that, one day soon, we will not need information management and IT any more, so why should we bother to think about where we are going in the next decades? Why look to the horizon when nobody is interested in the direction anyway? In light of this situation, it is easy to understand why contemporary IT organizations are experiencing considerable difficulty. The perpetual zigzagging has gotten almost everybody confused, from the top management to the end customers.

The cost of this zigzagging is exorbitantly high. The cash consumed by recent IT startups alone is dizzying evidence of this cost, which is magnitudes higher in large organizations. Do these IT organizations know where they are now? No, they cannot know where they are because they do not have a roadmap for their IT architecture. *If you don't care where you end up, then you don't need a roadmap.* However, if you want to produce increasingly effective systems over time, and if you ever want to reach the long-term advantages of IT architecture, then a roadmap is the only way to get there.

The roadmap to the IT-architectural style is also a decisive factor in the quality of information and knowledge management in any organization. Contrary to what some modern marketing campaigns would have us believe, knowledge management is not something that parts of IT systems do; knowledge management is what all IT systems do. It is the *raison-d'être* of IT systems. Every IT system, even a computer game, is built specifically to put order into data, to organize data into information, and to formulate and connect information to increase human knowledge. Essentially, the design of every IT system is a design for information and knowledge management. There are, of course, good ways and bad ways to manage information: A good design is synonymous with good information and knowledge management.[1] Information management goes further than simply structuring information within a system. To design systems that truly help humans better manage information, in contrast to just data, an organization must figure out how it wants to define, structure, and relate information to make it more useful. This is one of the most important aspects of IT architecture: It forces an organization to address issues of how information will be best managed and used at all levels. This emphasizes IT-architectural style as the foundation for superior information and knowledge management not just at the level of the individual system but for an entire organization, well beyond the traditional scope of IT systems. Thus the Convergent Architecture, beginning with its roadmap, lays the groundwork for improved knowledge management by communicating how the process of IT development directly supports information design.

There is another, more subtle reason behind the roadmap. It has to do with the expectations placed on consultants by contemporary managers. Organizations require software to support complex, mission-critical tasks. This means that a consultant who has been engaged to build a system first must work with the business to understand and clearly structure, that is, model, the mission-critical tasks. He or she must construct a roadmap of the structures and procedures in the particular business domain, whether it is automobile production, financial trading, or state government, so as to design and build an effective IT system. In other words, the consultant has been hired to define and realize a roadmap for a business. As a prerequisite, we should expect the consultant to have a roadmap for his or her own business—the business of IT architecture—that clearly structures the mission-critical task of IT architecture. We cannot reasonably expect someone to develop a high-quality roadmap for another business domain if that person does not yet have one in his or her own domain.

The remainder of this chapter presents the top-level roadmap of the Convergent Architecture in terms of the important stops along the recommended route to building convergent IT systems. It shows the locations and milestones along the road of IT architecture as well as their orientation with respect to each other. This is the "big picture" of the Convergent Architecture, which will significantly simplify and expedite the entire IT endeavor, no matter how extensive that endeavor may be. Its primary objective is to begin simple and stay as simple as possible, ruthlessly abrogating unnecessary complexity at every step along the way.

Since the milestones of the Convergent Architecture are not necessarily everyday landmarks that we all know and understand—like highways, mountains, and lakes—the roadmap also must explain its own particular landmarks and elements of geography—the highways, mountains, and lakes of IT architecture. Thus, along with the roadmap, this chapter also presents the high-level anatomy of the Convergent Architecture in terms of its significant parts and the important function of each part in the overall organism. This anatomy lesson began in the preceding chapter, where the significant features of any IT-architectural style were explained. The four features of an IT-architectural style are clearly visible in the Convergent Architecture. However, they now take on additional character, the character of this particular style.

After introducing the roadmap and anatomy here, the remaining chapters of this book take us on a journey through the Convergent Architecture, according to the roadmap, and present a detailed map at each stop along the road to building convergent IT systems.

The Anatomy of the Convergent Architecture

Figure 2.1 shows the combined elements of structure, process, and tools that make up the Convergent Architecture. This is both its anatomy and the top-level roadmap. As with any roadmap, the orientation of its elements is significant. Layers of abstraction run from top to bottom and left to right. In other words, it should first be read from top to bottom and then from left to right. The top two layers represent the models of the style and indicate their long-term influence on the lower layers, which represent tool and technology categories. The time perspective flows from left to right and shows the relationship between development process flow, tool modules, and technologies in any given project.

The layers of the Convergent Architecture and their correspondence to the four features of an IT-architectural style are

1. **The Convergent Architecture metamodel.** This layer fulfills the role of the architectural metamodel, as defined in Chapter 1.

2. **The development model.** This layer fulfills the role of the full-cycle development model, as defined in Chapter 1.

3. **The architectural IDE and its associated reusable assets.** These two layers fulfill the role of the full-coverage tool suite, as defined in Chapter 1.

4. **The technology projections.** This layer fulfills the role of the formal technology projections, as defined in Chapter 1.

Each of these layers is introduced in the following sections before being covered in detail in a subsequent chapter.

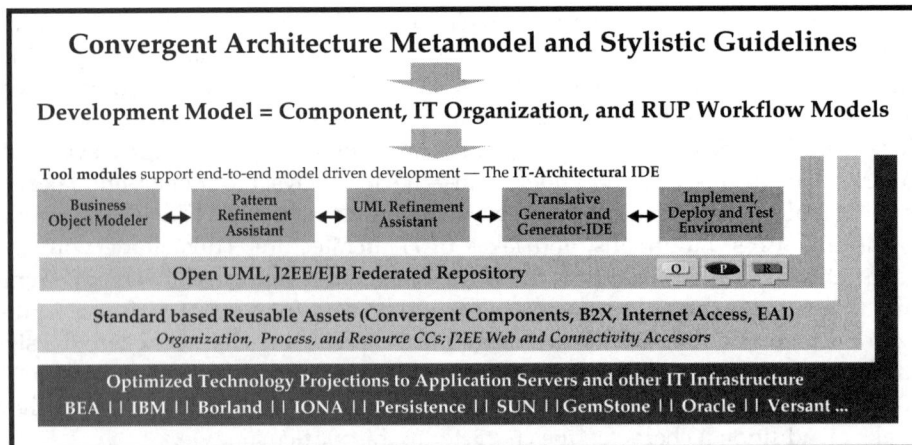

Figure 2.1   Roadmap and anatomy of the Convergent Architecture.

The Convergent Architecture Metamodel

The Convergent Architecture metamodel defines the long-term vision and fundamental design principles on which we base our design decisions. In summary, it comprises the following elements:

- **The three pillars of holistic architecture.** The intimately related themes of *project design, business design,* and *system design* are addressed to provide adequate coverage of the areas critical to an IT organization and its many interrelated projects. The project design pillar refers to how we set up, coordinate, and run the IT organization, its projects as well as its development workflow. It sets the stage for both effective business and system design. The business design pillar refers to the techniques and tools required to refine the business strategy and to represent it in a form that can be understood widely and mapped efficiently to an IT system. The system design pillar then indicates how we get from the business design to an IT system that optimally supports the business.

- **Convergence and Convergent Engineering.** Dr. David A. Taylor (Taylor 1995) formulated convergence in the context of IT systems in his introduction to Convergent Engineering. Convergent Engineering demonstrates how business and IT models can be united into one, simplifying model to resolve many of today's most complex operational and business-IT problems. It also recognizes the concept of integrated modeling and the proper use of object-oriented technology as critical factors for lasting improvement.

- **The machine shop metaphor.** Picture a well-run machine shop or workshop setting in any mature industry, and compare this picture with the settings of contemporary software development. It is clear that most, if not all, software settings allow significant room for improvement. The Convergent Architecture strives to achieve the level of a well-run machine shop by creating a comparable software shop. In contrast to a consultant arriving at a project with some ideas about how one could possibly begin building a software shop, the convergent architect is better prepared. He or she starts with a working, tried, and tested software shop that covers the whole process from conception to finishing, analogous to a well-organized machine shop.

- **Reduced Abstraction Set Computing (RASC).** Based on years of empirical research, IT architects have been able to identify a reduced set of design elements, or design abstractions, to significantly simplify many aspects of design and the design process. This improvement is analogous to the discovery of Reduced Instruction Set Computing (RISC) in computer hardware design, which was recognized as a desirable alternative to Complex Instruction Set Computing (CISC) in most situations. RASC constitutes a high-level language and lexicon that can be shared by both business and IT designers to achieve convergence in IT systems. The Convergent Architecture recognizes six significant RASC abstractions, from which it derives its family of components, the *convergent components*.

- **Conceptual isomorphism.** If a concept can be learned once and applied similarly in many situations, then we speak of *conceptual isomorphism.* The concepts of the Convergent Architecture are targeted for use across many domains. They resolve general problems at a general level instead of repeatedly solving the same problem differently at the level of specific systems. The Convergent Architecture can be used equally and with the same identifiable concepts across the diverse organizations of a bank, an automobile manufacturer, and a government agency, for example. A high level of conceptual isomorphism increases the understanding of models, tools, and systems across domains, simplifying communication while also reducing learning curves. Widely usable design patterns often are good examples of conceptual isomorphism.

- **Component metamorphosis.** There are few physical or material constraints to developing software systems. They are indeed "soft" in that we can conceivably manipulate and grow our designs any way we want. The principle of *component metamorphosis* invokes an intentional analogy with the metamorphosis of a butterfly. Instead of developing software systems as done today, in radical heaves of translation and reformulation of information, they can be evolved through steady stages of information enhancement and growth, comparable with the metamorphosis of a butterfly. It required a concerted effort in the Convergent Architecture to create structures, processes, and tools to enable component metamorphosis.

A detailed description of the Convergent Architecture metamodel is presented in Chapter 3.

The Development Model

The Convergent Architecture's development model formulates the principles of its architectural metamodel in terms of specific design structures, a development organization, and a development process. It distinguishes the following three interacting models:

- **Convergent component metamodel.** Convergent components are the most important structural vehicle for the principles of the Convergent Architecture. They realize these principles in terms of concrete component structures, behavior, and relationships. The metamodel defines technology-nonspecific concepts for organizations, process and resource components, utility components, accessor components (system-interface accessors, user-interface accessors), assembly components, and sentinels. It also organizes these components into architectural layers, specifies their mapping to technology and runtime systems, and defines their specific development process and tool support.

- **The IT-organization model.** This model defines a template IT organization in terms of the organizational structure, roles, and responsibilities required for effective support and management of the entire IT life cycle. It defines the canonical project organization and project team as well as organizations for IT architecture, development support, software development, and operational systems.

■ **The development-process model.**   Based on concepts from several professional frameworks for software development, the Convergent Architecture defines a specifically tailored approach, or instance, according the Rational Unified Process, known as RUP (Kruchten 1998), and the Object-Oriented Process Environment and Notation, known as OPEN (Graham 1997). The development-process model focuses on highly specific coverage of the core development workflow as well as on critical aspects of the supporting workflows according to the RUP.

A detailed description of these three interacting models is presented in Chapters 4, 5, and 6, respectively.

To simplify orientation from this point on, Figure 2.2 paraphrases the relationships between the three models outlined in this section, as well as their relationship to the remaining two layers, the architectural IDE and the technology projections, which are covered in the next two sections.

The Full-Coverage Tool Suite (Architectural IDE)

The full-coverage tool suite is an integral part of the Convergent Architecture. It is at the level of a preconfigured "machine shop" that has been designed specifically to meet the requirements of the architecture. The tightly integrated tools and automated

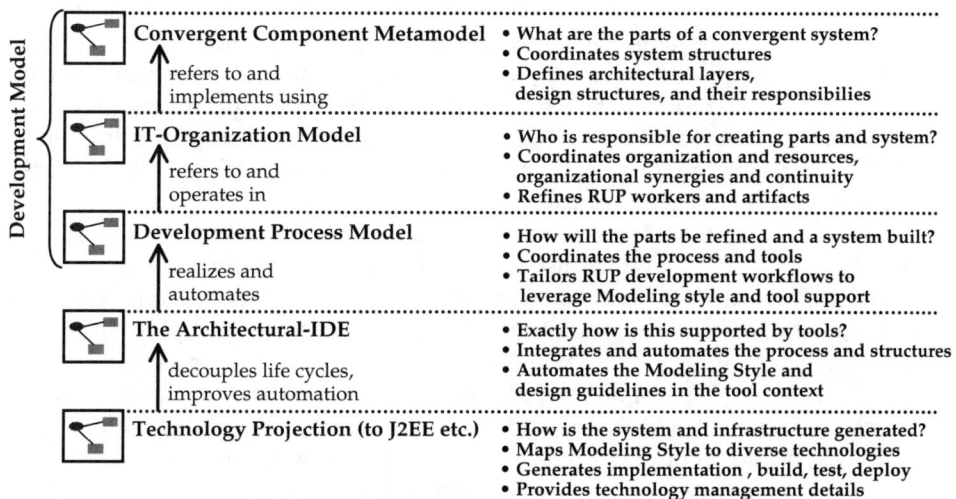

Figure 2.2   The development model and the layers below.

assistants support immediate and effective construction of architecture-conform IT systems. We call this comprehensive approach to high-level architectural tools an *IT-architectural IDE*.[2]

As emphasized in Chapter 1, the definition of the IT-architectural IDE must be part of the IT-architectural style. Thus, the Convergent Architecture specifies the modules of its own IT-architectural IDE. However, it does not specify who should provide the IT-architectural IDE or any one of its modules. To provide the reader with pragmatic, hands-on examples, a concrete IT-architectural IDE is used in this book, the ArcStyler (iO 2001). This IT-architectural IDE embeds the well-known modeling tool, Rational Rose (Rational 2001), as one of its central modules. Although the ArcStyler was developed to support architecture-driven development in general, it provides explicit support for the Convergent Architecture style.

A central aspect of the IT-architectural IDE is its support for mapping design models to available technologies. We call this mapping the *technology projection*, which is covered in its own section in the following. The Convergent Architecture leverages J2EE/EJB standards and J2EE-compliant application servers as its default technology projection. To properly illustrate the various levels of design and implementation independence provided by the IT-architectural IDE, two different J2EE application servers will be used with the ArcStyler in several examples in this book. The J2EE/EJB application servers used for the examples are those from Borland (Borland 2001) and BEA Systems (BEA 2001). However, other J2EE/EJB-compliant application servers easily could have been used in their place.

In the Convergent Architecture, the IT-architectural IDE is arranged into five major modules, as shown in Figure 2.3. These modules are not just tool descriptions. More important, they are used by the Convergent Architecture to simplify understanding and application of its development style. Each development technique is presented pragmatically in the following in conjunction with its specific tool support:

Convergent Business Object Modeler (C-BOM). This module assists both the IT designer and the business-domain expert in their joint task of requirements analysis and elaboration of the business structure and dynamics. It provides visual modeling assistance to help identify and document a convergent system using the RASC components described previously. It does this using the proven techniques of responsibility-driven design (RDD) and class responsibility cards (CRC), as prescribed by convergent engineering (Taylor 1995) and OPEN (Graham 1997). Cross-functional teams use this module during the highly collaborative task of modeling, documenting, and testing the business structure and business dynamics. This task also leverages analysis by design (ABD) and dynamic walk-through/run-through techniques to verify model completeness and quality, as described by convergent engineering. Run-through results are recorded both as formal state transition tables (STTs) and as a more intuitive graphical form. The graphical representation provides visual documentation, tracking, and playback. The rules of the modeling style are used to automatically verify and report on the model's integrity and completeness in both structural and dynamic aspects at any time. These reports, based on verified models, serve as design signoff documents. They also include test cases in the form of STTs and the visual scenarios documenting all run-through paths through the

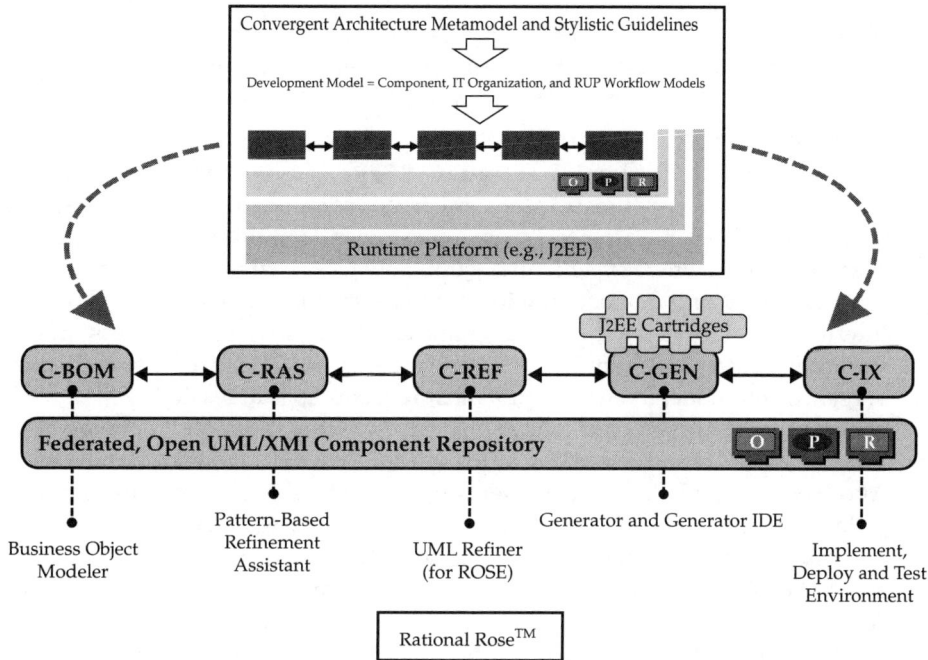

Figure 2.3 The modules of the IT-architectural IDE.

convergent business system. The results of the business modeling session are stored in a repository based on the standard Unified Modeling Language (UML) metamodel and the eXtensible Markup Language (XML). This repository is used in a federated manner by all other modules of the IT-architectural IDE to guarantee the translation-free, loss-less enrichment of design information according to the principle of component metamorphosis.

Convergent Pattern Refinement Assistant (C-RAS). This module picks up the results of the C-BOM and helps a designer graphically evolve the business model into a more detailed, more technically precise model representation in UML. This task proceeds in a structured manner according to the principle of convergent engineering. This is achieved by using refinement patterns based on those developed by the OPEN Consortium (Henderson-Sellers 1998), which are employed to guide the designer and to check the integrity of the refinement. With the visual support provided by this tool, the CRC component representations from the business model are mapped to UML component representations without losing track of their origin and without losing the existing information on the business components: The information is enhanced and refined, not translated or replaced. In the spirit of assisted modeling, much of the UML refinement is handled automatically by the tool itself according to the patterns and UML modeling style defined by the Convergent Architecture. For example, the projection to a standard J2EE/EJB component model starts here. The UML model is elaborated automatically into a J2EE/EJB-compliant design using reasonable defaults. The designer can influence these defaults, but the tool suggests a well-formed standard structure for the designer to build on or tune in the subsequent stages of refinement. Once again, all results are stored in the federated UML repository.

Convergent UML Refinement Assistant (C-REF).   This module reads the results of the C-RAS and now presents the convergent component model at the level of an advanced UML modeler for further enrichment and tuning of the design. This is the point where system interaction and access, whether via Internet[3] or other channels, and interaction with external systems, whether internal or via Internet,[4] is elaborated in detail using the standard UML. This tool provides several intelligent architecture assistants during this phase to further preserve convergence and model integrity and to ensure technological feasibility of the design. The first assistant checks at any time whether the detailed model is complete and well formed according to the UML, J2EE/EJB, and Java standards. Another assistant helps the designer proceed according to the specific modeling style of the architecture by providing specialized wizards, dialogs, views, and diagrams. A third assistant helps generate UML models for default user-access and test components (which we call *accessors*), based on the existing business-component model. This allows the designer to model and reuse complex Internet access and interaction logic in UML. A fourth assistant helps the user configure a particular technology projection and its runtime environment. Based on this configuration, the assistant then checks the model at any time for its technological feasibility. This verification step is analogous to a compiler, except it is working at the level of a UML model. Based on the capabilities and constraints of the configured technology projection, the assistant points out which aspects of the model cannot be mapped effectively to the selected implementation technology. With this just-in-time feedback, the modeler can better maintain architectural integrity and ensure the quality of the subsequent system generation.

Convergent Translative Generator (C-GEN).   This module reads the UML model in parts or in its entirety from the C-REF tool and generates the complete component infrastructure, including the environment for configuration, construction, and deployment of the convergent system. The generator translates the UML model to the particular infrastructure while preserving convergence. To do this, it uses transformation scripts, code-generation templates (for example, for Java, HTML, J2EE/EJB, XML, or a Java-IDE), technology capability tables (for example, for a J2EE/EJB application server), and other information. All transformation instructions belonging to a particular technology projection are encapsulated in a so-called generator cartridge, which can be installed, configured, and used as a unit by the developer. The generator cartridge is referred to simply as a *cartridge* when used in this context. There can be any number of cartridges, one for each particular infrastructure. The C-GEN is oblivious of the specific content of the cartridge. In addition, combinations of cartridges can be used in concert to guarantee proper modularity and separation of concerns between coexisting types of infrastructure, as explained with the C-BOB module below. The source code and other artifacts generated by the cartridge are of consistent, predetermined quality. The internals of the artifacts generated (for example, source code, deployment configuration, build configuration) can be modified at places deemed appropriate by the IT-architectural style. The cartridge uses several techniques to enable the controlled modification of generated artifacts. These techniques are presented in detail in Chapter 7. However, it is important to note here that the Convergent Architecture mandates clean model-based, model-driven development. This means that all artifacts that generated from the UML model can only be extended or modified in a controlled manner—as defined by the architectural style. This is an explicit enforcement of the model-driven development approach. However, the rigor of this enforcement can be regulated using the C-GEN-IDE (see the following) to modify the rules of the code generation.

Not all aspects of a system can be represented reasonably in UML models or derived and generated from UML models. These aspects must be developed at the source-code level. To do this, the IT-architectural IDE leverages one of the several programming IDEs available on the market. The programming IDE may be used to refine, compile, and debug artifacts generated by the C-GEN module. These artifacts include Java programs, configuration files, the build environment, test infrastructure, and deployment information. During the generation process, the cartridge clearly demarks and annotates the areas where additions can or should be made in the Java IDE. This helps the developer make rapid additions while maintaining structural integrity and synchronization with the UML models. In addition, the cartridge generates the artifacts required by the Java IDE to load, build, deploy, and test the system in the context of a specific runtime infrastructure. This includes default test code to permit evolutionary modification and testing of the system.

Convergent Generator IDE (C-GEN-IDE).   This IDE is the visual development environment for a generator cartridge. The development of a cartridge can be regarded as metaprogramming because the scripts developed here drive the translative generation of many other programs. The C-GEN-IDE is required only when a developer needs to extend or adapt a cartridge. In this case, the cartridge is developed visually, tested, traced, and debugged in a similar fashion to well-known programming IDEs for C++ or Java. The C-GEN-IDE is used, for example, to modify the HTML- and J2EE-generation templates in order to produce a different look and feel in compliance with a particular Web site branding or a corporate identity. Using the C-GEN-IDE, the chief architect and lead designers of large, multiteam IT organizations have a tool to tailor and adapt the IT-architectural style in a well-defined place and form. This helps guarantee a consistent level of well-documented quality and architectural integrity across all projects.

Convergent Implement, Deploy, and Test Environment (C-IX).   The models of the Convergent Architecture require that model-based development also cover the areas of user interaction and access to and from external systems. This is achieved in part in the C-REF module, as described earlier, where the appropriate modeling capabilities and assisted modeling style are provided. In addition, the UML models must be mappable to a stable deployment infrastructure to enable consistent generation, deployment, and testing of high-performance implementations. This infrastructure is provided by the accessor cartridge, which complements the modeling style by furnishing a stable, reusable framework in addition to its technology projection. For example, the accessor cartridge for J2EE provides a stable deployment and test infrastructure based on standards such as JSP, servlets, and Web archives. The framework complements these J2EE standards in areas required to enable effective model-based development in UML but not yet standardized in J2EE. It also provides a higher level of abstraction that increases model expressiveness while guaranteeing a transparent migration to relevant standards should they emerge.

A more detailed description of the IT-architectural IDE is presented in Chapter 7.

The Technology Projections (J2EE/EJB)

A *technology projection* in the Convergent Architecture specifies how convergent components and other modeled elements are mapped (projected) to standard component frameworks and then to various implementation technologies. By default, the Convergent Architecture recommends and specifically supports technology projections to infrastructures based on J2EE/EJB standards. This book covers the technology projections to standard J2EE/EJB infrastructures and uses projections to existing application servers from BEA Systems (BEA 2001) and Borland (Borland 2001) application servers in its examples.[5] However, several other technology projections to non-J2EE technologies have been developed already for the Convergent Architecture. These include projections to CORBA (Visibroker, BEA WLE), OODB Systems (Versant enJin), and pure-Java RMI frameworks.

There are two aspects to a technology projection:

1. Things that *can be generated automatically*, effectively, and with reasonable effort

2. Things that *cannot be generated automatically*

Both of these must be addressed to maintain architectural integrity because together they define the tangible results of the architecture.

The boundary between what can and cannot be generated reasonably often is fuzzy and usually changes with time. However, both aspects invariably exist in real-world projects. There will never be a way to automate everything because once we have automated one thing, we attack the next challenge, which we usually cannot automate immediately. In other words, our insatiable appetite for progress always keeps us out in front of the moving automation boundary. In addition, some things are not worth automating at all, namely, unique, nonrepetitive instances. For example, a complex adapter to a legacy system invariably must be written or tuned by hand using all kinds of proprietary technology. However, the component that cleanly encapsulates this adapter from the perspective of the architecture may be generated automatically from a UML model. Since the adapter is completely unique, it is not worth developing an automated technology projection for the special case.

In the Convergent Architecture, the design integrity of the automatically generated aspects is handled by the generator cartridge, which not only automates the management of technology, but also documents how the technology is managed. The concepts and workings of a generator cartridge were outlined in the preceding section and are detailed in Chapters 4, 7, and the bonus chapter on the Web site. The integrity of parts that cannot be generated automatically is addressed by so-called sentinels. A sentinel complements the generator cartridges by specifying the proper use of the technologies that are not managed explicitly by automatic generation. A sentinel is a document or some other structure in which the architect designates how a particular technology is to be used from the perspective of the architectural style. This is the only way to keep an IT landscape clean as a whole. It is one of the best investments against software entropy. Sentinel documents, or sentinels, are also important because they tell developers what is in bounds and what is out of bounds from the perspective of the architecture. They draw a boundary to more clearly delimit what is good and bad in terms of architectural integrity.

For example, large organizations usually want to integrate many packaged systems, such as Lotus Notes or Microsoft Exchange, into the overall system landscape. In such a situation, the architect[6] writes a sentinel defining which interfaces and features of Lotus Notes can be used in the company's software, as well as any constraints pertaining to their use. If this is not done, then parts of Lotus Notes' infrastructure will creep unnoticed and unhindered into the IT landscape, causing a complex, uncontrolled intermingling of the organization's systems with the external technology and design philosophy of Lotus Notes. Once this happens, the organization's IT-architectural style has been polluted: Creeping entropy has begun to take its toll. I call this process *creeping dilution* (or *pollution*) *of the architecture*. Once it starts, the company should not wonder why both IT complexity and the number of unpleasant surprises steadily increase. If a sentinel were in place, anybody could see where and how the Lotus Notes' infrastructure is used or should be used in a controlled, organized manner from the perspective of the architecture. Metaphorically speaking, the sentinel heads software entropy off at the drawbridge. It is an important measure taken by the architecture to guard itself from intruders. More details on sentinels will be provided in later chapters.

The technology projection (Chapter 4 and the bonus chapter on the Web site) simplifies risk mitigation by defining three distinct categories of sentinel. They are used to communicate and manage the long-term risks of change and coupling related to the use of externally developed technology. *Externally developed technology* refers to any design or implementation that has occurred outside the context of the IT-architectural style. The problem with externally developed technology is that its design, its implementation, and its life cycle are not controlled by the architecture, but it still must be managed effectively by the architecture. Defining the high-value, low-risk use of externally developed technology within an organization is key to achieving overall high-returns from technology. The following three categories of sentinels classify external technologies in terms of their potential for risk from the perspective of the architecture:

Ubiquitous technologies.   These are the technologies that are used widely to implement and interface the convergent components (see Chapter 4) across an entire IT landscape. These technologies include the corporate IT infrastructure down to its lowest level. Examples here begin with the networking infrastructure, computer operating systems that underlie all installed software, but also include other ubiquitous technologies, such as the Java Development Kit, XML exchange formats, and the myriad technologies bundled with or encapsulated by J2EE/EJB application servers (which includes databases). These sentinels ensure that the automated aspects of the architectural style also define how they use and remain in sync with the rest of the IT environment.

CC-encapsulated technologies. These are technologies that fall outside the ubiquitous technologies category. As such, they will always be cleanly encapsulated within convergent components. Such technologies are, for example, special communication middleware to access packaged applications and legacy systems, special B2B file and exchange formats, high-security mechanisms, or hardware interfaces. These sentinels define the architecture-conform use of the technologies they encapsulate.

Peripheral tools. The Convergent Architecture specifies the tools that directly influence the critical development workflows (see Chapter 6). However, other tools and their underlying technologies exist that influence IT development and operations indirectly (or peripherally). These tools still have an impact on the effectiveness and quality of the IT landscape as a whole and must be addressed by a holistic architecture. Examples of peripheral tools include e-mail systems, text-processing tools, backup systems, and virus checkers. These sentinels ensure that no tool is introduced into an organization without addressing its long-term, full-cycle effect from the IT perspective.

These sentinel categories are used by the architecture organization (see Chapter 5) to mitigate risks due to external technologies (both new and old) that cannot be addressed explicitly in advance by the architectural style. In the interest of holistic architecture, the style specifies how they will be handled appropriately in the given instance using sentinels. The IT organization now has a means to ensure uniformly clean, high-return use of technologies across its entire IT landscape.

The Operational Environment

Successful architecture in any field pragmatically must target existing operational environments. The architecture should enable an organization to make low-risk evolutionary changes in its operational environment instead of high-risk radical modifications. In addition, it must permit an organization to leverage reliable, cost-effective operating technology. This means rigorously avoiding the temptation of trends, marketing illusions, or wishful thinking at all times. The Convergent Architecture defines an operational environment that meets these criteria. It promotes the move to a standard-based environment with Internet-centric component technology. However, first and foremost, it shows how existing systems and external providers can be leveraged in a noninvasive fashion to become part of a convergent system. Figure 2.4 summarizes how the Convergent Architecture covers all the bases of enterprise IT integration in the operational environment. It is deceivingly simple. However, as described below, the

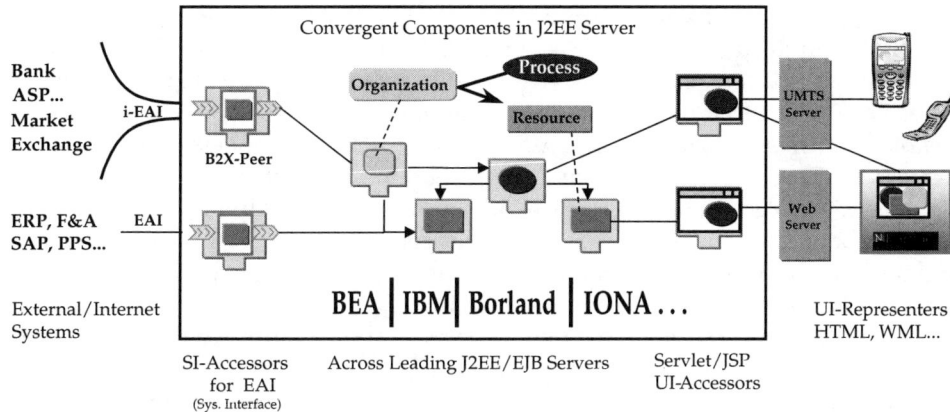

Figure 2.4 The operational environment.

convergent components in their respective roles meet all the requirements. Such simplicity is one of the major benefits of working out the IT-architectural style first, before diving into individual projects.

The elements in the figure represent those found in any IT infrastructure. Some organizations will have more of one element than another, of course. At the far left of the figure are the existing systems, packaged systems, and external Internet systems, including Internet marketplaces and application service providers (ASPs). The center of the figure shows the convergent components contained by a J2EE/EJB container.[7] At the right are examples of diverse user access channels. All elements are shown working together to form a single convergent system. A *convergent system* is defined as any operational system based on the Convergent Architecture.

Moving from left to right, the figure indicates that external systems, whether Internet or other external systems, are embraced as part of the convergent system via the system-interface accessors (SI-accessors). The SI-accessors are components that cleanly encapsulate the special interaction requirements of external systems. They are *model-driven*, which means that they are modeled in UML and generated in part or in whole from the model. The SI-accessors are within the *architectural boundary*. This boundary, indicated by the large rectangle in the figure, delimits the elements the architecture has under its design control from elements it cannot influence directly—the externally developed technology, as described earlier. The architecture must interface and adapt cleanly to the external systems to preserve its own internal integrity. This is achieved with the SI-accessors. The architecture-external side of the SI-accessors localizes and defines the interaction with external systems, whereas the architecture-internal side provides the components of the convergent system with common, well-formed structural and behavioral characteristics. This allows all other components within the architecture to be modeled and generated uniformly to leverage external systems without knowing the particular idiosyncrasies of those external systems. It allows existing systems to be integrated quickly as part of the overall convergent system without having to first redesign such systems according to the Convergent Architecture. For example, packaged applications for finance and administration (F&A), enterprise resource planning (ERP), production planning systems (PPS), or other modules from, for example, the company SAP can each be leveraged fully by convergent components via SI-accessors. This type of uniform system integration is often referred to as *enterprise application integration* (EAI). However, the same scheme applies for business-to-business (B2B) communications with systems on the Internet. Internet banks, ASPs, Internet marketplaces, and exchanges each become a model-driven SI-accessor that then can be used transparently by *all* convergent components. In the Convergent Architecture, this type of integration with Internet systems is simply a logical extension of EAI into the Internet, or Internet EAI (i-EAI).

The entities labeled as organizations, processes, and resources in the center of the figure represent elements of the organization's core business model. Directly below them are the convergent components that directly represent the elements of the business model within the IT system. These components use, on the one side, the SI-accessors to interact with the external systems and, on the other side, the so-called user-interface accessors (UI-accessors) to interact with humans. This system-to-human interaction aspect is shown to the right of the figure.

In addition to the classic user interfaces in local area networks, the interaction with humans via diverse Internet communication channels, such as Web browsers and mobile assistants, has become very significant. This type of interaction is often called *multichannel business-to-client* (B2C) *interaction.* Complicating the multichannel aspect are the many look-and-feel technologies possible for each of the possible communication channels. To communicate with any given client, there may be several different look-and-feel technologies, such as Hypertext Markup Language (HTML), Wireless Markup Language (WML), and XML/Swing dialects, just to name a few. To be successful in the Internet Age, convergent systems will have to flexibly handle all these forms of human interaction as well as new, currently unknown forms of interaction in the future. To achieve this, the Convergent Architecture introduces UI-accessors and UI-representers. The design and mechanisms of UI-accessors are congruous with the design and mechanisms of the SI-accessors. In fact, they are identical in almost every aspect, which further simplifies the architecture. The only significant difference is the requirement for multiple look-and-feel technologies when interacting with humans. This difference is cleanly localized by the architecture in the user-interface representers (UI-representers) shown at the right in the figure, which are also model-driven components. As shown in the figure, a UI-accessor may interact with human users via one or more UI-representers. Both UI-accessors and UI-representers are present in the design model. This enables a designer to model the user-interaction dynamics and structure, including the interaction of the user interface with business components, and then to generate the end-to-end infrastructure from the model. Of equal significance is the documentation and reusability of the UI-accessor and UI-representer components provided by the model.

As indicated in the figure, all convergent components, including the accessors, are physically located in a J2EE/EJB environment and can access external systems using the best-available technology for the situation at hand. The UI-representers run wherever the particular look-and-feel technology requires this.

Summarizing the Cumulative Improvements

The final task in creating the roadmap is to provide a "big picture" summarizing how and where major improvements can be harvested based on the Convergent Architecture. This interim summary of benefits is important for several reasons. First, the roadmap will not be used unless it is worth the trip. Second, although many experienced developers and IT project managers will understand the benefits without this summary, many of the benefits are not obvious at first glance. Many of them are cumulative, with the highest returns emerging from the holistic combination of elements over time: The music is often in the concert, not the individual instruments. Third, non-IT managers and skimming readers will find this digest of the highlights very useful.

Table 2.1 provides a top-10-style overview of cumulative improvements observed in different instances of the Convergent Architecture. The numbers are conservative. Although percentages are provided to indicate the time saved while simultaneously producing higher quality, there is no intent to infer a high level of mathematical precision. The increases in quality are more important than the increase in speed: Building poor systems faster cannot be our goal. The estimates are averages based on several years of consulting experience using the concepts in various organizations. There are neutral sources outside the current users of the Convergent Architecture who also have

Table 2.1 Overview of Cumulative Improvements

AREA	TIME REDUCTION, ~%	QUALITY INCREASE*
Business and requirements modeling	20%	++
Design evolution and UML modeling	30%	+
Web (B2C) and system (B2B) accessor development	50%	++
Implement, build, deploy cycle	60%	++
Testing	50%	+
Development tool environment	70%	++
Documentation	60%	++
Runtime environment	60%	+
Project management and development process	50%	+

*+ = significant.

endorsed the advantages slated here. However, the main objective of this section is to explain briefly and justify how these slated improvements are achieved, based on what you have already read in this chapter.

The area of *business and requirements modeling* is concerned primarily with structuring the way an organization can and should operate in the future. The principal challenge at this level is to work with a group of non-IT-domain experts to unambiguously formulate the structures and processes of a business. To be successful, the business clients must understand the requirements and the model at this level. Modeling with the RASC organizations, processes, and resources using the CRC technique is so intuitive to non-IT-domain experts that they immediately feel comfortable with this form of refining and structuring their requirements. They can participate actively in the responsibility-driven design sessions; they become codesigners of their convergent system. The walk-through/run-through technique is a simple and fun way to debug and verify the integrity of business logic before time and effort are wasted refining ambiguous, incomplete business requirements.

The resulting CRC structure and dynamic scenarios document complex business situations using simple visual techniques almost anybody can understand immediately. Due to its universal understandability and high-fidelity representation, it is much superior as a project signoff document than traditional textual specifications. Because business-IT convergence is preserved in the subsequent development steps, this model remains valuable as the high-level documentation and specification of the IT system. Due to the highly human-interactive nature of business and requirements modeling, the time savings resulting from the use of the architecture and its tools, while still significant, is less here than the savings in subsequent development steps. However, the concomitant increase in quality is more significant than the time saved. This is so because many projects fail completely because of problems in business and requirements modeling. This emphasizes the conservative nature of the figures in the table.

The subsequent area of *design evolution and UML modeling* concerns the process of refining a business model into a convergent component model. In contemporary system development, models are converted from one to the other during the process of design. These conversion steps subsequently lose track of the original business model from which they were derived, if a business model even existed in the first place. In the Convergent Architecture, the sequence of model conversions is replaced by the evolution of a single model: The components in the business model are the components in the resulting system. The refinement of the model can be tracked visibly throughout the development process. The developer can move freely between each level of the model in incremental refinement steps instead of major, error-prone conversions. The model and its evolution remain understandable. In addition, intelligent verifiers, debuggers, and assistants in the IT-architectural IDE help a developer stay on the most direct, high-quality path toward a convergent system. The specific application of patterns and standards, such as J2EE/EJB, by the architecture allows the tools to automate many of the error-prone and redundant tasks still handled by hand in traditional development scenarios.

In most, if not all, development organizations, the area of *Web and system accessor development* is still at the level of hand-made craftsmanship. This is not only costly, but also produces proprietary, complex systems that few understand. This type of handcrafted access to a system is a far cry from model-driven development. The Convergent Architecture improves this situation by promoting the design and delivery of system access components to the same level of model-driven development used to develop the business components of the system. The development of both UI- and SI-accessors is part of the IT-architectural IDE in the Convergent Architecture. The UML-based modeling of system access allows a developer to visually represent, document, and reuse both the structural and dynamic aspects of, for example, a B2C or B2B design. The interactions with the convergent components are also part of the UML model, so code can be generated for the end-to-end system, from the server-side business components to the user's Web interface.

The steps in the *implement, build, and deploy cycle* traditionally have involved extensive hand coding, even though many of these tasks are highly redundant and repetitive. The tools traditionally used for each of these steps are extremely generic and unaware of each other. As such, they are unable to assist each other. In addition, these activities still take place at a relatively low, complex, and error-prone level. For example, contemporary code design and implementation usually are performed in a programming IDE. UML models are still used rarely as a proactive structuring tool to guide subsequent code generation from the UML model. This is where the mutual awareness of the development model and the IT-architectural IDE in the Convergent Architecture provides extensive benefits. The payoff is in terms of turnaround time, structural quality, and reduced coding effort in all three steps of the frequently repeated implement, build, deploy cycle. The translative generation from a verified UML model automatically produces major portions of reliable program code, the build environment, and deployment artifacts. Using the UML model as a basis provides reliable documentation and ensures the structural quality of the implementation generated. Using the generator IDE, the extent of generation from the UML model can be increased with time to further reduce both the cycle time and the cycle quality. This also reduces the number of programmers and testers required to produce a given result.

The task of *testing* always has been accompanied by an intensive effort in test development. There are two ways to reduce the testing effort while increasing quality. First, raise the quality of the code produced in the first place. Second, simplify the definition and development of effective test instruments. The Convergent Architecture addresses both these areas. The code generated is of superior quality for two reasons. First, UML models are verified for their style compliance and completeness in the C-REF module before being used for code generation. Second, the generator itself repeatedly produces reliable results, much faster and with fewer errors than a programmer. This is known as *implicit quality* because the source of errors is removed transparently as a by-product of the development process. Although reduced in magnitude, explicit testing is still required. Such explicit tests are particularly important to verify that business logic has been implemented accurately. This requires precise business test scenarios. The definition of business test scenarios is an automatic result of the business-modeling task in the Convergent Architecture. The C-BOM module generates both graphical and tabular-state flowcharts from the recorded business run-throughs. These can then be used to model and generate test accessors, leveraging once again—this time in the area of test development—the advantages of model-driven components and accessors mentioned earlier. The end result is not only less testing overall, but also well-documented, higher-quality tests using specifications produced automatically by the domain experts during the process of business modeling.

An effective *development tool environment* is always required for successful progress in IT projects. However, an adequate environment rarely exists at the onset of a project. In addition, the intense effort to develop and integrate a mature tool environment is chronically underestimated. There are ample accounts of projects succumbing to what is known as "death by tools." This is the problem addressed by the IT-architectural IDE in the Convergent Architecture. With it, the tool coverage of the critical development path is completely stable before a project starts. This also means that the project effort and risks can be better estimated because it is clear how the project will proceed and how tools will support the development.

Documentation always has been a burden for IT projects, often resulting in the production of poor user documentation and little or no design documentation. The model-centric, convergent approach of the Convergent Architecture alleviates this burden by producing high-quality design documentation as a by-product of development. The model-driven code generation ensures that the technical aspects of the system are accurately documented and up-to-date at all times—automatically, with no extra effort. This also increases the quality and usability of the documentation. Due to the convergence of the business and technical models, the same applies to documentation of the business model. The business model documents the current business and its supporting system behavior. It is automatically up-to-date and may be used as a basis for training literature and handbooks.

The effort required to adapt development and tools to a particular *runtime environment* traditionally is very high. A project often will spend much of its time experimenting with the best way to leverage the selected runtime infrastructure, for example, a particular application server. This lengthy trial-and-error process results in a zigzag path of wasted programming effort, wasted modeling effort, and project plan alterations. The generator cartridges alleviate this problem by defining a place to reuse and cumulatively improve knowledge on the runtime environment across projects. The cartridge packages the results of experiments done by others and allows a developer to repeatedly produce effective mappings from UML models to the particular infrastructure. Moreover, this infrastructure-specific knowledge is used to check the UML models to avoid wasteful zigzagging during the modeling phase. The generator IDE is then used to further tune or adapt the technology projection, thus reducing the need to alter models and hand-written code.

The areas of *project management and the implementation of a development process* are broad areas that always constitute an inexact science. However, much of the effort and some of the inexactness are reduced by the development model and, in particular, the IT-architectural IDE in the Convergent Architecture. First, not only is the development process more specifically tuned; it also is supported explicitly and automated by the IT-architectural IDE. Thus, the effort required to implement and support the process is reduced. Second, tracking the project from the project manager's perspective is more effective and more precise. The modules of the IT-architectural IDE each present a window into the current status of design evolution. The verifiers in these modules present just-in-time information regarding the completion, integrity, and technological feasibility of the model. The immediate generation of a complete system infrastructure including user access aspects from a model allows the developer and the project manager to continuously verify the state of the design at the most reliable feedback level possible—the level of a deployed, running system.

Summary

This chapter presented the "big picture" and high-level roadmap of the Convergent Architecture. It served as both an overview and a common reference frame for use by any stakeholder in projects applying the architecture. It also covered the anatomy of the architectural style, including the role of its parts, how they are related, and how they support one another. It brought the concept of IT-architectural style to life by summarizing how each of its four features is realized in the Convergent Architecture.

Chapters 3 through 7 and the bonus chapter on the Web site follow the roadmap presented in this chapter. Each chapter details a major part of the Convergent Architecture, following the same order in which they were introduced in this chapter. Chapter 8 is the place to go from here if you are anxious to first see a hands-on tutorial example using the Convergent Architecture.

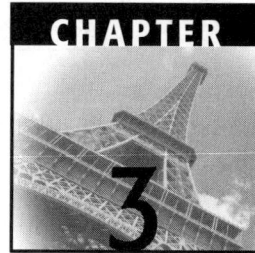

The Convergent Architecture Metamodel

The vision and principles of the architecture.

The Convergent Architecture metamodel defines the top-level vision, principles, and rules by which decisions are made within the architectural style and its instances. It constitutes a common reference frame of engineering and project-management principles shared by all stakeholders of information technology (IT) systems built according the Convergent Architecture. The general purpose and positioning of this metamodel within any IT-architectural style were described in Chapter 1. Chapter 2, then, presented its role in the top-level roadmap of the Convergent Architecture and summarized its contents, which consist of the following major themes:

- The three pillars of holistic architecture: project design, business design, and system design
- Convergence and convergent engineering
- The machine shop metaphor
- Reduced abstraction set computing (RASC)
- Conceptual isomorphism
- Component metamorphosis

This chapter covers these themes in detail. It should be read to get a firm grasp on the foundations of the Convergent Architecture. Architects, lead designers, and project managers need to be familiar with these topics to properly apply this IT-architectural style.

The Three Pillars of Holistic Architecture

It is obvious that every IT architecture has something to do with large-scale system design. However, a holistic approach to IT architecture requires a broader perspective. It also must address the critically important areas of project design and business design. Project design says how projects are set up, organized, managed, and coordinated. This goes beyond what typically is known as the *software development process*. Business design specifies how a business strategy is refined and represented to enable effective IT support of the business.

These three design areas-project design, business design, and system design—play a complementary role in the effective development of modern IT systems (see Figure 3.1). They are intimately related, considerably influencing each other in many ways. If a development project starts without a well-prepared project design, then it should be no surprise when the project slips due to coordination problems. Similarly, if a system is developed without a proper business design, then it should be no surprise if the resulting IT systems do not support the business adequately. To neglect the intimate relationships between these three themes is to ignore significant factors influencing large-scale system design. Neglecting any one of the three throws the other two off balance. The significance of their mutual reinforcement makes them the three pillars of holistic IT architecture.

Many of the problems experienced by contemporary IT organizations can be attributed to the fact that the areas concerning the design of a business and the design of a project are handled in an ad-hoc manner. Attempting to design complex IT systems without first designing an appropriate project organization, its roles, and its processes is the best way to waste time and effort. Sadly, many IT consultants do not possess clear project design concepts when they enter into an engagement, leaving the crucial project design component up to the customer, who often has little experience with modern IT development. In such cases, system development takes place without a proper frame of work, often in an unchanneled, chaotic manner, resulting in systems that reflect this chaos.

Even greater problems can occur when projects are set up using antiquated project management methods having little to do with modern IT development. Software development projects have unique requirements. Project management organizations and techniques that still may be well-suited for traditional (non-IT-centric) projects often will fail or be extremely inefficient when it comes to modern software development. The application of inappropriate project management principles to software design is the single most significant reason for the high failure rate of software projects. Large companies and government organizations with a long tradition of project management are the most susceptible to this hazard. It is no coincidence that software projects in these large traditional organizations are notorious for their ineffectiveness, and the resulting software is notorious for its inadequacies.

Often, the only counterbalance to a completely inappropriate project design in these organizations is their high tolerance of inefficiency and their extensive cash reserves. In the past, these cash reserves have been accrued through traditional product or service lines that had, at most, only a tangential dependency on IT systems. These business units could make money independent of the quality of their IT support. This situation is changing fast. Even the most resilient cash cows in large companies and government agencies are becoming critically dependent on IT. The cash cows are becoming the victims of the very IT inadequacy they subsidized. The traditional tolerance of software-inept project design in these organizations now has led to a vicious circle that already has begun to take its toll.

A similar situation exists in the area of business design. In the burgeoning Information Age, software no longer just supports isolated parts of the business, but the business in its entirety. Business strategies are no longer achievable without intensive IT support. This means that business design is now essentially synonymous with IT design. Business design and IT design can no longer be seen as separate entities: Future business designs also will be, to a great extent, IT designs. This evolution is reflected by the increasing significance of corporate information officer (CIO) positions in large organizations in recent years. In fact, many companies at the forefront of the Information Age have even abolished the CIO position in favor of a general IT awareness among all employees. The entire organization, starting with the chief executive officer (CEO), is IT-centric: Every employee is actively aware of the central role IT plays in the business. It is obvious, then, that a successful IT architecture for modern organizations clearly must communicate how the business and its IT systems fit together as one consolidated system. It must consciously address the intimate relationship between business and system design. Once again, this is not the case in the great majority of today's IT systems. The intimate relationship between the business and its systems has not been a central theme in IT development.

Traditionally, IT development has focused on secluded operational problems of a business, not on the business design itself. In fact, most organizations do not even possess a business design, not to mention a visible mapping of the business design to its commensurate IT support. Even worse, if you ask five coordinators in any large organization to give you a consistent picture of how the business works, that is, what its goals and priorities are and how things work together, you will get five very different descriptions. Usually, none of these descriptions is consistent and concise enough to design an IT system. Each of these persons has his or her unique perspective of the way things should work. There is nothing fundamentally wrong with this situation except for the fact that it is a terrible basis for creating an effective IT system. If IT systems are to integrate the business, then there has to be a consistent model of the business. There is no way to build an effective IT system that caters to numerous, imprecise opinions of how the business should work. This is why most contemporary IT systems are so woefully inadequate. Someone must be in charge of consolidating the various cross-functional opinions into one big picture, one consistent scheme that can be used to build a system that supports all the units of an organization—the entire organization, not just parts of it. Logically, one of the persons who must play a decisive role in creating this big picture should be the IT architect, since he or she also must ensure the IT component of the business model, which, as we have seen, cannot be developed as an afterthought. They are intimately related. Thus, the IT architect must possess powerful techniques and tools to assist in developing and evolving the big picture of the business domain in conjunction with its supporting IT systems.

In the vast majority of cases, the act of business design as part of IT architecture will lead to an overall increase in business quality. The simplifying conciseness required by

IT designs forces a business to get serious about defining and representing how it operates. The resulting business model alone is an important step toward improving business quality, regardless of the IT system. Above all, it unambiguously communicates to everyone in the business how the business works. The five business coordinators mentioned earlier now have one clear model instead of five different models. If this business model has been developed as part of the IT architecture, the corresponding IT aspects are now visible and positioned correctly as an essential part of the business equation. A continuous, positive cycle of change and feedback can now take place—first the business design, followed by its IT support, followed by operational feedback, leading to adjustment of parameters in the business equation. The IT systems have now become valuable tools to represent and optimize the business instead of just being a troublesome source of risk and cost. However, this cycle of continuous optimization cannot begin until business design and system design take place within the context of joint projects. Combining these themes into joint projects has the pleasant side effect of removing the traditional impedance wall between business and IT organizations. Here again, an appropriate project design is key to successfully integrating business and system design.

Lastly, it is interesting to note the relationship between the theme of business design and so-called standard or packaged software. Packaged software comprises a partial, common-denominator business model to solve common, widespread business problems. However, many organizations have been seduced into thinking that their entire IT needs can be met adequately by using packaged software. This is rarely the case in medium and large organizations. Usually, these organizations must add value by providing unique products or services. At some point, these products and services will require unique IT systems that must be either developed from scratch or integrate packaged software in unique combinations. In this sense, packaged software can be compared with the refrigerators or washing machines in a modern household. These machines package services required by most households. However, there is no pack-

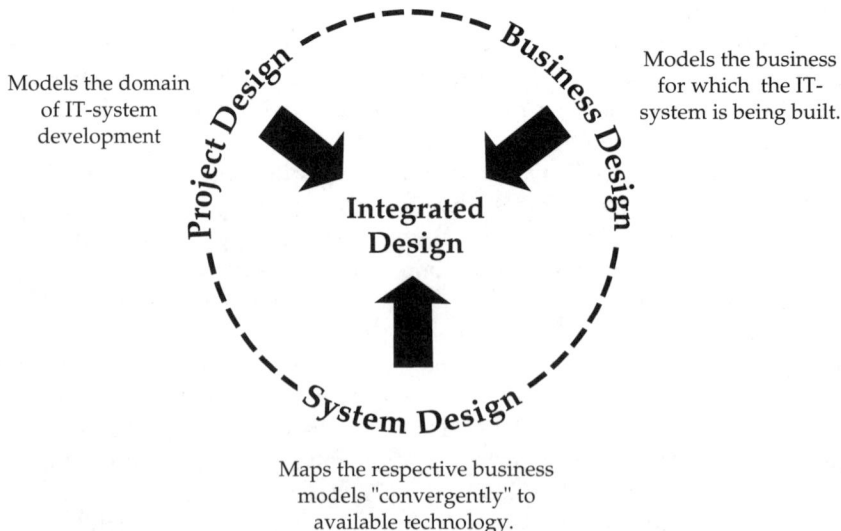

Models the domain
of IT-system
development

Models the business
for which the IT-
system is being built.

Project Design

Business Design

Integrated Design

System Design

Maps the respective business
models "convergently" to
available technology.

Figure 3.1 The three pillars of a holistic architecture. IT-architecture is only complete when it covers these three intimately related themes.

aged solution for the entire house. The house must meet the particular needs of its builder. Custom integration work is required to position and integrate the washing machine and refrigerator properly into the house. The parts in between the machines—the rooms, the cabinetry, an so on—must be custom-designed. Both an architect and an architecture are required if the whole house is to be constructed effectively to meet the special needs of the builder. Most businesses and their IT systems are orders of magnitude more complex than a house, making professional architecture orders of magnitude more important, above and beyond packaged solutions.

The following sections detail each of the three pillars of a holistic architecture. The principles in each section are formulated as requirements because the charter of the architectural style is to meet these requirements. These requirements are then fulfilled in the subsequent layers of the Convergent Architecture. In addition, as will be evident later in this chapter, the principles in the Convergent Architecture metamodel influence each other. This is quite natural because requirements are not necessarily unidirectional or independent.

Project Design

The project design theme is concerned with the optimal coordination of single and parallel projects operating at various levels of an organization. It must address the needs of consolidated business and system design.

From the perspective of project design, the architecture should do the following:

- Define the IT organization structure, roles, and responsibilities before beginning IT projects.
- Define the development team structure, roles, and responsibilities.
- Define procedures for the setup, planning, organization, and coordination of projects. In particular:
  - Project conception and bootstrapping.
  - The software development process in the context of an IT organization, where multiple projects may exist in parallel.
  - Project management, in particular project definition, estimation, planning, coordination, and tracking.
- Provide tool and infrastructure support for the critical project workflow and the most critical supporting areas.

Business Design

The business design theme is concerned with the consolidation and optimization of the entire business in conjunction with consolidation and optimization of its supporting IT systems.

From the perspective of business design, the architecture should do the following:

- Define the relationships between the business as a whole and its IT organization.

- Show how the business model and IT model interact as parts of the overall business equation and how to represent this to the various stakeholders in combined business and system development.

- Show how to represent the business strategy in terms of a business model, including its needs for flexibility and change.

- Define how IT models emerge from the business model without losing track of the business model.

- Enable IT systems to be modeled and evolved through active participation of business-domain experts and IT designers.

- Provide tool support for the activity of business design in close conjunction with the design of its supporting IT system.

System Design

The system design theme is concerned with simplifying the development of effective IT systems in the context of an entire organization.

From the perspective of system design, the architecture should do the following:

- Define the use of unambiguous structures and mechanisms covering critical design areas such as design layers, components, human access, system access, applications, and packages.

- Provide clear development guidelines and constraints to meet the technical requirements of enterprise systems (for example, transactions, persistence, security, scalability, availability, operations) using available technology. In addition, it should be as specific as possible in order to avoid complexity due to ambiguity and to replace fussy alternatives with clear guidelines.

- Address subtle *epiphenomena*.[1]

- Provide tool and infrastructure support for the critical-project workflow and the most critical supporting areas.

- Formulate the insuperable constraints of run-time and deployment technologies and leverage this knowledge to provide highly feasible design structures and mechanisms.

- Provide tool and infrastructure support for the activity of system design in accordance with the project and business design themes: modeling, documentation, automation, environment, and development flow.

Convergence and Convergent Engineering

In 1995, Dr. David A. Taylor coined the term *convergent engineering* to name the vision and techniques he presented in his milestone book entitled, *Business Engineering with Object Technology*. In his book, Dr. Taylor outlines in no uncertain terms why IT system development as practiced today will no longer succeed in the burgeoning Information Age. He then provides a solution to this dilemma by clearly explaining the appropriate use of object technology (object-oriented technology) to achieve a form of evolutionary business and system design unattainable with traditional techniques. The central concept of convergent engineering will be described briefly in the following sections. For greater detail, Dr. Taylor's book should be consulted as the ultimate source of these concepts (Taylor, 1995).

Convergent engineering essentially is concerned with completing the paradigm shift to object technology in an unadulterated manner and realizing its full potential despite numerous distractions along the way. You may be surprised at the power of object orientation exhibited in convergent engineering because it goes beyond what is commonly in use today.

The essence of convergent engineering is the consolidation, or *convergence*, of business and system design into a single harmonious whole. The critical reliance of today's organizations on information technology requires us to think of them as a single, intimately related system. The business cannot succeed without technology. By the same token, technological innovation drives the capabilities of the business. However, most contemporary organizations treat business strategy and its IT support as two separate worlds. These worlds rarely communicate, and when they do, they do so via obscure, poorly defined channels. This causes a continual divergence between the worlds of business strategy and IT strategy. *Divergence* means that it is not clear how IT really supports the business. The mapping between the two is at best vague and in most cases essentially unknown. Normally, divergence is synonymous with intractable system complexity. This leads to a myriad of familiar problems, for example, IT systems that impede business change, ad-hoc IT designs, and constant communication problems between an organization's core business management and its IT departments.

Convergence is the simplest solution to these critical problems. It says that an organization may represent both its business and its IT design with a common model. This common model can be viewed from two perspectives, the business perspective and the software perspective, as shown in Figure 3.2. The business and IT stakeholders have

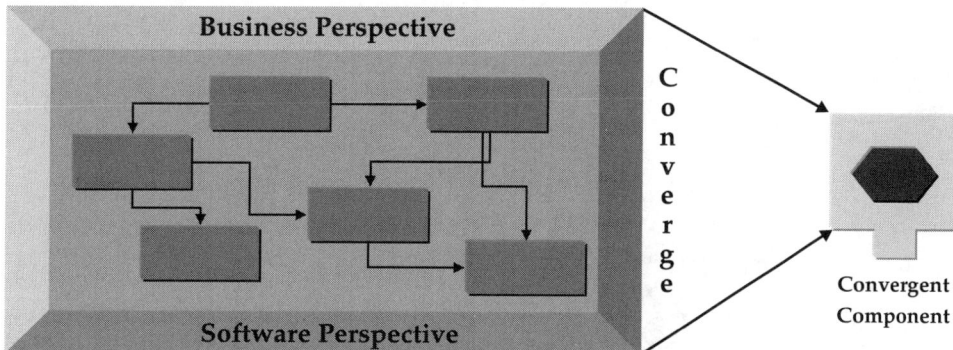

Figure 3.2 Converging business and IT models. Convergence = two perspectives of one model.

two views of one common model. To achieve this, convergent engineering applies the simplifying concepts of object-oriented design equally to both business and IT design. Historically, object-oriented design has been associated with simplifying the development of IT systems. This is an injustice to the powerful concepts of object-oriented design, which are a means of dealing with complexity in general and have no inherent connection with IT. Thus object-oriented design serves equally well to simplify the development of business models. Convergent engineering recognizes and leverages this strength to simplify business models. The most significant simplification is achieved by having an object-oriented business model, which can then be mapped easily to object technology.

To achieve convergence, the business is modeled incrementally using the concepts of object-oriented design one critical piece at a time. The central objects used in this process are *organizations, processes,* and *resources.* Since the resulting business model leverages the concepts of object technology, it also can be used as the software model. This convergence into a single model is maintained throughout system development and even into the run-time system. This is achieved by using IT components that directly represent the modeled business objects (that is, business organizations, processes, and resources), as shown in Figure 3.3. A system based on these concepts is called a *convergent system*.

Contemporary business analysts often stress the benefits of "aligning the business with technology." In doing this, they emphasize one of the many advantages of convergence. Clearly, a convergent system aligns the business with technology in that it keeps track of how business processes and organizations are supported by the IT system. A change in a business process may be realized quickly in the operational environment by changing the corresponding process representation in the IT system. Another benefit is that the process of convergent engineering improves communication between business managers and the IT department. Since they refer to the same model, they develop a common understanding of organizations, processes, and resources. This simplifies discussions regarding changes in the business and commen-

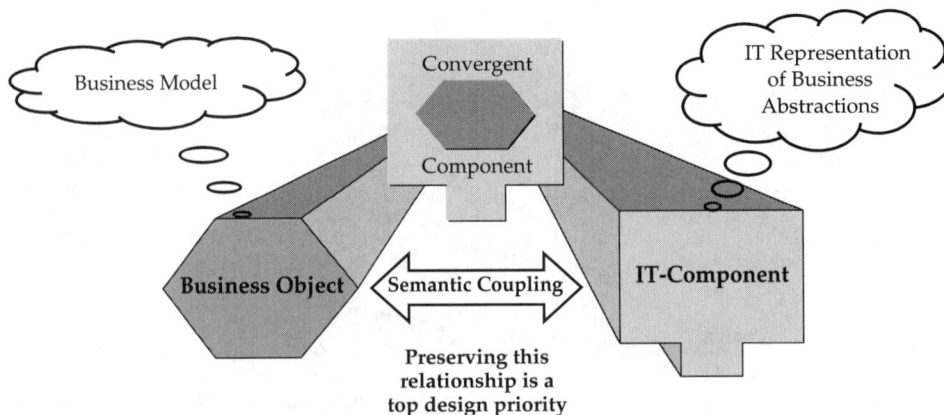

Figure 3.3 The convergent component.

surate changes in the IT system. In addition, due to the common concepts and language used in both worlds, the IT department can make considerable contributions to business optimization. Another advantage is the reduction in development effort and risks. This is so because fewer translation steps are required between the business concept and the IT system. There is a visible correlation between business-domain design and technical design. Projects no longer have to take the one-way street of translating business models into technical models. These translation steps are often the greatest source of error, cost, and risk in projects.

Despite its conceptual simplicity, convergence cannot be achieved overnight. This is so because organizations and their systems are already entrenched in the traditional problems. A rapid overhaul of the organization and its IT practice is not practical. A long-term migration to convergence is the only pragmatic approach. However, each small step along the road to convergence can bring measurable benefits. For example, modern application and middleware vendors are moving toward object-oriented, component-based systems. Thus, an architecture that focuses on convergent engineering is the best way to prepare businesses and IT departments to leverage new technologies as they become available in the mainstream IT market.

Lastly, it is important to note that, like all ideal models, convergent engineering may never be completely achievable in its purest form. This, however, does not reduce its applicability or value as a basis for IT architecture. This point is emphasized by the OPEN Group, which refers to convergent engineering as a basis for its third-generation object-oriented development process, the OPEN process (Graham, 1997).

In summary, convergent engineering is the cornerstone of simplification and the key to resolving many of the pathologic problems suffered by IT organizations. It drastically simplifies both business and software development by consolidating the aspects they have in common. It correctly recognizes the object-oriented paradigm as a universally applicable means of simplification. Consequently, the reader will see me use object-oriented concepts in some unexpected places—everywhere from business design, to project design, to system design. The ubiquitous use of object-oriented concepts may look like the easy way out, and as a key simplification, it is.

The Machine Shop Metaphor

Effective IT development requires an operational environment to support highly specialized techniques, templates, and tools to be used by teams of developers. Sadly, most projects start without such an environment and often fail for this very reason. The well-known concept of a machine shop exemplifies the environment used in mature industries to build complex systems. When comparing the outset of a typical IT project with the outset of a typical machine shop project, it is clear that the IT field has a lot of catching up to do. The Convergent Architecture uses the symbol of a machine shop to represent its target development environment. It strives to provide IT projects with an operational development environment commensurate with that of a well-run machine shop.

The metaphor of a machine shop is particularly applicable in the context of an IT-architectural style. This is so because an effective machine shop is always designed with particular types of products in mind. It is sensitive to the style of systems being built and has been highly tuned to build such systems, for example, motors, boats, or skis, but not all three at once. Thus, in the IT field, the effectiveness of a machine shop can only be achieved realistically in the context of an IT-architectural style where the style of system is also known. Like a machine shop, the development process, tool modularity, design partitions, and skills distribution all can be tuned to the specific requirements of the style. These requirements are formulated in the architecture and development models of the Convergent Architecture. The fact that these models are not project-specific enables a style-effective shop to be built and tuned outside the limited context of a particular project and to be reused by many projects. Just as in mature industries, the shop can be in place and operational before a project begins, thus reducing time, cost, and considerable uncertainty in the area of project estimation and management.

The machine shop approach has other advantages. The IT architecture in all its many facets will be best understood and applied most effectively in an operational environment similar to a machine shop. In this environment, relatively abstract concepts, such as the development guidelines, design patterns, and structures of the architecture, can be experienced directly in conjunction with work cells and tools supporting their proper application. The shop embodies the abstract forms of architecture as tangible, operational forms in a working environment that can be learned easily and applied effectively by a wide audience. Since the shop is tuned for development according to a particular IT-architectural style, once a developer has learned how the shop works, this knowledge can be reused in other projects or to train other developers. In addition, each time the shop is used, important feedback is gained that leads to consistent improvements in the quality of the shop environment.

Most contemporary organizations are in dire need of the machine shop approach for several other reasons. First, when a group of developers gets together at the onset of a new project, experience shows that they have a hard time agreeing on a common approach—to put it mildly. Second, even if they can agree, they are usually not experienced in the complex area of tool design and integration at the level of IT architecture. The endeavor to define the IT architecture and its procedures and then to construct an effective development landscape all within the context of a project is unrealistic. Such attempts have led to the demise of countless projects. Third, experience shows that if this all takes place within the framework of a single project, the resulting development environment will not be well-suited to other projects. Lastly, once the project is completed, who will make sure that the environment continues to evolve with modern concepts, technologies, and tools? These points make it clear why mature industries always start critical projects with a well-tested machine shop. Starting without a machine shop is equivalent to experimenting: It almost guarantees that nothing will be built effectively. Moreover, a newly conceived machine shop is not a whole lot better because high-quality, effective work can only occur in a shop environment that has been tuned across many project generations.

In summary, the effectiveness of IT projects can be increased significantly if they begin with a well-tuned, style-specific development environment comparable with machine shops found in mature industries.

Reduced Abstraction Set Computing (RASC)

The principle of *reduced abstraction set computing* (RASC) says that the core abstractions of convergent engineering (that is, organizations, processes, and resources) form the basic types with which we can model all business-domain aspects of a convergent system regardless of the actual business domain. This also includes technical businesses, such as manufacturing and government domains. These three core abstractions can be mapped directly to available technology with minimal translation loss. Two additional abstractions complement the core abstractions to complete the RASC set. These are the *accessors* and the *utility components*. Accessors address the access to and from human users and external systems. Utility components denote the purely technical utilities of an IT environment. The set of RASC abstractions is embodied by the convergent components in the Convergent Architecture.

The RASC organizations, processes, and resources (OPRs) are the basic building blocks in the convergent approach. The number of distinct building blocks, as well as their type, is extremely important from the perspective of a designer. RASC addresses this aspect of design by proposing a set of generally applicable abstractions as the optimal set of building blocks for designing and developing convergent systems. RASC says that there exists a certain set of building blocks, the RASC set, that enables us to maximize the expressiveness of models while keeping the models simple and easy to understand. More than this set of building blocks would be "too many," which would lead to unnecessary complexity and confusion. Fewer building blocks would be "too few," which would hinder adequate expression. The RASC building blocks form a pattern language consisting of this optimal set of abstractions. This set is used consistently in the Convergent Architecture to express (model) and build all three pillars of a holistic IT-architecture, not only the IT system. For example, from the perspective of business design in the Convergent Architecture, the three OPR building blocks, that is, the core abstractions of the RASC set, have been found to provide optimal results: As shown later in this section, four abstractions turn out to be too many, and two abstractions are too few.

The intended analogy with reduced instruction set computing (RISC) designs in the hardware industry emphasizes the benefits of using a useful set of reduced abstractions to deal with complexity successfully. The following statements from "mips RISC Architecture" (Kane, 1988) bear witness to the similar problems faced by both hardware and software designers and emphasize the benefits of what Kane refers to as "a simplifying architecture":

- "The uniform instruction set is easier to use."
- "There is a closer correlation between instruction count and cycle count, making it much easier to measure the true impact of code optimization activities."
- "Programmers can have a higher confidence in hardware correctness."

Similarly, by focusing on RASC, corresponding levels of simplicity and design effectiveness can be achieved in the software world. Several aspects contribute to the improvements. First, the small set of effective abstractions form a simple, common language to improve the quality of discussions and designs. Second, anybody and everybody can understand this small set easily at the appropriate level. Third, this small set of abstractions can be refined and tuned over time to produce high-performance systems while still maintaining the simplicity of models. In addition, just as with RISC, the tools used to develop and maintain the systems can be more focused, more specific, and more highly tuned while still remaining easy to understand. Lastly, the RASC set enables a small set of canonical components, the convergent components in the Convergent Architecture, to be introduced and refined over time. From the designer's perspective, the components are in many ways analogous to the concept of the canonical C++ class proposed by Jim Coplien (1992) in his book, *Advanced C++ Idioms*. The components simplify modeling, models as well as code style, while enabling more effective automatic code generators. This all adds up to reduced software entropy with increased design power and design communication.

In addition to its analogy with RISC in the hardware industry, important evidence of a RASC-type approach exists in the software industry. First of all, the RASC set used in the Convergent Architecture builds on the three core business abstractions proposed in 1995 by convergent engineering. These are the organization, the process, and the resource abstractions. Convergent engineering recognized three abstractions, not two and not four, to provide an optimal working set. These three core abstractions and their basic relationships are shown in Figure 3.4. However, Convergent engineering is not alone in selecting these three abstractions. The respected Advanced Network System Architecture (ANSA) (Iggulden, 1994), the predecessor and principal basis for ISO Open Distributed Processing (ODP) standards, also recognized a universally optimal set consisting of three core abstractions. It is interesting to note that both the

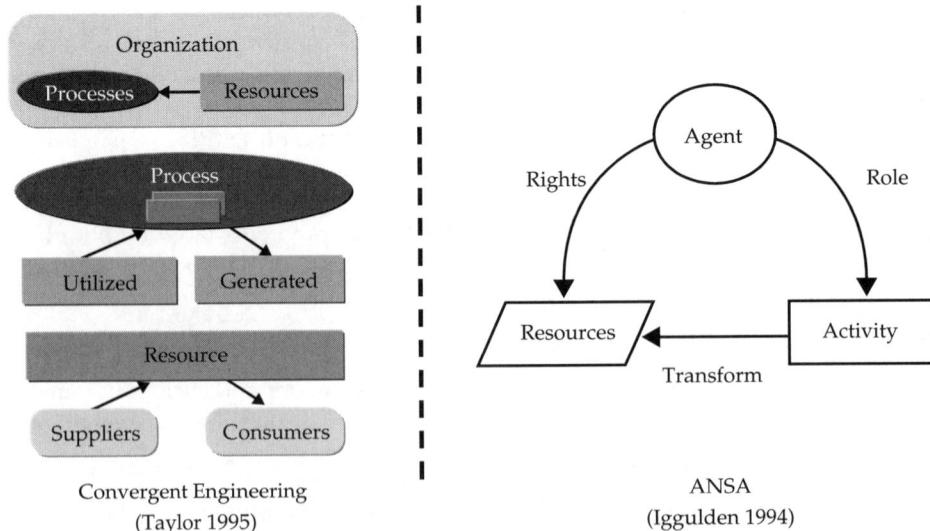

Figure 3.4 Independent derivations of RASC (simultaneously on different sides of the world).

ANSA/ODP architects, and Dr. David A. Taylor arrived at a reduced abstraction set consisting of three core abstractions independently of one another at approximately the same time.

Even more significant than the timing and number of these core abstractions is the similarity of their types, their semantic similarity.[2] Not only did these experienced designers arrive independently at the same number of abstractions (building blocks) to achieve the optimum, but also the types of abstractions they defined as optimum are essentially equivalent. The rigor, substance, and reasoning that lead these two groups to the same result are evident in the respective sources, but the results can be observed by comparing the two RASC sets. In Figure 3.4, the ANSA agents clearly fulfill the same role as the convergent engineering organizations. They manage the access and life cycle of activities (that is, processes) and resources. The ANSA activities clearly correspond to convergent engineering processes. The activities transform resources, whereas in convergent engineering, it is said that the processes use, consume, and produce resources—essentially identical. Resources are the intelligent units of work and value common even in name to both models. The only real difference between the two sets is that convergent engineering names its abstractions using common business terminology and positions them in the context of convergent engineering, whereas ANSA has chosen more technical terms, in particular the term *agent*, and has positioned them in the context of ODP. The Convergent Architecture recognizes and builds on the mutually confirming results of convergent engineering and ANSA.

In summary, RASC in the Convergent Architecture builds on the concepts of convergent engineering and stakes the following claim: The most useful set of abstractions to use in all cases of domain modeling, whether the domain is a global financial institution or a machine manufacturer, is organizations, processes, and resources. These are embodied by their respective convergent components throughout the entire architecture. More than these three is too many, and fewer than these three is too few. Other types of abstractions are less effective. In addition to the three core business abstractions, two others exist to simplify the technical and access aspects of design. These are the utility components and the accessor components, which also belong to the family of convergent components.

Conceptual Isomorphism

Part of simplifying anything is the consistent use of familiar terms and concepts wherever possible. When a concept has been reused in a similar form in two different areas, then we say that *conceptual isomorphism* has been achieved.[3] Conceptual isomorphism in the area of software development means that a design concept is applicable in diverse development situations while still maintaining its familiar form. It means that all stakeholders in an IT project can reuse the concepts and that the knowledge and experience regarding these concepts can be reused effectively in other projects. Although the reuse of technology and, more recently, modeling languages has become widely accepted as just plain common sense, the reuse of design concepts at the level of IT architecture across projects and domains is not yet widespread. The Convergent Architecture strives to raise the awareness and use of conceptual isomorphism to the level of convergent business and IT design. The goal is for the concepts of the IT-architectural style to be both understood uniformly and applied uniformly across diverse organizations, projects, and technologies.

There are several different areas where conceptual isomorphism can be used immediately to simplify and optimize both business and IT design. The first of these areas concerns the applicability of development concepts across all IT projects of an organization and across multiple organizations. An experienced IT architect selects development concepts that increase the effectiveness of developers and systems while at the same time being equally applicable in any organization, new or old. These are not vertical, domain-specific development concepts. They have the exact opposite, horizontal focus. Their goal is to counter the effect of the perpetual focus on vertical point solutions found in most organizations today. Just as a government must strive to avoid the disarray of compounded individual or point solutions in a society, so must an IT-architectural style help organizations to avoid repeatedly developing vertical point solutions to very general design problems. To replace redundant point solutions, architectural concepts are selected that may be reused everywhere to improve the vertical, domain-specific systems. These concepts solve general problems at a general level instead of expecting projects to repeatedly solve the same problem differently at the level of specific systems. This may sound like common sense—and it is—but it is not being achieved very often in today's IT organizations. The positive side effect of putting horizontal, cross-project, cross-functional architecture concepts in place is the creation of domain-specific systems that can be understood by persons from outside the domain. These systems have become conceptually compatible, and often technically compatible, with ones in other domains. There is a whole lot of room for these architecture-level concepts in most organizations. Substantial improvements are possible in the extensive areas of business modeling, technical detailing, technology mapping, and tools, for example. The convergent components are one example of such horizontal concepts in the Convergent Architecture. The convergent components may be applied equally to the convergent representation of human organizations, for example, a business unit or a train station, and to the representation of more technical organizations, such as a fabrication cell or an automobile motor.

Another area where conceptual isomorphism can make a big difference is in the IT organization or IT department of any company. There is no reason why the IT organization should not become part of the overall business model. If the IT architect can model a business, then there is no reason why he or she should not start by modeling his or her own business, which is the business of building IT systems. The organization responsible for this part of the business is, of course, the IT organization. It seems very reasonable to expect an IT architect to possess a model of his or her own business domain as a prerequisite to modeling someone else's domain.[4] If the same concepts are used to model the IT organization as those used to model other organizations—and there is no reason why this should not be the case—then the pleasant side effect of conceptual isomorphism results. The model shows all stakeholders not only how the IT organization works, but also how the design concepts will be used to model and support other business organizations. In addition, it substantiates the architecture itself by applying its own concepts in the spirit of "practice what you preach." As described earlier, the project design pillar of the Convergent Architecture requires this form of conceptual isomorphism. The result is the IT organization model of the Convergent Architecture, which employs the same concepts used to model other business domains.

One of the most significant advantages of conceptual isomorphism is its positive influence on the longevity and usefulness of knowledge. One of the biggest problems large organizations have today is the short half-life of expensive knowledge. The people who understood the concepts used in one project one year are in another project the next year. The design concepts and the way they were applied in the one project are invariably different in the other project. A simple move between IT-related projects within a traditional organization makes much of the knowledge from a previous project obsolete. If these projects used similar concepts in places where this is readily possible, then the knowledge could be reused and would be more valuable to the individual as well as to the company. Thus, shared architectural concepts enable persons who have been involved in one project to use more of the acquired knowledge later on in other projects. The longevity of the knowledge has been increased. This fuels the motivation to learn because the mileage of learning is increased. This form of conceptual isomorphism is also an indispensable step toward simplicity and efficiency in large organizations because, without it, nobody, not even the IT gurus of a company, can keep up with the number of different design concepts applied across diverse projects.

Conceptual isomorphism in IT system development does not happen by itself or as a by-product of everyday IT projects. This is so because these projects are not concerned with the subject of conceptual reuse across other projects. Trying to reapply design concepts from the narrow problem domains addressed by everyday IT projects across many domains will not work. To the contrary, this approach would increase software entropy rapidly because every project would have to modify the design significantly. Instead, it takes a major concerted effort to figure out which concepts can be reused readily and widely as part of an overall architectural approach. In addition, these concepts can only be used effectively when structured within the context of an IT-architectural style that has been designed specifically for this purpose. For these reasons, little conceptual isomorphism in the area of IT is found in organizations today.

Lastly, conceptual isomorphism is not the same thing as convergence. It does not mean that we should attempt to converge all business domains into a single uniform domain. Domains are separated logically according to their differences. Convergence focuses more on the vertical integration within a business domain. We converge business-domain designs and IT, but we do not try to converge reasonably distinct business domains with each other. Such attempts would be counterproductive because the result would be more complex and less effective than treating the business domains as logically separate categories. Conceptual isomorphism complements convergence from the horizontal perspective; it says that we can reuse many of the same concepts across diverse business domains.

In summary, the first step to high-value reuse of both technology and knowledge begins with the use of common concepts across diverse projects. This is known as *conceptual isomorphism*, which provides several significant advantages. First, it reduces learning effort and increases the longevity of knowledge. Second, the uniform application of design concepts, abstractions, and patterns across domains permits both knowledge and tools to be improved incrementally through reuse.

Component Metamorphosis

There are few physical or material constraints to developing software systems. They are indeed "soft" in that we can conceivably manipulate and grow our designs any way we want. The principle of *component metamorphism* invokes an intentional analogy with the metamorphosis of a butterfly to express a better way to manipulate and grow software designs. Component metamorphosis says that we can leverage the context of an IT-architectural style to create active software components that assist in their own development. As illustrated in the Figure 3.5, a component can become an active entity beginning with its conception early in the analysis process. It can then actively participate in its elaboration throughout its entire life cycle.

There is no reason why a component should first spring to life late in the development cycle, after days or weeks of development. In its embryonic stages, a component can act in concert with its tool environment to significantly assist the developer with many tasks associated with its development. This includes such tasks as the acquisition and coordination of analysis information and business requirements, creating and manipulating models, and recording documentation and test scenarios. In addition, it can actively ensure that a healthy component is evolving at each step along the way. Based on the design features in the models of the IT-architectural style, a component can possess knowledge early on in its development regarding its style-consistent growth. It can use this knowledge to check and report on its style-consistent progress, as if it had an active immune system. For example, it can actively report on the structure and quality of its contents, whether it has adequate information to proceed to the next stage, or whether its current design provides adequate support for its intended

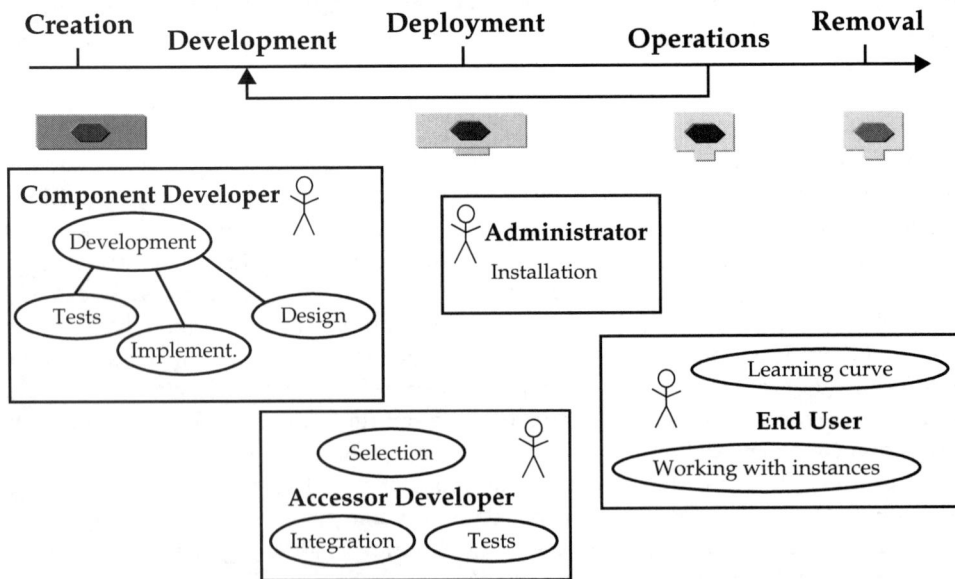

Figure 3.5 Component metamorphosis. Convergent components actively support users during a given life-cycle stage and work context.

role in the system. The component can take an active role in maintaining the integrity of the overall architecture by ensuring, at every step along the way, that it evolves according to the IT-architectural style. It can even tell us whether its current design status will permit it to be mapped appropriately to a particular technology.

Component metamorphosis is indeed possible if the IT-architectural style meets two principal requirements. First, it must stipulate how components evolve in the development model. Second, it must provide proactive support for this evolution in its tools and development infrastructure—its IT-architectural IDE. The process of metamorphosis can then replace the current mode of developing software in radical heaves of translation and reformulation of information. Components can be evolved through steady stages of information enhancement and growth—comparable with the metamorphosis of a butterfly. Mother nature achieved this for the butterfly over several million years, but we would like to move a little faster.

Component metamorphosis requires that we sharpen the tools of IT development. However, it turns out that sharpening our tools is probably the simplest step to take. This is due to the ironic imbalance between the systems the IT industry develops for others and the systems it develops for itself. As if dutifully fulfilling the proverbial truism of the cobbler's children having the worst shoes, we observe software in many business domains that does a much better job of managing information than we currently observe in our own ranks—in the business of building IT systems. It is a well-kept secret that the analytical and information-management capabilities of common finance and accounting systems, for example, put contemporary IT development tools to shame.

There is no good reason for this situation. However, there are reasons. First, IT designers have just been too busy improving tools for other domains to do the same in their own domain. Second, plenty of money is being made without good tools. Third, given the relative youth of the IT industry, customers are not IT-savvy enough to readily recognize how rudimentary and ineffective the contemporary techniques and tools are. Nor are they experienced enough to suggest—or better, to insist on—improvements. Fourth, and probably most important, the "softness" of software makes it possible to jerry-rig anything at any time, making tools appear to be a luxury. This could not be further from reality, as pointed out in Chapter 1. Component metamorphosis requires that we finally sharpen our own tools. It says to take the knowledge and experience that have been formulated in the models of the IT-architectural style and use them to create more intelligent components and tools. Together, this constellation will be the next best thing to cloning an experienced IT architect. The components become the vehicles of architectural knowledge and active architectural assistants, ready to help any developer anytime.

The principles of RASC and the machine shop metaphor are important prerequisites to achieving component metamorphosis. Without RASC, the components could not know much about their role in the architecture or anything about their intended features as mature components. Without the machine shop metaphor, tools could not optimally leverage the intelligence of the component or the high quality of information it provides. Combining the style-specific intelligence of the RASC components with the synergy of the machine shop approach in the IT-architectural IDE of the Convergent Architecture will ensure higher architectural fidelity even among less experienced designers and developers.

Component metamorphosis is not very trendy. It precludes for the most part code-derived architecture or code-driven modeling. This is in direct conflict with the so-called round-trip engineering (RTE) features currently endorsed by some tool vendors. Component metamorphosis requires a channeled, architecture-driven approach. Any structural changes made in source code following a model-driven code generation constitute an afterthought or ad-hoc change to the architecture. Such changes should constitute a rare exception and should be avoided if at all possible. In any case, they should not be encouraged. This is so because the component and tools cannot proactively coach to the evolution of features when they are changed late in the development chain. In such cases, the component has no way to ensure a well-balanced, healthy infrastructure. Such code-level structural changes bypass the features of a well-formed architecture, which begins early in the development cycle, and revive the very problems architecture is intended to solve.

Consider, for example, just one aspect of a component, its documentation. Component metamorphosis means that the documentation of a component will be enhanced and maintained at every stage of its development, each stage adding information regarding use, associations, risks, side effects, and so on. This type of documentation can be compared with the information sheet one receives with pharmaceutical products, such as a box of aspirin. The documentation is product-specific and is of extremely high quality. This quality cannot be achieved as an afterthought. It is the result of a long and well-controlled process that accompanied the development of the pharmaceutical product over its entire life cycle. If this process permitted late, ad-hoc modifications to the product, outside the defined process, there would be no way to ascertain the true quality of the product or its documentation. The mere fact that late, out-of-stream changes are allowed reduces the credibility of any information regarding the product, regardless of whether actual changes take place or not. The documentation becomes practically useless, despite the effort involved creating it. Similarly, if the controls of architecture-driven development are abrogated by arbitrarily modifying code at the end of the cycle, then high quality cannot be reasonably expected.

To ensure integrity, such changes must be made to the component by returning to the proper stage of metamorphosis (this is indeed possible in software in contrast to the real world). The changes can then be guided by the component and the IT-architectural IDE through all stages of development. Changes made without returning to the proper stage of metamorphosis constitute tumor-like growths in a design, which must be repaired later at a high cost. If this form of ad-hoc development persists, then the number and size of the tumors increase, causing a proportional degradation in the health of the overall system. In fact, a healthy component should even resist changes when these are attempted at inappropriate stages in its development. By doing this, it can proactively counter software entropy and irreparable pollution of the architecture.

In summary, component metamorphosis requires that components actively support their complete life cycle, in an entire community of components, beginning with the first identification of the component in the phase of business analysis. Once a component has been identified, it actively assists the designer throughout its architectural conform enhancement and evolution. It matures through the refinement stages of development from a basic, skeletal component to a fully functional component. This process resembles the metamorphosis of a butterfly and has been named accordingly.

Summary

This chapter presented the architectural metamodel of the Convergent Architecture. As we saw in Chapter 1, this is the highest-level model of the IT-architectural style. This chapter described the visions and principles of the Convergent Architecture, which directly influence the forms and mechanisms found in its subsequent layers. These visions and principles serve to define the spirit and goals of the architecture as a whole. They help diverse stakeholders at all levels of system design share a mutual understanding and mutual sense of direction across all IT projects in an organization. They instill a common sense of style in the entire organization, which results in more effective decisions and more compatible progress despite highly diverse projects.

The sections on the individual principles revealed how important synergies emerge from the cumulative contributions of the principles. They explained how the vision and the principles interact to influence the design of the structures and mechanisms in the IT-architectural style. The resulting structures and mechanisms are found in the development model of the style, which is covered in the next three chapters.

The Convergent
Component Metamodel

Components as the vehicle of architecture.

The development model of the Convergent Architecture is comprised of three subdivisions. The first of these is the convergent components metamodel, which is covered in this chapter.

The convergent component metamodel defines components as vehicles that transport the principles of the architectural style into elements of concrete design, tools, and technologies. It formulates the architectural style at the level of component design. It is a metamodel because it describes how to create a convergent component model that leverages particular standards (for example, UML or J2EE/EJB) and end technologies (for example, application servers) while fulfilling the requirements of the architectural style at large. Its requirements encompass project, business, and system design. As such, the metamodel has an impact on much more than just the way components are structured. It influences how they are derived, refined, and reused to achieve model-driven development using available standards and technologies such as UML, XML/HTML, J2EE/EJB, and Java.[1] The architectural IDE described in Chapter 7 is a prime example of the broad influence exercised by the convergent component metamodel. Every module in the integrated development environment (IDE) is more capable as an architectural assistant because the metamodel defines how such aspects as business design, project management, and technology management are related at the level of component development.

At a high level of abstraction, the structures and concepts in the convergent component metamodel are independent of particular standards and technologies. However, it would be contrary to the principles of the Convergent Architecture to stop at a high level of abstraction. The convergent component metamodel is explained and applied at ever-increasing levels of detail as we move through this book. Along the way, it is interesting to note how important the metamodel is as a visible and driving element of style and to discern its positive influence on the IT organization, the development process, and the architectural IDE.

This chapter presents the convergent component metamodel, its structure reflecting the logic in which the model moves from abstraction to detail. Each section addresses aspects of component structure, modeling style, patterns, and the technology projection:

- **Overview and fundamentals.** This section presents the underlying concepts and structure of the metamodel.

- **Architectural layers.** This section outlines major aspects of the layered component infrastructure and introduces the various types of components and their hierarchical organization.

- **Common aspects of all convergent components.** This section deals with the basic design and structures common to all convergent components to prepare the stage for the subsequent description of individual components. These commonalities comprise aspects such as component dimensions, modeling styles, and a technology projection. They address and build on the concepts known as Model Driven Architecture (MDA) as currently envisioned by the OMG (MDA 2001).

- **Convergent components.** This section provides detailed descriptions of component structure, modeling style, patterns, and the technology projection of the following components:

  - **Assembly components.** The top-level units of design and deployment.

  - **Accessor components.** For multichannel user interface and system interface access.

  - **Convergent OPR components.** Representations of business organizations, processes, and resources.

  - **Utility components.** Technical services supporting the superior layers.

Overview and Fundamentals

The convergent component metamodel does not build everything new from the ground up. Rather, it uses a solid foundation of existing concepts and standards, as shown in Figure 4.1.

To the left, this figure shows that significant aspects of the convergent components are *based on* the concepts of convergent engineering (Taylor 1995). Above all, convergent engineering prescribes the types and meaning of the business-relevant components-organizations, processes, and resources. It defines why and how these types of components are best suited to simplify both the process of business modeling and the software representation of the business model.

The UML shown at the center of the figure is used to *represent* the component structures, types, and concepts in a standard, semiformal modeling language. Based on the

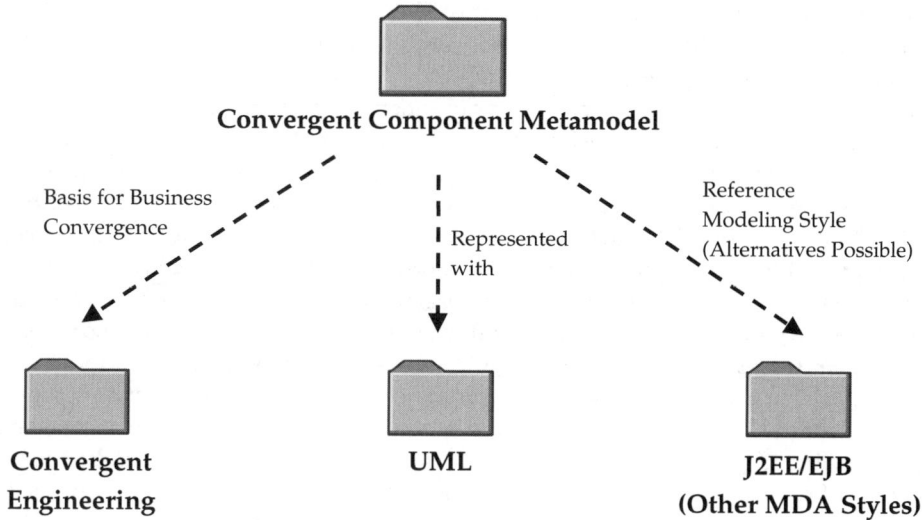

Figure 4.1 The foundation of convergent components.

UML representations, the component models can be communicated, reused, and manipulated more easily by teams of developers using modern tools. More important, the UML models used for convergent components serve to abstract the design from the particular implementation technology. The model then serves as the basis for automatic infrastructure generation using the technology projection, as introduced in Chapter 2. This *model-centric approach* to development is often referred to as a *model-driven design* or *model-driven architecture*.

The right of the figure shows that the J2EE/EJB specifications are used as the basis for the *reference modeling style*. The modeling style, which is covered in more detail later in this chapter, defines how we effectively manage and tune standards and technologies using high-level UML models. The term *reference* is also significant and has several implications here. First, the reference modeling style provides a concrete proof that the approach works: The reference modeling style can be used by default to build real systems, as will be seen later in this book. However, it also is a learning reference, used to effectively teach modeling styles and model-driven development in detail. It also serves as a starting point to build modeling styles for other platforms. The reference modeling style documents, in detail, how components and their relationships are unambiguously represented in UML. It provides an important basis for simpler, more expressive designs that, in turn, enable higher levels of model verification, testing, and code generation.

The current reference modeling style uses 100 percent J2EE/EJB. Other modeling styles also meet the requirements formulated by the Convergent Architecture. For example, in the context of specific projects, modeling styles and their respective technology projections have been developed for pure Java/RMI (not J2EE), CORBA, and OODB (Versant enJin) infrastructures.[2] A modeling style for the .NET platform is clearly possible but has not been attempted yet. The modeling styles, their technology projections, and the corresponding features of the architectural IDE are evolving in conjunction with the MDA initiative at the OMG. This projected evolutionary path is also indicated in the figure.

It is important to emphasize that our requirement for specificity produces modeling styles that are intentionally sensitive to a particular standard or platform. However, specificity is not necessarily synonymous with counterproductive dependence on specific implementations. The following sections explain how we achieve a best-of-both-worlds approach—models that serve as precise drivers of high-quality technology projections while still retaining maximum independence from the individual implementations. Using this approach, the convergent components have been mapped to many specific J2EE/EJB containers without changing the common UML models of the business components and without mitigating the expressiveness of these models.

Summarizing this in one sentence, it can be said that the convergent components apply standard UML in the context of convergent engineering with a default technology projection to J2EE/EJB. For this constellation, the full set of documentation for the convergent component metamodel, including its reference modeling style, consists of the material presented in this book plus the following base specifications:

- The UML Foundation Metamodel Specification

- The Java 2 Enterprise Environment and the Enterprise Java Beans Specification

- Convergent engineering as described in the book, *Business Engineering with Object Technology* (Taylor 1995)

- In the near future, the finished works addressing MDA as it evolves at the OMG (MDA 2001)

The goal is to always keep up with the newest release of each of these specifications, of course. Central to the convergent component metamodel are the convergent components themselves, which define a meaningful set of named design entities for use throughout the Convergent Architecture. They serve as a focal point for development organizations, development activities, design techniques, and tools. There are four distinct classifications or types of convergent components (CCs): *assembly components, accessor components, business components,* and *utility components.* A single type of convergent component may comprise closely related variants or subcomponents. The convergent components are partitioned into *architectural layers,* which are described in the next section, followed by sections detailing each type of component individually.

Architectural Layers

The convergent components form a layered component infrastructure, as depicted in Figure 4.2. The following list summarizes these layers, the convergent components they contain, and the important abbreviations for these components before each layer is examined in detail later in the section:

Assembly component layer.   Contains assembly components (ASCs).

Accessor component layer.   Contains accessor components (ACCs). These accessors are subdivided into two categories: the system interface accessors (SI-acces-

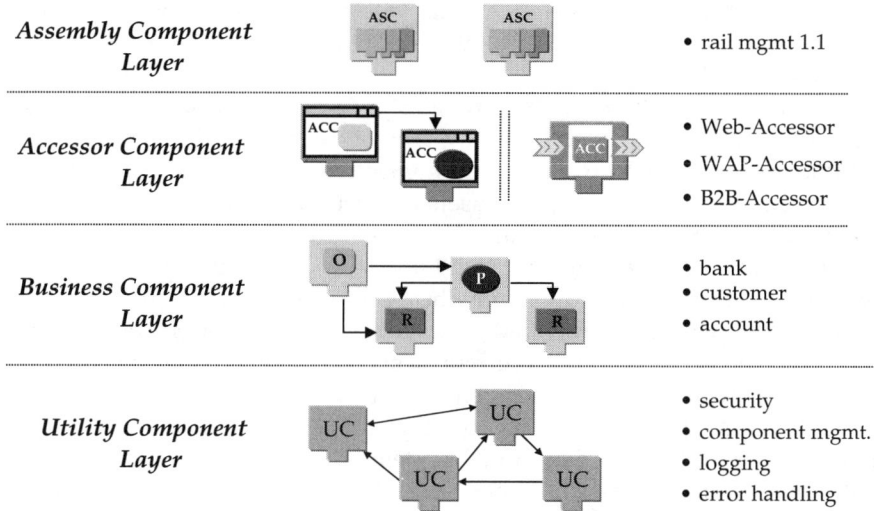

Figure 4.2 The architectural layers. Convergent components form four layers to best manage a design.

sors) and the user interface accessors (UI-accessors). In addition, each accessor component is associated with one or more representers, one for each type of interface channel.

Business component layer. Contains organization (O), process (P), and resource (R) business components, also known as the *OPR*s.

Utility component layer. Contains the utility components (UCs).

The intent of these layers is to reduce undesired coupling while increasing cohesion in design models, tools, and runtime infrastructures. Each layer corresponds to one or more convergent component types found in the layer. Thus, the component types are the primary vehicles for enforcing these layers. Each layer is hierarchically superior to the ones below it. This means that components are used, managed, and controlled by specific components in the same layer or the next higher layer.

The *assembly components (assemblies)* form the layer of packaging, distribution, and installation in the architecture. The clients of the assembly components are the operational and administrative personnel who install and maintain the IT landscape for end users. These components contain the intelligence required to install, update, adapt, and test an installation without requiring the operations personnel to possess detailed knowledge regarding the internals of the assembly. Instead, the assembly provides operational personnel with information and facilities to tune the installation and to monitor and adjust the steady-state operation of the assembly. From the perspective of the software developer, the assembly manages all convergent components required by a particular business application and ensures a clean evolution of these components into the operational environment. It integrates and intelligently manages every aspect of the deployment process. It takes care of the interaction with other assemblies, including migrational aspects concerning versions of assemblies. It proactively reduces software entropy and ensures the preservation of convergence in the runtime environment.

The *accessor components (accessors)* form a layer of interaction with all entities external to the architecture. They support any type of interaction channel or technology required to interact with the external environment. The external environment is partitioned into two major groups: human users and external systems. A family of related accessors exists for each of these groups. UI-accessors cater to the special requirements of human-to-system interaction, whereas SI-accessors cater to the special requirements of system-to-system interaction.[3] From the perspective of the software developer, accessors are modeled and developed as first-class, reusable components of a system. Each accessor manages one or more representer components, one for each type of interaction channel or interaction technology. Thus, a single accessor may interact with multiple channels. On the inside, the accessors encapsulate the interaction with OPR components in the next lower layer of the system. An accessor may be specific to a single OPR component, or it may be associated with an assembly and interact with many different OPR components. This all adds up to a style-specific constellation corresponding to the well-known model view controller (MVC) pattern. The use of many other well-known patterns and less commonly known design patterns can be observed in the UML modeling style and technology projection of the accessors and the other convergent components.[4]

The *business components (OPRs)* form a layer of organization, process, and resource components according to convergent engineering. They represent the core business aspects of the IT system. Their clients are the accessors and other OPRs in the context of an assembly. From the developer's perspective, the OPRs use non-business-relevant utility components in the next lower layer as well as a well-defined modeling style, such as the J2EE/EJB modeling style used in this book, to represent the core business functionality. In addition, the business-representation aspects of these OPRs, the so-called business dimension (discussed later), is explicitly separated from the purely technical-representation aspects, the so-called IT dimension.

The *utility components (utilities)* form a layer of reusable services that are, on the one hand, indispensable to the development and maintenance of high-performance convergent systems but, on the other hand, are not provided by standards or implementations of these standards. Other convergent components use utility components as necessary enhancements to the capabilities of the underlying standards. They are also employed to insulate the life cycle of the superior layers in the architecture from the very different life cycle and high-risk aspects of the implementation technologies.

Based on the components and their layers as just described, Figure 4.3 shows how convergent relationships are attained between use cases in the business domain and convergent components. To the left of the figure are the three types of use-case models employed to represent distinct aspects of the business domain. Note that the business-domain partitions correspond in a very logical manner to the architectural layers and their respective component types.

The intuitive convergence illustrated in Figure 4.3 simplifies many aspects of development. First, in the upper left of the figure, business use-case scenarios capture both

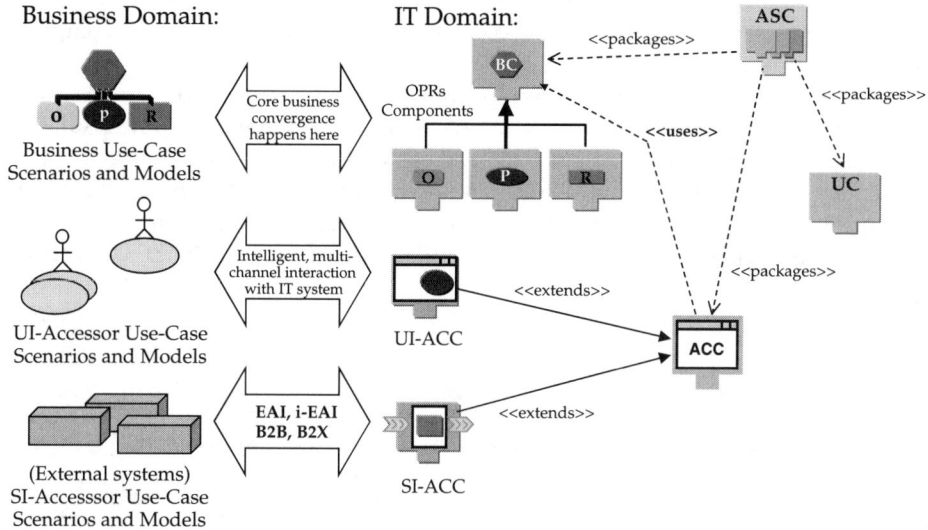

Figure 4.3 Convergent model-to-component relationships.

structural and dynamic aspects of the core business in a business model. The business model represents both requirements and business entities in terms of organizations, processes, and resources (OPRs). The business OPR components then serve to map the business model directly to its corresponding representations in the IT domain. The OPR business components are represented in UML. This allows the OPRs to be mapped (projected) automatically to a particular IT infrastructure. The figure also indicates that commonality among the OPRs is cleanly represented in a base business component, labeled *BC*. This and other details of the OPRs will be discussed later.

The center and bottom rows in the figure show that, similar to business scenarios, system-access scenarios are also modeled and mapped explicitly to a corresponding technical representation. The left side of the figure outlines the requirements and scenarios for human interaction. The accessor use-case scenarios are represented by a UI-accessor model in UML. Similar to the OPRs, these representations are technically refined in UML and are then projected (generated) to a particular IT infrastructure. The same schema applies to access to and from external, nonhuman entities, as shown at the lower left in the figure, where SI-accessors are produced. Just as with OPRs, commonality among the accessors is cleanly consolidated into a common base accessor component. Lastly, the architectural layers are also evident in the figure: The accessors use the OPRs hierarchically, and the assembly is used to package the convergent components.

It is now possible to show how the architectural layers cover the needs of an entire IT landscape in both modeling and runtime environments. The first of the following two figures (Figure 4.4) is an example of the runtime configuration for a typical e-payment intermediary portal. Figure 4.5 shows how such a runtime configuration is generated automatically based on the convergent components in a UML component model.

In Figure 4.4, a single assembly component contains the sum of convergent components for the e-payment portal. The SI-accessors to the left of the figure encapsulate the access idiosyncrasies of the external back-end systems required by the e-payment portal. Each external system may use a different representer to serve its particular communications and format requirements. However, these representers use a single SI-accessor for a given task. To the right, a similar scenario applies to the UI-accessors.

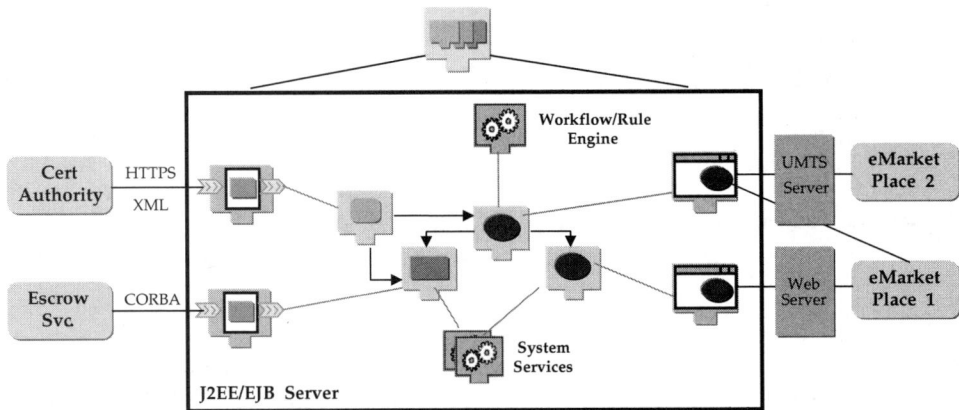

Figure 4.4   Example: Components in an e-payment portal.

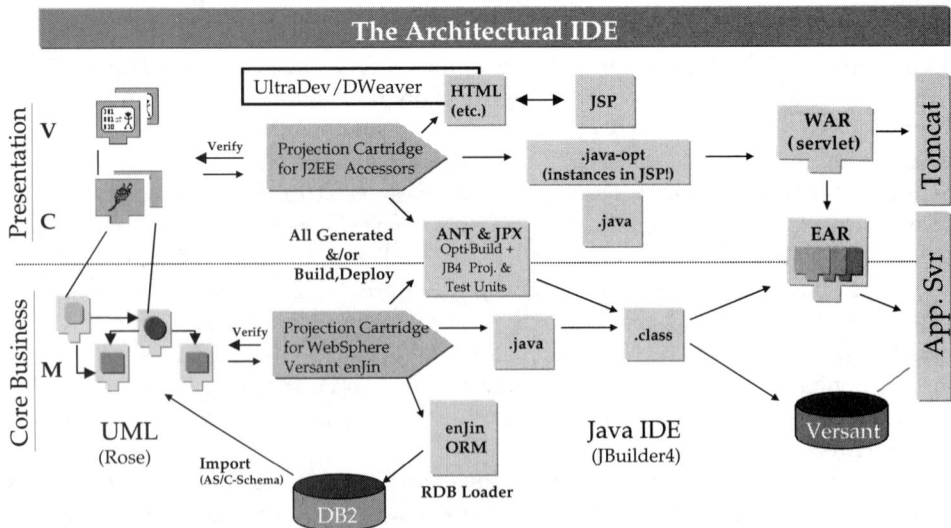

Figure 4.5   Example: Model-to-infrastructure relationship.

Each UI-accessor may serve several different representation channels via its different representers. The OPR components representing core business organizations, processes, and resources are situated in the middle and are accessed via the accessor components. These OPRs are the "decision makers" that determine the implementation of the business strategy. In this example, the process components delegate complex work-flow decisions to a utility component specialized in rule-based workflow control.

Figure 4.5 illustrates how most of a deployed assembly component and its environment is derived automatically from convergent components in the UML model. The bar at the top of the figure indicates that the entire process takes place in the architectural IDE (see Chapter 8). The UML model of convergent components created in Rational Rose is illustrated at the far left. In the model, the classic separation of presentation and business models is clearly visible: the accessors with their representers at the top and the OPR components at the bottom. The accessors and the OPR components each have a technology projection that, as shown to the right of the UML model, manifests as a technology projection cartridge in the architectural IDE. All arrows emitting from the projection cartridge (or simply cartridge) indicate artifacts generated on the basis of the UML model. The projection cartridge for J2EE accessors at the top generates all the artifacts required for a working Web archive (WAR), including its build and test environment. These generated artifacts are all shown to the right of the cartridge. At the bottom, a cartridge for WebSphere in conjunction with Versant enJin generates the artifacts required to create the rest of the assembly. The build and test environment generated by both technology projection cartridges is configured to leverage an advanced Java IDE, in this case JBuilder, shown at the lower right of the figure. JBuilder is used to implement low-level Java business logic and to automate the build, test, and deploy cycle. The assembly generated in this J2EE technology projection is a J2EE enterprise archive (EAR), as shown to the far right in the figure. The EAR is deployable as an intelligent unit into the combined WebSphere/Versant/TomCat application server represented at the far right of the figure.

This section presented the "big picture" of the convergent component metamodel at the level of architectural layers, the four convergent component types, and their use in both runtime and development environments. The next section moves down one level of detail and covers the metamodel from the perspective of each convergent component. The discussion begins with a description of the aspects common to all convergent components and moves on to detailed explanations of each type of component in subsequent sections.

Common Aspects of All Convergent Components

Several features are common to all convergent components. Before getting into the structural and stylistic features, let's take a short look at the components from the economic perspective of the IT organization.

Convergent components are important resources of an IT organization. They are named entities consisting of manifold models, documentation, and various forms of implementation technology. They are planned, built or bought, deployed, and maintained. They consume significant time and personnel. In short, they are extremely costly resources. In the interest of return on investment (ROI), an organization should be sure that these costly resources also turn out to be valuable resources. In order to measure and track the value of a resource, it must first be visible and have characteristics that can be measured. To this end, all convergent components are visible and measurable as managed resources of the IT organization, as you will see in the next chapter. The emphasis here is on the term *resource*. Although convergent components will represent many aspects of a business in its IT systems (for example, organizations and processes, as mentioned earlier), they all share the common property of being a clearly delimited resource within the IT organization. For example, a convergent component representing the sales process in a business system is also a resource from the perspective of the IT organization. The IT organization is the owner of this valuable resource and manager of its entire life cycle, ultimately being responsible for its ROI. This relationship showing that convergent components are managed resources in the IT organization is illustrated by the managed IT resource at the top of Figure 4.6.

Aside from their common home as resources in the IT organization, convergent components share several structural and stylistic features. These features are grouped into two categories, each covered separately in the following sections:

Technology projection component.   This contains the modeling style, guidelines, and artifacts defining how convergent components are associated with specific standards and implementation technologies.

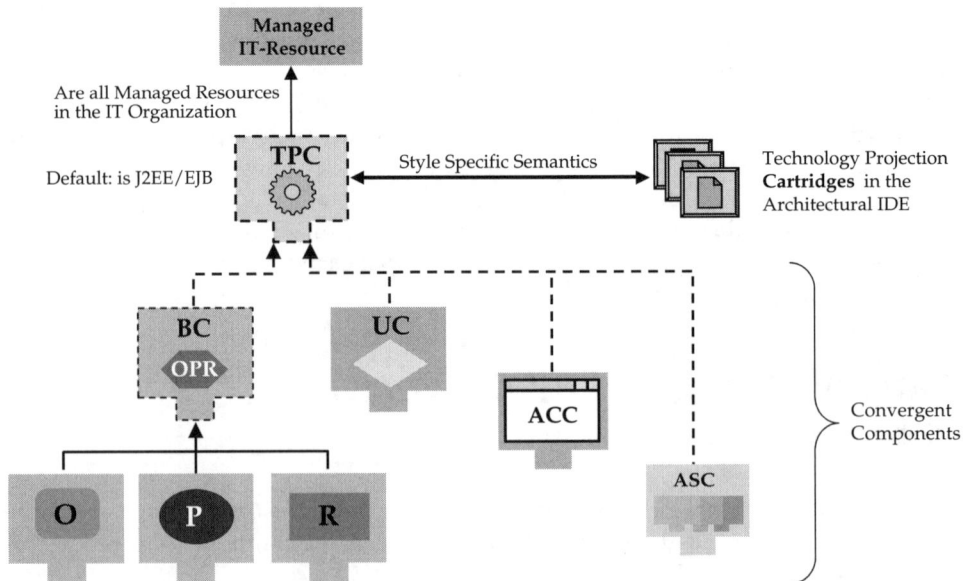

Figure 4.6   The technology projection component.

Component dimensions and personalities. This defines the basic internal structure of all convergent components.

The Technology Projection Component

Figure 4.6 shows the technology projection component (TPC) as a central feature, common to all convergent components. The TPC defines how we create convergent components models that meet the following three criteria:

1. They provide a level of (UML) detail that enables the automatic generation of well-tuned, standard-based technology, including its build and test environment, from the model: support for reality-scale model-driven automation.

2. The model must be expressive enough for power developers, meaning persons highly skilled in the respective technology. It must provide them with adequate, powerful tuning features within the model-driven approach so that these developers will not be tempted to circumvent the model-driven process.

3. Its partitioning and abstraction levels must permit effective, automatic projections to multiple implementations of a common platform or standard.

Meeting these three criteria at the same time is challenging, but it can be achieved by defining, first, an appropriate *modeling style* and, second, how the modeling style will be mapped to various technologies. When a model that conforms to a modeling style is mapped to a particular technology, this is called a *technology projection*. The term *technology projection* is also used to denote the definition of this mapping. The TPC represents a particular modeling style and its respective technology projections and defines how these are related to the rest of the architecture.

As indicated in Figure 4.6, the TPC is situated above the hierarchy of convergent components. It is not itself a convergent component. However, it significantly influences the modeling, refinement, and generation of the convergent components. All convergent components inherit the modeling style and its associated technology projections from the TPC. We call this type of inheritance *style-trait inheritance* because there is no direct, one-to-one correspondence between this component and a single physical component in the runtime infrastructure. Instead, it imposes traits of the particular style on its descendants. Such style-trait inheritance is designated by dashed lines in the figure.

As its name suggests, the TPC contains detailed information about how a model and its technology projection are related. It is where the rubber hits the road: *The TPC manages (in the form of modeling style guidelines and other artifacts) design properties and the development process in order to preserve maximum independence from implementation technologies.*

The modeling style is a core feature of the TPC. A *modeling style* is a set of guidelines used equally by system developers, development-process experts, and tool developers. It provides a UML profile for named technologies. Usually, these technologies are based on a standard. The *UML profile* is a detailed definition of UML modeling primitives based on the features or on the UML metamodel of the technology. Based on the

UML profile, the modeling style defines the precise meaning of the UML modeling primitives and the way a designer uses them to manage and tune real-world infrastructure. It also provides explicit modeling extensions to allow power users to tune systems at the model level without coupling the entire model to an implementation. The modeling style also possesses information about the rest of the architectural style, its upstream origins, and the downstream intent, which can be used to automatically complete and tune significant aspects of a model.

Needless to say, UML, as a generalized notation and modeling language, and generalized UML modeling tools cannot provide these specifics. Such tools are used rather to support one or more modeling styles.

The modeling style complements the generalized UML standard by adding precise meaning to elements of the UML notation relative to the architectural style and selected technologies.

It defines how these primitives relate to the structures and behaviors on both sides of the UML model in the development stream. On the upstream side, the modeling style defines how business concepts are expressed in UML, and on the downstream side, it defines how each UML representation influences the actual system implementation. This is analogous to defining the playing rules in a particular sport. If the rules are not clear, then every game is different, complex, and fraught with dispute about what the rules are. Moreover, it is hard for a team to prepare for the season if the rules of the game are not set. Finally, before we can define clear rules of the game, we first need to know what type of sport we are defining the rules for. The rules required for chess or horseback riding are quite different from those required for rugby or soccer. The analogy drives home the point that a modeling style is the prerequisite of a well-working development process. It is also a prerequisite for developing an architectural IDE to effectively support the development process.

The TPC is key to enabling the Convergent Architecture to achieve the advantages of specificity while avoiding the downside of coupling. It addresses the influences of technology while remaining independent of these influences. This sounds contradictory at first. However, it is not. It just requires due respect for the designer's paradox (see Chapter 2). Formulated for the situation at hand, the designer's paradox says that significant requirements and constraints due to a technology projection must be accommodated explicitly by the architectural style (its models and tools) in order for the style to remain independent of these constraints. The TPC contributes to this goal by addressing how upstream aspects of the development models and process must be adjusted to flexibly handle these downstream constraints. If this is not done, then the early stages of design are being carried out in a vacuum, and the resulting models can only be used to communicate concepts at best.

For example, in the J2EE technology projection, the TPC defines the necessary influence of the EJB component standard and environments on the UML modeling style for convergent components. For a .net technology projection, the TPC would be different. It would define the UML modeling style for convergent components based on the requirements of the COM component model and other constraints of the .net environment. Each of these component standards, J2EE/EJB and COM, place manifold, rigid requirements on the structure of the convergent components and thus on their respective modeling styles. In addition, these component standards result in many subtle but important constraints on the way developers and their tools work. For example, the J2EE/EJB standard specifies how documentation properly accompanies code down to the exact positioning and JavaDoc syntax of the documentation within the code. This will affect, at some level, the way developers document their design and how the architectural IDE acquires, formats, generates, packages, and stores documentation.

The TPC is indeed abstract, as denoted by its dotted outline in the figure, because it may take on different forms depending on the particular technology projection. This flexibility of content is required because TPCs will need to address platforms in the future, not just the platforms we recognize today. By default, as you will see in subsequent chapters, the TPC defines (contains) the technology-sensitive UML modeling style in the form of a specifications and guidelines document. In addition, it is associated with the corresponding set of technology projection cartridges and the support for these cartridges in the architectural IDE.

There is nothing mysterious about the TPC. It simply applies the fundamental object-oriented principle known as *factoring commonality*. In this case, stylistic aspects of design related to its mapping to technology are being factored and packaged; that is all. However, as shown in detail in the bonus chapter on the Web site, it is important to note that the TPC is more than a UML profile as foreseen by the UML standard: *It is a UML profile plus detailed guidelines for the modeling style and its comprehensive technology projection*. The modeling style constitutes the combination of a UML profile and stylistic guidelines.[5] Improved quality and more powerful tool support are two of the good reasons to complement UML profiles with the additional characteristics of the TPC. Just one example: The objective is to represent business invariants using the Object Constraint Language (OCL) (Warmer 1999) in UML models. Both the Java language and the J2EE/EJB standard place constraints on how such invariants can be implemented reasonably in the runtime infrastructure. Thus, the technology projection must deal with these constraints in order to generate working systems based on the model. This, in turn, places a requirement on the modeling style for J2EE/EJB. The style guideline in this instance is: All attributes associated with an OCL invariant must be private and exclusively accessible via set and get operations.[6] Only then can the generator properly generate the code to check OCL invariants without coming into conflict with the UML model. If this stylistic guideline is defined as part of the TPC, then it can be enforced in the tools—the architectural IDE can better assist the developer.

The next section will look at the common structural features of convergent components, including some examples of how these look when projected to different standard technologies.

Component Dimensions and Personalities

At the highest level of design abstraction, all convergent components also have a common internal structure. Figure 4.7 presents this top-level anatomy of a convergent component. It shows that every convergent component can be seen as consisting of quadrants formed by partitioning it into two distinct dimensions, the business and IT dimensions, each dimension consisting of two personalities, the client and server personalities.

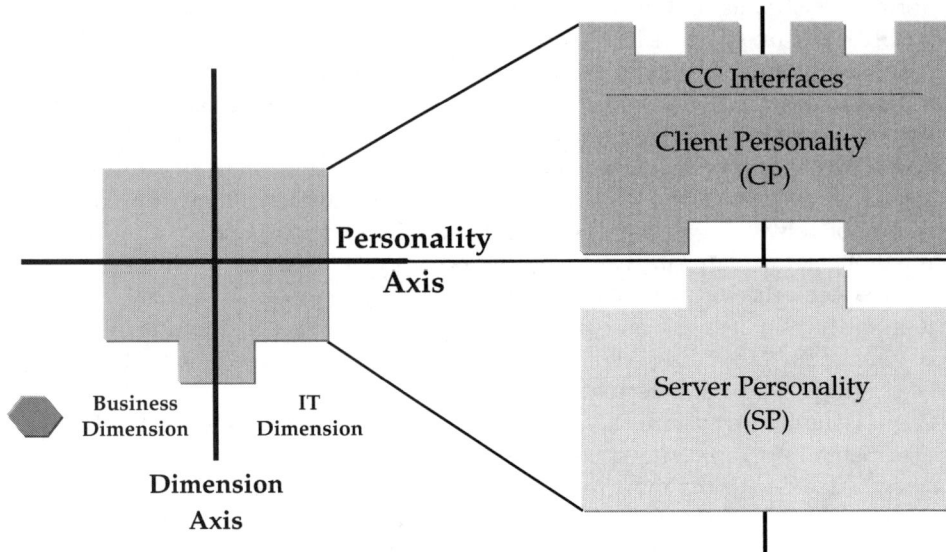

Figure 4.7   Convergent component dimensions and personalities.

The Business and IT Dimensions

Every convergent component starts out as a technology-independent representation of a business entity in a business object model (BOM). The characteristics of the BOM and how it is derived will be covered in subsequent chapters. The business-relevant aspects of a convergent component are clearly identifiable early in the development process and should remain so throughout the component's life cycle. I refer to these purely business-relevant aspects of a convergent component as the *business dimension*. The content and life cycle of the business dimension should remain independent of all non-business-relevant aspects of the system. These non-business-relevant aspects of a component constitute its ancillary technical infrastructure. Although this infrastructure makes up a significant portion of a component, it is only there to allow us to support the business dimension in a particular IT environment. I refer to these ancillary technical aspects as the *IT dimension* of the convergent component. Every running convergent component has an IT dimension, and if the component has core business relevance (in contrast to pure IT relevance), it also has an explicit business dimension.

An analogy is perhaps best to explain the reasoning behind these two dimensions: When you tune a radio, you have to deal with two things. First, you select the channel (content) you want. This is comparable with the *business dimension*. It is the content that you are concerned with in this dimension. You do not care how it gets here. The platform vehicle could be a television, a car radio, a portable radio, whatever. Second, you select the proper platform and make sure that the reception is ok. This is comparable with the *IT dimension*. Dealing with the complexities of reception, that is, the spectrum of poor to very good, frequency type, location and position of the antenna, the quality of receiver, and the quality of sound filters are all technology-related "annoyances" that have nothing to do with the content. If you swap the platform, you still get the same content, but with different technological properties. For example, if you switch from a waterproof portable radio to a living room stereo, you still get the same content, but the delivery platform has changed. Switching these two platforms to deliver the same content is equivalent to swapping technology projections in the Convergent Architecture to deliver the same business dimension to different IT dimensions.

Such clear separation of domain content versus technology content is highly desirable but has not been achieved by many IT systems. Attaining this clean separation of concerns is the intent of the explicit recognition of business versus IT dimensions in the very basis of the convergent component metamodel.

Put more concisely, we identify and maintain the following partitions of a convergent component throughout its life cycle:

- **Business dimension.** This dimension of a convergent component represents the core business or domain aspects in the IT world. This is the business object being "represented" by the component.
- **IT dimension.** This dimension comprises, quite simply, everything that is not part of the business dimension. These are the IT-specific "representation" aspects of a convergent component. This is the ancillary part of a convergent component that does not contain any information or logic pertaining directly to the core business.

Although both dimensions always exist, the business dimension is only present when required. If a component is initially purely technical in nature, then the business dimension is simply empty. If this component takes on business-relevant intelligence at some later stage, then this functionality is positioned in an explicitly designated business dimension, not just anywhere within the component.

The Client and Server Personalities

Each convergent component is partitioned into a so-called client personality (CP) and a server personality (SP). These personalities exist to cleanly encapsulate and denote the two design partitions inevitably required of any component if it is to be distributed. They exist to optimally support a component's use and reuse within a distributed environment. The client and server personalities permit a component to be physically distributed while remaining logically intact, that is, logically centralized. This enables a design to support the inevitable component-specific optimizations for use in a distributed system without becoming unduly complicated, as will be shown by the following examples. The actual distribution of the convergent component is optional but always possible. It is intended by the base design but not required, thus providing the designer with maximum flexibility.

The principal justification for a client personality as a separate design entity is to provide designers and programmers with a uniform place to put important client-side aspects of a distributed environment. It supplies a defined structure in which to tune distributed systems without having to subvert the encapsulation of the component as a useful design abstraction.

Both client and server personalities may have a business dimension and an IT dimension, as indicated in Figure 4.7. Thus, at the highest level of abstraction, *a convergent component consists of named quadrants: the business and IT dimensions of its client and server personalities, respectively*. How the business dimension is distributed between the two personalities depends on the type of system and the particular role of the component in the system. Various distribution models often are required even within a single assembly, depending on such things as the number and type of clients or whether the component must operate in a local network, an intranet, the Internet, or a nomadic environment. For real-world applicability of the architecture, all these distribution models must be equally possible within the component metamodel because none of them can be predicted in advance of the particular assembly design.

The quadrants of a convergent component in conjunction with the architectural layers make it easier to represent and communicate the design permeations required by distributed systems, including Internet-centric systems. Figure 4.8 shows how various distribution models are realized using convergent components with their respective client and server personalities. The examples in the figure are just points along a continuum between the two poles of 100-percent server-side implementation and 100-percent client-side implementation. These poles apply not only to the physical distribution of the component, but also to the partitioning of the business dimension between the client and server personalities. Once again, this is a constellation that corresponds to interwoven design patterns as applied by the architectural style first at the abstract design level and then at the level of technology projections to particular technologies. Several of these patterns were documented recently in the context of J2EE (J2EE Patterns 2001).

An EJB container fills the role of object factory shown in the figure when the components are projected to J2EE application servers. J2EE currently is the preferred technology projection because it provides standards onto which we may project any of

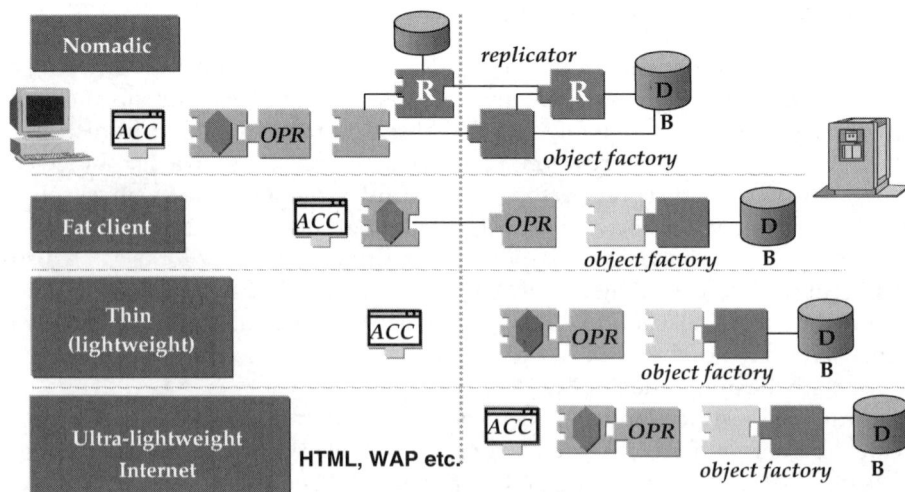

Figure 4.8 Enabling various distribution schemes.

these distribution constellations. Figure 4.9 shows how, for example, the ultra-lightweight constellation is projected to any J2EE application server that conforms to the J2EE blueprints (J2EE Blueprints 2001).

The next two figures provide a more detailed illustration of the client and server personalities of a component and their projection to various technologies. Figure 4.10 shows how ultra-lightweight constellations are projected to J2EE. Figure 4.11 shows how the personalities have been projected equivalently to a mixed-language (Java/C++) CORBA-based infrastructure.

In Figure 4.10, client personalities of an OPR component are shown in an EJB container. The OPRs are implemented as entity beans and are accessed by a distributed accessor. The server personality of the accessor is projected to a session bean in the EJB container. The client personality of the accessor is projected to one or more Java server pages (JSPs) and Java classes, both of which are deployed to a servlet engine. In the figure, the accessor's client personality manages three HTML (or any other lightweight protocol) representers to serve an Internet browser as its access channel.

Figure 4.11 shows the quadrants of a convergent component projected to a mixed-language CORBA infrastructure that also encapsulates a legacy infrastructure implemented in embedded SQL (ESQL). The client personality shown in the figure corresponds to the fat client scheme because it contains both the Java/Swing user access implementation and the entire business dimension. The C++ server personality simply serves to encapsulate database access and legacy ESQL code and make these available to one or more fat client personalities.

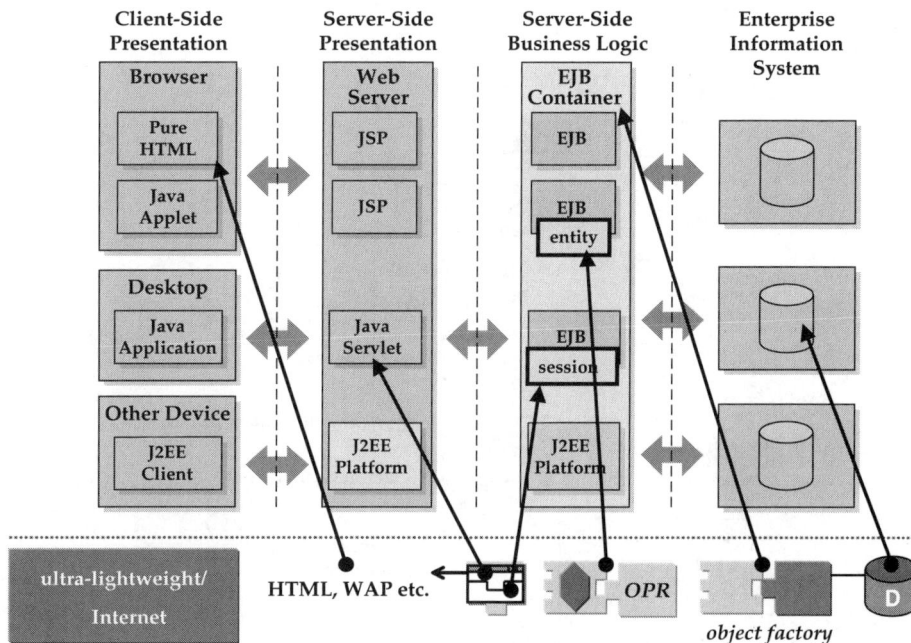

Figure 4.9 Projection of an ultra-lightweight client constellation to J2EE.

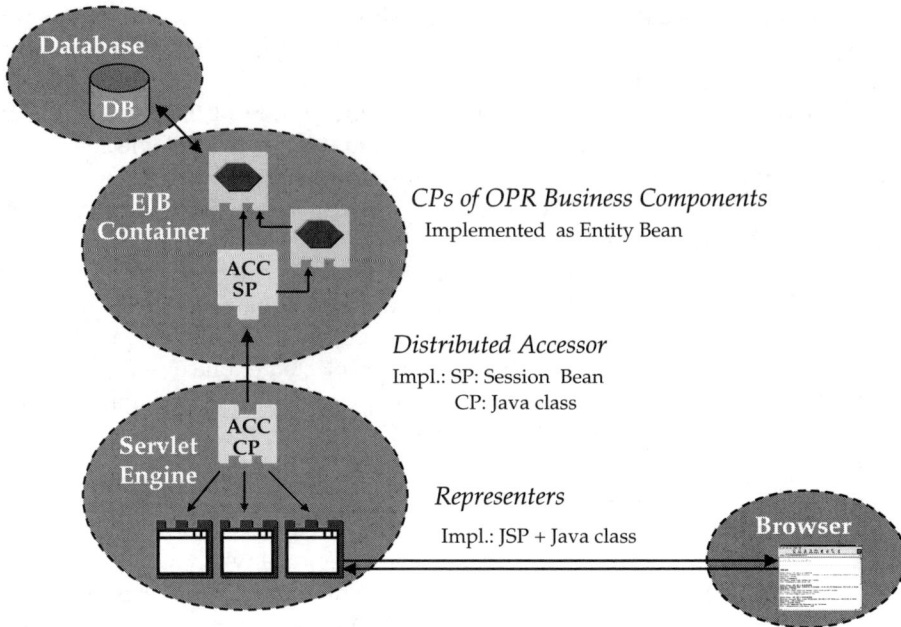

Figure 4.10   Detail: Ultra-lightweight client constellation to J2EE.

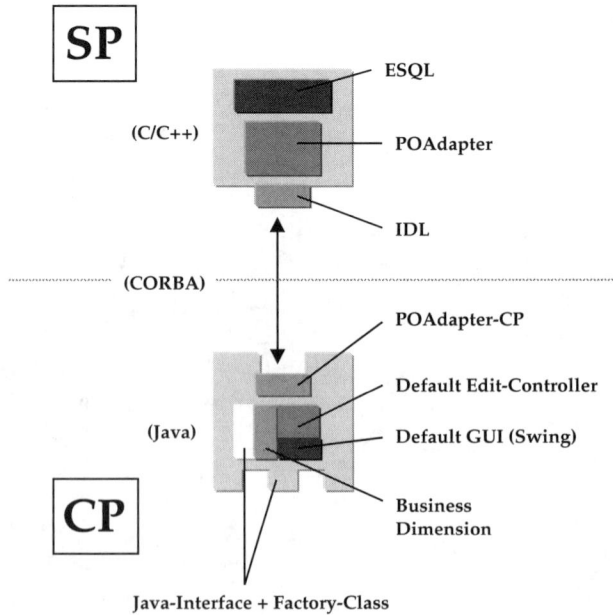

Figure 4.11   Projection of a fat client scheme to a CORBA Infrastructure (Java/C++).

We now move to the next level of detail for each type of convergent component, one section for each of the four architectural layers.

Assembly Components

Assembly components (assemblies) actively coordinate constellations of reusable components in both the development and deployment phases of the component life cycle. These constellations often correspond to traditional applications. The coordination provided by an assembly also extends into the operational phases of the life cycle. As shown in Figure 4.12, assemblies constitute the top-level, macro unit of system packaging and deployment. As the macro units of a system, they also drive the macro planning and development process.

Assemblies are convergent components that exist to manage and package other convergent components. Normally, assemblies are the only convergent components deployed alone as units. All other convergent components are deployed in the context of an assembly. During the deployment phase, the assembly component helps manage the installation process. This concept of an assembly component corresponds to the CORBA components' (CCM) definition of an assembly. In the J2EE technology projection, an assembly maps to a J2EE EAR.

Convergent components can be reused by several assemblies. In Figure 4.12, Assembly 2 uses components B and C from Assembly 1. Thus, an assembly can be referred to and used by other assemblies at the level of its convergent components. However, a convergent component is always owned and managed by a single assembly. Assembly 1 owns components B and C. Using a term explained in more detail in Chapter 5, every convergent component has a single resource owner. These reuse relationships are tracked and managed by the assembly development team (also defined in Chapter 5)

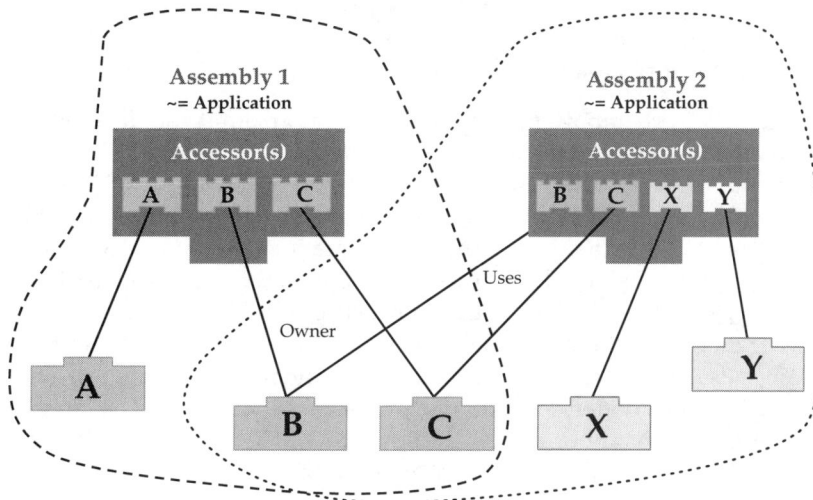

Figure 4.12 Assemblies as macro units.

during system development. This explicit ownership ensures that the reuse is managed throughout the entire life cycle of a component in the context of a single assembly. This means that although individual convergent components are still installable units, they are always installed in the context of an assembly. The assembly is responsible for the integrity of the overall system. For example, to update a single resource component in an assembly, a new version of its assembly is installed. The assembly may in fact only update this single resource component, but the assembly also must guarantee the continued integrity of its entire development and runtime environment. Guaranteeing such integrity is no small task. This is one reason why this task is clearly assigned to a component, the assembly component, and to its corresponding team, the assembly development team (for details, see Chapter 5) in the Convergent Architecture.

Accessor Components

As indicated by their name, accessor components (accessors) provide access to and from external entities. The definition of an *external entity* is very simple: It is anything that is not installed as part of an assembly or part of its direct runtime platform.

At the highest level, it is possible to distinguish between two basic types of accessor components. The similarities between these two types actually outnumber their differences, as will be seen:

1. **User interface accessors (UI-accessors and UI-ACCs).**   These are the mediators between an IT system A and a human user B. These user interfaces are not limited to graphical user interfaces (GUI); they can also be voice-based, text-based, and so on.

2. **System interface accessors (SI-accessors and SI-ACCs).**   These are the mediators between two systems A and B. They can be used to integrate different architectures (system integration) or different installations (an interface between the installations of the same system in different organizations).

Accessors serve two important purposes. First, they delimit and defend the architectural boundaries throughout the system life cycle. They are used to coerce and convert things external to the architecture into things that conform to the architectural style. This is the best way—and probably the only way—to ensure long-term architectural integrity no matter how many external entities are involved in an integrated system. Second, they separate the modeling of system access from the particular implementation of the access to provide developers with a clean separation of concerns.

The separation of the access model from its implementation permits us to develop long-lived, reusable models independent of the underlying technology and the life cycle of the implementation technology. This separation allows developers to effectively reuse accessor components at the level of UML models, thus promoting the advantages of model-driven, component-based development into the important field of system access and system integration. In addition, the clean separation of the accessor component layer from the business component layers of the architecture permits different development tasks and roles to be carried out independently: Business-model design, application development, and B2C or B2B design now can be performed by different, specifically trained specialists using specialized tools. This improves flexible adaptation, reuse, and maintenance at many points in the system life cycle. For example, with this separation of concerns, it is possible to redesign the type of user access or external system access at the UML level without touching the business component behind the scenes. By the same token, new use cases can be realized and new user interface technologies can be leveraged with little or no change to existing accessor models.

To date, the IT industry has been slow to address model-driven development in this area of user and system access—the terrain covered by accessors. This has not been due to neglect; it is simply because the IT industry at large has been more focused on improving the central, server-side aspects of system design. There is nothing amiss here; it just means that the accessor components have less standard infrastructure on which we can base their modeling style and its model-driven technology projection. Although the accessor design leverages the standards available in this space, they must currently define more of the model-driven infrastructure than the other convergent components. For this reason, the accessor metamodel and the runtime environment, which will be introduced in the following sections, are the most extensive parts of the Convergent Architecture.

The Accessor Framework

Figure 4.13 illustrates the use of accessor components to support different channels of access to a software system. It shows that an accessor component actually consists of

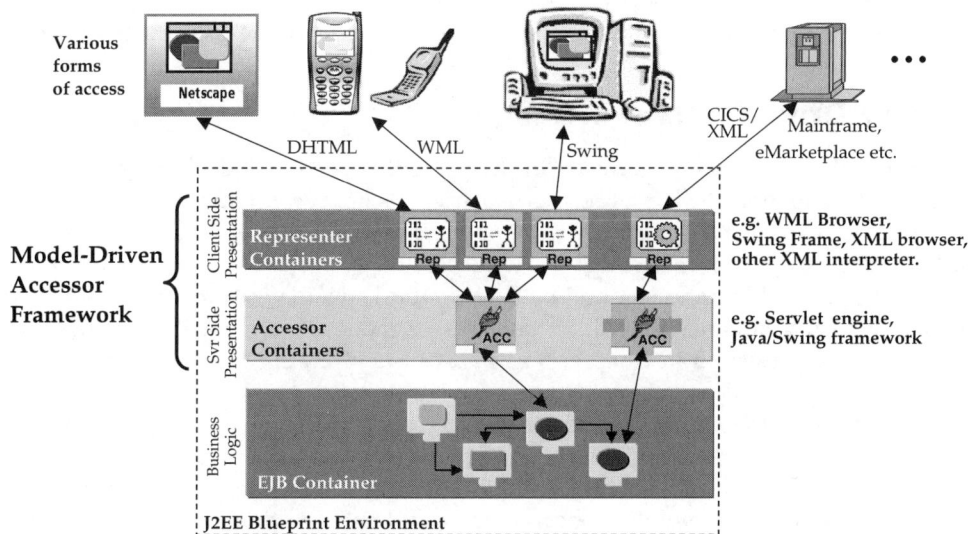

Figure 4.13 The model-driven parts of the accessor framework.

several separate parts. Many of these parts are modeled separately in the interest of the clear separation of concerns. However, they are interrelated as parts within a system of patterns. Together they form what is called the *accessor framework*.

This figure manifests some additional separation of concerns that has not been mentioned yet. First, beginning at the top of the figure, the accessor framework recognizes that various forms of access may differ only at the level of their external representation; all other aspects, such as information content, information flow, and event flow, remain equivalent across the various representations. In addition, new forms of access may arise at any time, while other existing forms may be deprecated over time. Thus, the modeling and production of these various representation channels are encapsulated by so-called representers. These representers run in so-called representer containers. A representer container is another important abstraction: It encapsulates a specific runtime environment for a group of interrelated representers. For example, an HTML browser is a representer container that may manage one representer per HTML frame. This level of model-driven granularity is required by modern Internet portals. Nothing less will suffice for a model-driven production of such systems. Another important advantage to this constellation is that it permits representers to be reused in different accessor models.

A single accessor may support any number of representers. Figure 4.13 shows three representer channels being supported by a single UI-accessor. It also shows a single representer being supported by the SI-accessor. Similar to representer containers, accessors are also housed in accessor containers. An example of an accessor container is a servlet engine or a Java/Swing framework. Based on this separation of concerns in both modeling and runtime environments, a single, reusable accessor may serve significant functionality to multiple representation channels, that is, to multiple representers. This is called *multichannel access to a single accessor.* Moreover, new channels may be added or existing ones removed at any time via the UML model without having to circumvent, and compromise, the model-centric architecture.

The following sections provide more detail on each part of the accessor framework.

Model-Driven Accessors

The accessor framework introduced in the preceding section complements the OPR business components during all phases of a system's life cycle. Thus, we require a corresponding level of model-driven development and IDE support for accessors. To achieve this, an accessor modeling style with technology projection has been defined to consolidate available standards and the architectural style. These are introduced here, while detailed guidelines regarding the accessor modeling style and its technology projection are presented in Chapter 8 as part of the J2EE/EJB technology projection component.

An *accessor model* is used to describe the accessor components in the context of an assembly. Every accessor model is an instance of the *accessor metamodel*. The accessor metamodel, in turn, is an extension of the UML metamodel. The accessor metamodel addresses the *view* and *controller* aspects of the well-known *model-view-controller* (MVC) paradigm. It is used to model interactions with the underlying business model, which fills the model role in the MVC paradigm.

The accessor modeling style specifies how to use the elements of the accessor UML metamodel to create a particular accessor model. An accessor model *defines both the control flow and the data flow* to and from an external entity (external as defined previously). The model contains the information necessary to generate deployable accessors and representers as part of the accessor framework. This information includes, for example, aspects covering display structure, reading and interpreting events, user or system interaction, and interaction with underlying OPR business components to handle input or output. This procedure applies to both UI- and SI-accessors alike.

Accessor models usually are based on well-defined application use cases, so-called accessor use cases. These use cases describe how a user in a specific role interacts with the IT system to perform a specific task. Identifying accessor use cases is part of the analysis-by-design workflow covered in Chapter 6. In accessor modeling, these use cases are transformed into accessor components in UML. Based on the accessor model, the technology projection then generates an implementation and environment for a particular technology. The J2EE technology projection generates, for example, Java server pages (JSPs), Java servlets, HTML representations, and their ANT build and test infrastructure.

SI-accessors are identical to UI-accessors from the modeling perspective. The differences between the two are in their respective technology projections. The technology projections must be different because SI-accessors support various system-interface technologies in contrast to the user-interface technologies supported by the UI-accessors. To keep the following sections in proportion, only an overview of the accessor metamodel will be presented, with a focus on UI-accessors and their J2EE technology projection. Extensive detail on the accessor metamodel can be found on the Convergent Architecture Web site.

Accessor (MVC Controller)

An *accessor* is the key concept within the accessor metamodel. An accessor is a specialization of the UML metatype *class*. It represents an external interface of a software system. External interfaces can be of two types: user interfaces and system interfaces. A (graphical) *user interface* is an interface that enables a human user to interact with the software system. Further, a software system often must be integrated with other existing systems. The interaction between systems is made possible through *system interfaces*. Examples of such interfaces are CORBA interfaces, Java JMS-based communication interfaces, XML-based standards for enterprise application integration (EAI), and so forth.

All UML foundation modeling constructs may be used to describe the structure and behavior of an accessor. Thus, accessors can have attributes and methods, they can be freely associated with other classes, and they can inherit from other classes and can implement interfaces.

In the context of the MVC paradigm, an accessor fills the role of the *controller*. UML activity/state diagrams are used to model the dynamic behavior of an accessor. UML states and stereotypes have been configured and extended especially to represent accessors. One of these UML-conform extensions is the presence of *representers* (see the following section) in the activity/state diagrams. Representers are the parts of an accessor model that define the content and dynamics of an external interface. However, the accessor model does not have to specify explicitly whether a representer is intended for a user interface or a system interface. This is important and emphasizes the similarities between modeling user and external system interaction. The selected technology projection determines whether a user interface or system interface is produced based on the model; the model itself may be used for both. This means that one model potentially can serve both user- and system-interface channels.

Accessors extend the model-driven component paradigm into the world of system and user interaction. Accessors, meaning entire accessor models, including structure and dynamic aspects, constitute components with clear interfaces that may be embedded in other accessors' models. Thus, the arbitrary composition and reuse of accessors are possible.

Representer (MVC View)

A *representer* is used to model an interface element, in particular its input and output properties. It is a specialization of the UML metatype *class*. As such, it can have attributes, methods, and associations with other classes, and so on. An external interface may consist of one or more representers. For example, a multiframed HTML interface consists of one representer per frame. The accessor model handles interactions between representers. Output properties of a representer are information originating from convergent components and being presented to the external entity. For example, output could be to a field in a GUI presented to a human, or it could be to an element within an XML document to be presented by the representer for interpretation by an external system. Similarly, input properties specify the input facilities the representer provides. Based on its input, the representer triggers activities in other convergent components. In the context of the MVC paradigm, the representer fills the role of the *view*. However, in contrast to most MVC interpretations, when modeling a representer, the designer only specifies the kind of information and input facilities to be provided by the representer, not the concrete form and layout of the information. The layout, which may be derived directly from the model information, is handled in a channel-specific manner by the technology projection.

Accessor and Representer Containers

Accessor components do not imply a particular runtime environment. Instead, accessor models may be mapped to different runtime environments. Examples of such different runtime environments are J2EE servlets (for example, HTML or WML), Java applets, Java/Swing environments, or portable mobile assistant environments. As shown in Figure 4.13, the accessor and representer containers are abstractions of runtime environments that enable us to model and configure important aspects of these environments.

An accessor container provides basic, standardized runtime services that will be leveraged by the accessor. This corresponds to an EJB container that provides standardized runtime services for OPR business components. For example, the accessor container normally is capable of activating accessors, managing interaction with the operating environment, and providing facilities to manage communication protocols in a highly robust, standardized framework.

An accessor container also may be a central object in a stand-alone application. Examples of such objects include servlets in the context of stand-alone Web applications and executable Java classes that create and manage a Swing frame component. The accessor container can be seen as the leading controller object in the MVC paradigm. All other accessors are created and managed either by the leading controller or by an accessor in the same accessor container. As an abstraction for the technical runtime environment, accessor containers normally are not visible in accessor models. Instead, they are configured automatically as part of the technology projection.

A *representer container* is an abstraction of a runtime environment for representers. An example of a representer container is an HTML/XML browser such as Netscape or Internet Explorer or a WML browser in a portable mobile assistant. The representers in these examples are then the HTML/XML pages or WML frames. Such representers often exhibit complex interaction relationships within the context of the representer container, such as the relationships between HTML/XML frames. Thus, these relationships may be modeled explicitly in an accessor model.

The representer container houses and manages the active representers and displays their graphic interface to users or, in the case of SI-accessors, provides another form of interface to the external entity. Representer containers may be composed freely to form a hierarchy of representer containers. The root container in the hierarchy is the top-level representer container, which is managed by its associated accessor container.

Lastly, from the perspective of the convergent component metamodel, both accessor and representer containers are utility components (defined later).

The Extended State Machine Model

The accessor metamodel also defines a UML-compliant extension to activity/state diagrams in order to model the behavior of an accessor effectively. This extended state machine model consists of several specializations of the UML type *state.* These are as follows:

RepresenterState.   This describes the state of a representer in a representer container. In a GUI, the state determines whether input or view elements are to be displayed. For example, in a system interface, the transition to a RepresenterState can trigger an XML document to be dispatched. In this case, the interface would wait for a response document containing input information provided by the external system. The events triggered through inputs of a representer are handled as *InputEvents.* InputEvents can trigger transitions in the activity diagram of an accessor.

EmbeddedAccessorState.   This describes a special state in the accessor's activity diagram composed of many (reused) accessors. A transition to an Embedded AccessorState initializes and activates the subordinate accessor. The originating accessor remains in the EmbeddedAccessorState until the embedded accessor reaches its terminal state. When the subordinate accessor reaches its terminal state, it triggers a *TerminalStateEvent,* which usually triggers a transition in the originating accessor. Optionally, the originating accessor can provide its own representer(s) in an active representer container. In this case, transitions to the originating state also can be triggered by InputEvents from the representer(s); the subordinate accessor is deactivated without reaching its terminal state.

JumpState.   This defines a special terminal state in the accessor's activity diagram where the accessor hands over control to another accessor, the jump target. In contrast to the EmbeddedAccessorState, the current accessor loses control; that is, on activation of the jump-target accessor, the current accessor is deactivated. If the current accessor is embedded in another accessor, its encapsulating accessor will be deactivated when a JumpState in the activity diagram of the current accessor is reached. If the encapsulating accessor is itself an embedded accessor, this deactivation mechanism will recurse up the entire active accessor stack. Afterwards, the jump-target accessor is initialized and activated, now being the only active accessor.

Activities and *decisions* are standard features of UML activity/state diagrams that take on special meaning in the context of an accessor. They are used to describe all behavioral aspects of an accessor that are not involved in activating and transitioning between representers (RepresenterState) or involved in managing accessors (EmbeddedAccessorState or JumpState). Typically, activities and decisions express the interactions of the accessor with its supporting convergent components. Activities and decisions trigger various *ProcessEvents*. In particular, activities can produce *Exception-Events*, which are a special kind of ProcessEvent used to handle exceptional situations. The exception-handling mechanisms are detailed in the bonus chapter on the Web site.

Resource Mapping

Using the elements described thus far (that is, special states, activities, decisions, events, and transitions), it is possible to model the control flow of an accessor. To describe the data flow within the accessor's state model, the accessor metamodel defines the *ResourceMapping* abstraction. A ResourceMapping is used to pass parameters within the accessor model. In general, a ResourceMapping is a rule for passing a single value from a source element to a target element on the occurrence of a particular event. The ResourceMapping consists of source and target references that specify the source and target elements, respectively. A reference is described by a *ReferencePath*, which refers to the referenced model element. The ReferencePath can be composed of an arbitrary number of ReferencePaths, thus forming a navigation path through the model.

ResourceMappings are used in the following places:

- **In RepresenterStates**.   A ResourceMapping in a RepresenterState typically is used to map values of accessor attributes to attributes of the representer(s) associated with that RepresenterState.

- **In EmbeddedAccessorStates**.   A ResourceMapping in an EmbeddedAccessorState typically is used to map values of attributes in the superior accessor to attributes of the subordinate accessor associated with the Embedded-AccessorState.

Further levels of detail are necessary to completely describe the model-driven accessor components, their modeling style, and their technology projections. This detail is provided in the bonus chapter on the Web site, which covers the entire Technology Projection Component.

OPR Business Components

The business component layer defines a finite set of component types, the OPRs, according to the principles of convergent engineering and RASC as described in Chapter 3. The most important advantage of the business components is their business relevance, the business dimension, regardless of their technical representation, the IT dimension, which may change quite often. The process of modeling with these components helps business and IT experts communicate, represent, evolve, and tune business operations. During the definition of an IT system, business components are first considered from this business perspective. The resulting business model is then evolved into an IT infrastructure according to the clear patterns and rules of the architectural style, thereby automatically avoiding the pitfalls of complex translation losses and conceptual drift—in other words, avoiding divergence. Avoiding divergence is the job of the convergent OPR components, each covered in its respective section here.

The OPR Business Perspective

In this section we focus on the business dimension of the business components. In addition to the extensive use of object-oriented design techniques in the IT dimension, they are also used at the level of business design. When applied properly, the object-oriented approach simplifies the entire modeling process at both technical and business levels. This is due to the fact that anybody can learn quickly to read an object-oriented model. It is easier to understand an object-oriented model than any other representation because object orientation leverages everyday concepts that we are all familiar with. For example, the concept of inheritance, one of the three pillars of object orientation,[7] and its power to simplify business models can be understood immediately even by persons with no previous exposure to software development. Thus, object-oriented design can be used by anyone to simplify both the representation of the business and the communication of this representation. However, there is one catch: Someone still has to define how these powerful concepts will be used to best represent a business as well as its respective IT systems. A set of guidelines, the modeling style, must exist to define how object-oriented and other concepts will be applied uniformly across the many projects and systems in an organization. In the Convergent Architecture, the modeling style for OPR business components begins here in the convergent components model. However, it also influences the activities of the development process and the UML modeling style, both covered in later chapters.

For the OPR components, the modeling style starts with the business model. It defines a set of modeling abstractions that will be used uniformly in all business models. These abstractions are the OPRs, from convergent engineering (Taylor 1995).

Figure 4.14 uses a typical constellation of OPRs to exhibit how they can be used to represent any business operation. Remember, the term *business* used here is relative to the domain or industry. A technical business domain also may be represented using the OPR abstractions.

In the figure, the business designers have recognized a business unit, its reception, and its departments as significant organizations. Purchase-order documents and personnel and product information sheets have been determined as significant resources. Lastly, the fulfillment process has been identified as a significant process in the operation of the business. The act of representing the business OPRs alone often reveals immediate possibilities for improvement. When carried out in the context of an overall IT architecture, the task of business modeling is an investment in the successive improvement of the entire business operation. These improvements may be the result of better automation of the business using information technology. However, immediate, non-IT-related operational improvements often outnumber the IT-related improvements in the initial stages of business modeling. The reasons for this are explained in Taylor (1995).

In addition to defining the three intuitive OPR business abstractions, the modeling style also can provide information on how these abstractions are related. Such predefined types of relationships help create more uniform models. More important, they are in the interest of constructive foresight down the development channel. They

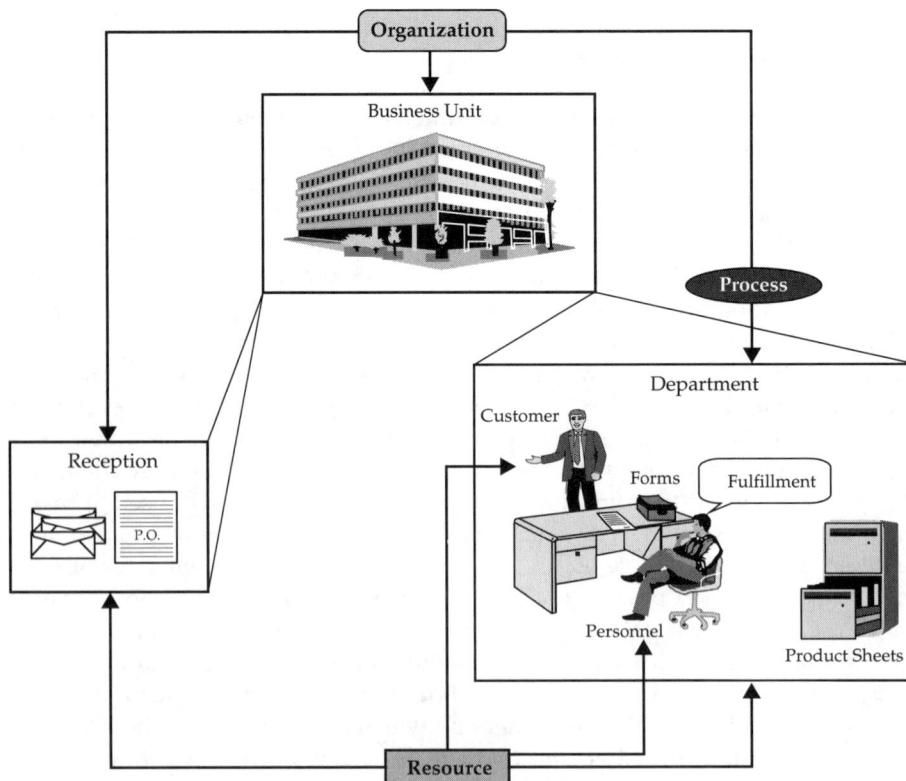

Figure 4.14 Business engineering with object technology.

enable effective preparation downstream in the development process without constraining the expressiveness of a business model. This is analogous to traffic rules stating that you may drive anywhere you want as long as you drive on the right side of the road. This simple constraint in the way we drive enables the entire signage and signaling of roads to be prepared effectively, once and for all, without having to ask every driver what side of the road he or she intends to drive on.[8] It also simplifies the rules and signaling at intersections, making them easy to learn and uniformly enforceable. Without this constructive foresight, a driver would never know what the intention of another driver is at a crossroad, and the definition of standard signaling (the automation and the tools) would be impossible. Just as the clear rules of the road significantly reduce the risk of driving, the constrictive foresight of the modeling style reduces development risks and enables, for example, more effective security mechanisms. The days of arbitrary rules of the road are gone forever. By the same token, the days of arbitrary object models as the default approach are passé in the Convergent Architecture.

The OPR business abstractions and their relationships form a pattern, as shown in Figure 4.15. To achieve convergence, this top-level pattern visibly evolves to other, more detailed patterns throughout the various levels of refinement, from the business model to various IT representations to the final running system. The objective is to preserve the basic relationships shown in the figure throughout all phases of system development.

In the figure, the base *business object* leverages inheritance in order to simplify the model. All OPRs inherit its common features, including its relationships: All OPRs are business objects. The association line and caption to its left indicate that all business objects are, by default, searchable and traded via their designated owning organization. The dotted line denotes that this mechanism is possible and, in the absence of overriding circumstances, is the default relationship. This means that all positions downstream in the architecture provide features enabling effective searchability and

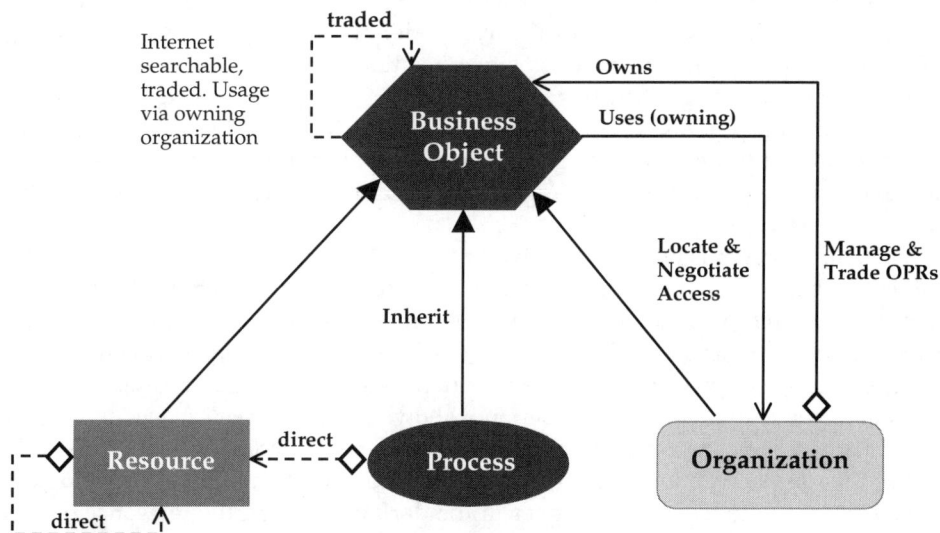

Figure 4.15 The basic OPR relationships and the semantics of OPRs.

trading. However, the precise meaning of "Internet searchable, traded" is not defined by the business model. It is defined by the technology projection chosen for a particular instance of the Convergent Architecture. The business model and subsequent UML models only define how searchability and trading features are configured, not their precise implementation. The models are not simply a notational translation or visualization of a particular implementation. Instead, depending on the technology projection, they may be mapped to many different implementations. The architectural IDE actively supports the task of configuration according to the constraints of a specific technology projection. This well-defined relationship with the technology projection downstream in the design flow is important because, in order to remain simple and compatible, models cannot arbitrarily define how such complex mechanisms as searchabilty and trading will work, nor should they be ambiguous about such business-relevant aspects of a system.

The relationships associated with the *organization* in the figure show that organizations are managers of all OPRs and are the centers for trading and dispatching these contained OPRs. All business objects locate OPRs and negotiate their access and use via the organization. Thus, the organizations are the top-level enforcers of security policy as well as the principal quality of service (QoS) query interfaces by which potential users locate the OPRs best suited to their needs.

Aside from being a business object, the *process* has the possibility (denoted by the dotted line) to more directly associate itself with resources. This direct association means that it may possess references to specific resources over long periods of time. Such direct binding, like all other relationships in the diagram, brings with it a certain set of tradeoffs downstream in the development process. The architectural style's preference for the set of tradeoffs associated with trading is expressed by the presence of trading as the top-level default, automatically inherited from the base business object. However, the fact that processes often require an explicit, direct association is also recognized by the style and indicated by the potential to overload the business object's default with the direct alternative—at a cost. Once again, the precise tradeoff set associated with the alternatives can only be defined by the selected technology projection—more evidence of the sensitive relationship between business design options and system design reality.

Analogous to a process, a *resource* also may have direct relationships with other resources. As all business objects, a resource has a particularly intimate relationship with its owning organization. Once again, the precise properties of this relationship depend on the technology projection.

This focus on the business perspective of the OPRs in this section emphasizes the relationship between the business, project, and system design, this time at the level of business modeling. Alas, not even the business model is exempt from the designer's paradox. Even the business designers must somehow deal with engineering realities to keep such realities from creeping up and, often, wreaking havoc on projects downstream in the development effort. Experience shows that *investments in models, business models or other models, that cannot be projected easily to available technologies are at best dubious regarding their effectiveness and returns.* One step toward avoiding such dubious investments is not to leave the designer in the dark concerning the relevance of constraints that await him or her downstream. Reformulating this from the perspective of a project manager, modelers, including business consultants, should no longer work in the optimistic bliss of zero constraints until the project hits the wall of reality downstream in the development flow. To avoid this, the realities of the technology projection (including the programming and implementation phases) must be propagated at the appropriate level of abstraction upstream, producing a higher level of design sensitivity. This does not mean that the designs are any worse or any harder to produce. In fact, just the opposite is the case: They are cleaner, simpler, and more effective because they express the business strategy, the OPRs, using a modeling style that understands how the model should evolve, by hand or automatically, and with higher quality into the next level of refinement. To come back to the analogy: Who cares whether we drive on the right or the left side of the road? Simply by specifying this inert driving constraint up front in the design stream, we improve the quality and effectiveness of the entire transportation system downstream. Moreover, such design sensitivity does not mean that the business and system design are inextricably coupled. To the contrary, although some level of coupling must exist in the interest of engineering reality, unnecessary coupling is avoided by explicitly dealing with the existence of these realities in the architectural style—the designer's paradox.

The OPR Convergent Components

This section complements the preceding section by focusing on how a business model is transposed via components into an IT system. Figure 4.16 illustrates the convergent mapping of the business design into IT components. To the left, we see the model from the *business perspective,* as developed using the reduced set of abstractions: organizations, processes, and resources. The right side of the diagram shows the same reduced abstraction set from the *software perspective.* This alignment of the business model with the component model is a high-priority goal in the Convergent Architecture.

In the software perspective, we see that the components add the IT dimension aspects while visibly preserving the features of the business dimension in the business components. The figure also shows the relationship between utility components (defined later) and the business-component hierarchy. The utility component does not

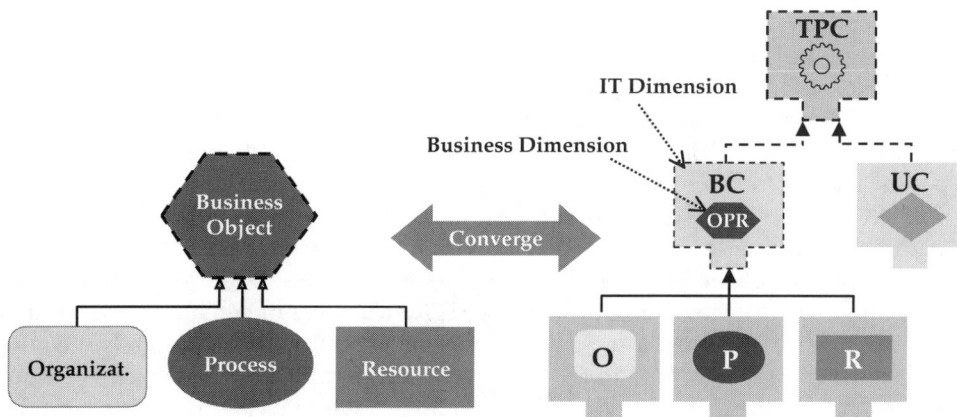

Figure 4.16   The convergent OPR components.

inherit from the base business component because it is, in effect, the antithesis of the business component: By definition, it has no business relevance.

The business component is shown as the first component with business relevance and, as such, with a visible business dimension. Its dotted outline suggests that it too is abstract and serves primarily to factor out common characteristics of the OPRs. The visibility of the business dimensions in the OPRs exists to preserve convergence, emphasizing that the designer and tools are to map the OPR business object model at the left of the figure to the convergent components at the right of the figure. Alone, the visibility, tractability, and reversibility of this convergent mapping simplify both technical and conceptual aspects of a design.[9] The process, patterns, techniques, and tools for convergent mapping are covered in Chapters 6 and 7 in conjunction with their concrete application using the architectural IDE. From the perspective of the convergent component metamodel itself, the UML modeling and technology projection of the OPRs remains to be discussed.

UML Modeling and Technology Projection of OPRs

Starting from the business model, it is important to keep the OPRs clearly visible through the UML models and into the runtime environment. The modeling style, part of the TPC, defines how the quadrants of the OPRs are modeled using standard UML for a given technology projection such as J2EE/EJB. Maintaining the business and IT dimensions as separate entities throughout the design flow is particularly valuable. First, it permits the workers on a team to be more appropriately allocated: Business logic developers can focus on the clearly visible business dimension. In addition, due to the model-level support of these dimensions, the IT dimension can be generated automatically from the model for a particular technology projection. The architectural IDE also can better support the very different life cycles of the two dimensions. The business dimension, which contains the majority of an organization's business logic, can be modeled, versioned, documented, and stored as separately managed entities. Even the generated build and deployment infrastructure (that is, directory structures, files, and build scripts) and the resulting runtime system (that is, components, classes, and objects) can separate the two life cycles. For example, a J2EE technology projection generates the business dimension into a completely different directory structure, separate from one or more IT dimensions. This single business dimension can then be used together with several different IT dimensions. Thus, different application servers can be deployed or tested in parallel with the same business dimension, or a version upgrade from one server infrastructure to another can be handled simply by regenerating the IT dimension from the model. These improvements by themselves result in significantly higher development quality in less time with fewer resources.

Developing an effective technology projection for the OPRs is far from trivial. This is not due to any inherent problems in the OPR structures or semantics; rather, it is caused by the fact that the business dimensions of the OPRs are, by design (see Figure 4.15), closer to the business than they are to currently available technology. The challenge of the specific technology projection is then to place as few constraints on the business dimension of the OPRs as possible while still supporting a robust, assisted, or automatic projection to available technology. This turns out to be a real challenge because the OPRs, as simple as they appear, push the limits of even the best technologies. In addition, our basic principles require that the technology projection avoids coupling with short-lived, proprietary implementations, which, quite correctly, narrow the options available to the designer of a technology projection.

To date, essentially two approaches have been taken to technology projection. These approaches affect to some extent the technology projection of all the convergent components. However, the OPRs, as the core business components, define the driving tradeoff set. These approaches represent two ends of a spectrum of reasonable tradeoff sets. Different IT organizations invariably select different positions within this spectrum. The first approach is to complement available technology by implementing high-level features of OPRs. This approach enables more powerful OPRs from the business design perspective at the cost of requiring some proprietary extensions to standards-based technologies. The extent of these improvements currently strains our requirement that we avoid coupling with proprietary technology. The second approach, and the one taken by the default J2EE technology projection described in this book, represents the other end of the tradeoff spectrum. It maps the OPRs to the robust features of available standards-based technology, such as a J2EE server, and avoids any significant extensions. Nevertheless, we do allow it to smooth out the rough edges of a particular J2EE server without drifting from the standard. This approach turns the tradeoff set around: The OPRs are no longer in the driver's seat. Instead of placing hard requirements on the infrastructure, the OPRs willingly submit to its limitations. In this approach, the OPRs are more limited in their capabilities, whereas the technology projection is better aligned with mainstream technology, more portable, and easier to communicate.

Any point in this tradeoff spectrum is equally well supported by the Convergent Architecture as long as the point is specifically selected. A closer look at the two approaches, the two ends of the spectrum, shows how this works.

The first approach has been around longer than the second approach. This is because component standards and standards-based infrastructures have only recently reached a level where they can reasonably support reality-scale systems. Before the advent of J2EE/EJB, the first approach projected organizations to CORBA-trader-compliant components in CORBA-centric infrastructures. Process and resource components were the traded CORBA objects. Process components leveraged proprietary workflow technology in order to reasonably support UML process models. Oddly, de facto standards for modeling process workflow in UML were available before any implementations of these de facto standards. Thus, the TPC and the architectural IDE could support standards-based UML modeling for processes, such as the method of event-driven process chains (EPCs) (Aalst 1998), while having to project these UML models to proprietary implementations.

Using current J2EE/EJB standards and technology for the first approach is similar. In these constellations, organizations are modeled and projected to EJB components that have been extended to use the EJB query mechanisms in the form of a component trader. CORBA-trader concepts often are leveraged here. Alternatively, an entire EJB container represents a single organization. The EJB modeling style for organizations is explicitly extended to expose relevant trader features in UML, and the technology projection is extended to map these features to the particular J2EE implementation. Similar to the CORBA-centric approach earlier, processes are modeled using a process-modeling extension in the UML modeling style. These models are then projected to proprietary, organization-specific extensions to EJB or, preferably, to purchased workflow engines.

In the first approach, it is important to note that any extensions may be generated to several different technologies. However, the effort required to maintain the technology projection for each platform may be significant—an important consideration in the tradeoff set.

In the second approach, the IT organization decides that the advantages due to standards and mainstream alignment outweigh the advantages of high-end OPR semantics. In this approach, the capabilities of the OPRs submit to the constraints of available technologies. Although still valuable, the OPRs are not as powerful as we would wish. Over time, developers can increase their power based on improvements in standards and mainstream technology. This is a slower incremental approach, but it is low risk and low resistance from the perspective of the IT organization. On the other side of the coin are the compromises that must be made in the OPR designs. Organizations are designed in UML as EJBs that are preconfigured to use the *best available* query features and association management features, as long as these features remain close to the EJB standard. The technology projection then selects and tunes the best configuration of these features for the particular implementation technology. In other words, there is no standard way to use the implementation of a standard. There are several ways to skin a cat, and a good technology projection, while remaining close to the standard, differentiates itself from run-of-the-mill code generators by providing expert tuning of the features of a particular J2EE/EJB implementation. Such tuning is complex but important because the various J2EE/EJB application servers do differ significantly in the implementation and tuning of their standard-conform J2EE features.

In the second approach, the same basic rules apply to processes and resources. Processes are, of course, much more challenging to map than resources. In fact, processes are the place where the most compromises must be made when using current J2EE/EJB technologies. Several major problems can occur when implementing EPCs (discussed previously) using current state-of-the-art standards and their implementations. These problems range from coordinating concurrency in the presence of isolated transactions (the so-called lost update problem) to the severe limitations on multithreading that arise as a side effect of transactional constraints in the EJB standard. The list of problems here is long and complex, but the bottom line is that without proprietary extensions, projecting processes modeled along the lines of EPC is out of the question. This is improving, but the currently available technology just does not make it possible using standard-compliant features. Instead, the modeling style in the second approach requires process models to be simpler. Currently, this translates to some restraints in the concurrency and asynchronous behavior of processes. Since the UML modeling style is explicit as to its capabilities, the architectural IDE can still check whether a process in the UML model complies to the specific constraints of a projection or not. The advantage of this approach is found in the long-term perspective. When standards and their implementations improve, the modeling style and the technology projections can cash in immediately on these improvements. This is so because they have not deviated previously from the mainstream flow. The restraint and resistance to the temptation of proprietary features can result in significant returns in the long run. The only prerequisite to this payoff is a clear, consistent path, a consistent architectural style.

Utility Components

Utility components, short for *technical utility components,* are convergent components without any business-domain relevance. They are not (do not inherit from) business components and as such do not possess any predefined business behavior or relationships. Similar to accessors, utility components encapsulate external technology to explicitly ensure the integrity of the architecture. In contrast to accessors, the technologies encapsulated by utility components are coinstalled as part of the convergent system: They are either physically part of an assembly, that is, installed as part of the assembly, or they are part of the prerequisite installation platform required by the assembly.

Utility components are used to implement any purely technical aspects of a convergent system and to abstract the other convergent components from fast-changing aspects of implementation technologies. Thus, as shown in several of the preceding figures, a utility component does not normally implement a business dimension; its only active dimension is its IT dimension. Typical examples of utility components include logging facilities, administrative or monitoring facilities, security servers, key servers, and configuration servers used uniformly by all convergent components.

Summary

The convergent component metamodel presented in this chapter plays a major role in the architectural style. It defines convergent components as a vehicle to assist business designers and developers along the path from high-level business modeling to effective design representations to running IT systems.

The metamodel first defines how the concepts of convergent engineering, the UML standard, and component design standards such as J2EE/EJB are combined to model and implement convergent components. It partitions convergent components into architectural layers and specifies how each of these layers contributes to the model-centric development of a convergent system.

The responsibilities, relationships, and structure of each convergent component are described in conjunction with its positioning as part of a UML modeling style. In each case, the important properties of the technology projection are discussed as well as the factors realistically influencing projection to current and future technologies.

In the following chapters, convergent components and the associated concepts seen in this chapter will be used to streamline the IT organization, the development process, and the architectural IDE and to increase the effectiveness of each one of these cogwheels in the clockwork of holistic architecture.

The IT-Organization Model

The business of building IT systems.

The development model of the Convergent Architecture is comprised of three subdivisions. The second of these is the IT-organization model, which is covered in this chapter.

The information technology (IT) organization is one of the most significant organizations of any modern business. Its services are critical to the success of the business as a whole because the systems it produces are the lifeblood of other organizations in the business. This means that the IT organization is essentially responsible for representing and optimizing the operational aspects of other business organizations. We saw in previous chapters that the process of building the IT systems is synonymous with the process of understanding and optimizing the business. The business, however, consists of many various organizations, each striving to improve the business as a whole and each crucially dependent on IT systems to achieve this goal. The IT organization is the only organization in a position to facilitate cross-functional optimization across all other organizations and to help these organizations represent, optimize, and support their strategies as part of a holistic whole. However, to be successful in this central role, the IT organization must first win the confidence of other business organizations. It must itself lead the way as the role model of effective design and IT support. If it did not, every effort to help other organizations optimize their work would be regarded, quite correctly, as pretentious. An organization responsible for business optimization must itself practice what it preaches. This professionalism is important not only from the perspective of credibility, but also from the perspective of being effective in the business of building IT systems. This is why the Convergent Architecture positions the

IT organization first and foremost as the business organization that must get its respective house in order before attempting to help others improve theirs. From this perspective, the task of the architectural style is to define what its house should look like and how it should be run in order to optimally produce systems according to the style.

The following sections provide a structured representation, or model, of the IT organization as it should operate to best support the other features of the architectural style. When creating an instance of the Convergent Architecture, this model is used as the roadmap to set up a new IT organization. It is also employed for the evolution of existing organizations. The result is a situation-specific representation, or model, of an IT organization. As explained in Chapter 2, the Convergent Architecture "uses what it sells." This means that the IT organization is modeled using the same concepts the Convergent Architecture uses to model any business organization. These are the business abstractions: organizations, processes, and resources.

The IT-organization model focuses on organizational structure and the resources that populate this structure. These are the resources relevant to system development, such as workers, development teams, and software. When referring to an IT organization as defined by the Convergent Architecture, I use the spelling IT organization. The IT organization is where both resources and processes live. It defines the structure in which the entire development process operates. It is where the components of the development process find the resources they require and deliver the resources they produce. It adds an aspect of calming continuity and order, which effectively directs the ever-changing landscape of development projects. Thus, the IT organization, as covered in this chapter, is the prerequisite foundation on which the development process is built. The corresponding process model—the development process model—presented in the following chapter is based on this foundation.

Before getting into details, let's turn our focus to the IT organization and its positioning within a business organization, as illustrated in Figure 5.1. In this and subsequent figures, organizations are represented as rounded rectangles in accordance with convergent engineering. Figure 5.1 depicts the IT organization as an integral part of the overall business. The outermost organization represents the top-level business organi-

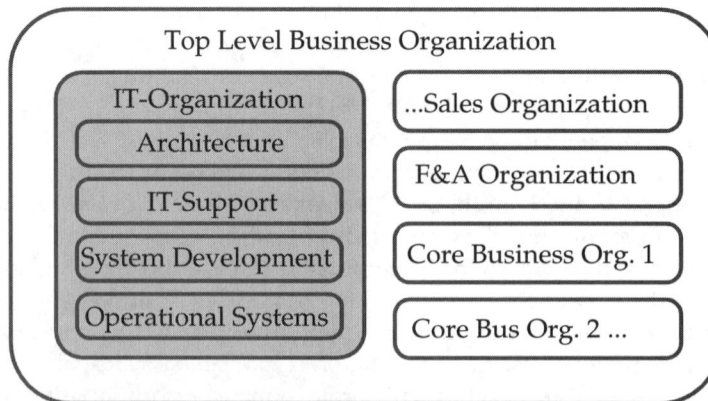

Figure 5.1   The IT organization in a business context.

zation. The organizations to the right in the diagram (that is, the sales and finance and administration organizations) are typical examples of other core business organizations. All the organizations outside the IT organization are the organizations it supports. They are its clients or its customers. The figure also shows the internal structure of the IT organization. It is comprised of its internal or suborganizations. Each of the IT organizations is summarized here:

- **IT organization.**   This is concerned primarily with project design as well as the environment and mechanisms required to effectively coordinate manifold IT-related projects. It sets up and manages the following four internal organizations and represents their cumulative responsibility as the interface to external or client organizations.

- **Architecture organization.**   This is responsible for defining and maintaining the Convergent Architecture and ensuring its proper use. It also has technical, project management, and mentoring responsibilities focused on achieving the high returns of professional IT architecture across all organizations.

- **IT-support organization.**   This is responsible for critical support services shared by the other IT organizations, including all software development projects. It can be seen as the operational systems organization supporting the business of IT development. The IT-support organization is comprised of suborganizations for change and configuration management, base infrastructure administration, project information management, and test center management.

- **System-development organization.**   This houses and manages the system-development teams. It coordinates individual software projects and the skills pool of developers working in these projects. It also defines the goals and guidelines for a successful software development project, as well as the structure, roles, and responsibilities for a successful software development team, the so-called canonical development team.

- **Operational-systems organization.**   This is the operational runtime organization responsible for deploying systems and maintaining their production use by other business organizations. The operational-systems organization is comprised of suborganizations for software deployment, user support, and base infrastructure administration.

The following sections cover each of these organizations in more detail.

Features Common to All IT Organizations

In accordance with the principles of the architectural metamodel, we use the techniques of responsibility-driven design and object-oriented technology to describe the IT organizations. This begins by defining the features common to all IT organizations and outlining the structure and terminology used to describe all IT organizations. Readers familiar with object-oriented technology would intuitively call this the *base IT organization*.

The characteristics of the organization, process, and resource abstractions (OPRs), common to both the IT-organization model and its related development process model, are covered in the remainder of this section. OPRs are design patterns introduced by Dr. David A. Taylor in his book on convergent engineering (Taylor 1995). The models of the Convergent Architecture leverage and build on these patterns; however, Dr. Taylor's book should be consulted for the rationale and detail behind these patterns. To assist readers who are not yet very familiar with convergent engineering, the necessary OPR fundamentals are reviewed here in conjunction with descriptions of how they are applied specifically in the IT organization. You may want to refer to Figure 3.4 while reading the following descriptions.

Organization, Process, and Resource Abstractions (OPRs)

OPRs are units of well-defined responsibility. Such responsibilities also include the relationships OPRs maintain with each other, as described here. In general, OPRs are fractal in both structure and behavior. This means that they may be nested to any level, with each level maintaining compatible behavior. This applies to all subtypes of OPRs. For example, as you will see, the IT organization contains an architecture organization. They are both organizations, and as such, they inherit the compatible structures and behavior of an organization. The architecture organization may contain other organizations. Such nesting may go on indefinitely. This constitutes what is known in convergent engineering as a *fractal structure* because no matter how far you drill down into the details of the structure of the IT organization, you still see the familiar forms and behavior of organizations. Persons familiar with object-oriented technology recognize that the power of fractal structures and fractal behavior is the result of applying the three pillars of object-oriented technology: data abstraction (encapsulation), type abstraction (inheritance), and function abstraction (polymorphism). However, you do not have to be an expert in object-oriented technology to understand and apply these powerful concepts to simplify the IT organization.

Organizations

Organizations manage processes, resources, and other organizations. They group people and other resources charged with carrying out specific business processes. An organization coordinates and represents the cumulative responsibilities of its contained OPRs. For example, just as in "real" business organizations, an organization prioritizes the access and use of its OPRs, implements security measures, and tracks their use. In the IT-organization model presented here, organizations are defined according to their responsibilities, their workers (see "Resources"), and the responsibilities of these workers.

Processes

Processes are goal-directed sequences of activities or tasks that are enabled by resources. They access or consume resources in order to enhance or produce other (hopefully more valuable) resources. For example, a process may consume a person's time to produce a document describing another new process. The document is a resource that has been produced by the process. Since processes may be nested to any level of granularity (all OPRs are fractal), they can represent high-level workflows as well as highly granular tasks. In the IT-organization model, we distinguish two types of processes to represent the granularities we require. The granularities and names used for these processes are in full alignment with the rational unified process. They are

- **Workflows.**   Long-term, identifiable groupings of logically related activities.

- **Activities.**   Identifiable groups of logically related tasks. Tasks are measurable, atomic units of work that usually are associated with a specific technique. They are the smallest unit of planned and assigned work in an organization.

Resources

Resources are intelligent units of value, cost, and action in an organization. They represent sources of business value, work, and information used by other OPRs. Three types of resources of particular relevance exist in the IT organization:

- **Workers.**   Humans are important resources for an organization, of course. Moreover, the roles a person can fulfill are resources. In the IT-organization model, the relationship between a human resource and a role fulfilled by a human is known as a *worker*. This corresponds to the term *worker* as used in the rational unified process. A single person may have many worker relationships. For example, if Susan possesses the skills to fulfill the role of component developer or lead developer in a project, she may be assigned as the worker fulfilling both these roles. This explicit separation of humans from their potential roles, as well as the representation of the worker relationship between these two, is another important pattern in convergent engineering. As part of their responsibilities, workers coordinate all other, inanimate resources within an organization such as machinery, money, time, and so on.

- **Artifacts and change sets.**   Also in line with the Rational Unified Process (RUP), we denote the resources produced or used by the IT organization in the context of system development as *artifacts*. Artifacts may be versioned alone or grouped into versioned sets. Such versioned groups are known as *change sets*. A change set may contain one or more artifacts. Change sets are managed using a configuration and change management (CCM) system, as described later. Thus, for our purposes, change set and artifact are synonyms, except that a change set may contain several named artifacts. We use the term *change set* when we speak of the artifacts grouped by the change set. In the IT-organization model, the artifacts and the change sets to which they belong are presented together with their respective managers. How and when these artifacts are created, and by whom, is the topic of the process model.

- **Technologies (reference technologies).**   The IT organization practices the same rules of technology management that it applies to other organizations of a business. Just as the IT organization rigorously plans and optimizes the application of technologies in other business organizations, the coordinated and planned use of technology is important for its own effective operation. Technologies developed outside the IT organization have been conceived in their own technological scope, oblivious of the concepts unifying a particular architectural style. This requires that certain critical technologies be positioned properly within the architectural style to avoid pollution of its concepts. At the same time, the architecture should leverage modern technologies effectively. To this end, the IT organization recognizes externally developed technologies as a special set of artifacts. It specifies those technologies used to support *highly specialized* activities in the IT organization. It does not specify a technology in cases where the choice of technology is noncritical (tangential) or noninvasive (for example, general office tools) from the perspective of the architectural style. In addition, the manager of the technology and its intended use in the IT organization are presented. Naming specific technologies in critical areas helps an IT organization get off to a running start. Clearly, the technologies specified here are *reference technologies* because they may be somewhat different in a particular instance of the Convergent Architecture. Even so, it is easier to get started based on a concrete, tried-and-true reference set. These technologies also will evolve with time, but the types of technologies used and their roles will remain stable. In other words, their evolution will be steady and clearly visible, not abrupt and obscure. As time goes by, the experience of the chief architect, in accordance with this worker's responsibilities, certainly will suffice to make the appropriate adaptations.

Using this new OPR terminology, we can now say more precisely that the IT-organization model covered in this chapter focuses on the IT organization, its contained organizations, and the artifacts (resources) associated with the organization. The development process model covered in the next chapter then explains how activities (processes) operate in conjunction with these organizations and how the activities use, produce, and manage artifacts.

Worker roles are always defined within the context of a particular organization. Thus, the sum of the worker roles in the organization essentially defines the responsibilities of the organization. In addition, a worker fulfilling a particular role is always working in the context of a specific organization, not just a process. This is important for two reasons. First, skills and roles should be grouped to achieve synergies. These groups are the organizations. Second, it is important to know which organization is responsible for coordinating the person fulfilling the role—the worker. If a person fulfills roles in two different organizations, then, by default, this person is managed on the level of the next higher organization. This is necessary because only the next higher organization possesses an undisputable authority to coordinate the time allocated by this person to each of the suborganizations.

A detailed description of the organizational structure begins by presenting the roles and responsibilities common to all IT organizations. Although some of these roles and responsibilities may appear obvious to the seasoned developer or project manager, experience shows that many of them are not being defined and fulfilled effectively in projects. Ironically, the largest projects are often the worst offenders. A realistic project manager or other stakeholder in a software project will not permit himself or herself to get pulled into a situation where these roles are being ignored. Each one of them is critical to the project's success. Ignoring any of them increases the project's risk.

Worker Roles and Responsibilities

The roles and responsibilities of workers common to all organizations are as follows:

- **Organization manager.** The organization manager is responsible for the overall fulfillment of an organization's responsibilities. The term *manager* simply communicates a higher level of responsibility and commensurate authority.[1] Not only do managers coordinate in the context of the Convergent Architecture, they also may do hands-on content work, depending on the organization, and they may engage staff to help them carry out their responsibilities. Above all, the organization manager focuses on optimizing investments with respect to the overall business priorities as agreed with the management of higher-level organizations. More important, the organization manager is the safety net, picking up all the ad-hoc tasks and responsibilities that were not predefined explicitly but are deemed to fall logically in the organization. In particular, the organization manager

  - Is the highest escalation point and top-level decision maker in the organization.

  - Is the principal communications and management interface to external organizations—the clients. This includes constructive feedback regarding designs and procedures in the form of requirements channeled to the requirements manager (defined later).

  - Defines, plans, tracks, and optimizes projects in the interest of client organizations. This includes coordinating and prioritizing requirements placed on the organization by others.

  - Is a member of the steering team (discussed later) in the next higher organization and convenes and leads the steering team meetings in his or her own organization.

  - Plans and coordinates the suborganizations and is fully responsible for them.

  - Performs functional management of the personnel and facilities of the organization. This includes procurement and administration of all resources required by the organization.

  - Is a Convergent Architecture-specific instance of the RUP worker: a project reviewer primarily from the IT-organization perspective. The project reviewer from the IT architecture perspective is the chief architect (discussed later).

- **Project manager.** Analogous with the organization manager but responsible for the overall fulfillment of a defined project's responsibilities, the project manager is the manager of a well-defined project. Once the organization manager has defined a project, the project manager runs the project from its initial planning through to the final project closure. He or she reports to the organization manager and may be asked to participate in steering team meetings.

- **Sponsoring client.**   The sponsoring client is a person or organization (external or internal) that sponsors a project. The sponsoring client may be an external software client or a representative of an entire software market (for example, a software product manager). In cases where the sponsoring client consists of a group or consortium, a *client steering team* is defined to provide an authoritative, representative body acting in the interest of the sponsoring client. The IT organization manager initiates the client steering team, if required, and coordinates its interaction with the rest of the IT organization.

- **Workflow owner, activity owner, resource owner.**   This worker takes full responsibility for the completion of a named workflow, activity, or life cycle of a named artifact, respectively. Each workflow, activity, and resource has a single owner.

- **Steering team.**   The steering team is responsible for global (horizontal) planning and optimization in organizations that contain multiple suborganizations. This includes the identification, bootstrapping, or modification of projects, as well as handling escalation situations. The steering team convenes at the discretion of the organization manager. It consists of the organization managers of the next lower level of organizations in the hierarchy. For example, the steering team of the IT organization consists of the organization managers of the architecture, IT support, system development, and operational-systems organizations. Each member of the steering team represents the perspective of his or her managed organization. This mixture of competence and responsibility ensures well-informed, rapid decisions as well as proactive optimization across the entire organization. The IT-Organization Steering Team

  - Officially kicks off system development projects based on the results of the project initiation activity.

  - Terminates system development projects based on iteration planning or review results and in escalation situations.

These worker roles and responsibilities exist within all IT organizations. They will not be listed repeatedly in each of the organization-specific sections to follow. However, any of these roles may be refined or specialized in the context of a particular organization. In such cases, the specialized aspects of the role are described and simply will refer to the common or base role it refines.

The IT Organization

The top-level IT organization (IT-O), shown in Figure 5.2, is the highest instance of decision and escalation concerning the development and operation of IT systems. Its customers are the non-IT-focused organizations of the business. Its steering team consists of the manager of the IT organization and the organization managers of the

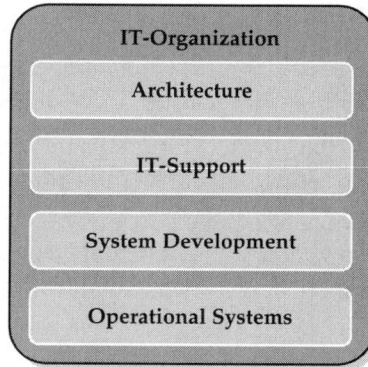

Figure 5.2   The top-level IT organization.

four organizations it contains, as shown in the figure. This particular steering team is the official interaction interface to all customers and stakeholders outside the IT organization.

Worker Roles and Responsibilities

Worker roles and responsibilities in the IT organization include the following:

- **IT-organization manager.**   In addition to responsibilities as an organization manager, the manager of the IT organization is specifically responsible for

  - Developing a situation-specific IT-organization model and implementation plan based on the IT-organization model. He or she carries out the implementation of the IT organization by kicking off workflows (see Chapter 6); that is, he or she is the top-level operational owner of the development process.

  - Initiating the four internal organizations and the top-level steering team. This begins with the architecture organization, which then bootstraps the Convergent Architecture and participates in the detailed planning and buildup of the other suborganizations.

  - Procuring and administrating the human resource pool. This is the central pool of all human resources allocated to the IT organization and all its fractal suborganizations. This responsibility may be delegated in part to other organizations.

  - Administrating the client relationship with both sponsoring clients and other non-IT organizations of the business.

  - Producing and administrating project proposals.

  - Performing centralized facilities management, procuring resources, and handling bookkeeping. This responsibility may be delegated in part to other organizations.

- Administrating the relationship with external partners. This includes centralized legal and contract management.

Owned resources:

- **Change sets (artifacts):** The IT-organization model and implementation plan, project proposals, and contractual and administrative artifacts.

Owned activities: Bootstrap the IT organization, project initiation and tracking, top-level owner of all operational workflows (not of workflow definitions, which are owned by the chief architect as part of the architectural style).

The Architecture Organization

The architecture organization (Arch-O), shown in Figure 5.3, ensures a high return on IT investments by providing professional system engineering skills to the entire IT organization. It prevents the ad hoc growth of incompatible infrastructures and competing design philosophies. It unites the most experienced IT personnel with a professional chief architect to ensure that the Convergent Architecture is communicated, established, and enforced properly.

Worker Roles and Responsibilities

Worker roles and responsibilities in the architecture organization include the following:

- **Chief (convergent) architect.**   The chief architect is the organization manager of the architecture organization and the single top-level authority on decisions regarding the Convergent Architecture and its use. In addition to a high level of technical and communication skills, the chief architect must have a wide range of hands-on experience with various roles in real-world development

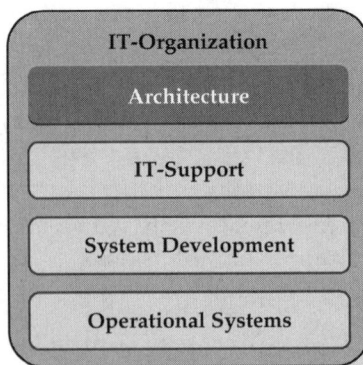

Figure 5.3   The architecture organization.

projects. The logical career path leading to the required skill set starts with work as a component developer, then lead developer, and then convergent architect. These worker roles are defined below. The chief architect has the following specific responsibilities, which may be delegated to another convergent architect (discussed later) in the organization:

■ Defines a specific instance of the Convergent Architecture for the IT organization and consistently evolves the instance. This includes the coordination and prioritization of requirements on the architectural style together with the requirements manager (discussed later). It also includes working closely with the architectural Integrated Development Environment (IDE) specialist (discussed later).

■ Monitors and controls proper use of the style across all system development projects. This includes reviewing all system project plans and monitoring development-process workflows. Operational problems in workflows are delegated to the IT-organization manager, whereas modifications in workflow definitions are worked into the instance of the Convergent Architecture.

■ Assists in detailed planning and buildup of the IT support, system development, and operational systems organizations. The chief architect regularly reviews these organizations and works with them to simplify and optimize overall operations from the perspective of the three pillars of holistic architecture: project design, business design, and system design.

■ Selects technologies and designates the resource owner for the technology. The chief architect identifies the need for sentinels for specific technologies and works together with the respective resource owner to define the sentinel.

■ Reviews project teams to ensure adequate skill sets and preparation.

■ Assists lead developers as a participant in system development projects (discussed later), particularly in the project inception and elaboration phases.

■ Is a Convergent Architecture-specific consolidation of the following RUP worker roles: architect, process engineer, business process analyst, architecture reviewer, design reviewer, business model reviewer, and project reviewer from the IT-architecture perspective.

> *Owned resources:*
> ■ **Change sets (artifacts):**
>> ■ **Convergent Architecture style reference.**   This describes an organization-specific instance of the Convergent Architecture as defined in this book. The instance may be a one-to-one application of the entire style as described in this book or a documented variant that remains compatible with the architectural and development models as described in this book.
>> ■ **Assembly architecture review.**   This is a review report confirming and explaining the architectural compliance of a particular assembly component.

- **Unified glossary.** This consolidates all glossaries produced by assembly developers (discussed later).

- **Sentinels.** All sentinels describing the architecture-conform positioning and the use of technology within the IT organization, including its system development projects.

- Top-level OPR business model and context diagrams.

- Specialized Technologies: None pre-defined.

Owned activities: T-bar business analysis and architectural evolution.

- **Convergent architect.**[2]   This apprentice or assistant to the chief architect gains experience as a convergent architect while assisting the chief architect in day-to-day activities. The number of convergent architects required depends on the size and maturity of the IT organization. A convergent architect accompanies each system development project and serves as the technology-versed counterpart to the system project manager (discussed later). His or her primary role is to guarantee cross-project integrity of the architecture, timely feedback between the architecture organization and other IT organizations, and mentoring of lead developers. The number of convergent architects also must suffice to ensure adequate redundancy and long-term continuity in this critical area. This worker is a Convergent Architecture-specific instance of the following RUP worker role, the same as the chief architect previously.

- **Speaker of the architecture.**   This communicator professionally explains and teaches the architecture to its many stakeholders at all levels of the organization. Due to the critical importance of the IT architecture in all aspects of the entire business, it is important that it be properly communicated at all levels of the business. The speaker of the architecture focuses on this specialized task. This person must be a master in the skills required to communicate the features, goals, status, advantages, and plans of the architecture and the architecture organization. The chief architect does not necessarily fulfill this role. In fact, in large organizations, this speaker frees up the chief architect to carry out his or her core responsibilities.

- **Requirements manager.**   This central figure organizes, refines, and prioritizes the continuous stream of business and technical requirements from all sources. The requirements manager is the single, official sink for all requirement requests that do not have a predefined sink in another IT organization or software development project. Any requirement without a clearly defined and receptive sink lands with the requirements manager. Once requirements have been sifted, sorted, and prioritized, the requirements manager then dispatches the requirements to organization managers (according to their organization's responsibilities) for the planning of new projects or organizational changes. This worker is the Convergent Architecture-specific consolidation of the following RUP worker roles: requirements reviewer and change control manager.[3]

Owned resources:

- **Change sets (artifacts):** Requirements pool.
- **Specialized technologies:** Rational Requisite-Pro.

Owned activities: Global requirements management

- **Architectural IDE specialist.**   This tool specialist is the single top-level authority on the use and evolution of the IT-architectural IDE and other development-support tools used in the IT organization. He or she defines, refines, and maintains the reference tool topology. The primary responsibility is to ensure that the tools optimally support the goals and features of the architectural style and that the tools remain consistent and compatible across projects. This worker normally has extensive experience as a development toolsmith (discussed later). This worker is a Convergent Architecture-specific instance of the following RUP worker role: tool specialist.

Owned resources:

- **Change sets (artifacts):**
  - **IT-architectural IDE.**   Technology projection component (modeling style guides, cartridges), installation kit for IT-architectural IDE modules, and installation verification tests.
  - **Tools integrated by the architectural IDE.**   JBuilder Java IDE, Rational Rose Modeler, J2EE Application Server (for example, Borland BAS, BEA WLS, IBM WebSphere, and so on), Apache WebServer, persistent resource manager for J2EE application server (for example, TopLink, Oracle, Sybase), Cygnus GNU Tools.
- **Specialized technologies:** Same as change set.

The IT Support Organization

The IT support organization (IT-Sup-O) provides the technical infrastructure and services for all IT organizations except for the operational systems organization. In other words, it provides support for the complete development-oriented infrastructure. Often, development support environments are neglected in project plans or are delegated to the persons responsible for the operational systems of an organization, and both approaches result in major problems. Just as the environment in an automobile factory does not much resemble that of a service station, the environment required for effective IT system development is much different from the environment in which the IT systems eventually operate. In addition, the system developers cannot be responsible for both development of new IT systems and development and maintenance of their supporting environment at the same time. These are two completely different jobs. Experience has shown that it is much more effective to have a well-defined IT support organization to handle the myriad support activities required by system development projects. Since the system development projects adhere to the same

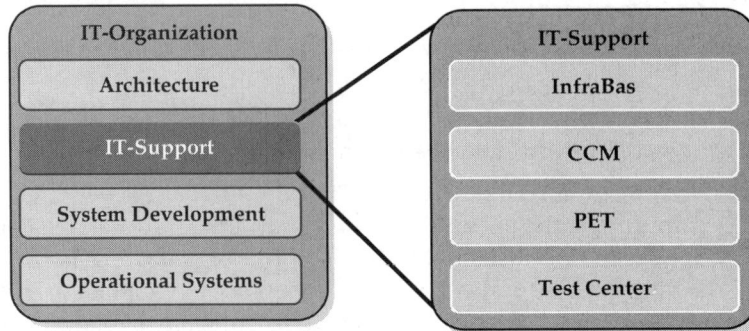

Figure 5.4   The IT support organization.

IT-architectural style, the IT support organization can better reuse its systems and services across development projects. As always, such reuse enables superior optimization of support procedures and systems—everybody wins.

As indicated in Figure 5.4, the IT support organization is partitioned into four suborganizations. All its responsibilities and roles, aside from those common to every IT organization, are delegated to the suborganizations, which are covered individually in the following sections.

The Infrastructure and Base Systems Organization

New, innovative systems can only be developed effectively once the fundamental base systems on which the development effort depends are robust and well organized. The infrastructure and base systems organization (InfraBas-O) is responsible for providing these fundamental base systems. The chief architect defines the common-denominator system environments together with this organization. The infrastructure and base systems organization then implements and supports the environment for all IT organizations except for the operational systems organization. Continuity and consistence with the operational systems organization are maintained through frequent, iterative project interaction in the due course of system development projects and the activities of the test center organization (see the following section).

Worker Roles and Responsibilities

Worker roles and responsibilities in the infrastructure and base systems organization include the following:

- **Infrastructure and base systems organization manager.**   In addition to the responsibilities of an organization manager, the manager of the infrastructure and base systems organization is specifically responsible for the following:

  - Defining the basic system environment and services with the chief architect and ensuring the robust implementation of this environment.

- Procuring, installing, administrating, supporting, and maintaining the infrastructure (both hardware and software) in at least the following areas: networks, file servers, and application servers for general use; operating systems; office applications; security and backup systems; and basic utilities as defined by the chief architect.

- Defining and maintaining the tools and associated procedures used to support the base infrastructure.

  Owned resources:

  - **Change sets (artifacts):** Infrastructure and base systems guide. This guide documents the structure, installation, maintenance, and use of the infrastructure and base systems for the respective user of the base system.

- **System administrator.** This specialist in system administration operates and maintains the infrastructure. This worker is a Convergent Architecture-specific instance of the following RUP worker role: system administrator.

The Change and Configuration Management Organization

The change and configuration management organization (CCM-O) houses the team and the systems required to effectively manage the versioned and archived artifacts of the IT organization. *Versioned artifacts* are things such as source code that are managed online in terms of their precise versions. These versions must be reproducible at any time. A change and configuration management system supports this complex task. *Archived artifacts* are one of two things: They are either artifacts that do not require the precise tracking of version history, or they are artifacts that cannot be managed reasonably within a configuration management system. The latter may still be versioned as part of a system configuration. In both cases, mechanisms must exist to identify and manage these artifacts outside the configuration management system and in many cases offline. Examples of offline archived artifacts are CDs containing software kits or specialized, software-version-dependent hardware such as a smart-card reader.

Worker Roles and Responsibilities

Worker roles and responsibilities in the change and configuration management organization include the following:

- **Change and configuration management organization manager.** In addition to the responsibilities of an organization manager, the manager of the change and configuration management organization is specifically responsible for the following:

  - Defining the system and service levels for both archived and versioned pools of artifacts based on the projections of the other IT organizations. This is done in conjunction with the managers of each IT organization and the chief architect. The granularity, partitioning, and quantities of versioned and archived artifacts can be reasonably estimated due to the common component and process models and the common architectural IDE employed across all projects in the architectural style.

- Managing the software inventory, library, and licenses, as well as the hardware inventory.

- Cataloging existing convergent components for reuse and assisting others in locating them. This includes maintenance of consistent naming conventions and a clean, unambiguous name space at the level of convergent components.

- Maintaining offline software archive and literature library.

- **Configuration manager.**   This specialist in configuration management operates and maintains the versioned and archived pools. The configuration manager has the following specific responsibilities:

  - Structuring and optimizing the versioning and archiving activities according to schemes defined by the rational unified change management (UCM) methodology for the artifacts and change sets in the Convergent Architecture. The development model and the architectural IDE specify many artifacts and change sets, such as the convergent components, as well as their partitioning.

  - Supporting the users in the entire IT organization in effectively meeting their specific change and configuration management requirements. In particular, this entails creating a configuration management reference according to the UCM for each assembly component.

  - Creating a base or template configuration management reference and using it as a basis for assembly-specific configuration management references.

  - Assuring that all artifacts required to reproduce assemblies are versioned or archived. This is carried out in conjunction with the test center organization (discussed later). Examples of these artifacts include models, generated sources, build environments, tools, and utilities, that is, essentially everything required to reproduce the development environment.

  - Convergent Architecture-specific instance of the following RUP worker role: configuration manager

    Owned resources:

    - **Change sets (artifacts):** Versioned UCM pool, archived pool, UCM usage guidelines, base UCM configuration management reference.

    - **Specialized technologies:** ClearCase UCM system including clients.

- **Repository toolsmith.**   This CCM system expert defines, deploys, maintains, and evolves the UCM infrastructure and tool environment. The specific definition of the CCM system and accompanying tools is carried out together with the chief architect. The repository toolsmith is also responsible for tailoring the CCM-related tools for effective use with the architectural IDE and for supporting users in this context. He or she works closely with the development toolsmith and configuration manager.

Owned resources:

- **Change sets (artifacts):** None.
- **Specialized technologies:** ClearCase UCM system including clients.

The Project Information, Events, and Training Organization

The project information, events, and training organization (PET-O) helps the IT organization achieve optimal use and reuse of information across organizational and project boundaries. It is responsible for the proactive definition of effective communication and learning mechanisms for the entire organization. It provides a pragmatic platform for the timely flow and availability of valuable information, which is often lost in system development organizations. It achieves this, for example, through the proactive design of how information will be harvested and structured both in the IT organization and for the end-user of its system development products. It then provides well-defined access channels to this information such as a Web site, regular events, and educational material. In addition to planning and structuring the information, an important goal of this organization is to support the direct, well-coordinated contribution to the information pool by all stakeholders. Lastly, this is the organizational home of all workers specializing in the consolidation, presentation, and publishing of information in the IT organization.

Worker Roles and Responsibilities

Worker roles and responsibilities in the project information, events, and training organization include the following:

- **Project information, events, and training organization manager.**   In addition to the responsibilities of an organization manager, the manager of the project information, events, and training organization is specifically responsible for the following:

  - Working with other organizations and projects to define their particular information, documentation, and training requirements.

  - Coordinating and administrating educational and information events appropriate to the size and plans of the other organizations.

  - Providing the central definition, coordination, and support for the suite of electronic office tools used by the entire IT organization.

- **Technical writer.**   This specialist in technical documentation produces the final forms of any official documents. He or she is also responsible for the selection, preparation, and maintenance of publishing tools and the production of document styles and templates. These preparatory artifacts are defined together with the chief architect. The technical writer participates in system development projects to ensure that high-quality documentation is produced in the course of the normal development activities leveraging maximum synergies between contributors. This worker is a Convergent Architecture-specific instance of the following RUP worker role: technical writer.

Owned resources:

- **Change sets (artifacts):** Documentation development set (documentation style guide, document style templates), design documentation, end-user documentation.

- **Specialized technologies:** FrameMaker, Quadralay Webworks.

- **Course developer.**   This specialist focuses on the development of educational material and is otherwise analogous to the technical writer. He or she is often an experienced educator (discussed later). This worker constitutes a Convergent Architecture-specific instance of the following RUP worker role: course developer.

  Owned resources:

  - **Change sets (artifacts):** Training development set (training style guide, training style templates), developer courses, and end-user courses

  - **Specialized technologies:** PowerPoint.

- **Educator.**   This expert delivers training courses in his or her particular field using materials prepared by the course developer. This worker is often also the course developer.

- **WebDirector.**   This specialist in Web site definition sets up, administers, and supports the use of a central Web site for the IT organization, the *IT-Org-Website*. This Web site directly reflects the structure of the IT organization. The WebDirector works with all other organization managers to define and fine-tune their Web content, provision, and maintenance. He or she is also responsible for the selection of tools and maintenance of the entire Web infrastructure. IT organizations are instructed by the WebDirector on how to enter and manage their own pages and content in the Web site. He or she continually supports, monitors, and optimizes the process of distributed information contribution.

  Owned resources:

  - **Change sets (artifacts):** The IT-Org-Web site, which is where *all* project documents, reports, and general information are published in standard HTML format.

  - **Specialized technologies:**

    - HTML is used for *all* IT organization internal documents and internal communications. Microsoft FrontPage (or an equivalent tool) is used for editing, just-in-time team contribution, and content management. Transmission of documents is either via e-mail of via the IT-Org-Web site depending on the target audience and information half-life.

    - Visio (or equivalent) with HTML output is used for context-free graphics such as context diagrams.

- **Graphic artist.** This specialist in graphic design and related tools is responsible for the end production of all graphic design-intensive artifacts. Examples of such artifacts include user-interface icons and graphics for packaging, logos, Web logos, installation logos, stereotype logos, documentation figures, and educational and presentation graphics. The graphic artist also defines the specialized graphic tool and format landscape with the chief architect and the other specialists in the PET organization. He or she maintains the tools and provides user support for others using the tools and formats produced by the tools. This worker constitutes a Convergent Architecture-specific instance of the following RUP worker role: graphic artist.

- **Computer ergonomics and GUI expert (CEG).** This specialist in the layout, flow, and general usability of GUIs assists accessor developers (discussed later). The CEG (pronounced "keg") is in particular involved in the production of ergonomic, aesthetically pleasing representers. Thus, he or she must be an expert in the high-end Web page design tool selected for representer customization. This worker also develops the look-and-feel guidelines for the specific organization or industry segment and may develop reusable accessor components and accessor-generation templates at the request of the architecture organization outside the context of a system development project.

  Owned resources:

  - **Change sets (artifacts):** GUI look-and-feel guidelines, representer GUI of UI-accessor components.
  - **Specialized technologies:** Macromedia UltraDev (or equivalent).

The Test Center Organization

The test center organization (TestCenter-O) ensures that nonpartisan, effective testing skills and coordination contribute to timely quality control in the IT organization. Professional testing is a complex area. It is an extremely nonstandardized field involving complex technologies as well as difficult tradeoffs regarding effort and payoff. A well-run test organization can save an organization significant time and money, whereas a poorly run test organization can cause more problems than it solves. Thus, a professional testing organization is required to ensure that the proper decisions are made, that proper preparation takes place, that well-managed testing is performed, and that the results contribute to improving overall quality and efficiency. In addition, since test design, preparation, and execution affect every IT organization at some point in the development life cycle, this organization is required to provide the necessary expertise, focus, and continuity in this important area.

Worker Roles and Responsibilities

Worker roles and responsibilities in the test center organization include the following:

- **Test manager (test center manager).** The test manager is the organization manager of the test center organization and the single top-level authority on decisions regarding the Convergent Architecture and its use. In addition to the responsibilities of an organization manager, the test manager is specifically responsible for the following:

- Defining and maintaining the test infrastructure corresponding in character with the current or planned infrastructure in the operational systems organization, including all real constraints of the operational environment.

- Working with the chief architect to customize the test features of the development model (for example, unit testing features of convergent components) and the architectural IDE to meet specific requirements of the organization. This results in the specific testing guidelines document and, in some cases, the addition of specialized testing tools and infrastructure to the architectural IDE.

- Working with the lead developer and deployment manager in each system development project to specify the assembly test plan, including the test environment. Then the test manager allocates and coordinates one or more testers to assist with unit testing and to carry out assembly testing.

- Reviewing tester results and test reports and determining in the later iterations of a project whether an assembly has reached the initial operation capability and, as such, may be released for deployment by the transition organization (discussed later).

- Developing long-term evaluations and statistics regarding not only the quality and end results of tests in general, but also the quality of testability in the IT organization, and providing this as regular and timely feedback in the form of a consolidated quality evaluation report to the other IT organizations or through the requirements manager.

Owned resources:

- **Change sets (artifacts):** Testing guidelines document, including guidelines for the organization's specific test infrastructure, assembly test plan, and consolidated quality evaluation report.

- **Tester**: This test specialist sets up and administers the test environment (application server, assembly components) and carries out the test according to the assembly test plan as a participant in a system development project. This is a Convergent Architecture-specific instance of the RUP worker role: tester.

Owned resources:

- **Change sets (artifacts):** Assembly test results report.

- **Specialized technologies:** None pre-defined.

- **Testing toolsmith.**   This specialist in the test tools and infrastructure supports the integration and operation of test tools in the architectural IDE. This expert user of the testing components and capabilities of the IDE supports users of these features throughout the development life cycle.

Owned resources:

- **Change sets (artifacts):** Specialized testing tools if required.
- **Specialized technologies:** JUnit.

The System Development Organization

The system development organization (SysDev-O) is where the actual development and delivery of all convergent components take place. In this organization, effective system development projects are set up in terms of two predefined teams, as shown in Figure 5.5. These teams are specially configured to best address two different types of development projects. *Assembly development teams* are specialists in the highly integrative aspects required to deliver entire assembly components. *Component development teams* specialize in the reusable parts of assemblies and usually work in the context of an assembly development team. The teams define the sets of workers and responsibilities that best complement each other during the system development life cycle.[4] The development process described in Chapter 6 will cover the coordination and flow of activities in and around these predefined teams.

Worker Roles and Responsibilities

Worker roles and responsibilities in the system development organization include the following:

- **System development organization manager.** In addition to the responsibilities of an organization manager, the manager of the system development organization is specifically responsible for the following:

  - Supporting the effective production of convergent components by providing an optimized organization environment for the entire pool of system development projects. This worker is involved in the initiation of each project and accompanies all projects from the perspective of organizational support and synergies. The significance of this responsibility increases with the number of projects in the project pool.

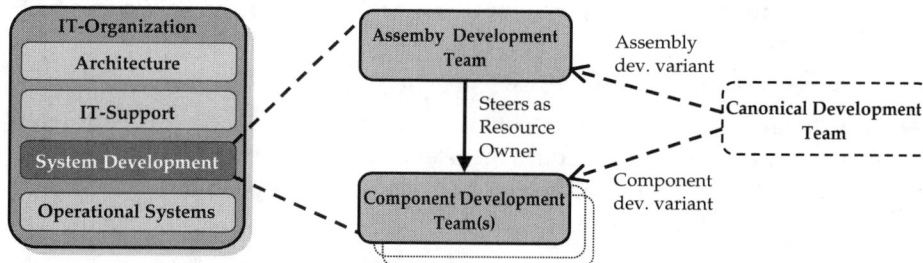

Figure 5.5 The system development organization.

- Assuring optimal allocation of developers and resources to and across system development projects.

- Pro-active training of developers and establishing an optimal team development environment.

- Providing consolidated feedback based on the observations of manifold parallel system development projects, formulating feedback in the form of requirements to the requirements managers, and working with the chief architect to refine and optimize the definition of the system development project and the canonical development teams (discussed later) for the specific organization.

- **Development toolsmith.** This trained and experienced user of the architectural IDE makes a project-specific configuration of the IDE and architecture-compliant extensions/modifications to the IDE in the context of specific projects. He or she helps developers effectively apply the IDE by setting up and tuning the development environment together with each developer. He or she continually evaluates the IDE from the project perspective and submits new requirements or change requests to the architectural IDE specialist or requirements manager.

- **System project manager.** In addition to being a project manager, this is a specialist in system development projects, as defined in the following section, and is specifically responsible for the following:

  - Bootstrapping and accompanying a system development project as defined in the following section according to the development process model as presented in Chapter 6. This includes initial project analysis and planning and managing project iterations according to the project management workflow (see Chapter 6).

  - Building and supporting assembly development teams and their component development teams (discussed later).

  - Convergent Architecture-specific instance of the following RUP worker role: project manager.

    Owned resources:

    - **Change sets (artifacts):** System project plan (long-term development strategy, current iteration plan with work orders for both assembly and component development projects), but no predefined specialized technologies.

    - **Specialized technologies:** None pre-defined.

- **Developer.** A collective term denoting any developer in the system development organization. This includes the lead developers, assembly developers, component developers, and accessor developers, covered in this chapter.

The System Development Project

A *system development project* is something specific in the Convergent Architecture. Just as in most organizations, the IT organization sets up explicit projects to create valuable processes and resources. The processes and resources produced by a project are then used by organizations in ongoing processes or as building blocks in other projects. Thus, projects are the central driver in an infinite cycle of progress and change. Although projects in all organizations share common features, my focus here is on the development of IT systems—on system development projects.

I speak of system development instead of software development because the resulting systems are not limited to pure software. Although my focus here is on IT, these projects also include aspects of business organization that have little to do with technology. A system development project also addresses the infrastructure and operational elements of systems that have more to do with the configuration and maintenance of hardware, packaged-software, and human infrastructure than they do with software development. The consolidation of these various aspects helps us produce more effective systems, not just a piece of software.

System development projects in the IT context are the *raison d'être* of the system development organization, regardless of whether the system is actually developed in-house, is outsourced, or, as is most often the case, is a mixture of both. Although still called *development* projects, these projects also address the long-term aspects of the system life cycle. To achieve this, the structure and focus of these projects must deal explicitly with the dichotomy of short-term deliverables versus long-term returns.

The short- and long-term perspectives of system development form two competing poles in any development organization. Whereas the clients of development projects normally are interested only in their short-term, immediately tangible deliverables, IT architects are also concerned with the long-term, often hidden qualities of systems. Most clients have an acute problem. They only want to pay for the minimum effort required to solve their particular problem. On the other hand, the IT architect realizes that a purely short-term focus to system development will cause significant long-term problems. Ironically, the costs to rectify these problems eventually are borne by the client, so professional IT architecture also is in the client's interest. The IT architect determines how long-term planning and investment can significantly reduce the costs of each client over time. On the other hand, a purely long-term focus to system development often ends up in an unchecked academic exercise, which, sooner or later, will be condemned by clients as "utopist"—usually with good reason.

Although a modern iterative development approach helps a project deal with these poles within a single project, it is not very specific about how they should be dealt with across multiple projects and across multiple generations of systems. The system development organization emphasizes the following specific short- and long-term aspects of development to help projects and project teams improve the equilibrium between these two poles.

Long-Term: Deliver Business-Centric OPRs

When a convergent component is identified as significant during the business-modeling workflow, particular attention is paid not to refine it into an accessor-specific component that meets only the punctual requirements of a particular application. Instead, care is taken to also represent the inherent features of the business domain, regardless of the particular application. To achieve this, domain experts and the lead developers do not focus only on the accessor use cases associated with a particular accessor component. They know that the OPR components of the business may be used by any number of accessors, many of these accessors being currently undefined. Thus, the business use case scenarios are employed to help the domain experts and designers identify more business-centric, in contrast with problem-centric, OPRs. These OPRs result in cross-application convergent components that can be reused and evolved over time more easily from the long-term perspective, according to the requirements of the business at large. However, to prevent this from becoming an academic exercise, this evolution takes place in the context of individual system development projects, each driven by the needs of a particular assembly component. This approach is compatible with the short-term aspect discussed later.

A good example of this long-term aspect is the classic situation of a customer component that will be used by manifold assemblies in many different business contexts. In the case where a customer is required by a particular application, that is, by an accessor component, the design team first attempts to locate an existing assembly that owns a customer component. It then reuses this component from within the new assembly. In the advent of new requirements, the team adds or adapts the responsibilities of this component in the business object model to also fit the requirements of the new assembly. Manipulation or adaptation of the customer component is coordinated with its resource owner. Depending on the number of deployed assemblies already using the customer component, more planning and coordination effort may be required than just developing a new one for the specific case. Thus, at first glance, the process of reuse and evolution is more costly. However, the investment clearly pays off in the long term by avoiding expensive and error-prone coordination of multiple customer representations across systems. If this investment is not made at this point in the development life cycle, risks and quality problems due to software entropy increase, and the costs to reverse this trend rise steadily.

To keep the activity of long-term optimization from digressing into an academic exercise in business design and component reuse, I introduce the second aspect of equally high priority.

Short-Term: Deliver a Business-Relevant Assembly Component

System development projects need measurable short-term goals. This priority is addressed by setting up each project around a deliverable assembly component. The assembly components are application-driven. As described in the convergent components metamodel, they exist to encapsulate and install a well-defined business application with all components required by the application. This application-specific focus also serves to channel and drive the project toward its concrete deliverable.

The concrete application is represented directly by the accessor components of an assembly. Accessor use cases formulate the client's immediate requirements on the system. Reusable accessor components also may be leveraged or created, of course. The requirements of the accessors drive and channel the detailed planning and implementation of an assembly component, the short-term deliverable of a system development project.

The subtle balance between the two poles of long- and short-term focus has a significant impact on the return on IT investments. Moving too close to either of the poles can cause the IT organization to miss its potential by several orders of magnitude. It is difficult to avoid the temptation of short-term focus in today's world, where the horizon often ends at the next quarterly report. One of the best ways to keep an organization on the right track is to have the proper constellation of experience and skills in system development teams. This is the focus of the next subsections.

The Canonical Development Team

The canonical development team defines the critical workers in each system development project, as shown in Figure 5.6. The shaded area of the figure indicates the core team. The workers shown within this area are known as *core project workers* because their responsibilities lie in the critical path of the development project. In other words, without the core workers, the project could not proceed. Other important workers whose participation usually is required in a project are shown straddling the edges of the shaded area. These workers are known as *participating workers* because, in general, they participate in several teams simultaneously. Core project workers normally are allocated to a single team. Both participating and core project workers have official work plans in a project. The responsibilities of each worker in association with his or her role in the canonical development team are presented below.

Two predefined specializations of canonical development teams exist, as shown in Figure 5.5. These specialty teams are the ones used in concrete development projects. The canonical development team serves as the basis for both these teams because they both have the same basic structure, core workers and participating workers. *Assembly development teams* focus on the highly integrative aspects required to deliver assembly components. *Component development teams* specialize in the reusable components that the assembly owns and manages. How each specialty team differs from the canonical

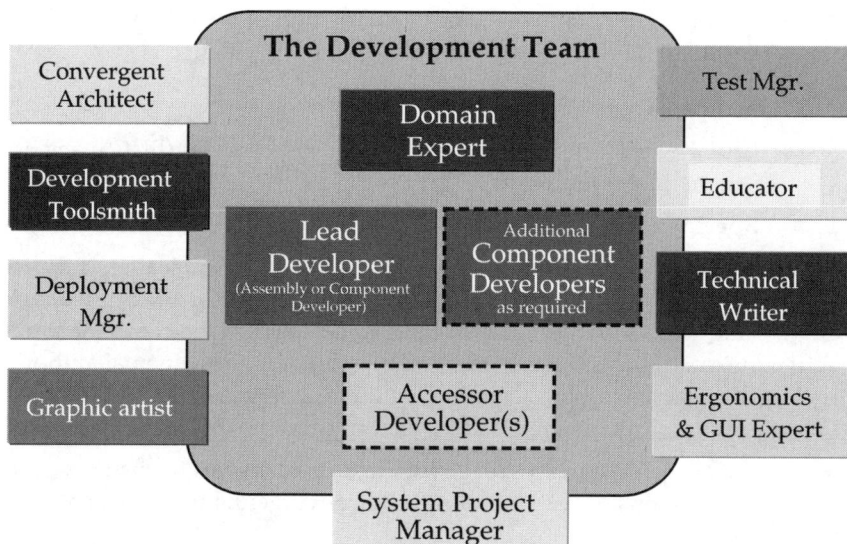

Figure 5.6 The canonical development team.

development team is covered in the following respective subsections. If a project only has one team, then this team must be comprised of the workers and responsibilities of both specialty teams.

Worker Roles and Responsibilities

Worker core roles and responsibilities in the canonical development team include the following:

- **Domain expert.**   This experienced business operator possesses up-to-date, practical knowledge on the workings of the business. He or she accompanies the project as its business domain "champion," modeler, and advisor throughout all phases of the project to ensure the business relevance and correctness of the system. This person is the primary communication channel to business organizations influenced by or influencing the development of the component. Due to other business obligations, this worker normally cannot participate as a full-time team member. However, this worker must be intimately involved in development and share responsibility for success of the team. In particular, the domain expert does the following:

  - Provides rapid, authoritative decisions on the essential and "nice to have" future requirements of the domain.

  - Develops applied work scenarios covering the relevant business domain, including potential use scenarios of a new system. The development of scenarios may be delegated to other domain specialists under the direction of the domain expert.

  - Works with the lead developer to drive development from the business perspective.

  - Convergent Architecture-specific consolidation of the following RUP worker roles: business designer and use-case specifier.

    Owned resources:

    - **Change sets (artifacts):** Business use-case scenarios (BUCS) and accessor use-case scenarios (AUCS).

    - **Specialized technologies:** C-BOM components of the architectural-IDE.

- **Lead developer.**   This is the single authoritative technical leader of the team. In addition to fulfilling the role of *assembly developer* in the assembly development team (discussed later) or of *component developer* in the component development team (discussed later), the lead developer is the principal authoritative technical contact for all participating team workers and external stakeholders of the team. In particular, the lead developer does the following:

  - Carries out all design sessions with the domain expert to ensure a concise definition of business terminology and convergent, business-relevant results.

- Works with the convergent architect to consolidate the convergent business model and terminology across all projects and, in general, to ensure architectural integrity across projects.

- Remains resource owner of the respective convergent component across all generations until it is retired from use.

- Defines best-fit CCM change-sets for the convergent components together with the convergent architect and configuration manager.

- Convergent Architecture-specific consolidation of the following RUP worker roles: component developer (discussed later) or assembly developer (discussed later) depending on the development team, plus RUP business designer and RUP code reviewer.

Owned resources:

- **Change sets (artifacts):** See component developer or assembly developer depending on the development team.

- **Specialized technologies:** The entire architectural-IDE.

- **Component developer.**   Depending on the scale of the project, there may be additional component developers as described later in the chapter in the component development team. There should be a maximum of six component developers in a single team.

- **UI-accessor developer.**   This expert in UI-accessor development develops any human interfaces required by a convergent component. This worker is a Convergent Architecture-specific instance of the following RUP worker roles: user-interface designer, designer, and implementer.

Owned resources:

- **Change sets (artifacts):** UI-accessor component (accessor models, documentation, implementation).

- **Specialized technologies:** The component of the architectural-IDE from C-REF on down.

- **SI-accessor developer.**   This expert in accessor development develops any SI-accessors required to interact with external entities. A UI-accessor developer may fill this worker role because there may be an overlap in development skills. In addition to understanding accessor development, this worker should, at best, already be familiar with the types of external systems that will be accessed by the component. This worker is a Convergent Architecture-specific instance of the following RUP worker roles: designer and implementer.

Owned resources:

- **Change sets (artifacts):** SI-accessor component (accessor models, documentation, models, implementation).

- **Specialized technologies:** The components of the architectural-IDE from C-REF on down.

Participating Workers

The system project manager plans participating workers in the same way core workers are planned. Two differences exist between participating and core workers. First, participating workers may not be needed in every project or may not be required in each project iteration. They are not the permanent spearhead of the critical development path. Instead, they participate at different stations along the critical development path. Second, participating workers usually provide special services to several projects in parallel. This cross-project participation is important to ensure integrative or "horizontal" synergies and design uniformity in each highly specialized area. The participating workers are measured by the system project managers concerning their individual project contributions and by the steering team regarding their optimizing contribution across all projects in which they participate. Each participating worker contributes as follows to the development team:

■ **System project manager (participates from the system development organization).**   This manager accompanies the team effort as team initiator, planner, organizer, and facilitator. He or she is the escalation interface to the steering team in the IT organization. His or her principal goal as participant is to enable technical personnel to optimally apply their respective skills toward critical, measurable project goals. This is rarely a full-time job for a properly staffed project.

■ **Convergent architect (participates from the architecture organization).**   The convergent architect consults the system project manager and lead developer on project and iteration planning activities. He or she is a design coach and reviewer who normally is assigned to these activities at the beginning and end of each project iteration. He or she assesses and enforces intraproject quality through reviews and consulting and ensures interproject quality through parallel participation in many projects. This worker also ensures timely feedback regarding quality and optimization potential of the architectural style. The convergent architect also may spend considerable time as a coach and codeveloper within a single team.

■ **Development toolsmith (participates from the system development organization).**   This worker helps team members configure and tune the architectural-IDE and other tools to the requirements of a specific project.

■ **Graphic artist (participates from the project information, events, and training organization).**   This worker develops project-specific artwork. This artwork normally is associated directly with the convergent component.

■ **Computer ergonomics and GUI expert (participates from the project information, events, and training organization).**   This worker assists the UI-accessor developer with representer design and development.

■ **Educator (participates from the project information, events, and training organization).**   This worker helps assess training needs in the initial planning stages of the project. This includes both the training needs of the project team and training for end users of the developed system. He or she arranges the timely education of team members, develops end-user training with the technical writer, and coordinates the delivery of training with the domain expert and deployment manager.

- **Technical writer (participates from the project information, events, and training organization).** This worker plans and compiles both design and user documentation. He or she also may produce educational materials. This includes ensuring that other team members understand their responsibilities as contributors to quality documentation. For example, well-documented models, in-code documentation, and usage samples are produced by developers for documentation, not produced from scratch by the technical writer. In the course of creating high-quality documentation, the technical writer verifies the accuracy of the documents and samples and provides continuous feedback to the developers.

- **Test manager (participates from the test center organization).** This worker plans, designs, and coordinates project-specific testing with the lead developer. He or she provides each component developer with clear testability requirements and instructions for individual testing responsibilities such as unit testing.

- **Deployment manager (participates from operational systems organization).** This worker contributes project-specific requirements from the operational systems organization, including deployment, transition, and education aspects. He or she works with the system project manager and lead developer to ensure fulfillment of these requirements early on in the project and coordinates and carries out operational deployment tests and the operational transition.

The Assembly Development Team

The assembly development team specializes in the highly integrative aspects required to deliver an operational assembly component. Figure 5.5 shows that component development teams operate in the context of a single assembly development team. This is so because the assembly component encapsulates and exclusively manages convergent components. The assembly development team, in particular the lead developer of the team, is the resource owner of the assembly component, and the lead developer of the respective component development team is the resource owner of its convergent components. Any development teams outside the context of the assembly must coordinate design changes to the convergent components with their respective resource owners.

The assembly development team may manage several component development teams. Alternatively, at the discretion of the assembly development team, a single component development team may develop more than one of its convergent components.

As discussed in Chapter 4, an assembly may be comprised of accessor components that are particular to the assembly but not uniquely associated with any single component within the assembly. The assembly development team normally develops such accessors.

Many assembly components may exist in various stages of development or deployment at any time in the system development organization. The lead developer of each assembly component remains its resource owner throughout its entire life cycle and accompanies its evolution through generations of development and deployment.

Worker Roles and Responsibilities

Worker-specialized roles and responsibilities in the assembly development team include the following:

- **Assembly developer.** This is the lead developer of the assembly development team who normally has extensive experience as a component developer. This worker has the following additional responsibilities as owner of the assembly component:

  - Begins with the inception phase of a development project to delimit and define the project and help the system project manager produce the long-term development strategy.

  - Develops the BUCS, AUCS, and the convergent business object model for the entire assembly together with the domain experts involved in the assembly.

  - Works in the project planning stages to define the component development teams required by the assembly, partitions development among the teams, and works closely with the lead developers of these teams.

  - Develops the assembly-specific configuration management reference together with the lead developers and configuration manager.

  - Produces the assembly architecture reference, which describes the overall design of the assembly in the context of the Convergent Architecture style reference. The assembly architecture reference consolidates the component design references produced by its component development teams.

  - Defines, implements, and carries out integration tests, business-case tests, and installation and deployment tests for the entire assembly. Assembly tests are carried out in the test center organization assisted by its respective workers.

  - Defines and carries out the deployment plan for the assembly with the deployment manager. The deployment plan covers both tests and operational releases.

  - Develops the assembly installation kit, which drives the intelligent installation and deployment of the assembly.

  - Coordinates the development of design and end-user documentation with the technical writer and the component development teams.

  - Coordinates and tracks the reuse of any of its enclosed convergent components by other assemblies. This tracking information is recorded in the assembly models. By the same token, he or she communicates the reuse of external convergent components with the respective assembly developer.

■ Remains resource owner of the assembly across all generations until it is retired from use.

■ Convergent Architecture-specific consolidation of the following RUP worker roles: same as component developer (discussed later) plus RUP system analyst and RUP integrator.

Owned resources:

■ **Change sets (artifacts):** Assembly component (assembly architecture reference, assembly glossary, assembly configuration management reference, architectural IDE artifacts [convergent business object model, assembly UML model, project configuration files, generation cartridges, build and test environment, Java-IDE environment], assembly installation kit, user documentation, developer documentation, application server configuration). The following specifications apply:

   ■ The convergent business object model is comprised of the structural CRC model and dynamic state-transition-flow models (visual and recorded run-throughs) of BUCS and AUCS.

   ■ The assembly UML model is comprised of the cumulative accessor component models and business component models (optional UML representations as required for explanatory or documentation detail: use-case representations of BUCS and AUCS, sequence diagrams, and activity diagrams for convergent components).

   ■ The assembly installation kit normally deploys an enterprise archive (EAR) in the J2EE technology projection and is comprised of all convergent component installation sets (discussed later), J2EE Web archives containing accessors, EJB archives, client Java archives, uninstaller, consolidated user documentation, assembly installation guide and release notes, and the consolidated installation verification test.

■ **Specialized technologies:** Same as Lead Developer plus Zero-G Install Anywhere.

The Component Development Team

Component development teams specialize in the reusable parts of assemblies. Although the convergent components will be managed exclusively by their owning assembly, they often will be reused by other assemblies.[5] Thus, the component development team plays an important role in producing effectively reusable convergent components.

Worker Roles and Responsibilities

Worker-specialized roles and responsibilities in the component development team include the following:

- **Component developer.**   This worker is a developer in the context of the component development team. A component developer may be designated as the lead developer of the component development team, in which case he or she is the definitive owner of the following specific responsibilities as well as the responsibilities of the lead developer described earlier. If not designated as the single lead developer in the team, then the component developer works under the direction of the lead developer to help fulfill these responsibilities:

    - Further refines the convergent business objects allocated to the component development team by the assembly developer into deployable convergent components. This includes model refinement, technical modeling, model-driven implementation, and testing of the components.

    - Defines artifact partitioning (for example, UML models, Java archives, Java packages, and documentation) with the assembly developer to ensure effective consolidation of these artifacts into the assembly component.

    - Refines the accessor use cases specific to the assigned convergent components together with the domain expert and defines and drives accessor development.

    - Develops the convergent component installation set for the component in conjunction with the assembly developer.

    - Works with the technical writer to create design and user documentation materials.

    - Convergent Architecture-specific consolidation of the following RUP worker roles: test designer, developer, capsule developer, implementer, database designer.

    Owned resources:

    - **Change sets (artifacts):** Convergent components (architectural-IDE artifacts [UML models, configuration files, generation cartridges, build and test environments, Java-IDE environments, project configuration files], component installation sets, user documentation materials, developer documentation). The following specifications apply:

        - The component installation set for the J2EE technology projection (Chapter 8) comprises: J2EE WebArchives containing accessors, EJB archives, client archives, and an installation verification test.

    - **Specialized technologies:** Same as lead developer.

The Operational Systems Organization

The operational systems organization (OPS-O) is where assemblies are deployed and put into operational use. The specialty and prime responsibility of this organization is to provide a robust, stable environment as specified by the assembly development teams in the assembly installation guide. The assembly, including its operational installation, is developed in conjunction with the operational systems organization (deployment manager) to ensure feasibility and realistic expectations of all stakeholders regarding deployment, test, maintenance, and long-term operation of the assembly. The chief architect works with the operational systems organization to ensure that the simplest possible operational environment evolves to fulfill the diverse requirements of assemblies.

The operational systems organization *also exists when the IT organization is developing software to be sold to external customers. The only difference is the focus* on external customers in contrast to internal customers. The operational needs of these two customer groups are essentially identical from the perspective of the IT organization. In the case of external customers, the transition organization described later manages prerelease tests (beta-test programs) and the rapport with customers during the transition phase of system development. In parallel, it channels the rollout of the software product to the respective marketing, sales, and distribution organizations. With regard to the other organizations described in the chapter, the user support organization becomes the customer support organization and the local infrastructure and base systems organization provides necessary base systems for these activities. The feedback channels and relationships with the other IT organizations remain unchanged.

As indicated in Figure 5.7, the operational systems organization is partitioned into four suborganizations. All its responsibilities and roles, aside from those common to every IT organization, are delegated to the suborganizations, which are covered individually in the following subsections.

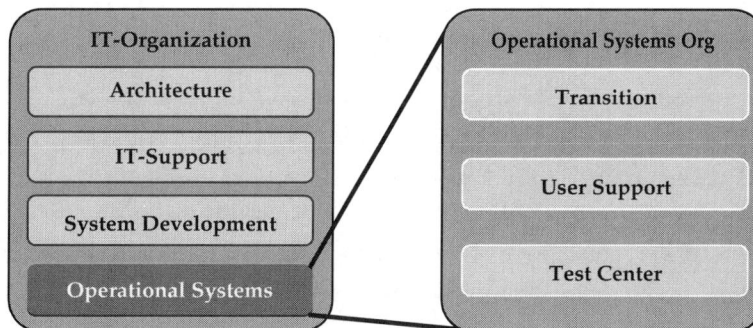

Figure 5.7 The operational systems organization.

The Transition Organization

The transition organization (Transition-O) is concerned with effectively moving assemblies into the operational environment. Such movements may occur not only at the end of the development cycle, but also at the end of iterations during elaboration and construction of an assembly. This organization is responsible for reducing impedance and friction between the development phases of the system's life cycle and the operational phases of its life cycle. To achieve this, the transition organization is involved in the entire life cycle of the system to ensure compatible planning and development of capabilities in both system development and operational systems organizations.

Worker Roles and Responsibilities

Worker roles and responsibilities in the operational systems organization include the following:

- **Deployment manager (participates in canonical development team).** This IT operations expert works in the context of system development projects to ensure that the requirements of the operational environment are met. This includes such aspects as infrastructure, installation, testing, training, administration, and upgrades. He or she also coordinates and manages the transition tests and final operational transition of an assembly. This worker is a Convergent Architecture-specific instance of the following RUP worker role: deployment manager.

The User Support Organization

The user support organization (UserSupport-O) provides professional front-line support to end users of assemblies.

Worker Roles and Responsibilities

Worker roles and responsibilities in the user support organization include the following:

- **User support specialist.** This worker is an experienced user of the assembly and has been trained to ensure an effective work environment for end users of the assembly. He or she fulfills the following specific responsibilities:
  - Sets up and configures the end-user environment for an installed assembly.
  - Provides everyday front-line user support and hot-line services.
  - The single escalation interface for end-users to the system development organization and the assembly developer. He or she provides change requests and feedback to the requirements manager.
- **End-user educator.** This experienced user support specialist is responsible for training groups of new assembly end-users. The trainings are organized with and coordinated by the project information, events, and training organization.

The Infrastructure and Base Systems Organization

Commensurate with the infrastructure and base systems organization in the IT support organization, the operational infrastructure and base systems organization (OPS-InfraBas-O) is responsible for supporting the operational systems organization. An operations-specific organization is required because the priorities and constraints of the operational environment differ significantly from those of the development environment. For example, security, availability, and migration aspects play a much more significant role in the operational environment than they do in the development environment.

The chief architect defines the common-denominator operational environments together with this organization. The infrastructure and base systems organization then implements and supports the environment for the operational systems organization. Continuity and consistence with the IT support organization are maintained through frequent, iterative project interaction in the course of system development projects and the activities of the test center organization.

Worker Roles and Responsibilities

Worker roles and responsibilities in the infrastructure and base systems organization include the following:

- **OPS system administrator.**   This worker is the operational counterpart to the system administrator in the IT support organization.

- **Container operator.**   The container operator takes up where the OPS system administrator leaves off. He or she is a specialist in a specific type of application server container and manages this environment in the interest of all deployed assemblies and their users. This includes professional management of the underlying data stores (databases) and proactive performance management such as clustering and load balancing. For the J2EE/EJB technology projection, this worker installs and manages a distributed J2EE/EJB container environment, including its associated databases. This worker also provides timely feedback on container-specific tuning requirements to the deployment manager and the requirements manager.

- **Assembly operator.**   Assemblies may be extensive, heavily used, and widely distributed. The assembly operator complements the container operator in large installations to ensure proper administration, maintenance, and tuning of a specific assembly in the operational environment. This worker also carries out assembly-specific activities in the operational environment such as online monitoring, security management, problem tracing, and infrastructure migration. He or she works closely with the container operator and provides feedback regarding operational improvements to the assembly developer, deployment manager, and requirements manager.

Summary

A properly prepared IT organization is fundamental to producing effective IT systems. Above all, a well-tuned organization simplifies things by adding continuity and order to the constantly moving landscape of development activities, workers, and artifacts involved in system development. The IT-organization model presented in this chapter defined such a well-tuned organization. It described a reference organization that has been streamlined to support large-scale system development according to the architectural style. The effectiveness of this reference organization stems from the fact that it is sensitive to the style of systems that will be built. As such, it can be more specific about the resources, processes, and tools used to create these systems.

In this chapter, the basic OPR concepts presented in Chapter 3 were used to structure the IT organization and to define the roles and responsibilities of workers in the context of concrete organizations. In addition, the artifacts created by these workers were specified along with any specialized tools these workers use to produce and manipulate these artifacts.

The reference IT organization may be used as a basis to prepare IT organizations, large or small, to consistently produce systems according to the Convergent Architecture. It also sets the stage to present the process—the specific flow of activities between workers, tools, and artifacts. This flow of activities within the IT organization is the focus of the process model in the next chapter.

CHAPTER

6

The Development Process Model

The preceding chapter addressed the design of the information technology (IT) organization. This chapter will focus on the development process model, also referred to as the *Convergent Architecture* (CA) *process,* that complements and leverages the responsibilities, workers, and artifacts of the IT organization. This is the third and last component in the development model of the Convergent Architecture.

The existence of hundreds of books covering the software process is clear evidence of the central importance of this process in professional software organizations. Although there is ample discord—with a touch of religious fanaticism—as to which precise approach is best, many of the modern methodologies exhibit more similarities than differences. Their principal differences lie in the structure of their presentation, their weighting or emphasis of particular process aspects, and their scope. Indeed, there is no precise definition of where process begins and where it leaves off. This is why the Convergent Architecture sees process as just one aspect of a holistic approach that addresses the three pillars of project design, business design, and system design.

The CA process is not yet another generalized development process or methodology. As you will see in the following section, the CA process refines aspects of existing methodologies. However, instead of taking a process-centric approach, it takes a style-centric approach: It considers process in the context of the rest of the architectural style. By doing this, features of the architecture can be tuned to assist each other in all directions. This is in stark contrast to many methodologies that expend considerable effort trying to make things work together that were not designed to work together. In other words, in the development of the CA process, two questions are of main concern. First, how can the CA process help us achieve our style-specific goals using the other features of the style—the organization model, the convergent component metamodel, the architectural integrated development environment (IDE), and so forth? Second, and most important, how can the other features of the style help us simplify the CA process? The answers to these questions results in a continuous fine-tuning from the perspectives of both the development process and its surrounding environment. Such comprehensive optimization from various perspectives enables efficiencies and synergies not possible from a unidirectional, process-centric perspective. This multidirectional tuning contributes to what I call *reference-frame continuity*, an intrinsic property of the architectural style: Every project benefits from it automatically and immediately.

Before moving into the details, let's look at one example of reference-frame continuity and how it simplifies the CA process. A good example is the interaction between the modeling style and the architectural IDE, which, although not themselves part of the CA process, are part of the style. As such, they are a dependable part of a reference frame that can be leveraged by other parts of the style. In this particular example, the architectural IDE and the modeling style combine forces to simplify several workflows, thus simplifying the CA process. Based on the modeling style, the IDE can actively assist the developer through many activities.[1] In many situations, the developer only needs to set a few key properties in the model to enable the IDE to automatically derive other models and properties. These derived design features are later used by the IDE to generate source code, also according to the modeling style. In such cases, the developer can be successful without having an expert background and/or having extensive experience with these activities. For example, during accessor development, complex design mechanisms such as user event dispatching or the interaction between the frames of an Internet representer are now carried out in the context of assisted modeling. As such, these aspects no longer need to be handled in the workflow description. They are delegated to the style-specific IDE. This new level of assistance and automation constitutes a logical step toward higher design capabilities similar to the improvements brought about by third-generation compilers. Just as no other development processes would describe the internal workings of a compiler as part of the workflow, the workflows of the CA process do not need to cover the aspects handled automatically by its architectural IDE. From the perspective of the developer, the complexity disappears (without being ignored by the architecture), and this aspect of development becomes a simple step in the workflow description.

Let's now look at the foundations and basic structure of the CA process before detailing each of its workflows in a separate section.

Foundations and Structure

As shown in Figure 6.1, the CA process is an *architectural-style-specific instance of the Rational Unified Process* (RUP) (Kruchten 1998). However, the RUP is only one of the modern methodologies that has influenced the CA-specific process throughout its evolution. The figure shows the other major contributors from which the CA process was derived. It also indicates the progression that took place over the years. The major players in this progression are explained below the figure.

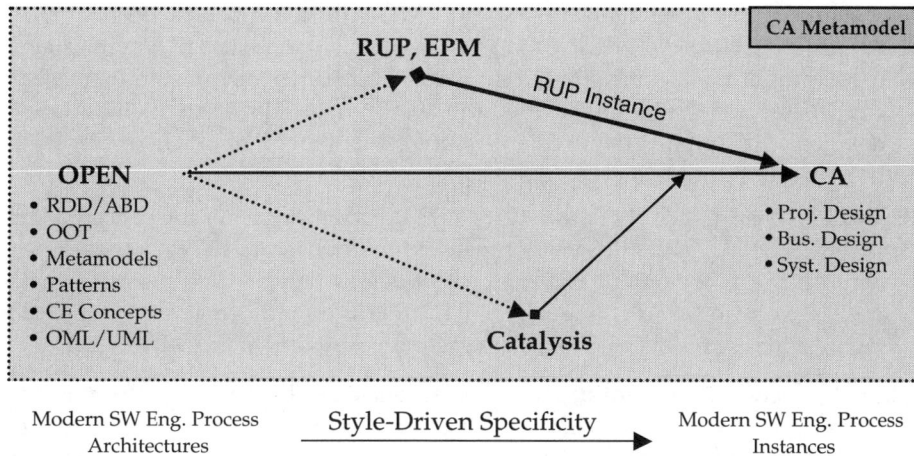

Figure 6.1 A specific instance of process architectures. CA's relationship to third-generation SW process frameworks.

The lines in the figure illustrate the process of combining and filtering several methodologies over the years to form the CA process as it stands today. It begins at the left with a very broadly scoped software engineering process architecture (Graham 1997). The methodologies in the center of the figure are more specific, each having its own specific focus, strength, and scope. Consolidated parts of these methodologies flow into a CA-specific instance shown at the right. Along the way, each of these streams is integrated and configured to best fulfill the principles and requirements from the other models of the architectural style. Moving from left to right, the contributing methodologies and their relationships from the perspective of the CA process are as follows:

The OPEN Process Specification (OPEN) (Graham 1997).   This is known as a third-generation methodology because it focuses on modern concepts such as the object paradigm, metamodels, and patterns in software development. This includes particular emphasis on the principles of convergent engineering, including responsibility-driven design (RDD) and analysis by design (ABD). The direct line between OPEN and the CA process indicates that the OPEN concepts were a mainstream basis for the CA process before being later influenced by RUP and catalysis.

The Rational Unified Process (RUP) (Kruchten 1998).   Although not a direct derivative of OPEN, RUP complements and refines many concepts found in OPEN. In addition to its different weighting of certain concepts, RUP adds structural clarity and pertinent management-level explanations of the modern development process. In particular, RUP recognizes and explains the importance of process instances and is designed to serve as a basis for such instances. This is one reason it is used as the foundation for a CA-specific instance.

The evolutionary project management (EPM) method (Gilb 1988/1999).
Although not based on RUP, EPM was found to complement RUP with pragmatic project-management features. The EPM features that most influenced the CA process were in the area of evolutionary team building and evolutionary development, implicit requirements management, implicit quality control, iteration planning, and team configuration.

The catalysis approach (D'Souza 1998).   This reflects many of the concepts found in OPEN or RUP and adds its own particular emphasis in the area of component-centric development and component design patterns. It also addresses the UML Object Constraint Language (OCL 1999) as a semiformal means of specifying design constraints as a complement to the fundamental UML notation.

The CA process at the right of the figure emphasizes that these contributors influenced aspects in all three pillars of the Convergent Architecture. As such, the influence is not localized to the CA process but is also evident in the other features of the architectural style.

The following subsection introduces the structure and content of the CA process.

Overview: Workflows and IDE Support

To achieve the goals of the Convergent Architecture, RUP is streamlined—as is fitting when creating an instance of RUP. Some aspects of RUP are repartitioned or weighted differently. As set forth by RUP, the CA process comprises workflows that are subdivided and detailed in the form of activities. Similar to RUP-based workers and artifacts in the IT organization, the workflows in the CA process are derived from corresponding RUP workflows. Then adaptations are made according to the models of the architectural style. No aspect addressed by RUP has been left out, but aspects may be implicitly or explicitly handled elsewhere in the architectural style. As pointed out in the introduction, there is no reason to explain an activity that has been taken care of implicitly or automatically elsewhere in the style.

A case in point: Many of the activities in the RUP environment workflow correspond to responsibilities in IT organization in the Convergent Architecture. This is because the IT organization is a separate model in the Convergent Architecture; it is the entire environment of the CA process, and it is not a workflow. *Workflows in the CA process define activities above and beyond the responsibilities of the IT organization.* These are activities that can be well defined to enhance the responsibilities of the IT organization; however, they do not replace the IT organization. The IT-organization model exists to handle the myriad important aspects of software development that cannot, and should not, be defined as an explicit workflow or activity.[2]

As explained in the preceding chapter, RUP workflows and activities denote hierarchies of processes. I have already defined the concept of a process in the Convergent Architecture. Applying this definition in the context of this instance of the RUP, *workflows and activities complement the ongoing responsibilities of the IT organizations by defining and naming goal-oriented sets of tasks. These tasks describe how specific aspects of the IT organizations and their respective resources are used to produce more valuable resources.*

Lastly, the CA process considers the multiproject scope of an entire IT organization, no matter how extensive this organization may be. This is important because today's IT landscapes consist of many distributed contributors across many organizations and projects. In addition, significant optimizations due to an architectural style occur at the cross-project, cross-system, and cross-organization levels. For example, the workflows in the CA process describe how we use information gained in one project to optimize both the design and development workflows across other projects. It covers how projects come and go in the normal course of the overall workflow cycle or how projects drive their own reconfiguration in the interest of business optimization. Here again, much of this happens through interaction with the IT-organization model.

To achieve this, the workflows in the CA process are partitioned into two major categories:

Preparatory and cross-project workflows.   These workflows are not associated with any particular project. They are initiated before the first development project and act in a cross-functional manner across all projects.

Canonical project workflows.   Similar to the canonical development team presented in Chapter 5, the canonical project workflow describes the development process used by the canonical development team.

I distinguish here between two categories of workflows:

Critical-path workflows.   These constitute the main, essential thread of the development effort. Without these workflows, we would not require the supporting workflows.

Supporting workflows.   These are tangential to the critical path and, as such, receive less style-specific attention than the critical-path workflows in this book. The reduced attention is necessary to maintain proper focus on the architectural style. For supporting workflows in particular, I refer to the guidelines and examples provided on the Convergent Architecture Web site. The supporting workflows are labeled as such in this chapter.

The following sections are breakdowns of these categories. Each section contains a summary description of the workflows in the category. It also lists which aspects of the architectural IDE are used to support each activity.

Preparatory and Cross-Project Workflows

The IT organization begins business by initiating the following workflows:

IT-environment workflow.   This bootstraps and maintains the IT organization. The IT-organization manager develops an IT-organization model tailored to the specific situation based on the model described in Chapter 5. He or she then implements the model by populating each of the IT organizations and preparing each organization to fulfill its responsibilities. The extent, speed, and scale of this preparation are determined by the two cross-project workflows indicated below that define system development projects, their extent, their training requirements, and so on.

- **Activity owners.**   IT-organization manager.
- **Specialized technologies.**   None.

T-bar business modeling and requirements workflow.   This manages the top level of an overall analysis-by-design workflow (see the following section) according to the *T-technique* as unanimously endorsed by convergent engineering (Taylor 1995), Microsoft (Ambler 1997), and RUP (Kruchten 2000). This workflow applies the responsibility-driven design (RDD) concepts as formulated by convergent engineering and RUP's "Work Guidelines: Role Playing" (Rational 2000).

- **Activity owners.**   Chief architect, IT-organization manager, requirements manager.
- **Specialized technologies.**   Architectural IDE, primarily the C-BOM module; Visio (or equivalent).

Architectural evolution workflow.   This evolves, refines, adapts, and maintains the organization-specific instance of the Convergent Architecture.

- **Activity owners.**   Chief architect.
- **Specialized technologies.**   Architectural IDE.

Canonical Project Workflows

Assembly and component development teams proceed hand in hand as described in the preceding chapter. They are logical subdivisions, each producing parts of one unit, the assembly. Each assembly development team has much in common with the component development team; they just have a different focus while moving along a similar path toward a common goal. For this reason, a canonical project workflow also corresponds to the canonical project team and its variants defined in the IT-organization model. In the description of canonical project workflows, the activities of the workers in both assembly and component development teams are pointed out as we step through the workflow. Whether a particular activity applies specifically to an assembly or component development team is clear by the worker designated as the activity owner of the individual activity. The workflows are as follows:

Project management workflow.   This consists of a four-pass iteration planning and tracking activity to detail and monitor the RUP phases and iterations at the level of measurable criterion and personal accountability.

- **Activity owners.**   System project manager.
- **Specialized technologies.**   Architectural IDE for tracking and monitoring.

Development environment workflow (supporting).   This sets up and verifies the development environment for each team member.

- **Activity owners.**   Development toolsmith.
- **Specialized technologies.**   Intimately familiar with the setup and test of the entire suite of development tools and technologies used in a system

development project. The basic set of tools consists of the architectural IDE, unified configuration management (UCM) tools, unit testing tools, application server environment, and Web server environment.

Configuration and change management (CCM) workflow (supporting).   This defines and sets up the CMM features required by a particular team member.

- **Activity owners.**   Configuration manager.
- **Specialized technologies.**   ClearCase UCM system.

Analysis-by-design (ABD) workflow.   This consolidates the RUP business modeling, the RUP requirements, and the RUP analysis and design workflows into three phases of convergent refinement, each representing a critical stage in the metamorphosis of a business strategy into the OPRs of a convergent system.

- **Activity owners.**   Assembly developer.
- **Specialized technologies.**   Architectural IDE with focus on the upstream modules C-BOM, C-RAS, and C-REF/Rose; ClearCase UCM clients; Front-Page (or equivalent); Requisite-Pro (or equivalent).

Implementation cycle workflow.   This is the model-driven refine, generate, edit, deploy, and test cycle.

- **Activity owners.**   Developer.
- **Specialized technologies.**   Architectural IDE with a focus on downstream modules C-REF/Rose, C-GEN, and C-IX; Java IDE; J2EE application server with associated database tools; Apache server; Tomcat Web server; Cygnus GNU tools; ClearCase UCM clients; FrontPage; Install Anywhere; ANT-based build environment.

Test workflow.   This provides explicit quality checks and a just-in-time diagnosis at each stage of the development life cycle.

- **Activity owners.**   Lead developer (component testing) and developers (unit testing).
- **Specialized technologies.**   Architectural IDE; JUnit; installation of J2EE application server according to the constraints of the operational environment.

Documentation workflow (supporting).   This covers the production of documentation, help files, and training material.

- **Activity owners.**   Technical writer.
- **Specialized technologies.**   FrameMaker, WebWorks, Javadoc.

Deployment and monitoring workflow.   This provides a transition to the operational environment and monitoring within the operational environment.

- **Activity owners.**   Assembly developer.
- **Specialized technologies.**   Operations-level installation of J2EE application server.

Preparatory and Cross-Project Workflows

The preparatory and cross-project workflows exist outside of the context of individual projects. These workflows begin before the first project and continue across project generations. They are the continuum that initializes, accompanies, and controls the overall constellation of projects.

IT-Environment Workflow

The IT-environment workflow addresses the recurring, ongoing activities of each IT organization in support of the overall IT effort. These activities are in fulfillment of the organization's responsibilities as defined in the IT-organization model.

Activity. Bootstrap the IT organization.

Activity owner, principal participants. IT-organization manager, chief architect, steering team.

Artifacts produced/refined. IT-organization model and implementation plan.

Guidelines and artifact/tool usage:

- The IT-organization manager uses the IT-organization model as a template and develops a concrete IT-organization model for the specific situation. Based on the model, he or she then fills the organization manager positions of its direct suborganizations. The steering team now exists.

- In conjunction with the steering team, each organization owner refines the aspects of the IT-organization model relevant to his or her organization. Based on the refined model, the organization manager sets up and prepares the organization to fulfill its responsibilities. The rule of thumb for this activity is to start small and build once things work, that is, get things working at a small scale before scaling up.

- Once prepared, the architecture organization kicks off the T-bar business modeling and requirements workflow (discussed later), which, through the identification of system development projects, influences the speed and extent of the IT-environment workflow.

- With the establishment of the steering team and the kickoff of this first T-bar workflow, the self-regulating cycle of operational workflows has commenced. As stated in the IT-organization model, the active, operational workflows are owned as a whole by the IT-organization manager. This sounds like more work than it really is. Since each instance of an activity within a workflow has its own owner, the IT-organization manager is more a proactive monitoring and escalation point than anything else. It simply confirms the IT-organization manager as the top-level owner of the operational development process. This should not be confused with the owner of workflow definitions—the definition of the process. It is the chief architect who maintains these definitions as part of the Convergent Architecture-style reference.

T-Bar Business Modeling and Requirements Workflow

This workflow and the ABD workflow detailed here exercise different hierarchical levels of the *T-technique* as described in convergent engineering (Taylor 1995) and unanimously endorsed by Microsoft (Ambler 1997) and RUP (Kruchten 2000). In addition, both workflows and their respective tools in the architectural IDE constitute a style-specific application of the responsibility-driven design (RDD) concepts formulated by convergent engineering (Taylor 1995) and RUP's "Work Guidelines: Role Playing" (Rational 2000). Complementing the T-technique, techniques such as class responsibility collaboration cards (CRC) and walk-through, as described in convergent engineering and RUP, are used to derive and validate requirements and to ensure a high-fidelity business model.

The T-bar business modeling and requirements workflow (or simply T-bar workflow) derives its name from its focus on the highest level of business modeling as represented by the bar of the T—the crossbar of the T—in the T-technique. It serves to identify business requirements and business partitioning as a prerequisite to defining system development projects. This workflow initiates system development projects and, as such, initiates the project management workflow. It also serves as the top-level consolidator of feedback and requirements arising from the sum of all system development projects.

Effective global optimization of the business and its IT infrastructure is achieved by consolidating the feedback and requirements at this level, according to the T-technique. This is also where the non-IT-related organizational impact of system development projects is assessed, communicated, and coordinated with the entire business and its projects.

This workflow comprises the following ordered activities:

- **T-bar business analysis.** This produces the top-level OPR business model, including scenarios and analyses of contexts, constraints, and urgency, and it produces project proposals.

- **Project initiation and tracking.** This initiates system development projects or other projects in the IT organization.

- **Global requirements management.** This provides uniform prioritization, coordination, dispatching, and the tracking of requirements, including change requests from diverse sources and levels.

Activity. T-bar business analysis.

Activity owner, principal participants. Chief architect, business managers (sponsoring clients or their representatives) and domain experts, IT-organization manager, requirements manager, lead developers.

Artifacts produced or refined. Top-level business object model, context diagrams, project proposals.

Guidelines and artifact/tool usage:

- The chief architect or an appropriately experienced convergent architect heads up this activity to ensure effective information modeling and requirements gathering. The architect defines and mediates T-bar business analysis sessions. Another architect or lead developer may assist during modeling and results processing. The IT-organization manager coordinates and administers participation of the appropriate mixture of business managers and domain experts.

- The sessions normally last two to four days; the business managers and domain experts are only involved half-days. There are a maximum of three active business managers or domain experts per session plus the architect and, optionally, one lead developer. This constitutes a T-bar business analysis team (or T-bar team). During the morning, the joint requirements gathering and modeling activity proceed according to the convergent engineering schema shown in Figure 6.2. In the afternoon, the business managers and domain experts are freed up to carry out their daily business. During this time, the architect and lead developer work on consolidating, documenting, and generally improving the model. Above all, they advance into the invention phase shown at the right of the figure. The results of the consolidated business model and the tentative invention results are then the basis for discussion when the session resumes together with the business managers and domain experts on the next morning.

- Session results that include top-level OPRs and top-level business scenario models are recorded in the C-BOM tool. The analysis-by-design workflow (discussed later) and the C-BOM section of Chapter 7 provide details on this task. In addition, context information and constraints of the IT and organizational environment are recorded in sketches. The need for immediate, ad hoc responses to problems in the existing operational environment is also

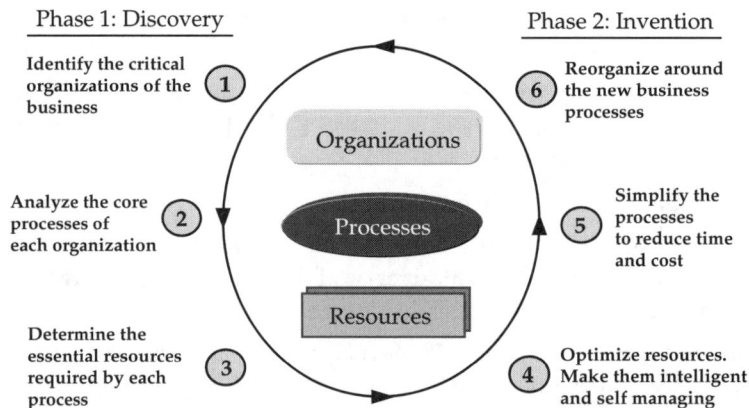

Figure 6.2 The core analysis-by-design process. Simple and effective. Business components evolve incrementally. The first model is usually a real eye-opener.

prioritized. Figure 6.3 exhibits the necessary effort split along the road to convergent systems.

- The session ends with one or more proposals for system development projects together with assessments of those proposals that address the organizational and business impact of the project. Requirements deemed as tangential, secondary, or of interest at a later stage are recorded, sanity-checked, and handed over to the requirements manager for further coordination and qualification in the normal course of the global requirements management activity.

- As part of the T-bar team, the IT-organization manager sanity-checks and refines the project proposals from the organizational perspective. The chief architect and lead developers ensure realistic development estimates in the project proposal, thus avoiding long, costly sanity-check cycles. The IT-organization manager then produces project proposals and proceeds to the project initiation and tracking activity. The T-bar business analysis is repeated regularly at the discretion of the chief architect or the IT-organization manager. Normally, this will occur at least twice a year. The very first T-bar business analysis may require numerous sessions to get past the initial organizational impedances and learning curve.

Figure 6.2 illustrates the core analysis-by-design process from convergent engineering. This process is used at two different levels of granularity in the Convergent Architecture. It is used by the T-bar business analysis activity to identify and structure the high-level OPRs and the associated constraints and requirements of the business at large. It is then used at the analysis-by-design workflow to successively refine the T-bar results into operational OPRs.

Figure 6.3 shows that migrating from a traditional IT landscape to a convergent system requires a planned effort split. An organization graduates over time from problem-driven responses to architecture-driven change. To ensure that this graduation

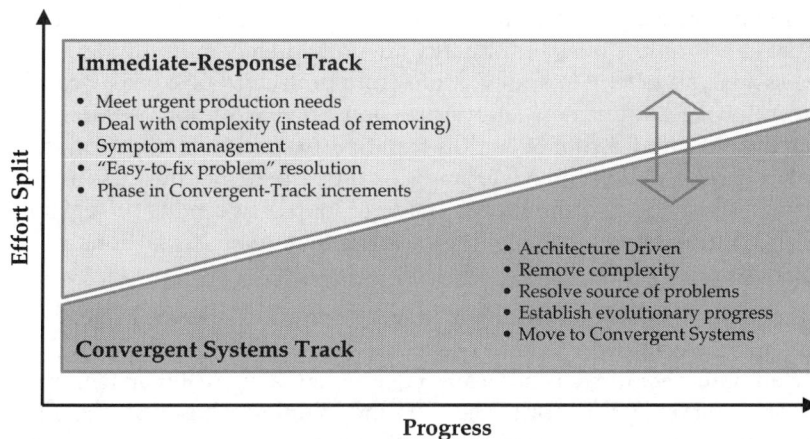

Figure 6.3 The effort split: Graduating to convergence. Convergent Arcihtecture deals with the reality of the existng IT environment.

takes place, the immediate-response track must be recognized and addressed by the convergent systems track. No matter how motivated the IT organization is, an entire enterprise cannot be migrated overnight. Instead, the convergent architect ensures that *new* barriers to convergence do not occur as a result of immediate-response efforts. As the capabilities of the IT organization and systems in the convergent systems track increase, the demands on the immediate-response track are reduced through the managed migration of existing IT systems or by the introduction of new project and system design techniques. The speed of progression into the convergent systems track is organization-dependent. An organization that is pushed too fast may go into a mode of destructive resistance to change. One of the primary reasons for regular T-bar business analysis activity is to constantly take the pulse of the organization and to adjust the correct speed and stride of change at the proper level before expensive setbacks occur during projects.

Activity.   Project initiation and tracking.

Activity owner, principal participants.   IT-organization manager, project manager/system project manager, steering team, sponsoring client, requirements manager, lead developers.

Artifacts produced or refined.   Consolidated project reviews.

Other end results.   Project kickoff or termination.

Guidelines and artifact/tool usage:

- The project proposals from the T-bar business analysis activity are used by the IT-organization manager to initiate new projects. This is a separate activity because the initiation of a project normally requires considerable effort, particularly in large organizations. Whether all proposed projects actually progress beyond the inception phase is determined during this activity. The IT-organization manager, as a member of the T-bar team, understands and can communicate the interrelationship between the project proposals and aspects of the business strategy. If a project does not progress beyond the inception phase, then adjustments in all related projects as well as consequential effects on the business strategy are immediately made at the T-bar business analysis level. Major deviations from project proposals may call for an exceptional T-bar business analysis session. Such exceptional sessions are, on the one hand, a sign of healthy iterative analysis by design and, on the other hand, should send a warning signal that the T-bar business analysis is not as effective as it should be. The tight loop between the project initiation and tracking and T-bar activities ensures that timely corrections and optimizations are made.

- In this activity, the IT-organization manager simply initiates the project management workflow (discussed later). As described in the workflow, project initiation requires the allocation of a potential project manager and the clear intent by a sponsoring client to fund the project based on the initial estimates in the project proposal. The project initiation activity proceeds in this scope until the project is officially kicked off or terminated by the steering team. The project manager drives the initiative to achieve kickoff. However, project kickoff and reviews are normal responsibilities of the

IT-organization steering teams, and they occur in the course of the regular steering team meetings as run by the IT-organization manager.

■ Successfully initiated projects are tracked at the steering-team level to ensure global optimization across all projects through timely input to ongoing T-bar activities as well as feedback to prevent a drift from T-bar goals. The procedure for tracking is simple: The organization manager of the system development organization presents the status of each active project, whereas the other organization managers, which include the chief architect (and all normal members of the steering team), provide input and feedback regarding problems and potential optimization or synergies.

Activity.   Global requirements management.

Activity owner, principal participants.   Requirements manager, chief architect, IT-organization manager, steering team.

Artifacts produced or refined.   Requirements pool.

Guidelines and artifact/tool usage:

■ Requirements tracking includes change management in the Convergent Architecture. It is a straightforward activity if taken seriously. However, it cannot be handled in an ad hoc manner. The key to success is having a dedicated and well-organized requirements manager working at the nonpartisan level of the architecture organization, as shown in the IT-organization model. The requirements manager organizes all requirements in a global requirements pool. The pool may be a simple document, but larger IT organizations require a more sophisticated tool such as Rational RequisitePro. At a minimum, the global requirements pool must order requirements according to the source, priority, responsible sink, and status. Once a priority is set, the requirements manager officially dispatches the requirement to a sink (defined later) and tracks the status of the requirement. There is no clear definition of what a requirement must look like or how it will be fulfilled. This is because requirement is a very ambiguous word. Nevertheless, a whole lot of these ambiguous requirements appear from all directions at all times in an IT organization. If these are sorted and handled with a due portion of discipline according to the following simple procedure, a whole lot of progress will be made.

■ Getting more specific, the requirements manager willingly accepts any sort of requirement, no matter how obscure, that has not found an *official sink* anywhere else in the IT organization. It is easy to locate an official sink for many requirements by locating the appropriate responsibility in the IT organization. However, just locating the responsible person is not all; the person must be able to accept and fulfill the requirement. Thus, an official sink is anybody willing to take on official responsibility for fulfilling a requirement. This means that the source and sink agree on the definition and priority of the requirement. Taking *official responsibility* means committing to fulfill the requirement along the lines of the official organizational and workflow stream of the IT organization. This includes all side effects (time, resources, risk, impacts) associated with fulfilling the requirement. If any doubt exists about the official sink, then the requirement is submitted to (through) the requirements manager. Such sinkless requirements can range from arbitrary good ideas to high-priority change requests from the operational systems organization that cannot be allocated directly to a particular assembly owner. Another example would be if the assembly owner and the source of the change request cannot agree immediately on the solution, priority, or fulfillment timing of the requirement. In this case, no official sink has been found, and it is immediately escalated to the requirements manager. Thus, everybody knows where to go with every requirement, no matter how obscure the requirement may be. There is no impedance to the flow of requirements, and all requirements find a responsible owner according to the path of least resistance. Requirements that fit into the normal work stream are handled properly without any extra administrative overhead. The remaining requirements are handled by the requirements manager as follows:

Once a requirement lands with the requirements manager, it is tracked in the requirements pool. Thus, all requirements in the IT organization end up either in the official plan of a workflow activity or an IT organization or in the requirements pool, or both. Once in the requirements pool, the requirements manager goes about finding an official sink for the requirement. To find the official sink, the requirements manager sorts, filters, and consolidates the requirement with the existing requirements pool. Based on his or her investigations and consolidation, the requirement may be dispersed into parts of other existing requirements. The requirements manager then sets out to achieve a consensus regarding priorities via the official responsibility hierarchy of the IT organization. Based on this consensus, he or she then dispatches the requirements into official sinks such as the owners of current project proposals, owners of assemblies, or organization managers. Another completely viable official sink is to declare the requirement as insignificant. Declaring a requirement as insignificant can only be done by the requirements manager as a nonpartisan representative of the entire IT organization. Requirements that cannot be resolved reasonably to an official sink are escalated by the requirements manager to the IT-organization manager, who may bring the issue to the steering team for resolution. The steering team is then in the position to immediately address any side effects due to an exceptional resolution that may be inconsistent with the currently active workflow.

Architectural Evolution Workflow

An instance of the Convergent Architecture defines the way the entire IT organization operates, including how it designs and delivers convergent systems. Clearly, this is a long-term approach that must take changes and the passage of time into account to be successful. The architectural style workflow makes sure that changes relevant to the architectural style take place in a proactive, constructive manner as part of the normal, self-optimizing activities in the IT organization. Through this workflow, the architectural style embraces change as part of its own design and ensures that it does not begin to impede its own goals with the passage of time. This activity starts with the creation of the very first instance of the Convergent Architecture.

Activity.   Architectural evolution.

Activity owner, principal participants.   Chief architect, steering team.

Artifacts produced or refined.   Convergent Architecture style reference.

Guidelines and artifact/tool usage:

- As outlined in Chapter 5, the Convergent Architecture style reference describes an organization-specific instance of the Convergent Architecture as defined in this book. The instance may be a one-to-one application of the entire style book or a documented variant that remains compatible with the architectural and development models, both described in this book. The chief architect allocates adequate time to maintain the Convergent Architecture style reference and to ensure that changes are understood and implemented throughout the IT organization. The extent of this effort will depend on how far the variant instance of the Convergent Architecture deviates from mainstream evolution of the architectural style. Although one of the principal goals of the style is to reduce the invasive effects due to change, change will occur. For example, even a stable, fundamental standard such as UML will evolve. Many, if not most, changes to the architectural style will have a minor impact so long as they are introduced incrementally. The trick is to handle this steadily and step by step. The best strategy an organization can take to avoid problems due to change while at the same time benefiting from new developments is this ongoing activity of observation and incremental change—that is, evolution. This allocation of the chief architect's time is a wise investment in constructive foresight to ensure that changes take place at the best time and at the right place.

- In addition to continuous investments by the chief architect, this activity will involve efforts from other members of the IT organization. For example, the architectural IDE may need to be adapted by the toolsmiths who are responsible for its usage in individual projects. However, timely adaptations to the reference IDE will help avoid costly problems in active projects down the road.

Project Management Workflow

The project management workflow applies the RUP phases, its milestones, and its concepts on incremental development. This begins with a canonical *iteration planning and tracking activity* that applies an optimizing four-pass approach. This planning activity is canonical in the sense already used in the IT-organizational model. It is applied equally to every iteration with slight variations relative to the current life-cycle phase of a project. This canonical planning activity in conjunction with conceptual proximity of the IT organization and the architectural IDE enables a simple, highly effective project management workflow.

The project management workflow coordinates and drives all other canonical project workflows. It also interacts with the cross-project workflows, in particular with the T-bar business analysis activity as described previously. This interaction is intentional along the lines of the T-technique: The project management workflow handles the lower levels of the T, as denoted by the vertical strut of the T, whereas the T-bar business analysis activity absorbs and consolidates information at the upper level of the T, the T-bar. This relationship is illustrated in Figure 6.4.

The figure also illustrates the logical orientation of the other canonical project workflows, from top to bottom, along the *critical path* of each iteration in a system development project. The project management workflow initiates and terminates each iteration, as indicated by the innermost arrow in the figure returning from the review and termination of an iteration at the bottom, back to the top of the workflow, where the next iteration is planned. Clearly, the project management workflow brackets the other critical-path workflows into the context of planned iterations of a project. As emphasized in the RUP, the workload distribution among the workflows is highly dependent on the current phase (and state) of the project. The intended distribution of workload across the iterations of a project is signified by the scales to the right of the figure. Lastly, the vertical positioning of two supporting workflows, the development environment workflow and the configuration and change management (CCM) workflow, indicate that, although important, they do not lie directly in the critical path of each iteration. These supporting workflows are ongoing in the context of a project with a peak load for workers from the IT support organization toward the beginning of the project.

Activity.   Canonical iteration planning and tracking (base activity), with phase-specific variants each covered individually later after the guidelines covering the canonical aspects:

- Inception-phase variant (project initiation)
- Elaboration-phase variant

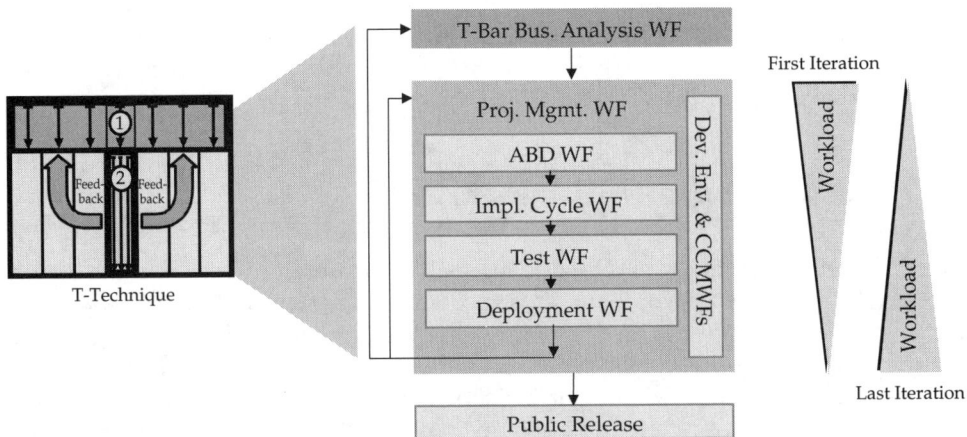

Figure 6.4   The flow and scope of an iteration.

- Construction-phase variant
- Transition-phase variant

Activity owner, principal participants.   System project manager, assembly developer, other lead developers in the system development project, convergent architect.

Artifacts produced or refined.   System project plan (long-term development strategy, current iteration plan with work orders for both assembly and component development projects).

Guidelines and artifact/tool usage:

- Each iteration of a system development project begins with a variant of the common canonical iteration planning and tracking activity described here. The canonical procedure combines the factors required for timely, reality-driven optimization of each project iteration. *Reality-driven* means that the participants in the project are consistently freed from their respective illusions (optimism, wishful thinking, overestimation of capabilities, quality of requirements) to arrive at a plan based on a consensus of the real constraints and requirements in the project.

- To achieve this, each iteration is planned using a rapid, four-pass process. This process produces, or updates, the long-term development strategy document and the current iteration plan. The current iteration plan exists in the form of a features summary and a simple *task ownership matrix* (TOMA), which is covered in more detail with Figure 6.6. Each task in the TOMA comprises a work order specifying the five W's (who, what is done, when, with whom, and where do the deliverables go), as described later, for each specific task. This short four-pass session and its resulting TOMA are all that are needed to guarantee that each participant contributes the maximum to the progress, synergy, risk management, tracking, and steering of a project in harmony with other active projects. In addition, this approach leads to a significant reduction of the number of iterations required for a given set of features. This is so because the sanity-checking capacity of the iterative approach is amplified by the four-pass approach to planning. The following subsections explain how this works.

- The initial planning for each and every iteration proceeds according to this logic: The system project manager schedules a *four-pass iteration planning session* with the assembly developer and the other lead developers slated for the system development project. How the initial group of lead developers is defined is explained in the section on the inception-phase variant. The requirements manager also participates at the beginning and end of the session. In addition, the sponsoring client and domain experts should be on call in order to immediately clear up issues. The session can last anywhere from two hours to four days, depending on the extent of the project and, above all, on the number of illusions that still exist in the group's collective mind. The session takes place in a room equipped with plenty of whiteboard space and the capability to copy the contents of the white boards (copy boards). The four-pass iteration planning session then proceeds according to the flowchart illustrated in Figure 6.5.

Start

List requirement/features

Detail & allocate prio 1 s

Check sanity & adjust

Work Plan Consensus

Features + TOMA

With Lead Developers and Convergent Architect:

1. Talk through: List requirement/feature blocks for both core business and IT-Organization features and prioritize.

2. Allocate and Estimate: For prio 1 s: Further detail each block in terms of deliverable features. Allocate resources and estimate iteration development effort.

3. Walk-through: consolidate plan and compare to available constraints (features, time, worker-skills). Repeat step 2 adjusting free-variables: features, time, worker-skills until plan and constraints match.

4. Run-through.

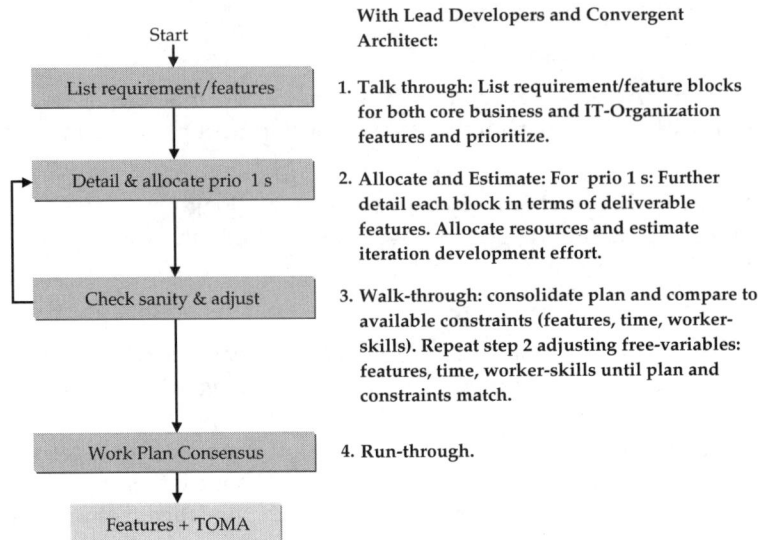

Figure 6.5   Planning an iteration: The four-pass approach. Carry out these steps with the lead developers and primary customer.

The four-pass approach is as follows:

Pass 1 (talk-through).   In pass 1, the assembly developer groups and lists the requirements to be fulfilled as blocks on the white boards. The requirements are grouped into major requirements and related subrequirements. The assembly developer normally has a good idea of the requirements on the iteration. The source of these requirements is the review of the previous iteration (if available), the project proposal, and any new input from the requirements manager. Then all requirements are broken down in terms of deliverable features, core business features, technical features, and project-specific IT-organizational aspects. The core business features are listed in terms of business models or convergent components. Features are broken down into subfeatures if necessary to enable the realistic estimation of resource requirements: worker skills, time, and infrastructure. While listing the blocks of requirements/features, they are also prioritized: 1 being highest priority and 3 the lowest. Things that must be accomplished together or as prerequisites for others are recognized in the priorities. Also, the dependencies from other projects (other assemblies) that depend on the assembly being planned must be reflected in the priorities—a clear responsibility of the assembly developer. The participants set the priorities as a group by reaching a consensus or through a consensus via democratic majority if reaching a complete consensus proves difficult. This step ensures that priorities, sequencing, and prerequisites are agreed on among participants, both project management and developers, from the start.

Pass 2 (allocate and estimate).   In pass 2, realistic resource estimates (worker, worker time, infrastructure) are made for all priority 1 features and requirements. Once a worker has been assigned, the fulfillment of the feature or requirement becomes a task for the worker. The resource estimate is for everything related to the task up to the delivery of the results at the end of the iteration. Thus, the estimate also includes testing and administrative efforts, for example. All participants in the session must agree on the resource estimate to ensure that the feature is defined adequately. If they cannot agree, then the features and requirements in question must be broken down into further detail. If this is not possible, an additional requirement for further investigation usually is the solution. At best, a person is immediately allocated to carry out the task instead of defining a worker role. This nails down the precise skill set and permits optimal developer synergies to be created by the experienced team of lead developers. Allocating the proper persons to requirements significantly influences the effort estimates both for the task itself and in other areas of the development effort. Thus, the immediate allocation of a person makes the estimate more precise. If no person can be allocated directly, then the details regarding required skills and experience must be recorded for the next pass.

Pass 3 (walk-through).   This pass is the first sanity-check and adjustment pass. The resource estimates from pass 2 are listed and compared with the available resources for the project. At this point, hard decisions are made by the planning team or, in case a problem cannot be resolved, must be escalated by the team. Three so-called free variables can be adjusted in this pass: *feature set (requirements), time invested,* and *available worker skills.* These are the only three variables that need to be considered. They are known as *free variables* to suggest their similarity to free variables in classic engineering and physical science disciplines. Each free variable may be adjusted and then the totals recalculated. Time and person skills can be converted to cost, of course, at any time. In contrast to some science disciplines, the three free variables noted here are not completely independent of one another. This is one reason why the experience of the lead developers is imperative in the planning effort. For example, dependencies between the features must be addressed with each change of the free variables. Also, the total time allocated for an iteration should not be stretched, contrary to the RUP's recommended practice for iterations. As a rule of thumb, the mean iteration length should not be more than 12 weeks.

Pass 4 (run-through).   In the final pass, the team runs through the results of pass 3, checks for consistency and consensus, finalizes the so-called W5 details (discussed later) for each task, and records the unfulfilled requirements/ features. The W5 details ensure that all features are planned at the level required by the system project manager to construct the TOMA and its associated work plans. Figure 6.6 illustrates a TOMA. The columns in the TOMA represent the named tasks to be completed during the iteration. The rows in the TOMA represent the workers (persons) available to the project. In the TOMA, each task has an owner, which is denoted by a large circle at a node in the TOMA, as shown in the figure. Also, tasks may have significant participants, denoted by the smaller squares in the figure. Each task-owner pair in the matrix (the large circles in the figure) is associated with its respective W5 work plan details. The W5 specifies *who* (the owner and participants), *what is done* (what are the deliverables), *when* (when are things due), with *whom* (the significant contributors), and *where* the

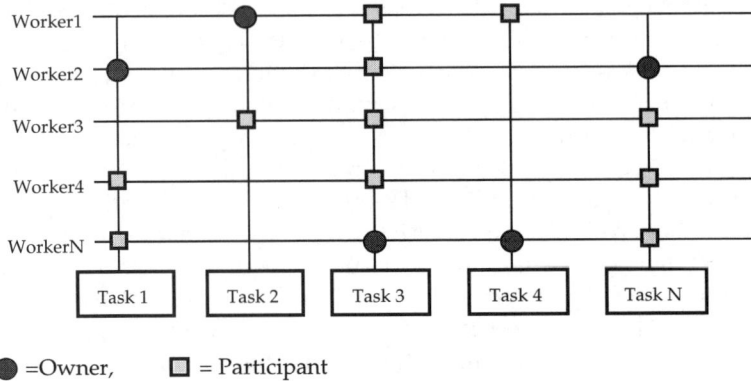

Figure 6.6   Work plan: The task ownership matrix (TOMA) is used to communicate work plans.

> deliverables go (where are the resulting artifacts to be delivered). Based on the run-through consensus, the system project manager then produces the final feature list, TOMA, and W5 work plans. In addition, the system project manager is the owner of a task for regular iteration reviews and the final iteration review. These cumulative results comprise the new current iteration plan.

Based on the information quality won during the iteration planning session, the planning team produces or refines long-term prognoses for the project. This long-term plan includes estimates covering the number and extent of projected iterations, staged releases, test versions, and RUP life-cycle milestones. It also formulates the strategy for achieving these goals. This information is compiled by the system project manager to produce or update the long-term software development plan. This plan enables the IT organization and its steering team to make long-term forecasts and proactive management decisions. Updating the long-term plan with each iteration plan ensures the maximum accuracy of forecasts. It also enables the team to gain experience regarding the quality of its estimates and to more objectively assess the state of the development process and the IT organization. Let's now look at project phase variations to the canonical iteration planning and tracking activity.

RUP Inception-Phase Variant (Project Initiation)

The project initiation activity begins with the results from the T-bar business analysis. Its primary goal is to delimit the project domain and define the solution strategy. It begins with a very small team consisting of an experienced assembly developer, the system project manager, and a few (not more) other developers, depending on the extent of the proposed project. This *initiation team* also must have access to the relevant domain experts and experts familiar with the existing operational IT environment. In addition, the convergent architect participates in the initiation team by providing constructive feedback regarding the development strategy on a regular basis. The initiation team works for a period of approximately one to eight weeks to produce the long-term development strategy. The length of this initiation activity is essentially dependent on the number of *T-prototypes* (investigative prototypes in the spirit of the T-technique) that must be developed. There are often many unknowns at this stage because we are at the very beginning of the project investigation. However, the project proposal often contains reasonable estimates. The precise number and length of T-prototypes and other tasks in this iteration are determined in the iteration planning and tracking activity, which the initiation team also uses to plan this initial iteration.

In this phase, the initiation team proceeds with a streamlined approach to the ABD workflow (discussed later). The streamlined approach focuses on the critical unknowns and risk factors in the project. The scope and content of the streamlined ABD workflow are at the discretion of the experienced accessor developer, with feedback from the convergent architect. The team produces a long-term development strategy that consists of critical results from the initial ABD workflow as well as an initial cut of the assembly architecture reference. It also includes the priorities, content, and coverage of the projected iterations, with more detail for the early iterations of the project. These initial results may change significantly during the elaboration phase. Overall, these results fulfill the requirements for the RUP life-cycle objective (LCO) milestone.

At the end of the phase, an LCO review is carried out with the initiation team, the steering team, and the sponsoring client. The results of this review determine whether

- The project should be continued according to the long-term development strategy, in which case the iteration planning and tracking activity for the first iteration of the elaboration phase is commenced.

- The project proposal should be revised and a second iteration carried out in the inception phase.

- The knowledge gained during the inception phase requires a complete review at the T-bar business analysis level, in which case the requirements and feedback are formulated for input into the T-bar analysis activity, and the cycle begins again at the T-bar level.

RUP Elaboration-Phase Variant

The elaboration phase begins with the first full-scale version of the iteration planning and tracking activity. Its focus is on the ABD workflow, as defined later. During the iterations of the elaboration phase, the system project manager and convergent architect ensure well-directed progress of elaboration. The system project manager checks that the agreed-on content and schedule in the work plans are being fulfilled. This is done in part by using the architectural IDE to track the progress of component metamorphosis in each view of the model. Each view can be checked for completeness and integrity with its respective model verifier in the architectural IDE. The convergent architect also monitors the views from the perspective of the overall, cross-project, cross-system integrity of the architectural style.

As elaboration progresses, the assembly developer ensures that each member of the assembly development team and its subordinate component development teams produce increasingly elaborated versions of their owned resources, with focus on the ABD workflow aspects. Remember, the owned resources and the worker responsibilities are also defined in the IT-organization model. Once well elaborated, the results of the ABD workflow, the owned resources, fulfill the requirements for the RUP life-cycle objective (LCO) milestone. This means that the assembly developer has arrived at a stable version of the assembly component (also defined in the IT organization) from the design and architectural perspective. At this point, significant structural changes have slowed to the level where UCM coverage becomes reasonable and necessary for many artifacts, as described in the CCM workflow (discussed later). The remaining effort now concentrates on the completion, tuning, and testing of the business logic.

Initial operational capabilities normally should be demonstrable at the end of the second iteration in the elaboration phase. Beginning with the second iteration, an *operational increment* of the system is presented in the operational test environment (in the test center organization). Each of these operational increments increases the operational scope of the system. However, they are not yet transitioned into the operational systems organization for end-user use. They remain in the operational test environment. This is so because radical changes may still occur in the design and realization of these increments until later in the construction phase.

RUP Construction-Phase Variant

The construction phase constitutes a smooth, practically unnoticeable shift of focus toward the implementation cycle workflow. In these iterations, the ABD workflow has diminished significantly, with a proportionate increase of time spent in the implementation cycle and test workflows. These workflows are now the center of activity, with the models from the ABD workflow still driving development and, in particular, code generation. In our model-driven approach, the ABD workflow does not come to an abrupt end. It just shifts focus during the iteration of the construction phase, leading to rapid increases in the visible capabilities of the system.

The assembly developer, deployment manager, and system project manager plan and drive the construction-phase iterations to fulfill the requirements for deployment into the operational systems organization. The last iteration in this phase concludes with the RUP initial operational capability (IOC) milestone, where the test center manager and deployment manager agree to release the assembly to the transition organization for prerelease testing by end users in the operational systems environment.

RUP Transition-Phase Variant

The goal of the transition phase is the public release of the assembly into general usage. In this phase, the assembly development team works closely with the transition organization and focuses on the deployment and monitoring workflow. During an iteration, problem reports from the deployment and monitoring workflow propagate via the deployment manager back into the implementation cycle workflow aspects of development and result in new prerelease versions of the assembly. New feature requirements and major change requests flow to the requirements manager, not to the assembly development team, as defined in the requirements management activity previously.

In addition to testing the deployed system, the operational user support organization and infrastructure and base systems organization (see the IT-organization model) are brought up to speed by the assembly development team. The end of this phase is marked by the transition manager declaring that the assembly is ready for public release. This also ends development for a single, versioned release of the assembly, which may be followed by subsequent versions during its entire life cycle. A final review is held with the assembly development team. This review provides constructive feedback to each of the IT organizations. In addition, the review addresses further releases and further ownership of the assembly. If the normal planning flow has not already foreseen a subsequent release, then the responsibility for further planning regarding the assembly lies with the IT-organization manager, as described in the IT-organization model. Alternatively, the ongoing T-bar business analysis and requirements workflow may reinitiate a project proposal for a new version of the assembly at any time in the due course of its activities. Ownership of the assembly and its contained convergent components remains with their respective developers. If this is not possible, then resource ownership for the artifacts reverts to the architecture organization until new resource owners can be assigned.

Precisely the same approach applies to projects developing software to be sold to external customers. The only difference, as already noted in the IT-organization model, is that the operational systems organization manages prerelease tests (beta testing) with external customers (as sponsoring clients) during the transition phase and, in parallel, channels the rollout of the software product to the respective marketing, sales, and distribution organizations.

Development Environment Workflow

The development environment workflow is a supporting workflow that sets up and verifies the technical environment for any team member. It also tunes the development environment for each new iteration of a project as the detailed requirements on the development environment change. This workflow is concerned primarily with verifying that the technical development environment is at its effective best throughout the development life cycle. This enables developers to concentrate on their core development duties along the critical development path.

Activity.   Set up and tune the development environment.

Activity owner, principal participants.   Development toolsmith, developer, or the other workers requiring a development-like environment.

Artifacts produced or refined.   None.

Other end results.   Tuned development environment.

Guidelines and artifact/tool usage:

- The development toolsmith and developer work closely together in this activity. By assisting the toolsmith in this activity, the developer is learning and influencing the environment he or she will use. The first thing the development toolsmith does is to engage the infrastructure and base systems organization to ensure that the basic hardware and software platform is operational.

- Then the toolsmith and developer proceed to jointly tackle the following tasks, more or less in this order:
  - Set up the developer's particular view of the project directory structure and ensure that the backup strategy is in order.
  - Create the physical UCM structure in the local environment and the views appropriate for the current phase of development. The detail and range of the views usually change as the project progresses. The artifacts that need to be managed in each phase of the project are covered in the CCM workflow (see Figure 6.7).
  - Set up the local architectural IDE and local runtime/test environment (see Chapter 7 and the following test workflow section). This includes the application server and its storage tier (for example, the underlying database). Configure these to use the CCM and backup strategy as appropriate for the current phase of the project (see the CCM workflow section).

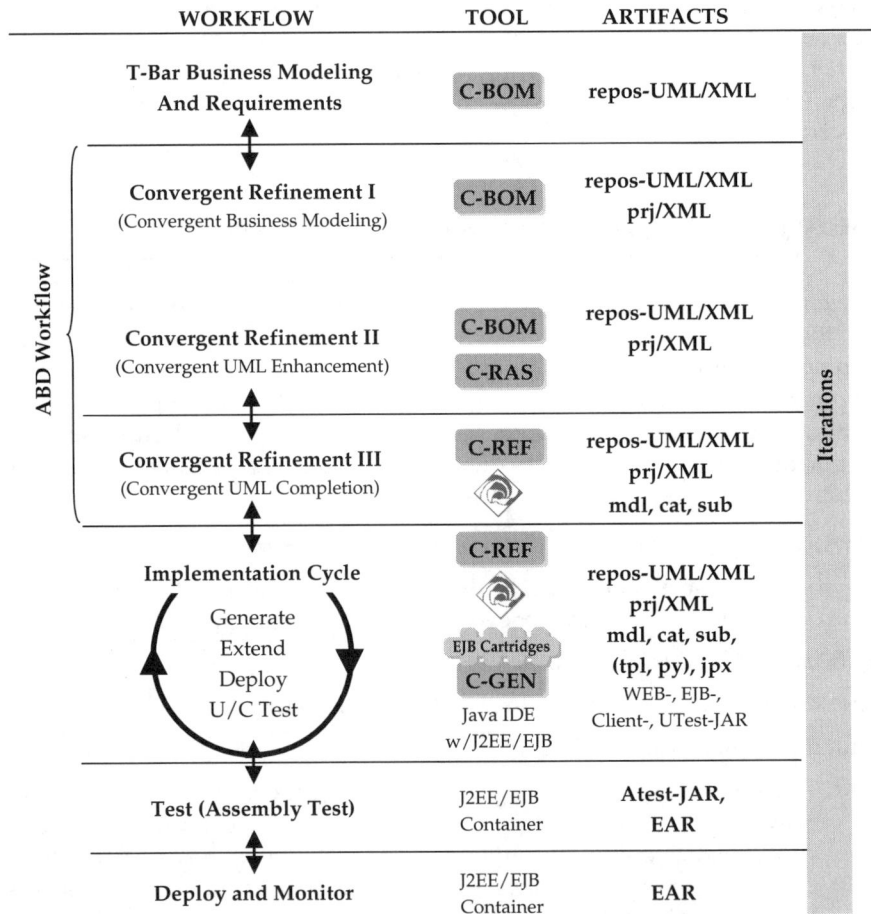

WORKFLOW	TOOL	ARTIFACTS
T-Bar Business Modeling And Requirements	C-BOM	**repos-UML/XML**
Convergent Refinement I (Convergent Business Modeling)	C-BOM	**repos-UML/XML prj/XML**
Convergent Refinement II (Convergent UML Enhancement)	C-BOM C-RAS	**repos-UML/XML prj/XML**
Convergent Refinement III (Convergent UML Completion)	C-REF	**repos-UML/XML prj/XML mdl, cat, sub**
Implementation Cycle Generate Extend Deploy U/C Test	C-REF EJB Cartridges C-GEN Java IDE w/J2EE/EJB	**repos-UML/XML prj/XML mdl, cat, sub, (tpl, py), jpx** WEB-, EJB-, Client-, UTest-JAR
Test (Assembly Test)	J2EE/EJB Container	**Atest-JAR, EAR**
Deploy and Monitor	J2EE/EJB Container	**EAR**

(ABD Workflow spans Convergent Refinement I through III; Iterations spans the right side.)

Figure 6.7 Workflow, tools, and core artifacts.

The technical CCM capabilities are set up and verified together with the repository toolsmith.

■ Test the development environment from beginning to end to reduce the possibility that problems will be discovered later when they may inconvenience the entire development team. Using the reference technologies described in this book, it is possible to carry out these tests completely automatically. This precedes using ANT procedures (ANT 2000) to call and exercise each tool used along the critical development path. An automated test procedure at this stage provides all the advantages it has anywhere else: predictable results, fast and simple, enabling incremental improvements. See the Convergent Architecture Web site for more information and resources regarding such test procedures.

■ Setting up the initial development environment entails most of the effort during this activity, but the activity normally must be revisited at the beginning of each iteration. For the sake of project efficiency, iterations each require a level of formal tool support appropriate to the phase. For example, as will be pointed out in greater detail, the rigor of CCM and the test support required will increase with the number of iterations. Enabling these features too early can, in fact, severely hinder development. The tools environment will be configured successively to enable, or even to enforce, the appropriate rigor as the project progresses.

Configuration and Change Management Workflow (CCM Workflow)

CCM is a supporting workflow that accompanies the entire critical development path and its tools. The requirements management activity (discussed previously) handles change management from the perspective change requests and the flow of these requests in the IT organization. CCM addresses the environment and mechanisms to technically manage the artifacts produced and changed within the IT organization, most notably by system development projects. CCM is concerned primarily with effectively partitioning, versioning, and archiving artifacts throughout the development life cycle. This requires a dedicated, highly technical workflow. For this supporting workflow, the Convergent Architecture leverages UCM, as recommended by RUP (Kruchten 1998). This section describes how special artifact types are handled in the UCM context. These are the artifacts that are specific to the architectural style and, as such, are not covered as part of the standard UCM workflow guidelines.

Since the CCM environment manages artifacts at the technical level, it is also close to the physical environment; it must deal with the diverse storage requirements of tools, frameworks, and operating systems. In fact, the architectural IDE leverages the CCM environment to help insulate it from the idiosyncrasies of the low-level physical environment. The Convergent Architecture Web site provides examples to help set up and manage CCM environments in conjunction with the architectural IDE and for large development teams.

Activity.   Activate UCM (manage CA-specific artifacts in a UCM workflow).

Activity owner, principal participants.   Assembly developer, configuration manager, repository toolsmith, developer, or other worker requiring the CCM environment.

Artifacts produced or refined.   Assembly configuration management reference, UCM repository.

Other end results.   Project-specific versioning and archiving of artifacts.

Guidelines and artifact/tool usage: This activity may commence any time after the development environment workflow has installed and tested the basic UCM infrastructure. However, it normally does not start until the second iteration of the project or even later. This is so because the UCM model, procedures, and tools are designed to manage relatively stable artifact topologies, not to handle rapid changes in topologies. The initial phase of a project is called the *inception phase* for a good reason: Much of the topology is not known yet. During the initial iterations, a team is rapidly inventing, creating, and concurrently changing the component and package topology. Artifacts are changed and exchanged many times a day between the members of the project. Experience shows that trying to introduce the complete UCM model too early results in hindering this dynamic team process due to the administrative overhead required to make changes. In the initial iteration, a canonical project team may go through 10 or 20 UCM cycles (integration-baseline cycles) per day. At this stage of a project, this amounts to high time consumption with essentially zero returns. Thus, this activity usually starts later, at the discretion of the assembly developer, who will know when the component topology and other artifacts can be managed reasonably using the UCM model. Up to this point, a basic client-server version control system, for example, a basic ClearCase infrastructure, is the best bet.

Similar to other supporting activities, the UCM activity is also a team effort, where the developer helps specify and set up his or her local UCM environment while learning and practicing its use. To ensure that the UCM partitioning is coordinated across the entire project as well as with other projects, the assembly developer participates in this activity. The assembly developer works with the developer to define the UCM contents and structure and the UCM views, access rights, responsibilities, and ownership issues. This task must be lead by the assembly developer because it has a lot to do with project planning and design foresight: Improper partitioning and assignment of artifacts at this stage will invariably lead to confusion and friction in the development effort. During this task, the configuration decisions are made in accordance with guidelines in the assembly configuration management reference or serve to extend these guidelines to handle a special case. The initial assembly configuration management reference is created by the assembly developer based on the template provided by the configuration manager. This ensures maximum CCM uniformity across projects. At the end of this activity, the assembly developer creates a new version of the assembly configuration management reference.

In addition to versioned artifacts, the team identifies archived artifacts. Archived artifacts are those entities that cannot, or should not, be handled by the UCM repository directly. These are things such as handbooks that do not exist in electronic form or things such as software installation CDs that would unduly burden the UCM repository. Such archived artifacts normally are represented as versioned proxy artifacts (also known as *reference artifacts*) within the versioned UCM pool. Managing versioned proxies of the archive artifacts enables a labeled release to be managed in the UCM system without losing track of the relevant archived artifacts.

Figure 6.7 illustrates the special types of artifacts produced along the CA process workflows using the architectural IDE. These artifacts lie in the critical development path and need to be under UCM management. Following the figure, I explain how each of these artifacts normally should be handled in the context of the IT organization and its canonical development team. Before covering each artifact, it is important to note that *we do not need to version purely generated artifacts in the UCM pool*. Instead, we only version and manage the source artifacts that are used to generate these other artifacts. The exception to this is at the end of an iteration, where the released assembly, including all generated and deployable artifacts, is versioned and labeled. Since the Convergent Architecture focuses on a model-driven approach along the entire life cycle, significantly fewer artifacts must be managed as compared with traditional development environments.

Figure 6.7 shows the evolution (metamorphosis) of a convergent model through the workflows of the CA process and the special types of artifacts created using the architectural IDE during each workflow. The following list describes the artifacts that must be UCM-coordinated among participants in the canonical development team. The design internals of these artifacts will be discussed in more detail in Chapter 7.

repos-UML/XML, prj/XML. The *repos-UML/XML* is the UML repository that manages the convergent model across all stages of development and across the various tool modules that operate on the UML representation of convergent components. The *XML* signifies that import-export and partitioning of the model among developers is achieved via XML/XMI-formatted modules. These XML partitions are units that may be managed on a per-developer basis in the UCM pool. In addition, the IDE configurations for the team and for each developer are managed in a XML project file, *prj/XML*. At some stage, this project configuration information also will need to be in the versioned UCM pool.

mdl, cat, sub, prp. Beginning with the convergent refinement III activity of the ABD workflow, the IDE embeds Rational Rose as a foundation for its UML completion assistants. This produces additional Rose-specific artifacts to support team development using Rose. These artifacts are the ASCII model files *mdl*, category files *cat*, subsystem files *sub*, and model properties files *prp*. You will see in the next chapter how these artifacts relate to the UML/XML repository. These artifacts also will enter the versioned pool on a team and a per-developer basis as soon as the partitioning of the model has stabilized.

tpl, py. Some projects require extensions or modifications to the default technology projection cartridges. These extensions normally are in the form of metaprograms consisting of template files *tpl* or JPython scripts *py* that have been developed and tested in the translative generator IDE. These extensions must be versioned in the UCM pool to coordinate them with other versioned artifacts that require these generator extensions.

jpx. To support the implementation cycle workflow, the IDE embeds JBuilder for completion, compilation, and testing of the business dimension. To support these activities, JBuilder-specific project files in XML *jpx* are generated from the UML model. If these artifacts are modified above and beyond their purely generated aspects, they too must be versioned similar to the project-specific configuration files.

WEB-WAR, EJB-JAR, Client-JAR, UTest-JAR, ATest-JAR, EAR. For the implementation cycle, test, and deployment workflows, the translative generator produces source code (for example, Java, C++, COBOL, XML, HTML), configuration files, deployment descriptors, build environment files, and test utilities. It also produces information to package these artifacts as deployable units. These deployable units are the JAR (Java archive) files shown in the figure, which together comprise the assembly. The assembly is packaged as an enterprise archive (EAR) file. Any of these files may contain style-conform refinements by the developer above and beyond their generated content. Any of these artifacts that deviate from their generated form must enter the versioned pool.

Analysis-by-Design (ABD) Workflow

The concept of analysis by design is central in convergent engineering, and as applied here, it consolidates the RUP activities of business modeling, requirements analysis, and design activities. The analysis-by-design workflow is divided into three phases, each representing a critical refinement stage along the metamorphosis from a rough business strategy into the OPRs of a convergent system. Each activity of the workflow covers one of these three phases:

Convergent refinement I (convergent business modeling). This begins with the results from the T-bar business analysis activity and produces a verified business object model, including its use-case scenario models using the C-BOM module of the architectural IDE.

Convergent refinement II (convergent UML representation). This begins with the results from convergent refinement I and produces an initial convergent UML model using the C-RAS module of the architectural IDE.

Convergent refinement III (convergent UML completion). This begins with the results from convergent refinement II and produces a fully elaborated UML model using the C-REF/Rose module of the architectural IDE.

Activity. Convergent refinement I (convergent business modeling).

Activity owner, principal participants. Assembly developer, domain experts, lead developers.

Artifacts produced or refined. Convergent business object model, refined context diagrams.

Guidelines and artifact/tool usage:

- The first activity in the three-phase refinement process is known as *convergent business modeling* or simply *convergent refinement I*. The only prerequisite is the results from the T-bar business analysis activity. The refinement activity takes high-level T-bar business models and requirements and refines them into a tested convergent business object model that includes both structural and dynamic detail. It uses the C-BOM and UML model repository modules of the architectural IDE to support this activity and to manage the resulting artifacts.

- In this activity, the assembly developer organizes business modeling sessions with lead developers and domain experts according to the convergent engineering approach (Taylor 1995). These sessions are, in many ways, similar to the T-bar sessions described earlier. At this stage, the focus is on further refining parts of the T-bar results, as defined in the project proposal and current iteration plan. First, business use-case scenarios (BUCS) and accessor use-case scenarios (AUCS) are created. These scenarios pick up where the top-level scenarios from T-bar activity leave off. These are normally textual scenarios. BUCS describe business operations, independent of the particular user or system access mechanisms. If required (discussed later), AUCS add scenarios specific to one or more access channels from the perspective of an external user or an external system. The AUCS simply specify the structure and interaction aspects of each of the accessor's representers (an access channel) from the perspective of the user. It takes a flat perspective: It just talks about how the user interacts via the particular representer; it does not cover the business logic stream behind the scenes, which is covered by the BUCS. The AUCS may refer to one or more BUCS, of course.

- Once *initial*, first-cut BUCS and AUCS exist, the rest of the activity proceeds as illustrated in Figure 6.8. This approach is summarized following the diagram; details and extensive examples may be found in the convergent engineering reference (Taylor 1995). Details regarding the C-BOM tool support and modeling style are also covered in subsequent chapters.

- In a talk-through, the developers discuss a scenario, step by step, with the domain experts. Along the way, convergent components are identified and

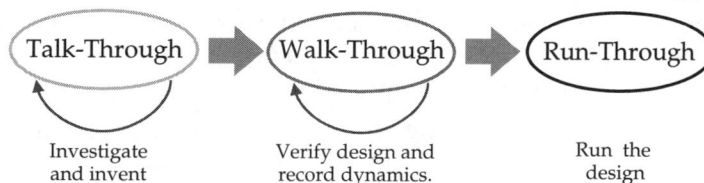

Figure 6.8 Recording and verifying business designs. Role playing verifies and debugs the design and achieves consensus with domain experts regarding requirements and priorities.

recorded as CRC cards with their respective responsibilities and collaborators in the model. During this process, the business use-case scenario is also refined into a *use-case scenario model (scenario model)*, a visual representation of the dynamic business flow and transitions between the convergent components. Scenario models only need to be created for BUCS; the accessor use-case scenarios are further refined in step 3 of the refinement process.

- The responsibilities on each CRC card are categorized in terms of *visible* and *hidden* responsibilities, corresponding to things of internal, private nature to the business component or things that must be exposed to collaborators of the component. In addition, each responsibility is allocated to one of the following three responsibilities categories:

  - **Knowing.** These are passive information entities held or referenced by the business object, an address or account number, for example.

  - **Doing.** These are active procedures or algorithms carried out by the business object, the act of transferring funds, for example.

  - **Enforcing.** These are preconditions, postconditions, and invariants that must be ensured by the business object. An example here would be an invariant indicating that a client cannot also be a member of staff.

- These categories are not always orthogonal in nature. This means that one may be expressed in terms of another—responsibilities are, after all, written in human language. For example, one could express a responsibility for enforcing the customer's good standing in terms of one doing a check on a customer's good standing instead. However, it is often easy to categorize the responsibilities, especially with some experience. Also, the nonorthogonality is not a critical problem at this point in design: The focus of this level of design is on high-quality business requirements, not on 100-percent orthogonality of representation. Using these categories still helps simplify and streamline the pattern-matching process in subsequent activities. Refer to the OPEN toolbox of techniques (Henderson-Sellers 1998) if you require more background on these three categories.

- In a walk-through, a RUP-compliant role-playing technique is used to further refine and check the completeness and business relevance of the model. A walk-through often results in changes to optimize the model. Several walk-throughs may be required until the entire team, which represents both business and system perspectives of the convergent model, is satisfied with the operational improvements and the feasibility of the model. Not only is each walk-through a refinement and optimization step, but it is also a debugging and sanity-check procedure.

- To ensure that all team members concur on the quality of the model, a run-through must be completed and recorded. In a run-through, the team runs through the scenario models, including each separately modeled path. A run-through is successful when no more errors are found, and all parties are satisfied with the content and quality of the model. Thus, this step represents a sanity-verification and consensus check. Each run-through produces a *state-transition table* that documents each of the respective paths through the convergent model. The results of the run-through are recorded together with the CRC and scenario models.

■ The three steps—talk-through, walk-through, and run-through—are repeated for a number of paths through the business operation and model, not just a single best-case path. The recorded results of each path define the acceptance tests for the resulting convergent system. They also serve as a signoff document for the life-cycle objective (LCO) milestone of the project.

■ In this activity, accessors may be modeled in the form of CRC cards with associated accessor use-case scenarios. However, since accessors are not core business objects, they do not have to appear in the business model. Often, accessors are introduced into the model in the third refinement stage, the pure UML stage. This is more effective because, once in the UML stage of refinement, default accessors and many aspects of custom accessors can be derived automatically from the business component model. Many accessor models can be generated automatically from the business component model once the UML stage has been reached. The decision is whether accessors should be detailed and documented in refinement phases I and II, the extent of detailing being left to the discretion of the assembly developer. By default, I recommend beginning with the automatic generation of accessor models in phase III of refinement.

Activity.   Convergent refinement II (convergent UML representation).

Activity owner, principal participants.   Assembly developer, lead developers.

Artifacts produced or refined.   Pattern-refined convergent business object model.

Guidelines and artifact/tool usage:

■ This second activity in the three-phase refinement process is also called *convergent UML representation* because it complements the business dimension with the structures to effectively represent both business and IT dimensions in UML. In this activity, the developer or developers from Convergent Refinement I sessions refine their results into a convergent UML model. Patterns from the OPEN Consortium (Henderson-Sellers 1998) are used to help ensure that trackable convergence takes place and that uniform refinement style is established across projects. Similar to the previous activity, this is a creative design process that cannot be 100 percent automated; however, it can be partially automated and significantly supported by an intelligent tool. This support is provided by the C-RAS module of the architectural IDE, which assists the designer with the process of pattern-driven refinement, design style checks, and other checks for completeness and quality. Details regarding the C-RAS tool support and the relevant aspects of the modeling style are covered in subsequent chapters. In particular, an example of the OPEN refinement patterns is shown in the C-RAS section of Chapter 7.

■ In this activity, the developer steps through the convergent business object model and refines each of the recorded responsibilities and collaborations of a CRC card. Each responsibility and collaborator is explicitly assigned a UML representation according to the defined (or configured in the case of a tool) UML modeling style. How such assignment takes place is determined by patterns mentioned earlier. The explicit assignment in the IDE according to patterns permits bidirectional trackability and convergence between the refinement stages.

■ After completion of this activity, the model has been detailed and partitioned to the point where the assembly developer can make effective assignments concerning resource ownership in due course of the project management workflow. Thus, at this point, further stages of refinement and implementation may be assigned to a number of component development teams.

Activity. Convergent refinement III (convergent UML completion).

Activity owner, principal participants. Lead developer, accessor developer, CEG.

Artifacts produced or refined. The UML model of convergent components has been refined and verified to the level of technical feasibility for a specific technology projection.

Guidelines and artifact/tool usage:

■ The third activity in the three-phase refinement process is known as *convergent UML completion* because it results in a UML representation that is complete enough to support automatic technology projection into a deployable system. To achieve this, the lead developers and accessor developers use the modeling style for one or more technology projections. This process of completion is actively supported by the C-REF module of the architectural IDE in conjunction with technology projection cartridges and their respective model verifiers.

■ The canonical development team starts by agreeing, together with the assembly developer, on the partitioning and unique ownership of the convergent components if not already completed in the previous phase. Accessors are usually allocated to accessor developers and other convergent components distributed among component developers. The relative responsibilities and interaction between these team members and other participants in the team follow the logic defined in the IT-organization model.

■ Once the developer knows which convergent components he or she is responsible for (resource owner), refinement can begin in the C-REF/Rose module. The first thing that the developer will notice on opening the detailed UML view is that much of the UML model has been completed behind the scenes by the architectural IDE. The IDE has accompanied each step of refinement with an automatic metamorphosis of the components according to the modeling style. In other words, the creative input of the developer thus far has been used by the architectural IDE to derive other models and properties. The developers now continue with this process of style-driven assisted modeling by setting key properties of the model at the UML level and letting the IDE derive other models and properties.

- The developer should now configure a particular technology projection cartridge in the architectural IDE if this has not already been done. As pointed out in Chapter 4, the technology projection cartridge extends the modeling style with aspects sensitive to a particular runtime infrastructure. The IDE uses this information to help the developer check or complete the model not only at the level of UML and J2EE/EJB standards (assuming the default J2EE/EJB modeling style), but also in terms of the capabilities (positive features and performance aspects) and constraints (the problems and limitations) of the particular infrastructure. It also adds defaults for infrastructure-specific properties that can be used reasonably to tune the generated system from the UML model.

Now the developer proceeds to refine the following four areas:

1. Business-relevant behavior (business dimension aspects) from the higher-level models is refined at the UML level. For example, exceptions that were noted in the business scenario models may now be detailed in the UML model according to the modeling style for exceptions. Similarly, the UML-level details of associations, multiplicities, and inheritance can now be completed in detail by the component developer. Business components are associated, for example, not only with each other, but also with their supporting utility components in the model. Examples of such utility components are logging sinks, specialized decoders, or device drivers.

   At this point, some projects may want to provide more detailed documentation to represent especially complex sequences of component interactions, for example. To do this, optional UML diagrams such as process model activity diagrams, sequence diagrams, and other activity diagrams may be created in the UML model. These are optional in nature because they are not necessary to generate the deployable infrastructure.

2. The accessor use-case scenarios are refined into accessor models. This normally begins by generating so-called default accessor models based on the existing business component models. Default accessor models may be generated automatically for common system access features such as viewing components, editing a component, querying and browsing lists of components, and so on. Based on these or in addition to these, custom accessors can be modeled and refined in UML according to the accessor modeling style.

3. To address specific physical requirements of the system, the IT dimension is tuned and the physical package structure of assemblies is defined in the UML model. Physical requirements concerning distribution, caching, querying, or database mapping may all be influenced by changing the J2EE/EJB properties of the components in the UML model. Based on the configured technology projection cartridge, every component has received defaults for these properties. These defaults may be changed to tune specific aspects of the runtime environment. During the generation phase, the technology projection interprets each of these tuning parameters, including combinatorial interactions with other parameters, and generates optimized features for the particular infrastructure. In addition to standard properties available from J2EE/EJB, separate property

sheets expose properties specific to the particular technology projection. Here also, the defaults in the UML may be changed to tune the specific added-value features of the respective implementation technology.

The developer then creates the assembly model, which consists of the physical partitioning of all other convergent components in the model into the deployment modules such as client-side JAR files, EJB JAR files, and Web archives (WARs). These are configured as physical components in the UML model with the help of modeling assistants.

Also, the developer may decide to repartition the IT dimension of a component to meet special distribution or query requirements. For example, EJB-dependent values may be split out to transport the state of an object between the client and server personalities of a component. Another such case would be the use of a special query-utility component to increase the performance of extensive, distributed queries. Such utility components often are generated by the technology projection cartridge to leverage special features of a particular application server.

4. Unit and component test aspects are modeled or configured to enable the automatic generation of test structures and test instrumentation. These aspects are covered in more detail in the test workflow section below.

In general, this refinement takes place as a series of development increments, each increment being a compressed iteration across the remaining workflows of the development process. In each of these compressed iterations, the model is verified, generated, and tested using the architectural IDE to provide timely feedback to all members of the development team. The UML model verifier is used frequently by the developer to check the style integrity, completeness, and technical feasibility of the model. Such verification permits the developer to make more extensive changes per increment before having to traverse the other workflows.

Refinement Continuity Across Workflows

Before moving to the implementation cycle workflow, it is important to address how continuity of refinement is achieved in the Convergent Architecture. The visibility of the business dimension and the IT dimension of components identified and refined in the ABD workflow is conserved in the subsequent implementation cycle and test workflows. In these workflows, refinement occurs in Java (or C++, COBOL, PL/1, and so on; Java is simply the reference example) using the Java IDE in the context of the architectural IDE. In the Java IDE, low-level business logic is added into the generated Java infrastructure. In a convergent system, adding source code is still part of the structured refinement process. The source code is another level of the model, visibly derived from the UML model. In the refinement process, the Java-level additions to the business dimension remain clearly visible and easily distinguishable from the generated business dimension and IT dimension aspects. This visibility is achieved by using intelligent *protected areas* in the Java code, as you will see in subsequent chapters.

The protected areas allow us to carry the model-driven paradigm and the clear separation of concerns into the code base. At the source-code level, the convergent component is still clear, and it is clear which aspects of this component were derived from the UML model. Everything outside a protected area is generated from a higher-level model; everything within the protected area is specified at the Java level of the model. The metamorphosis of the component is still visible: The model-driven approach does not dissipate when one gets to source code.

Each level of refinement and each view of the model, including its Java view, has its justification as a structured step in convergent refinement. This is because important things cannot be represented in UML. UML is, after all, just a level of abstraction. If we tried to represent everything in UML, then it would be just as complex as the machine code generated by compilers. Some aspects of the business dimension are best understood and represented at the Java level of the model, some are best understood and expressed further upstream in the UML model, and others are best understood and formulated as CRC cards in the top-level business model. The aspects best represented in Java are the low-level "if, then, else" aspects of business logic. This logic implements, for example, the conditional transitions that we captured upstream in the BOM scenario models or the complex algorithmic aspects of responsibilities described in the CRC cards.

In the Convergent Architecture, the Java (or C++, COBOL) compiler is viewed as just one of many model-driven automation steps. For example, the generator and technology projection cartridge (for one or more technologies) is used to get from the UML model to the Java level of the model, and the compiler (for one or more platforms) is used to get to the next level below Java. In fact, there are additional automation steps. On deploying an assembly, for example, the application server also generates masses of new code behind the curtain in order to complete the IT dimension in the context of the particular application-server environment. This application-server-specific automation step is driven by things (deployment descriptors and Java, for example) generated by the technology projection cartridge, which, in turn, is driven by the UML model.

To summarize the continuity across workflows, it can be said that the *model-driven development of a convergent system consists of a series of repeatable, style-driven stages of refinement and automation (metamorphosis) that begin with business modeling and progress consecutively through to the final runtime system.*

Implementation Cycle Workflow

The implementation cycle workflow describes the steps required during the stage of development following the ABD workflow. It is called a cycle because it is repeated quite often, beginning with the enhancement phase of a project and increasing in frequency through the iterations of the construction phase.

The implementation cycle begins in the Convergent Architecture with a mouse click. Based on the models developed in the ABD workflow, the generator module of the architectural IDE now takes over and generates somewhere between 50 and 90 percent of the environment required to build, test, and deploy the system further downstream.

The integrity of the generated code is the responsibility of the technology projection component (see Chapter 4 and the bonus chapter on the Web site).

The remaining percent of the system is low-level logic that is filled into the generated infrastructure by the developer. The environment generated from the UML model can be built, deployed, and tested immediately. However, since the Java-level business logic has not yet been implemented, many business-relevant features will not be completely functional. To add the Java-level (or C++, COBOL, and so on) logic, build the assembly, deploy the assembly, and test the assembly, a high-end programming environment, a Java IDE such as JBuilder, is leveraged. The complete configuration required to leverage the Java IDE is also generated from the UML model. Thus, after generation, the developer can load the generated artifacts automatically into the Java IDE and can get down to business immediately completing and testing business features. The individual tasks carried out by the developer during this cycle are described in the following activity.

Activity.   Model-driven implementation cycle.

Activity owner, principal participants.   Developer, test manager.

Artifacts produced or refined.   Assembly component or convergent components as defined by the IT organization (see Chapter 5) depending on the worker (assembly developer or component developer).

Guidelines and artifact/tool usage:

■ In this activity, the developer begins with results from the ABD workflow. These results consist of a UML model that has been verified for technical feasibility in the C-REF module of the architectural IDE. The next step is to generate the infrastructure and the environment for the implementation cycle using the C-GEN module of the IDE. To prepare for generation, the developer uses the dialog provided to configure details of the technology projection cartridges and other aspects of the project environment. For example, in addition to checking the configuration of the application server itself, the developer enters information pertaining to the database or persistent storage environment, the Java IDE environment, and the current operating system environment.

■ The developer then selects the UML model and activates the generator from the UML environment. Individual parts of the UML model or parts of the technology projection may be selected for generation. For example, to selectively generate the Web accessors, only the accessor cartridge is selected, and all the other cartridges are deselected for the generation run.

■ Once the generator is finished, the developer switches to the Java IDE and loads the generated project file (if this has not already been done by the Java IDE). At this point, the compile, build, and test cycle can be started right away using the generated infrastructure. This permits the developer to immediately test aspects derived from the UML model in the runtime environment. However, the business dimension is still incomplete, so not much business logic can be tested yet. The next step is to complete the business dimension in the Java IDE.

- To complete the business dimension and its interaction with the IT dimension, the developer edits protected areas that were generated into the Java/J2EE infrastructure. The location of these protected areas is also derived from the UML model. Depending on the quality and coverage of the modeling style and the technology projection cartridges (or extensions to these, respectively), the developer may have to edit protected areas within the IT dimension. In any case, anything written within the boundaries of protected areas remains unchanged across repeated generation runs.

- Implementation guidelines for hand coding also exist. These are the sentinels (see Chapter 7) that are defined or designated by the chief architect to govern the architecture-conform usage of certain technologies as required by the local instance of the Convergent Architecture. The default sentinel for the Java development kit, for example, contains a reference to widely accepted Java coding conventions found at java.sun.com/docs/codeconv/.

- Ensuring the testability of the components is a normal part of the implementation cycle workflow. Both unit tests and component tests are created and maintained by the developer as part of each convergent component. Similar to other artifacts, significant parts of these test artifacts can be generated from the UML model and completed in the Java IDE. The test workflow described later provides more information on test artifacts.

- At this point, the developer begins a rapid design and implementation cycle. Each cycle consists of an incremental increase in system capability and its commensurate test features. In each cycle, the developer moves back to the UML model, changes or extends the model, and regenerates the respective infrastructure.[3] The developer then proceeds to the Java IDE to add more custom code to the component and its test artifacts. The Java IDE is used to automatically compile, build, deploy, and run the components, including the accessors. The developer then runs the accessors and the test artifacts in the Java IDE to check the business and technical features of the system and to trace and debug any problems introduced during custom coding.

- In the later iteration or the construction phase, editing may be unnecessary. The developer or testers may want to regenerate, build, and test the system without accessing the UML tool or the Java IDE. This is especially true for automatic tests of assemblies and components, where entire models are checked out directly from the UCM pool and then generated, built, deployed, and tested without human intervention. Such automatic tests will be carried out on a regular basis, nightly, for example, once the project has matured well into the construction phase. To support the large-scale automatic testing of components, infrastructure, and tools, the technology projection cartridges also generate command-line scripts to carry out the cycle. Based on these scripts, command-line processing can be started by calling the generator (C-GEN module) from the command line to access the UML model (via the C-REF module) and generate the infrastructure. The scripts also provide command-line commands for the rest of the compile, build, deploy, and test cycles. The level of support for these phases depends, of course, on the particular technology projection cartridge.

■ Developers may need to modify or extend the capabilities of technology projection cartridges. This is done using the generator IDE module of the architectural IDE. A simple modification that is frequently made to a cartridge is, for example, to add the corporate logo and other graphics to the default HTML representers. As explained in Chapter 4, the HTML representer is the HTML front end generated by a cartridge. To modify the graphic design produced every time the generator is run, a developer or development tool expert may edit, test, and debug the new graphic design using the generator IDE. Once tested, this cartridge change may become part of the default cartridge to be used by all other projects. However, such changes to cartridges should only be made with consent of the chief architect. More details concerning the content of cartridges and their relationship to the architectural IDE are provided in the next two chapters.

Test Workflow

A mature model-driven approach significantly reduces the amount of code that must be tested. However, at least three good reasons remain as to why effective test coverage is needed. First, even the best UML models and their technology projections are not formal proof that the generated system will work as expected. Mature modeling and well-tested technology projection cartridges do reduce the source of error significantly, but one is never 100-percent sure until the system is tested. This uncertainty is inherent in the complexity of application-server and networked-system environments. Clearly, these servers and environments are themselves not without error. Second, any models and code entered by humans during the implementation workflow are subject to human oversight. Testing is the only effective way to check their correctness. Third, and most significant, we need to verify that the business representation, the business dimension, is really doing what we said it would. No matter how good we are at reducing errors, there will always be residual uncertainties—in the foreseeable future anyway—that can be reduced further only through adequate testing. The architectural style deals with this reality by encompassing a test workflow and its respective organizational and tool support.

Here again, the model-driven approach affords the most effective test coverage. Figure 6.9 illustrates this approach as supported by the architectural IDE. To the left are the UML models that conform to a well-defined modeling style. Thus, significant aspects of the test infrastructure can be derived and generated automatically from the models. Similar to the generation of default accessor models mentioned earlier, testing models also can be derived from the business component models—models used to generate other models.[4] Based on the default test models, a developer can add specialized testing features at the UML level. The right of the figure shows how test components, instrumentation, and the automation infrastructure are generated, as always, by

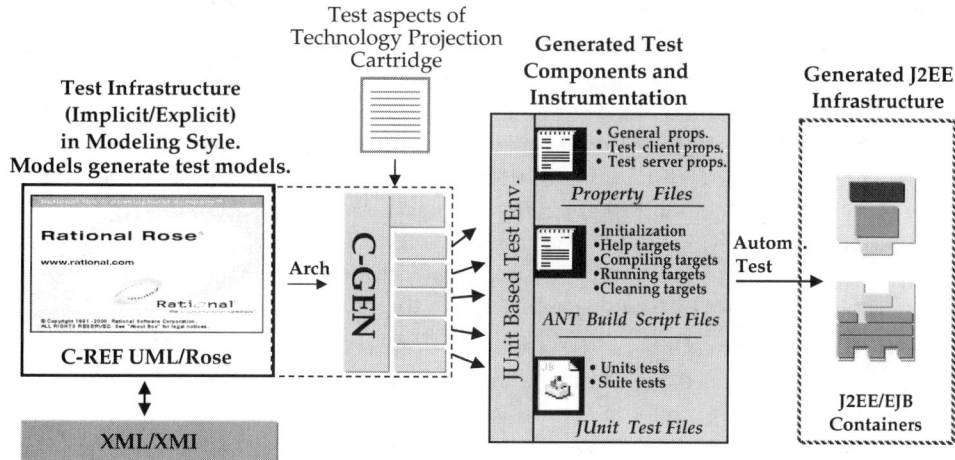

Figure 6.9 Model-driven test infrastructure. UML-driven (OCL) test generation, instrumentation, build, and runtime.

way of the technology projection cartridge. The generated infrastructure is now model-specific, enabling the test of both business logic and technical infrastructure. The level of automatically generated support for various types of tests is evolving rapidly and is, as always, dependent on the current state of the modeling style and particular technology projection.

The Convergent Architecture specifies the following test categories to enable optimal coverage and synergies during each phase of development:

- **Unit tests.**   These automate testing of individual technical units such as Java classes.

- **Component tests.**   These automate testing of entire convergent components.

- **Assembly tests.**   These automate testing of entire assemblies and their interactions with other assemblies (integration tests).

- **Interaction and response tests.**   These verify accessor use-case scenarios, user interfaces, and response performance.

- **Business flow and convergence tests.**   These check the fidelity of the system with respect to the business object model.

The test development and execution activity explains the tasks associated with each of these test categories.

Activity.   Test development and execution.

Activity owner, principal participants.   Lead developer, developer, test manager, tester.

Artifacts produced or refined.   Test models and environment, unit tests, component tests, assembly test plan, assembly tests, assembly test results report.

Guidelines and artifact/tool usage:

- Once the developer is sure that a particular unit in the UML model, a class, for example, is relatively long-lived, he or she creates *unit tests* to test this unit in the runtime environment. The structure of these unit tests may be modeled in UML, or the structure may be derived automatically from the model by the technology projection cartridge. For the J2EE/EJB technology projection, the JUnit (JUnit 2000) framework is used as a basis for testing, and the ANT (ANT 2000) framework is used to automate the tests. By stipulating JUnit up front in the process, both modeling style and technology projection can be tuned specifically for this framework.

- Based on the unit tests, the developer creates *component tests*. Component tests are suites of unit tests that test the sum of the features comprising a convergent component. In addition to testing the IT dimension and basic structures of the business dimension, business-logic tests occur at the component test level. The code required to test the business-logic aspects of the component is often as complex as the custom business logic itself. As such, it is currently added at the Java level in the Java IDE. However, the basis for these tests may be derived directly from the preconditions, postconditions, and invariants entered in the model for each operation of the component. These conditions and invariants were recorded as needed in the beginning in the convergent refinement II stage of the ABD workflow (using the C-REF module of the architectural IDE). If these preconditions, postconditions, and invariants have been specified using the Object Constraint Language (OCL) (Warmer 1999), then they are not only more concise than natural language, but they may, at some point in the future, also serve to generate business-level test logic. Significant progress is being made in the areas of formalizing OCL as part of a modeling style, thus enabling technology projections to automatically generate business-level test logic.

- The next level of testing happens at the assembly level. These are the *assembly tests*. In contrast to unit and component tests, which are developed continuously and run by developers in local test environments, assembly tests are specified and carried out carefully in conjunction with the test center organization. Late in the construction phase, they will be used by the test center to test both the assembly itself and significant interactions with other assemblies. The assembly tests are the ultimate level of automated testing. They are the basis for regression testing. The results of the assembly tests carried out in the test center organization determine whether an assembly is ready to be released into the transition phase. To this end, an assembly test plan is created by the test manager together with the assembly developer. The assembly developer is then responsible for ensuring that the assembly is testable according to this plan. For the most part, the assembly test consolidates and integrates the component tests. Thus, the assembly developer and test manager must ensure early on in the elaboration phase that all developers are working according to a common modeling style for the test framework. As stated earlier, in the Convergent Architecture, this modeling style and framework currently are based on JUnit and JUnit-compliant extensions for J2EE/EJB environments.

- Accessors that were modeled and built during the normal course of the ABD and implementation cycle workflows are extremely valuable test tools. Both custom and default accessors may be used by human testers or by regression testing tools such as Rational Robot to check two aspects of the system. First, they can be used for so-called interaction and response tests. These tests can be used to verify the access channels defined in the accessor use-case scenarios. More important, they may be used to test user interaction quality and system performance. The system performance is tested in this case at its most relevant point—the response times at the user interface. The automatically generated default accessors can be used right off the bat to test the general interaction and response behavior of the components without having to create any custom accessors.

- The second aspect tested using accessors is the fidelity of the system with respect to the initial business object model. This step is in fact also testing the degree of convergence that has been achieved, so it is called *business flow and convergence testing*. During the construction phase of the project, custom accessors have been derived and built from the scenario models developed in the BOM. Remembering back to the ABD workflow, each scenario model was

associated with a set of recorded run-throughs, each documenting a business-relevant path through the convergent system. The architectural IDE automatically documents this set of business paths in the form of state-transition tables. The tester or test recorder uses the accessors to test each of the documented paths through one or more state-transition tables. The results of these tests provide valuable feedback concerning the completeness of the convergent system, the quality of the current business dimension, and the ease of use of the system to support the intended business operations.

Documentation Workflow

Experience has shown that developing quality, high return on investment (ROI) documentation necessitates a dedicated support workflow that runs parallel to the critical development path. Above all, the same developers who are responsible for the critical development path cannot be expected to also be experts in documentation. Also, normally they are supposed to apply their special development skills to the critical path, not to documentation. Producing reasonable documentation is a highly skilled job of its own. Anyone without the proper skills and focus will produce poor documentation, which, in turn, may cast an unjustified shadow on the entire development results. To ensure that high-quality documentation is produced at lowest risk and lowest cost, the Convergent Architecture takes the following basic approach.

First, the organizational coordination of a worker with the proper skills is instated in the IT-organization model: the technical writer. Second, the model-driven approach and the architectural IDE are designed to produce much of the documentation automatically as an explicit side effect of component metamorphosis. The focus on convergence in the architecture creates an easily understood stream of artifacts that serves as the system documentation. Clearly, if the system can be generated from the UML model, then the model is accurate documentation of the system design. And if the UML model was visibly refined from a previous model, then we have the next level of design documentation, and so forth, all the way up to the highest-level business model. Thus, after style-conform development of a convergent system, the artifacts managed by the architectural IDE document the business design, not just the system design—the essence of convergence. Other important synergies also emerge in this constellation. The developer is in fact producing a whole lot of the documentation. The developer is essentially unaware that much of the documentation is being produced as a side effect of the critical development path. The approach also ensures that the documentation automatically reflects the real state of the design and its resulting system at all times.

The documentation preparation and production activity covered here describes the steps required to ensure the quality of the design documentation and to produce the end-user documentation for an assembly component.

Activity.   Documentation preparation and production activity.

Activity owner, principal participants.   Technical writer, developer, test manager, deployment manager.

Artifacts produced or refined.   Documentation development set, design documentation, end-user documentation.

Guidelines and artifact/tool usage:

- The documentation preparation and production activity is driven by the technical writer (the writer) as participant in every canonical development team. During the iterations of the enhancement phase, the writer begins work with the assembly developer to develop a documentation roadmap for the assembly. Then the writer works with each developer to plan his or her contribution to the documentation set in each phase. When properly planned up front, this contribution is not a particular burden on the developers; it simply specifies and coordinates how models are documented. The intent is to improve the quality of the models and to produce material for the documentation as a side effect. The writer ensures that each developer does the following.

- First, for each stable model element created by the developer, a description should be entered in the places provided by the architectural IDE. This includes documenting preconditions, postconditions, invariants, and other details of the business dimension and IT dimension in the respective view of the convergent model. The partitioning and structure for these documentation entries are provided by the architectural IDE. For example, preconditions and postconditions have their own editors. It is important to note that the developer does not have to document anything already covered by the architectural style itself: The principles and structures of the architecture are already clear across all projects, as is the modeling style and the technology projection for convergent components. All these are already documented. The developer just has to address his or her particular usage of the style. The developer and writer can use the verifiers in the architectural IDE to check that the elements of the model have been documented.

- Based on the UML model, the technology projection cartridge generates code with documentation in the standard JavaDoc format. When adding custom Java code, the developer may need to extend these JavaDoc entries to more precisely describe the behavior.

- *Design documentation*. Once the preceding tasks are completed, the models in the architectural IDE serve as ample design documentation. If required, special reports and special statistical views of the convergent design can be generated based on the information in the architectural IDE. The information exists and is easily accessible through the various views provided by the architectural IDE itself or by external tools via Java and XML, for example. *The model is the documentation of a convergent (business and software) design.* If this is not the case, then something is awry because this is one of the principal goals of the architectural style.

- The *end-user documentation* is a special compilation and extension of the design documentation for end users of the system. To create these documents, the writer derives the basic usage of the system from the existing accessor models and the look and feel of the accessors themselves. Little or no additional input is needed from the developers. As part of the end-user documentation, the writer begins developing tutorials for the end users during the construction phase of the project. This task has an important side effect to further increase the ROI of the documentation workflow: The writer is testing the usability of the system from the perspective of the end user. By developing tutorial documentation, the writer provides the assembly developer with early, impartial feedback concerning the usability of the system.

- The writer also produces online help documents. The end-user documentation serves as a single documentation source from which the online help is produced automatically. This is to prevent the online help from becoming a branch of the documentation that must be synchronized continuously with the main trunk of documentation. Such branches are error-prone and costly. The single-source approach is not as simple as one might think but is indeed possible with the reference tools defined in the IT-organization model (see Chapter 5). Using these tools, the online help becomes a by-product of a central documentation stream and does not constitute an extra documentation effort.

- As stipulated in the IT-organization model, all projects create documentation according to a single documentation style. This style is defined in the *documentation development set* created by a technical writer in the PET organization during the IT-environment workflow. Documentation templates and style guides for a documentation development set are publicly available for FrameMaker, the reference documentation tool in the Convergent Architecture.

Deployment and Monitoring Workflow

Deployment and monitoring, although directly in the critical path, turn out to be fairly simple in the Convergent Architecture—who said it has to be hard! This is primarily due to progress made in recent years in the area of standards-based application servers. When used properly, such application servers can provide a stable, high-performance, easy-to-manage platform that far surpasses that of many mature mainframe environments.

The trick is not just to install an application server, but also to leverage the powerful features of these new server infrastructures. Several aspects of the convergent components and the architectural IDE help developers and operators use these features to reduce deployment effort and risks while improving the monitoring and adjustment capabilities of the system. The deployment and monitoring activity covered here describes how participants on the canonical development team contribute to achieve these capabilities and how the workers in the operational systems organization use these capabilities.

Activity.   Deployment and monitoring activity.

Activity owner, principal participants.   Assembly developer, deployment manager, assembly operator, container operator, user support specialist, component developers.

Artifacts produced or refined.   Assembly component, application server environment.

Guidelines and artifact/tool usage:

- This activity is driven by the assembly developer and begins in the elaboration phase. Later, once the assembly component has been deployed into the operational systems organization, the assembly operator takes over the responsibility for proactive monitoring and adjustment of the operational assembly as well as for providing feedback to the assembly developer.

- In the late iterations of the elaboration phase, the assembly developer works with the deployment manager to define the special installation requirements, monitoring accessors, instrumentation, and model-driven tuning requirements from the operational systems organization. As participant on the canonical development team, the deployment manager represents the entire operational system's organization and may solicit direct participation from other members of this organization for this task. The significant development aspects to be addressed in this context are as follows:

    - Above and beyond the type of application server envisioned for the operational environment, there will be special requirements and constraints concerning the existing operational environment. These requirements usually will affect the development of the assembly installation set and may affect the tuning of the assembly model at the UML level.

■ In addition to standard application-server features that are set in the UML model, a particular system environment may require special instrumentation to enhance monitoring and logging capabilities. This proprietary instrumentation can be activated via a separate module in a technology projection cartridge for a particular environment without polluting the standard-based aspects of the UML model. If these features need to be adjusted at the UML model level, then the modeling style also can be extended modularly to expose these features in the UML model view of the architectural IDE.

■ Special accessors and utility components may be desired to allow a portable diagnosis or runtime tuning at the level of convergent components, regardless of the underlying application-server infrastructure or the particular access channel.

■ Assembly components are designated as the intelligent deployment units in the architecture. In the default J2EE/EJB technology projection, these units are enterprise archives (EARs). In the case of high-end J2EE/EJB application servers, EARs may be deployed automatically and configured into the J2EE/EJB containers via several paths, each path accommodating a particular phase of development and its deployment requirements. Assembly components can be generated to support three deployment paths: an ANT-script-driven deployment to be used for automated test cycles (such as assembly tests), a Java-IDE-driven deployment to support the implementation cycle workflow within the test environment, and a release-level deployment via the console of the operational application server to support the transition workflow and operational deployment.

■ After release, the steady-state operation of the assembly is handled by the assembly operator in coordination with the container operator. Two aspects are important when considering runtime monitoring and the adjustments to an assembly as a result of monitoring:

■ Some tuning parameters, such as EJB transaction modes and caching parameters, which were set in the UML model and generated into the runtime infrastructure, may be modified in the runtime EJB container environment from the monitoring console. Based on changes in the runtime environment, these parameters may require short- or long-term adjustments. In the case of long-term adjustments, a change is also fed back to the assembly developer for a permanent change in the source model for the next release. More important, if a change in the runtime environment is dubious or uncertainty exists regarding its possible side effects, the assembly developer can provide proactive, high-quality advice based on the originating UML model.

- The convergent components are visible in the management console of the application server. Here again, their convergence with the upstream models simplifies the monitoring and feedback channels. All stakeholders can communicate rapidly and unambiguously the source of problems to the responsible organizations. This is so because the convergent component is visible, so its resource owner, beginning with the assembly developer, is also clear. Also, the component in question can be located and inspected easily at any position along the development stream. This enables more rapid and professional responses to problems and suggestions from the field.

- Lastly, feature requests and major change requests may arise during the deployment and monitoring activity. Requests not willingly absorbed by assembly development teams are relayed to the requirement manager, as described in the global requirement management activity previously.

Summary

This chapter covered the system development process aspect of the Convergent Architecture. This is known as the CA process and is the third and last component in the development model. The introduction pointed out the rest of the architectural style, which enables both the optimization and simplification of the development process. This simplification is due to the inherent continuity between all elements of the style, a property referred to as *reference-frame continuity*.

The CA process is not a new development process; instead, it is a derived refinement of several other modern process frameworks and methodologies. Above all, it is a style-specific instance of the RUP (Kruchten 1998). In addition, it was influenced by OPEN (Graham 1997), EPM (Gilb 1988/1999), and catalysis (D'Souza 1999).

As an instance of RUP, the CA process consists of workflows that are subdivided into activities. The workflows are organized in terms of two major categories:

- **Preparatory and cross-project workflows.**   These workflows are not associated with any particular project. They are initiated before the first development project and act in a cross-functional manner across all projects.

- **Canonical project workflows.**   Similar to the canonical development team presented in Chapter 5, the canonical project workflow describes the development process from the perspective of the canonical development team.

Each of these categories was described in terms of the workers involved, the results produced, and the tools used to achieve these results. In addition, guidelines were presented within each activity outlining the tasks carried out by each worker and the usage tools employed to support the tasks.

The development model is now complete. The next chapter provides detail on how the architectural IDE supports the development model. The final chapter presents a tutorial to show how all the parts work together based on a concrete example using the architectural IDE. In this example you will see how key features of the architectural style work together to provide tangible advantages in a real-world environment.

In addition, the bonus chapter on the Web site provides complete details of the technology projection component in the form of a reference manual.

The Architectural IDE

Automating the architecture.

The third and fourth main features of an information technology (IT) architectural style as realized by the Convergent Architecture (refer to Figure 1.1) are the full-coverage tool suite and the formal technology projections. The focus of this chapter is the tool suite.

In the previous chapters we saw how the architectural integrated development environment (IDE) plays a central role in supporting and simplifying various aspects of the Convergent Architecture. Up to this point, the perspective has been from the various topics of the development model. The support provided by the IDE was pointed out with respect to the local topic of each section. Although important, the local perspective does not present the overall picture of how all these things work together. This chapter takes a close look at the sum of the parts: the interdependence of the individual pieces. It also analyzes some aspects not covered from the local perspectives of previous chapters. These aspects include the integrative and flow characteristics of the architectural IDE that enable it to better support the architecture as a whole instead of only covering parts of a development flow. Figure 7.1 summarizes the coverage of the architectural IDE with respect to the Convergent Architecture (CA) process.

The principal objective of the architectural IDE is to automate and assist the critical-path workflows in the context of the entire development model. In the figure, the critical-path workflows are shown as they progress with time from left to right. Situated below each workflow are major categories of artifacts that must be created, integrated,

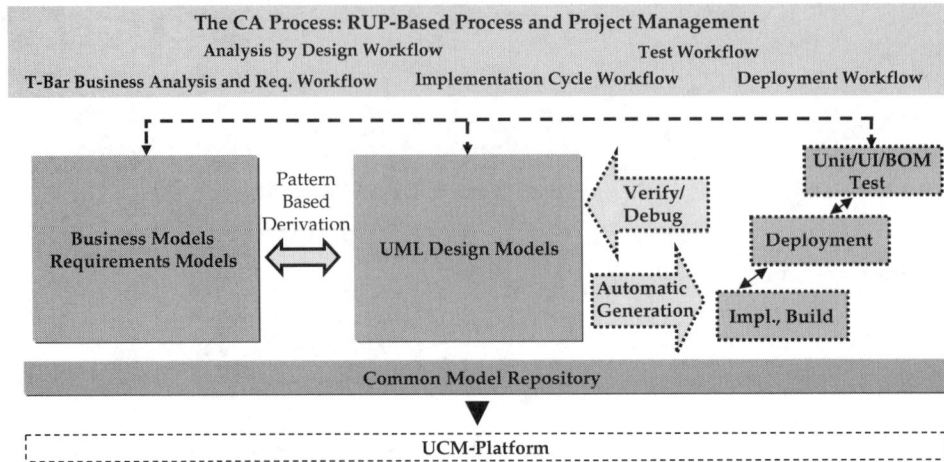

Figure 7.1 Architectural IDE: Critical path coverage. Covering the critical-path workflows.

and manipulated during the workflows. Analyzing the figure, we can briefly summarize the requirements on the architectural IDE as follows:

Concerning business and requirements models. The T-bar business analysis and requirements workflow requires tools to easily record and manipulate business structures and flows. The modeling activities in this workflow are highly interactive. Thus, the tool must help a designer to rapidly record and structure significant amounts of business information without hindering the dynamics of group-analysis sessions. The resulting models should then be equally valuable as a source of business information and for convergent refinement into software systems.

Concerning a common model repository. The business and requirements models should initiate a trackable thread of information and design refinement across all other workflows. To support this thread, both business and technical design information should be saved in a well-defined central format (Unified Modeling Language, or UML) or common model repository. This repository must be open to incremental exchange and integration at any time with other tools (XMI/XML, open Java API).

Concerning UML design models. The creation of UML models according to the analysis-by-design workflow should proceed in an automated or assisted manner using the patterns defined by the architectural style. Further automation should help the developer refine UML models according to the well-defined modeling style. This process of tool-assisted modeling should continue until the model is sufficiently complete to permit the automatic generation of all those aspects of a software system that can be reasonably represented in UML (as defined by the modeling style). To enable the generation of high-value artifacts, the tools must permit the developer to automatically verify and debug the UML model according to the requirements of the modeling style and the requirements of the target deployment environment.

Concerning implementation, build, deployment, and test artifacts. Significant portions of these artifacts can be generated automatically from any UML design models that conform to the modeling style. This generation occurs according to a technology projection that has been designed to map a style-conform UML model to a particular technology. Thus, the IDE must support the pragmatic, flexible configuration of technology projections and their automatic use in an incremental development process. Lastly, the tools must help developers create new technology projections or modify and extend existing technology projections.

The rest of this chapter shows how an architectural IDE meets or exceeds these high-level requirements. It also illustrates the individual features of the architectural IDE that were referred to in previous chapters on the development model. First, however, we need to see how the basic categories and requirements from Figure 7.1 are mapped to concrete modules of a real-world architectural IDE. This is done in Figure 7.2, which introduces the main modules of the *ArcStyler*, an architectural IDE as defined by the Convergent Architecture. The figure positions these modules of the IDE with respect to the critical-path workflows and the supporting workflows of the CA process. It also shows some of the major tools that are currently encapsulated or explicitly coordinated by the IDE: Rational Rose and JBuilder, J2EE/EBJ application servers, Web infrastructure, and so on.

The following sections describe each of these modules, one module per section:

- The convergent business object modeler (C-BOM)
- The federated UML/XML model repository (C-MOD)
- The convergent pattern refinement assistant (C-RAS)

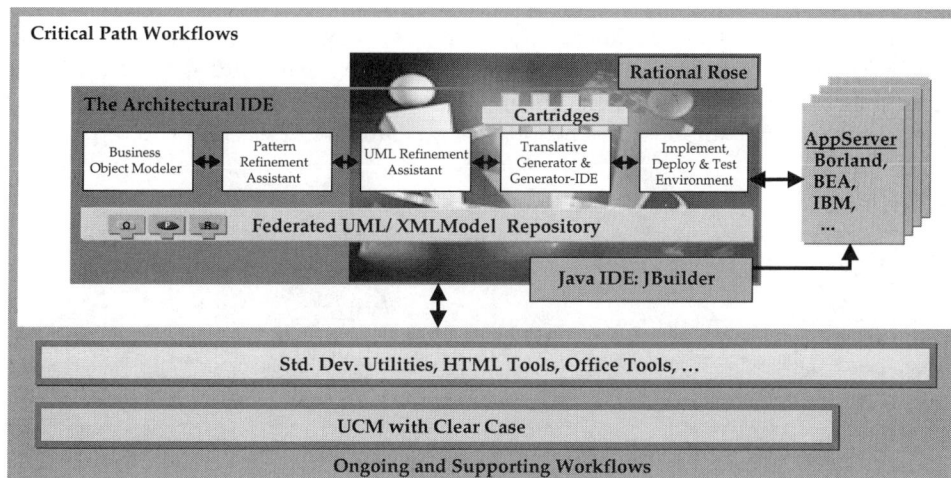

Figure 7.2 The modules and environment of the architectural IDE.

- The convergent UML refinement assistant (C-REF) with Rational Rose
- The convergent translative generator (C-GEN)
- The convergent generator IDE (C-GEN-IDE)
- The convergent implement, deploy, and test environment (C-IX) with JBuilder and a J2EE application server

Since the architectural IDE covers a whole lot of ground, the overview will be somewhat selective. To maintain the focus, each section is limited to one or two screenshots that exhibit several of the most style-relevant features of the module. Based on the screenshot, I explain how the module supports the development model of the architectural style. Only the highlights and the most critical features are explained; many features of the tool modules are not covered. Additional information at the user's guide or a user's reference level is available on the Convergent Architecture Web site.

The architectural IDE leverages a specific set of best-of-breed tools in its standard constellation (in particular, Rational Rose and JBuilder). These tools were selected to enable the most effective overall platform. However, as a pure Java component environment itself, the IDE is not inextricably coupled with these technologies. Alternatives to this particular set of embedded tools are conceivable.

The Convergent Business Object Modeler (C-BOM)

The C-BOM module (see Figure 7.3) supports both the T-bar and analysis-by-design workflows. It is used to capture and organize the business requirements and the business model. Figures 7.4 and 7.5 show its two primary views, first the CRC modeling view to capture the business components and then the corresponding scenario modeling view to capture the business dynamics. Together these views constitute a contract-based design.

The teams in the T-bar and analysis-by-design sessions record convergent components in the form of CRC cards, as shown in the figures. The CRC cards are used to record the business responsibilities, collaborators, private ownership, and inheritance relationships of the components. The tabs of each card are designed to hold the infor-

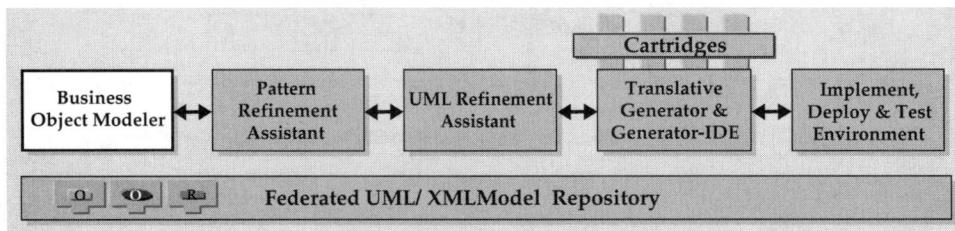

Figure 7.3 Orientation of the C-BOM module.

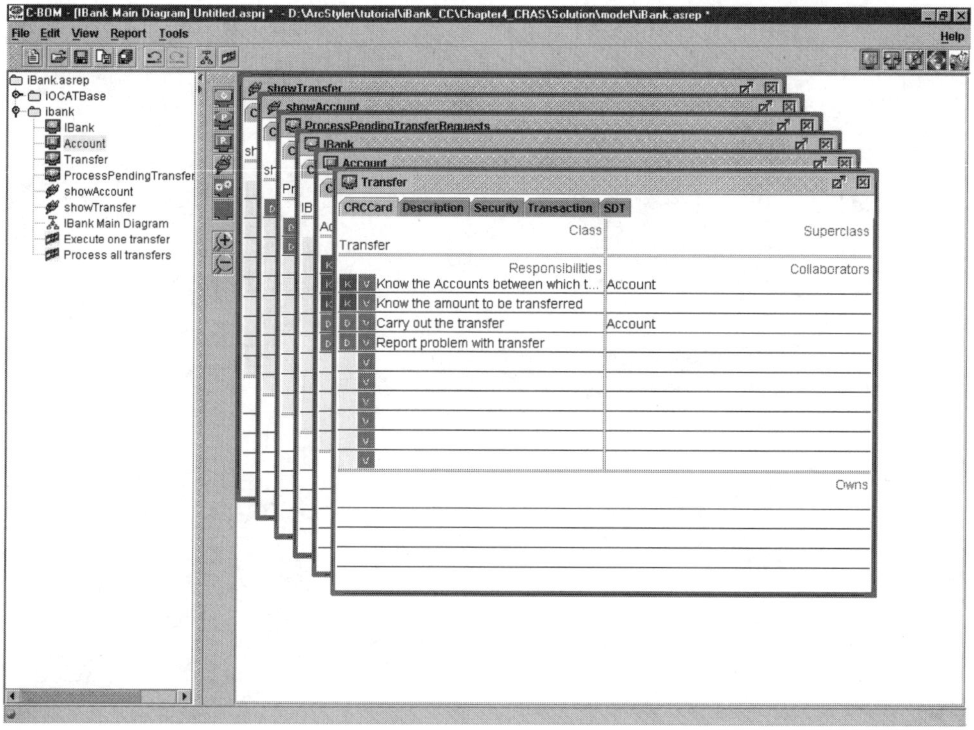

Figure 7.4   Business object modeling.

mation on both documentation and special requirements in areas such as security, migration, coordination with other components, and so on.

The hierarchy browser to the left of the figure serves to organize the design into logical groupings corresponding to organizations and assemblies. In addition, the scenario models and recorded run-throughs are organized in the hierarchy browser. The hierarchy browser remains visible throughout the entire development cycle in all tool modules. Each module of the IDE will show the hierarchy containing the artifacts from the previous module plus the additional, module-specific artifacts. This allows convergence to be tracked in both directions along the development path.

Figure 7.5 shows the scenario model view of the C-BOM module. It is used by the teams to investigate and record the business dynamics in terms of component message flow, conditional transitions, and visual run-throughs.

This figure exhibits a scenario model for the "Execute one transfer" scenario. Each node constitutes a contract between two components. It records a significant business action and how this business action is handled by one of the components in the CRC view. The scenario node documents the client component of the action and documentation describing the action. It also records the server component that fulfills the action as well as the particular responsibility of the server component that is used. Different paths through the model are determined by the transition conditions, as shown by the

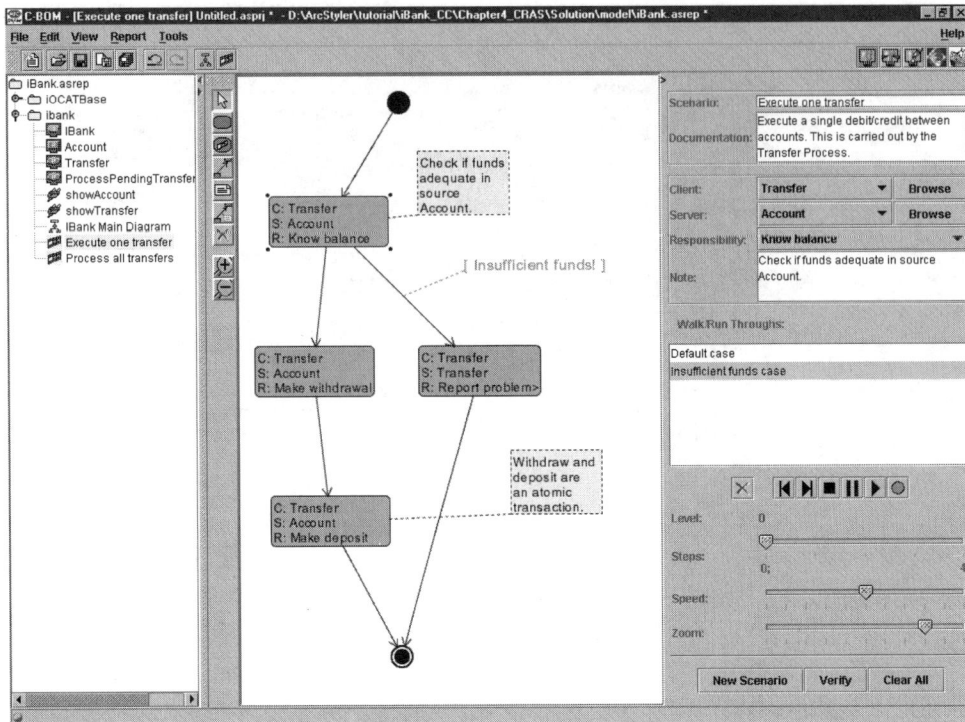

Figure 7.5 Use-case scenario modeling.

transition "Insufficient Funds" in the model. The paths in the scenario models allow designers to visually document the precise contract behavior among business components for any or all important business cases.

The run-through console shown to the right of the figure is used to record and store any number of business-relevant paths through the system. Each run-through can be stored and visually replayed at any time. These run-throughs are used to generate detailed state flow tables (SFTs) at the end of the session. As pointed out in the CA process, the SFTs play an important role in subsequent testing of the business system.

Both the CRC and scenario model views have verifiers. Each verifier checks the integrity of the view according to the contract-based business modeling style. As pointed out in the CA process, this modeling style is based on widely accepted concepts of responsibility-driven design. At this level of design, the modeling style is perennial and independent of a particular technology projection component.

The verifier also can be used to check the completeness and cleanliness of the model. The results of the modeling sessions are stored automatically in the federated UML/XML model repository (discussed later). In addition, consolidated HTML/XML reports and documentation of the model may be generated at any time from the C-BOM module. Once the run-throughs have been recorded and verified, these reports constitute the signoff documents for the business model. At the end of a business modeling session, the developer may move on to the next stage of refinement by activating the C-RAS module via its respective button in the toolbar. The buttons for each of the currently enabled modules of the architectural IDE are shown in the toolbar at the upper right of the figure.

The Federated UML/XML Model Repository (C-MOD)

The Federated UML/XML model repository (see Figure 7.6) automatically integrates and coordinates the results from the various modules and their respective views into one shared UML/XML model. The repository is a Java implementation of the UML foundation metamodel that accommodates input and output via UML-based Java interfaces as well as XML/XMI. The UML foundation metamodel is extended by UML-compliant profiles to support the modeling styles of the Convergent Architecture. The repository is integrated and synchronized with the repositories of other tools embedded by the IDE, in particular with Rational Rose.

The UML repository is invisible to the user of the architectural IDE except in a few well-defined areas as follows: First, a repository browser lets the developer view the precise contents and UML structure of the repository at any time. The user may import and export the entire model or portions of the model (merge) in standardized UML/XML format according to the OMG/UniSys XMI standard. The import or export is carried out via a menu in the architectural IDE.

Second, just as other IDE modules, the C-GEN and C-GEN-IDE both access the repository via Java programming interfaces and scripting interfaces. This scripting interface is used, for example, from the C-GEN module during infrastructure generation or from the C-GEN-IDE when extending and testing the technology projection cartridge.

Third, the C-MOD also may be used from any Java program via its Java application programming interface (API). This API is essentially an exposure of the UML metamodel and the additional UML-compliant extensions in Java. It is documented in JavaDoc and, aside from being used by the default modules of the architectural IDE, is used by a variety of other modules and programs for special tasks. Information and the

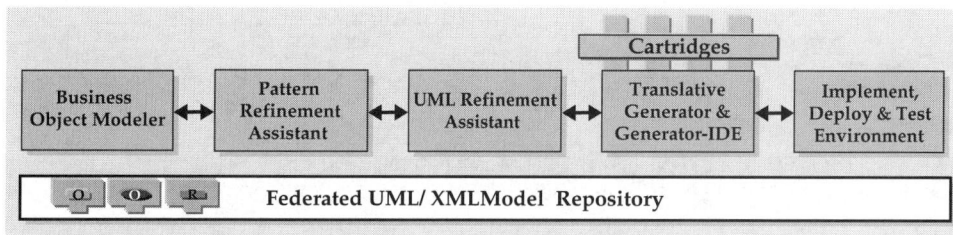

Figure 7.6   Orientation of the C-MOD module.

availability of such special modules, known as *reusable assets,* are provided on the Convergent Architecture Web site.

The Convergent Pattern Refinement Assistant (C-RAS)

The C-RAS module (see Figure 7.7) supports primarily the convergent UML refinement activity of the analysis-by-design workflow. It is used by a developer to further refine the business object model from the C-BOM module into a UML model according to the currently enabled modeling style-J2EE/EJB by default. The tool assists the designer in achieving style—conform convergence by channeling the development according to documented refinement patterns. Figures 7.8 and 7.9 show the C-RAS module and an example of one of the OPEN refinement patterns used by the module.

Figure 7.8 illustrates the refined state of the same model presented in the C-BOM section earlier. Here again, the hierarchy browser to the left of the figure shows the convergent components. When expanded, each component reveals its current state of refinement from the particular perspective of the C-RAS module. Note that the same business objects are still visible, but significant detail has been added. Each part of the CRC card for each convergent component is now displayed in the browser. In the figure, the account's responsibility for knowing/visible, "Know balance," is selected. To the right, in the work area, the results of this selection can be seen.

In the work area, an overview of the refined "Know balance" is shown. It can be seen that this responsibility has been mapped to an attribute and an operation, both residing in the default facet of the account component—an OPR resource component. Note that the facet is labeled with <none>. This manifests that the mapping patterns together with the J2EE-based modeling style understand that J2EE/EJB components currently only provide single interfaces. Facets are a component feature stemming from the CORBA component metamodel. They exist to support components with multiple interfaces, provided it is allowed by the modeling style (with its corresponding technology projection). In this case, the default J2EE/EBB projection is used. It is important to note that intelligent sensitivity toward the particular deployment infrastructure begins here. If the designer was allowed to model multiple interfaces, that is,

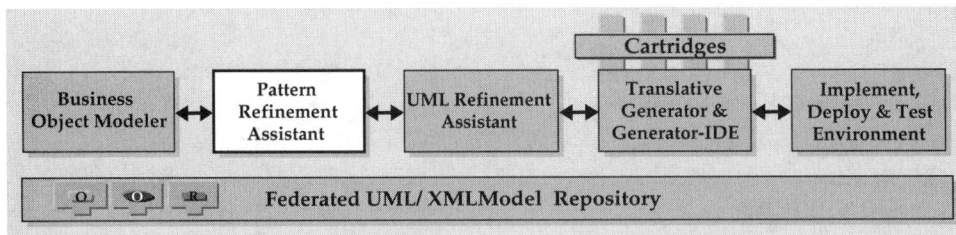

Figure 7.7 Orientation of the C-RAS module.

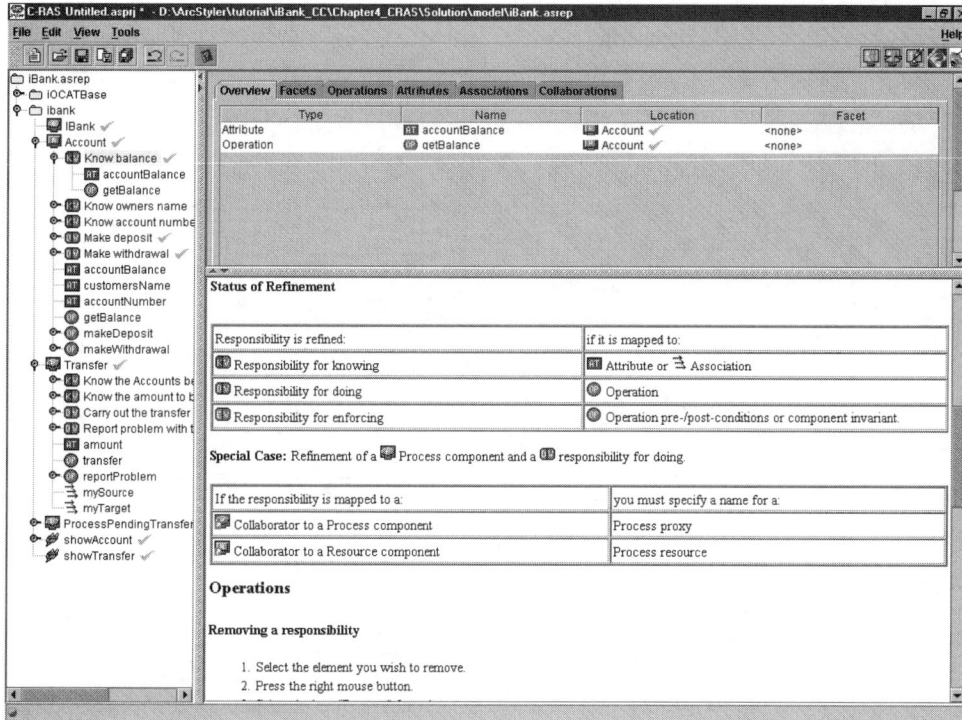

Figure 7.8 Pattern-based refinement.

facets, then the model could not be mapped cleanly (neither automatically nor by hand) to the intended J2EE/EJB infrastructures. By adding this constructive foresight, the developer is assisted in creating a model that can be used to effectively drive all downstream stages of development, many of them automatically.

The tabs at the top of the work area show how a developer refines a selected responsibility. Each tab presents the paths available for refinement according to the refinement patterns. One of these patterns is shown in Figure 7.9. This is the pattern for UML refinement of public/visible responsibilities from CRC cards in the business object model.

The pattern in the figure indicates that a public/visible responsibility for knowing, which corresponds to the currently selected responsibility, may be refined to visible operations or properties (attributes) of a component. When proceeding farther down in the pattern, it can be seen how these operations and attributes may be further refined. These refinement options are made available to the developer by the C-RAS for the selected responsibility. The developer then uses the tabs to create the required set of operations and attributes and to configure their details. Such details are, for example, the attribute's name, the operation's parameter list, or its preconditions and postconditions.

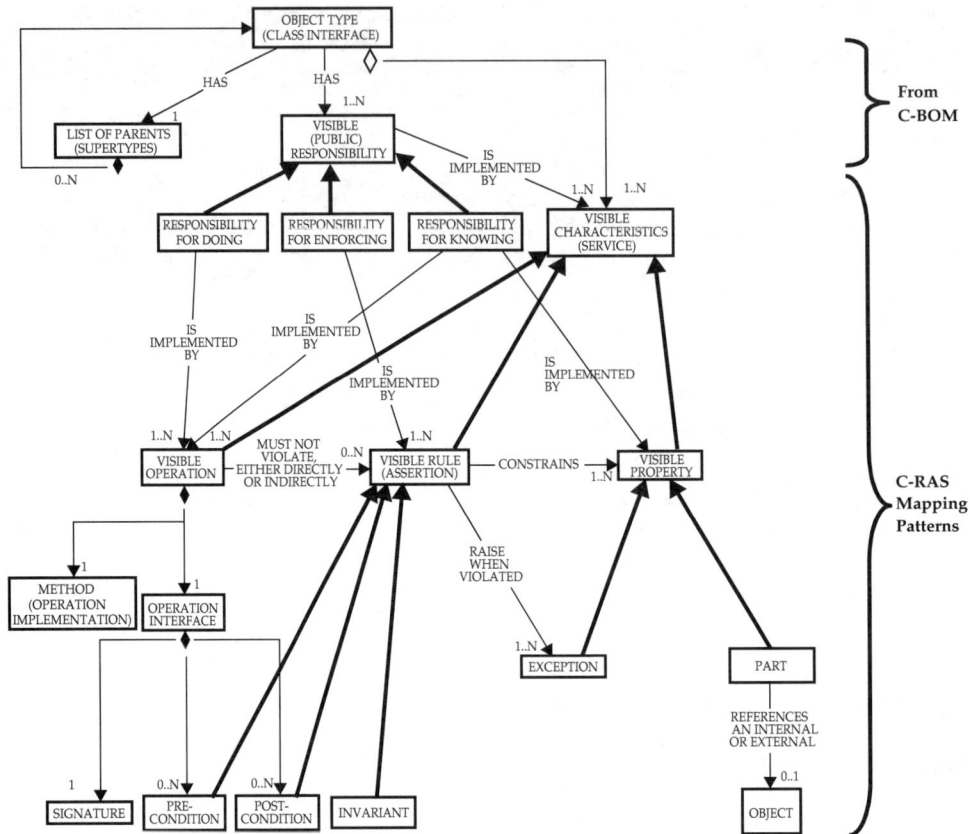

Figure 7.9 C-RAS-OPEN pattern example.
With permission (Henderson-Sellers 1998, Fig. 2.3)

The lower part of the workspace provides directions and explanations to the developer concerning each type of refinement according to the patterns. As in all modeling modules, a verifier helps the developer see the integrity and status of refinement for each entity in the model. The entities marked by a green check have been sufficiently refined to satisfy the pattern. A red exclamation point means that refinement is still incomplete for that entity. The developer does not have to refine all entities before proceeding to the next module; he or she can come back later and complete the model in increments, each time removing a new set of red exclamation points. This process can begin with changes at the C-BOM level as well, of course. At the end of each refinement session, the developer moves on to the next stage of refinement by activating the C-REF/Rose tool via the Rose button. This button is shown at the upper right of the figure in the toolbar of the architectural IDE.

The Convergent UML Refinement Assistant (C-REF)

The C-REF module (see Figure 7.10) embeds Rational Rose and supports the later phases of the analysis-by-design workflow and all model-driven activities downstream from the analysis-by-design workflow. It assists the developer during UML refinement of all convergent components according to the currently enabled modeling style— J2EE/EJB by default. It is also used to configure and manage model-driven activities (generate, build, test, deploy) from the perspective of a project team as well as from the perspective of the special configuration requirements of a particular installation.

Figures 7.11 through 7.14 exhibit several aspects of UML model refinement. This begins with a diagram of a completed business component model in UML, followed by a look at how details of the modeling style are managed in this module. Figures 7.13 and 7.14 are corresponding Internet accessor and process models in UML.

The figures shown thus far in this chapter originate from a development tutorial called *iBank*. The screenshots used from here on out in this chapter are taken from a completely different business case, a system for trip planning and flight booking. The trip-planning case bears witness to the universal applicability of the convergent components and the architectural IDE across business organizations and domains and allows me to show some more complex aspects of the architectural IDE. More extensive tutorial examples are also available on the Convergent Architecture Web site.

Figure 7.11 exhibits the trip-planning model in the C-REF/Rose module. In the C-REF module, Rational Rose is embedded as a component within the architectural IDE. The C-REF module (a Java system) adds numerous features to assist the architecture-conform use of Rose. In other words, Rose is configured and actively "driven" by the C-REF module to support the UML-related stages of development according to the architectural style. The intelligent feedback and automation provided by the C-REF ensure a more effective, higher-quality approach both at the individual developer level and at the cross-project or corporate architecture level.

Here again, the hierarchy browser in the C-REF displays the convergent components that were created and refined in the C-BOM and C-RAS modules. They remain visible so that their evolution can be tracked in both directions along the development path. The UML-level adornments of the components are now also visible. Many of

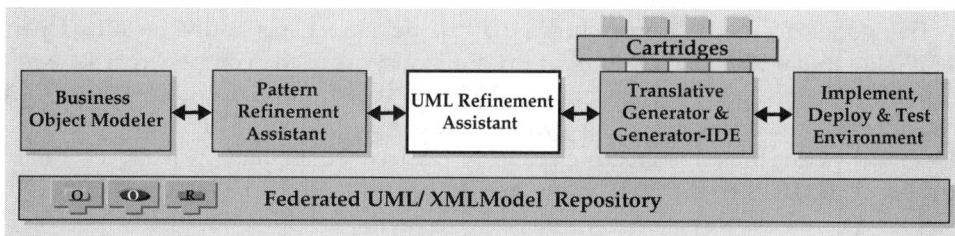

Figure 7.10   Orientation of the C-REF module.

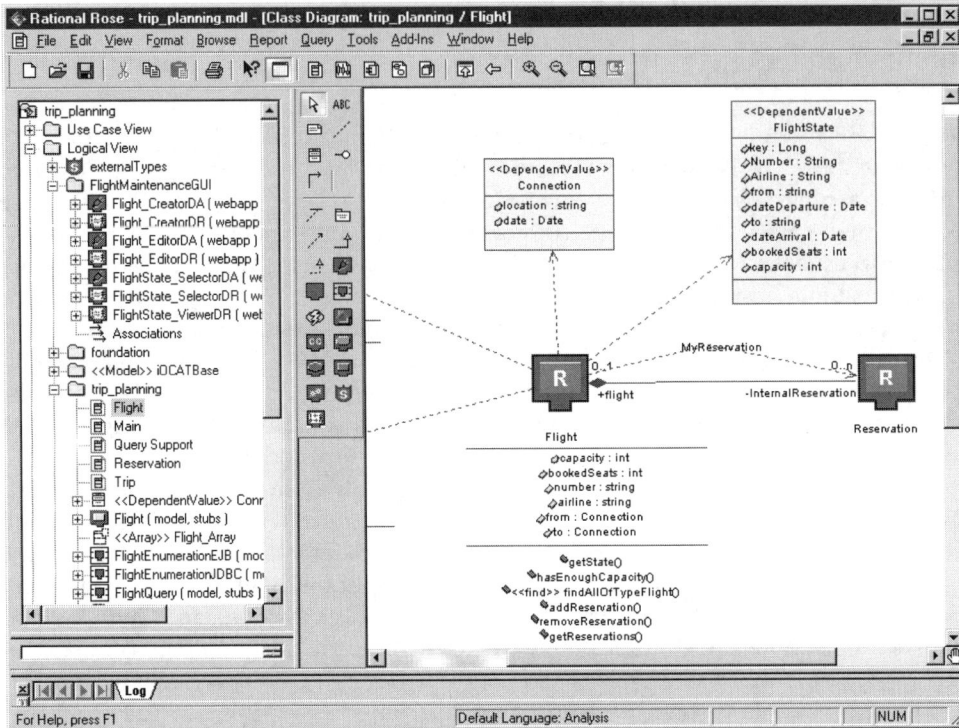

Figure 7.11   Convergent J2EE/UML refinement.

these adornments were created automatically by the C-RAS or via the wizards and modeling assistants in the C-REF. In addition to the elements imported from the C-RAS step, the developer can add new convergent components directly in the C-REF. Such newly added components are subsumed automatically to the C-RAS and C-BOM levels via the common repository. They can then be completely documented at the C-RAS and C-BOM levels later. This means that the developer can begin designing in the C-REF/Rose if appropriate for the task at hand. Beginning at the UML level is often reasonable when developing assemblies of utility components, assemblies consisting mostly of accessors, or for ad hoc testing and evaluation of alternatives in early investigation stages of the project.

The workspace in the figure shows that the developer has added an EJB DependentValue in the UML model to optimize the transport of the component's state in a distributed environment. As part of the J2EE/EJB specification, DependentValues are clearly addressed by the modeling style and the corresponding technology projections. This means that instead of creating arbitrary UML constellations, such aspects can be created or modified in the UML model according to the modeling style and then verified for a configured technology projection—a prerequisite for the extensive generation of a high-value infrastructure. How the C-REF supports each of these style-based enhancements is exemplified by the Figure 7.12.

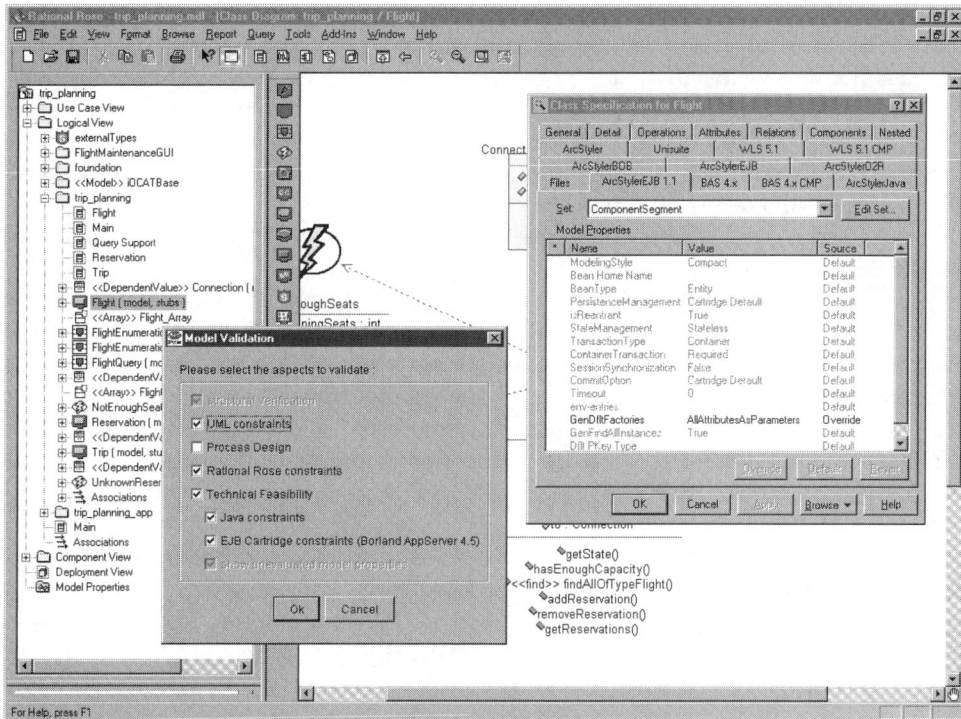

Figure 7.12   Details of the default J2EE/EJB modeling style.

In this figure, the convergent resource component "Flight" from Figure 7.11 is now being detailed and verified. The dialog to the right is the Rose specification dialog for the flight component. In the dialog, the Rose UML tabs have been complemented by a number of tabs to support the architectural style. The content of one such properties tab, the ArcStylerEJB1.1 tab, is selected and fully visible in the figure. This tab permits the developer to optimize the EJB configuration of the component. The properties in the tab are standard EJB1.1 properties. In addition, properties in the tab affect the generation of certain EJB conform features. The gray properties are the defaults provided by the technology projection component (that is, the modeling style in conjunction with the configured technology projection cartridge). These defaults are by no means arbitrary. They have been selected by experts based on extensive testing and experience to be the best default combination in this particular constellation. The developer may override these defaults. This is carried out within the tolerances of the modeling style, of course. Knowing these tolerances is good because they represent the real-world tolerances of the J2EE/EJB infrastructure. To override a property while remaining style-conform, the property in the dialog is selected to display the options available. The black-colored properties in the figure are ones where the default setting has been overridden by the developer. For example, the developer has modified the property determining the generation of default factory operations for the component.

In this case, the selected setting instructs the cartridge to generate factory operations that expose all attributes of the component as formal parameters.

The other tabs visible in the top of the dialog contain important groupings of properties for such aspects as tuning the object-to-relational mapping of the component or the container-managed persistence (CMP) engine of a particular J2EE/EJB infrastructure. In addition, tabs addressing unique features of a particular J2EE/EJB infrastructure appear with each newly installed technology projection cartridge. For example, Figure 7.12 shows the tabs for the Borland Application Server (BAS) as well as the tabs for the BEA Web Logic Server (WLS).

These separate property groups, as manifested by tab sheets in Rose, ensure a clean separation of concerns. Each grouping may change independently from the others. However, this does not mean that the technology projection cartridge is oblivious to interactions between the groupings. In fact, one of the primary advantages of having a well-defined modeling style and intelligent technology projection support in the IDE is the fact that such interactions can be checked and optimized. This is no small task when one considers the number of possible interactions between the various possible tuning parameters.

The technology projection cartridge can globally optimize the interactions between model properties when code generation occurs. During code generation, the currently enabled technology projection cartridge interprets each and every one of the properties and generates code and an infrastructure tuned to the particular EJB/J2EE infrastructure and its environment. This is in stark contrast to generators that produce lowest-common-denominator code. Such lowest-common-denominator code is essentially useless in real-world situations. Generating optimized code means not only that each parameter in the modeling style must be mapped intelligently by the cartridge, but also that the interactions between any number of parameters can be considered in order to generate a well-rounded, globally optimized implementation for the particular infrastructure at hand. Such global interactions of properties and structures in the UML model may affect myriad aspects of code generation, as clearly shown in the bonus chapter on the Web site. This is known as *fan-out coordination* and *fan-out optimization* because a single property change may affect many parts of an infrastructure. Proper coordination of the fan-out, the prerequisite to global optimization of the fan-out, precludes the use of so-called round-trip engineering (RTE) as it is currently defined by the tool industry. In addition, models produced via RTE of arbitrary code would make it impossible to maintain and automate a clean modeling style across designs, projects, and implementations.

Another advantage of the well-formed, clean modeling style is shown in the second dialog of Figure 7.12, the model-validation dialog. This dialog is used to automatically verify architectural integrity according to the architectural style. It asserts whether the current model or the selected model element conforms to the requirements of the currently configured technology projection component. The dialog shows that various levels of conformity can be checked at any given instant. In addition to structural conformity and completeness of the model, the "EJB cartridge constraints" allow the developer to verify the feasibility of any modeling decisions with respect to the available runtime infrastructure. In this particular case, the Borland Application Server (BAS) version 4.5 is currently configured and will be used to check the technical feasibility of the model. If the developer has used modeling constructs that cannot be reasonably (realistically) mapped to the given BAS version, then a warning or error dialog will display an explanation. Warnings dialogs signal possible design conflicts or dubious constellations, whereas error dialogs inform the developer of why an effective technology projection of the given UML construction is impossible in the current configuration. An example of an error situation would be the use of component inheritance in the UML model in conjunction with one of the many J2EE/EJB containers that do not support component inheritance.[1] Via the model validation dialog, the designer receives just-in-time feedback regarding the problem. This is comparable with the just-in-time feedback provided to a programmer by traditional compilers, now at a much higher level of design expression—the UML level.

Figure 7.13 shows part of an accessor design in the C-REF module. This particular accessor diagram shows a default editor accessor with its default representers for the same flight component shown in the preceding figures. The default accessor was generated automatically by selecting the flight component and then selecting the desired type of default accessor. Based on the information in the Flight convergent component, the accessor was derived automatically according to the modeling style. The developer can use the default accessors to then create custom accessors or can use the default accessor as is. The dialog in the lower part of the figure exhibits one of several accessor

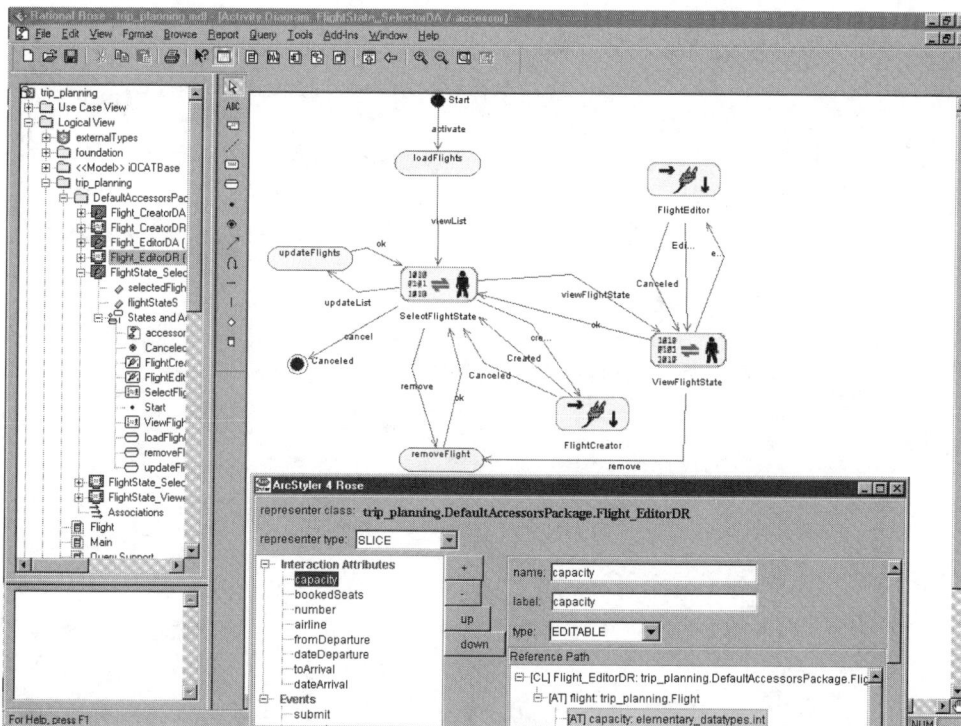

Figure 7.13   The multichannel assessor design.

configuration dialogs. It shows the interaction attributes and event-handling properties as created with the default editor accessor.

The accessor diagram itself is a UML-compliant activity diagram. The diagram in the figure exhibits two representers, two embedded (reused) accessors, and the event-driven transitions between these elements. Based on this information, the technology projection cartridge for J2EE accessors generates the servlet, JSP, and, in this particular configuration, the HTML infrastructure to access the flight component. The hierarchy browser to the left shows that considerable detail regarding accessors and representers is available to the developer and to other modules of the IDE as required.

The last C-REF figure (see Figure 7.14) displays a process design diagram for the same trip-planning system. The diagram to the right of the figure indicates the structural relationships between the process convergent component, BookingProcess, and other OPR convergent components in the model. A process flow diagram is visible in the center of the figure. Similar to accessor diagrams, process flow diagrams are UML-compliant activity diagrams that have been enhanced by the architectural IDE to support the overall architectural style. The small Process Component dialog to the upper left of the figure shows one example of such an enhancement. The dialog illustrates how the modeling style coordinates the creation and assignment of process roles to process types in the model. This is just one of several process-modeling dialogs that

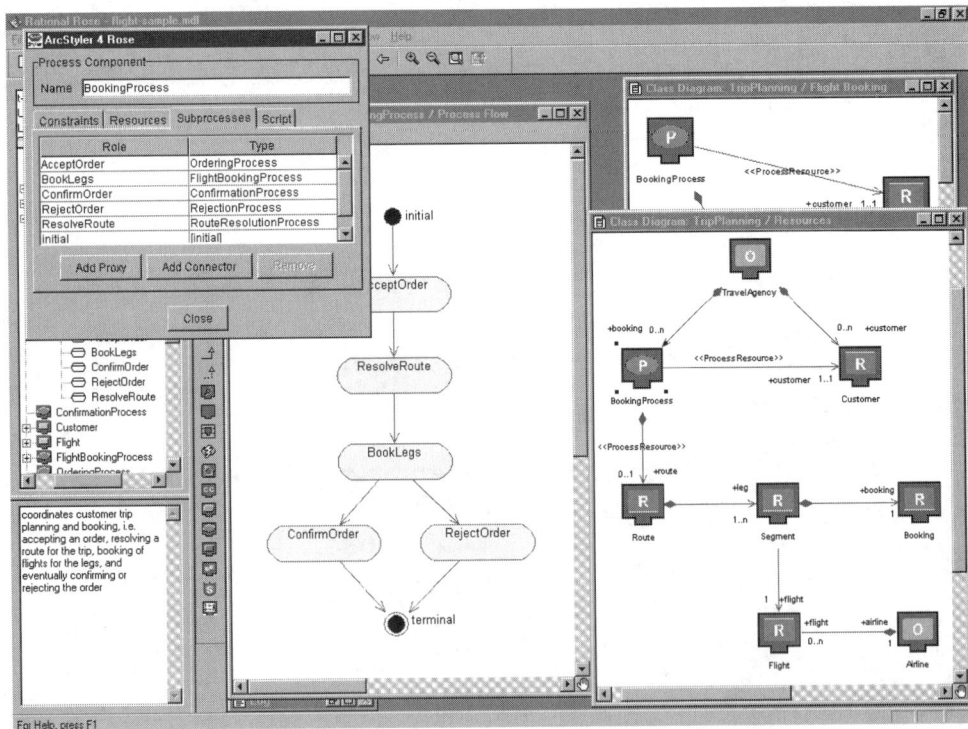

Figure 7.14 The process design.

may be used by the developer to refine the process (also known as *workflow*) aspects of the OPR model based on the concepts described in Chapter 4.

Once the model has been validated, optimized code can be generated without leaving the C-REF module. To this effect, the convergent translative generator (C-GEN) module is activated, as described in the next section.

The Convergent Translative Generator (C-GEN)

The C-GEN module (Figure 7.15) is another self-contained component in the architectural IDE. It is normally activated directly from the C-REF module so that the developer can perform rapid increments of UML modeling and subsequent infrastructure generation. However, the C-GEN also can be called as an independent Java component via a Java API or from the command line.

The basic concept behind translative generation as employed by the C-GEN also has been referred to as a third-generation design for code generators (Mellor 1999). The C-GEN implements translative generation by reading the C-REF/UML model from one source, the model repository, and reading the translation information on one or more infrastructures from another source, the technology projection cartridges. This constellation allows the developer to plug in various translation aspects in the form of cartridges. Once the cartridges are configured, generation can begin.

Figure 7.16 illustrates how technology projection cartridges are configured into the architectural IDE and stored as part of the project configuration. The figure shows the project configuration dialog that is used by the entire architectural IDE to edit and store project information. In this particular screenshot, the tab to configure the C-GEN has been selected, and a subtab, Projections, has been activated to configure the technology projection aspects. In this particular project, two cartridges have been configured, one for the Borland Application Server version 4.5 (BAS45) and one for J2EE/JSP accessors. The BAS45 cartridge is selected in the figure, which means that its cartridge details are displayed for configuration in the center of the dialog. Some of these details are set automatically on installation of the architectural IDE because they can be derived from the local environment. Others are initialized to cartridge-specific defaults. They can be modified to adapt to changes in the environment. For example, the parameters

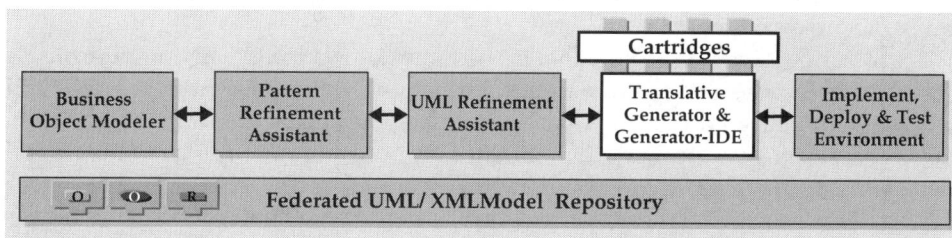

Figure 7.15   Orientation of the C-GEN/C-GEN-IDE module.

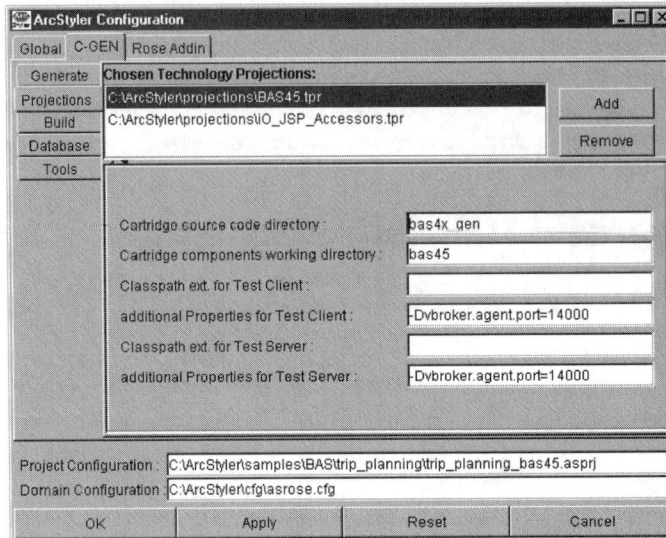

Figure 7.16 Configuring cartridges and projects.

affecting the generation, build, and execution of the test environment can be modified. In the case of the BAS45 cartridge shown in this dialog, test clients require a port number for the Visibroker Smart Agent. Since this port number may need to be changed, for instance, to enable parallel testing by several developers, the default port may be modified in the configuration dialog.

Figure 7.17 shows the graphical interface to the C-GEN module. In the C-GEN module, the convergent components are visible in the hierarchy browser to the left, as always. The figure shows that the trip-planning project from earlier is now ready to be generated using the configured technology projections. The tabs shown at the top of the work area are used to select the information and output consoles for each of the configured technology projection cartridges, respectively. The cartridges contain information regarding grouping and dependencies with other cartridges. This information is used by the C-GEN module to let the developer select various valid subsets for generation. For example, the developer can selectively generate the J2EE/JSP accessor aspects of the model or of a model element without having to generate its entire EJB infrastructure each time.

The lower portion of the work area in the figure shows the C-GEN output console. The cartridge writes progress and log information, in this case from the J2EE/JSP accessors, to this console. In this particular case, log information for the generated Tomcat servlet-engine configuration, JBuilder support, and ANT build support is visible.

What if the component developer wants to change or extend the behavior of the cartridge for a particular test environment? Or the chief architect and architectural IDE specialist want to change the behavior of the cartridge used in every project across the

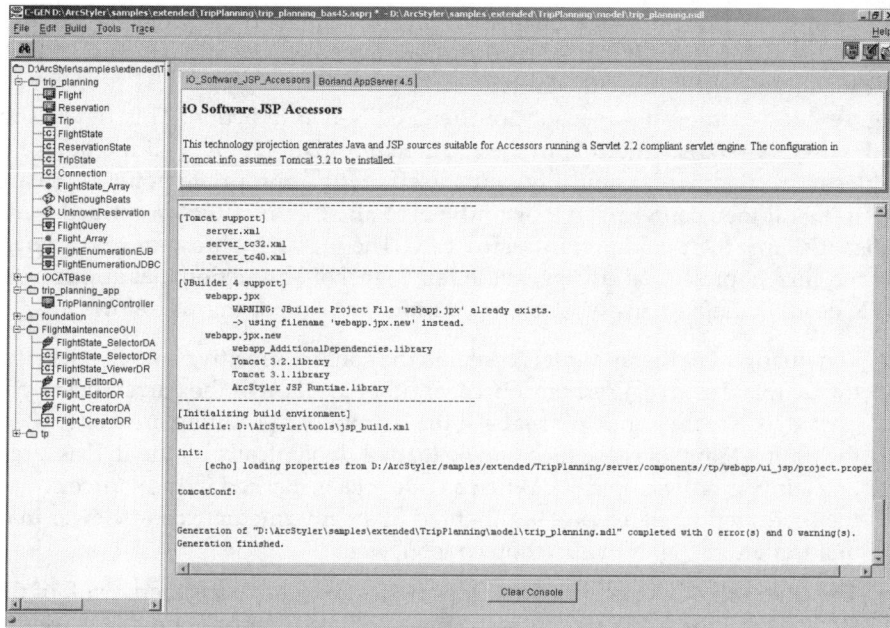

Figure 7.17 Generating infrastructure and environment.

entire IT organization? In such cases, they use the C-GEN-IDE module described in the next section.

The Convergent Generator IDE (C-GEN-IDE)

The C-GEN-IDE module of the architectural IDE is used to edit, test, and debug technology projection cartridges. Each cartridge contains templates, JPython scripts, and other artifacts that are organized according to the so-called cartridge architecture. It is important to note that technology projection cartridges themselves are extensive programs. They are referred to as metaprograms because they generate other programs and infrastructures via the C-GEN module. As such, it can be seen as a metaprogramming IDE that provides the developer with a modern environment comparable with familiar Java IDEs. In fact, much of the architectural IDE itself is generated based on UML models and technology projection cartridges. Thus, it is important that the cartridge infrastructure itself be well designed.

The cartridge architecture defines how cartridges are structured in order to guarantee all the things we expect from well-designed systems: the proper use of object-oriented design, locality of cartridge code, reuse of cartridge code, modular composition of the cartridge, modular extension points, evolutionary updates to cartridges, and so forth. However, only the architectural IDE specialists and, in rare cases, the development toolsmith (see Chapter 5) must understand the working features of the cartridge architecture. It is used by these workers to extend and develop cartridges according to the cartridge architecture.

Figure 7.18 is a typical screenshot of the C-GEN-IDE in action. This figure shows that the C-GEN-IDE is a module in the architectural IDE. Just like all the other modules, once activated, it (dynamically) adds itself at the appropriate point in the architectural IDE. It then conforms in look and feel to all other modules described thus far because it shares their common infrastructure. The hierarchy browser to the left displays the current project, as always, at the same level of abstraction that appears in the C-GEN itself. By default, the work area is divided into quadrants as follows:

- The quadrant at the upper left contains the context-sensitive source editor for the template source, JPython source, or other artifacts of the currently selected cartridge. The files appear as tabs at the bottom of the editing area, as shown in the figure. Many of these files will be loaded dynamically by the IDE as a result of testing or browsing tasks. When a code area is marked in the source editor, the corresponding areas are highlighted in the intermediate code viewer in the quadrant to its right: the JPython code viewer.

- The JPython code viewer to the upper right shows the translated result of the code in the source editor. This is the intermediate JPython code that is used to generate the actual infrastructure.[2]

- The quadrant to the lower left contains both the debugging toolbar and the output/log console. Debugging proceeds just like in any programming IDE. Break

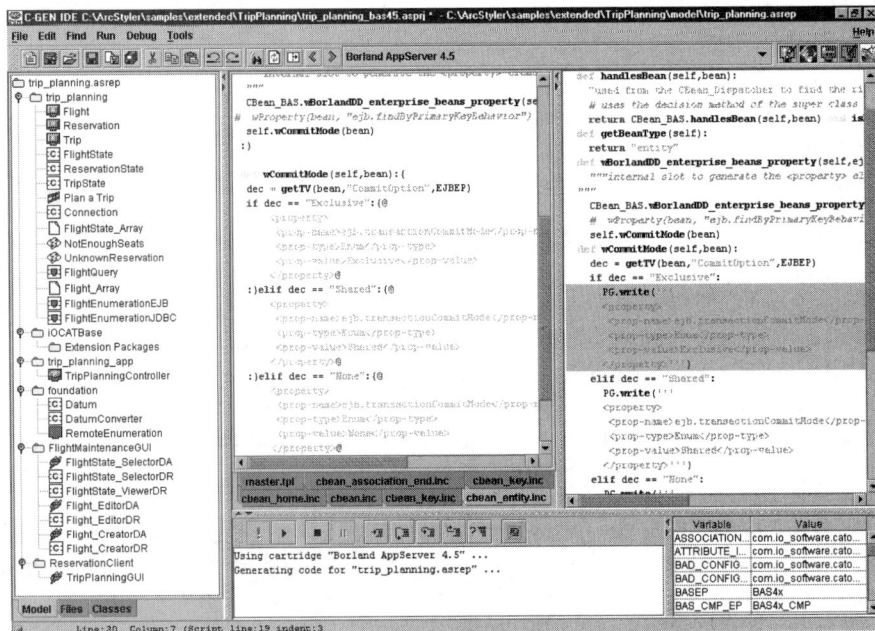

Figure 7.18 Using the generator IDE. The meta-programming environment.

points can be set, and then the generator can be started to run to the break point, using watch points along the way as required. Other normal debugger features such as single-step, step-over, step-into, and so on. are also available. The console area displays the cartridge output and log information just as in the C-GEN console. In addition, if selected, the console shows the end result of each generation step—the Java code, XML files, IDE project files, deployment descriptors, build scripts, test scripts, and so on.

■ The quadrant at the lower right is the extensible evaluation panel. It is comparable with a flexible register list or stack viewer in a source-code debugger. In addition to several standard watch expressions, it may be extended by the developer using arbitrary JPython expressions to watch any other aspect of the generator or cartridge.

The Implement, Deploy, and Test Environment (C-IX)

The implement, deploy, and test environment module (C-IX) (see Figure 7.19) leverages a high-end programming IDE (for example, Java or C++ IDE) and deployment and test tools. Similar to the embedded UML tool in the C-REF module (Rational Rose), the C-IX encapsulates, integrates, and drives these tools to assist the developer along the critical development path. Like the C-REF, the C-IX achieves this by enhancing and complementing the Java IDE (JBuilder in this case), tools, and infrastructure with two things. First, it seamlessly integrates the C-IX components with the rest of the architectural IDE; this integration applies to the modules conceptually before, after, above, and below the Java IDE and the other tools coordinated by the C-IX. Second, it adds architectural-style-specific features such as the modeling style and model-driven technology support for the code, test, build, and deployment aspects of the system.

The following three figures are used to exhibit several of the central features of the C-IX module. Figure 7.20 displays the generated code and test infrastructure as used to deploy and test the convergent components in the context of the Java IDE. Figure 7.21 shows the generated accessors as they are displayed for testing or refinement in either the Java IDE or, equivalently, in a Web-design tool such as DreamWeaver or UltraDev.

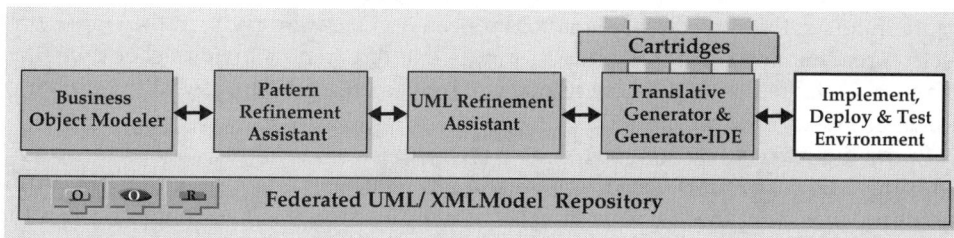

Figure 7.19   Orientation of the C-IX module.

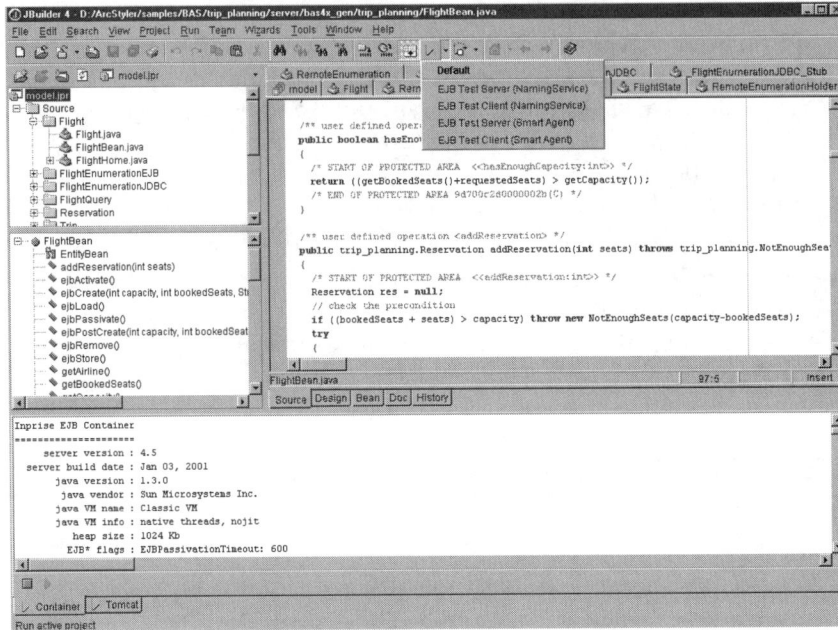

Figure 7.20   Implement, deploy, and test components.

Figure 7.21 illustrates the convergent components as deployed in the operational environment or the assembly test environment.

Figure 7.20 shows the trip-planning project in JBuilder. The JBuilder project files and build environment for the trip-planning project were generated automatically from the C-REF/UML model shown in previous sections. The two browsers at the left of the figure indicate that convergence has still been preserved at the source-code level: The flight component and other OPRs from the business model are clearly visible in the browsers. As always, the browser shows the accompanying artifacts relevant to the component in this life-cycle stage and to this module of the architectural IDE.

In the work area, we see one of the generated Java files, FlightBean.java, displayed in the code editor. In the editor, the generated comments and protected areas are colored green. The long number at the bottom of each protected area comprises so-called check-sum information and other information that is used by the C-GEN to intelligently manage the protected area across repeated generation runs. In the upper protected area, the developer has added a single line of business logic to check whether the sum of booked seats plus the number of requested seats surpasses the number of available seats.

In the tool bar, the developer has activated the Run Project menu. The menu presents the unit test projects for both client and server aspects of the assembly. This infrastructure, including the JBuilder project configuration required to build and run the tests, also was generated from the C-REF/UML model. The developer uses this menu to build and test the assembly or parts of the assembly. Remember that the packaging of the convergent components into testable units also was modeled in the C-REF/UML module as described in Chapter 6. This enables the generation of a properly partitioned test infrastructure.

The result of activating the generated menu item "EJB test server" is shown at the bottom of the figure. When the menu item is activated, the project dependencies are checked automatically, and the components are built. If compilation is successful, the test proceeds to automatically package the components together with the other generated artifacts required for deployment—the J2EE/EJB deployment descriptors, for example. Then the application server is activated, and the package is automatically deployed into the application server. In JBuilder, this all happens within the Java-IDE environment. The output at the bottom of the figure shows the active Borland Application Server as well as the active Tomcat servlet engine. Once the test server is loaded, the unit test clients and accessors may be built and started automatically in a similar fashion.

Figure 7.21 shows an example of such accessors in the trip-planning project. These accessors were generated from the C-REF/UML model shown in Figure 7.13. In this figure, the JBuilder project for the accessors package has been selected in the browser. This unit was given the name WebApplication in the C-REF/UML model. The browser shows the accessors and their corresponding representers just as they appeared in the corresponding C-REF/UML browser (the left side of Figure 7.13). These artifacts, including the JBuilder project and other infrastructures required to build, deploy, and test the accessors, were all generated directly from the C-REF/UML model.

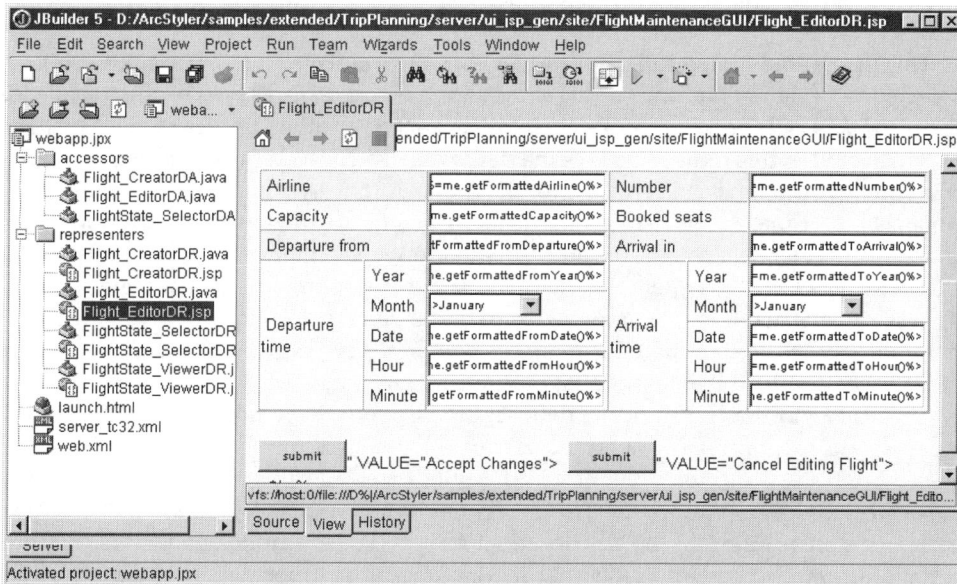

Figure 7.21 Implement, deploy, and test accessors.

In the figure, one of the representers, Flight_EditorDR, has been selected and appears in the JBuilder editor to the right. This is the default representer (indicated by the suffix DR).[3] This model is shown on right side of Figure 7.13. For the flight-editor representer, the HTML/JSP view has been selected by the JBuilder editor. This view allows the developer to visually edit the HTML/JSP representation in JBuilder. However, the graphic editing of representers normally is done by the computer ergonomics and GUI expert (see Chapter 5). As explained in the development model, this expert uses high-end Web page design tools such as DreamWeaver or UltraDev to polish the Web page layout. Such editing also occurs using exactly the same generated representers. Both Java-IDE and Web design tools are completely complementary components of the C-IX module. JBuilder is used by the accessor developer to manipulate, build, and test the accessor internals, whereas the Web design tool is used by the GUI expert to manipulate the HTML/JSP representers of the accessor—the optimal separation of concerns. Both the accessor developer and GUI expert operate in their area of expertise with their high-end tools, and the results are completely harmonious. The representer files saved by the Web design tool can be updated immediately in JBuilder and can be tested immediately with the rest of the assembly.

The steps taken to build, test, and deploy the accessors are identical to the procedure described previously (see Figure 7.20) for the server-side aspects of the assembly: The developer uses the preconfigured Run Project menu in the JBuilder toolbar, and testing proceeds via the test clients and accessors. In this particular example, the Web accessors may be started within the JBuilder environment or from a standard Web browser outside the environment, depending on the level of instrumentation required. The standard Web browser is used to test the look and feel of the application from the end-user's perspective. This brings us to Figure 7.22, which shows one view of the trip-planning assembly as deployed in the operational environment. As described in the CA process (see Chapter 6), this environment is also used to test the assembly before release.

This figure shows an application server console. In this particular case, it is the console for the Borland Application Server; however, it could just as well be the console for the BEA WebLogic Server, the IBM WebSphere Server, or other application servers. The view selected in this figure displays the deployed assembly. It provides clear evidence that convergence has been achieved for the trip-planning system. The convergent components are visible in the browser to the left of the figure: the business components in the EJB container branch and the accessors in the Web container branch. In this particular screenshot, the EJB references view of the business components has been selected. This shows the convergent components and their reference in the deployed J2EE/EJB environment. Note that the OPR business components—flight, reservation, trip—are still clearly visible in the operational monitoring environment.

This aspect of the C-IX module permits the assembly to be manipulated and monitored in the operational infrastructure during the various phases of its life cycle: Assembly tests, transition activities, and day-to-day and operational activities are all carried out in this environment. This level of automation makes operational tests possible in early iterations of the development project. For example, developers can integrate, deploy, and test the assembly in this operational constellation directly from JBuilder. This allows parts of the system to be instrumented and tested from the Java-

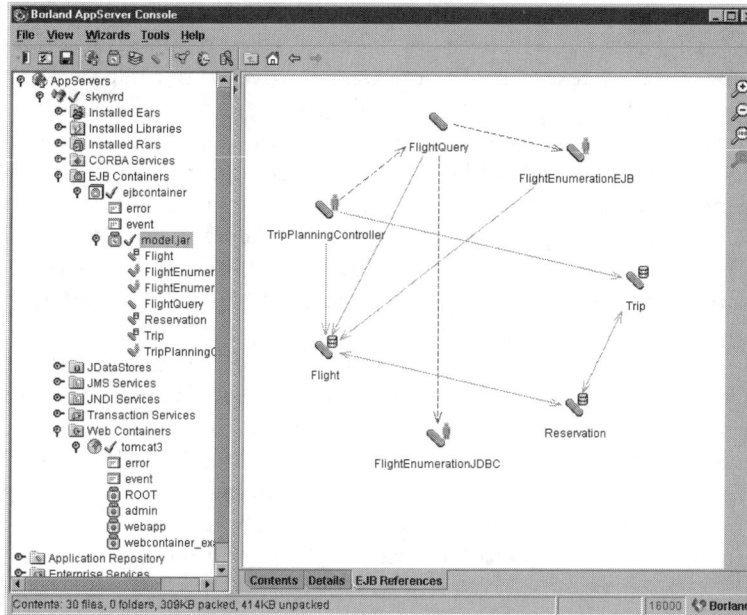

Figure 7.22   The operational deployment and assembly test.

IDE environment by one component developer while using other parts of the assembly that have been deployed by other component developers. In addition, it lets the assembly developer, the test manger, and the deployment manager verify the deployment and monitoring capabilities of the operational environment early on in the project. These diverse deployment and testing needs, each corresponding to different stages of the critical development workflow, are intelligently supported by the C-IX module as a part of the overall architectural IDE.

Summary

This chapter provided concrete illustrations and descriptions of the architectural IDE and its important role as a part of the Convergent Architecture. In particular, it addressed the mechanisms of the third and fourth features in an IT-architectural style described in Chapter 1 (refer to Figure 1.1). These features are the full-coverage tool suite and the formal technology projections, with the focus in this chapter being on the tools and their high-level support of the development model (see Chapters 4, 5, and 6). In the next chapter the focal point will be shifted to the formal technology projection aspects.

Screenshots from an actual architectural IDE, ArcStyler, were used to show how mature tools such as Rational Rose, JBuilder, and J2EE/EJB application servers are integrated and enhanced to intelligently support holistic architecture in reality-scale projects. Each section presented one major module of the architectural IDE and illustrated how it supports the development of convergent components, as described in Chapter 4, the in the context of the IT organization covered in Chapter 5 using the CA process defined in Chapter 6. This began with tool support for the business modeling and requirements workflow using the business object modeling module (C-BOM). It then proceeded through the three levels of convergent refinement using the pattern-based refinement assistant module and the UML refinement module for Rational Rose (C-RAS and C-REF). Finally, support for the implementation cycle, test workflows, deployment, and monitoring activities were illustrated using the translative generator and its metaprogramming modules (C-GEN and C-GEN IDE), followed by the module for the implementation, deployment, and test environment (C-IX).

Up to this point, the technology projection component (which includes the guidelines for a modeling style and its technology projections) has been covered from the perspectives of design rationale, positioning, and structure as a part of the architectural style, as well its pragmatic usage in the architectural IDE. The next chapter will cover the last, most detailed perspective of the technology projection component: its content. It will provide the reader with detailed insight into this important aspect of the Convergent Architecture before the final chapter will move back to a pragmatic usage level.

Tutorial Example: Applying the Convergent Architecture

This chapter demonstrates the Convergent Architecture at work. It consists of a short, step-by-step tutorial that applies significant portions of the Convergent Architecture (CA) process in the context of the architectural integrated development environment (IDE). It demonstrates the tasks required to develop a convergent J2EE/EJB system including its Web accessors (the Web application) using the ArcStyler with Rational Rose, JBuilder/ANT, and technology projection cartridges for JSP Web accessors and J2EE/EJB application servers. The particular examples used in this tutorial demonstrate the use of the J2EE/EJB cartridges for the BEA Web Logic Server (WLS) and the Borland Application Server (BAS).

The tutorial includes the following steps, each covered in its own section:

- Business modeling with C-BOM
- Refinement into an initial UML model with C-RAS
- UML modeling of the EJB components with C-REF
- Code generation for the EJB components with C-GEN
- Building, deploying, and testing the EJB system
- Unified Modeling Language (UML) modeling of the Web accessor components with C-REF
- Code generation for the Web accessor infrastructure with C-GEN
- Building, deploying, and testing the Web application

Needless to say, familiarity with the Convergent Architecture is a prerequisite to best understanding the underlying concepts and advantages presented in this tutorial.

The J2EE/EJB System: A Convergent iBank

In this tutorial, you will develop the heart of an Internet banking (i-bank) system: its account management features. In summary, the **iBank** consists of two components: an **Account** (resource) component and a **Transfer** (process) component. The **Account** component possesses an account number and a balance and is capable of making transactional withdrawals and deposits. The **Transfer** component can transfer funds between a source account and a destination account.

The **Account** component will be modeled and implemented as an EJB entity bean using container-managed persistence. The **Transfer** component will be modeled and implemented as an EJB stateful session bean. They will be modeled into a single assembly and deployed in an EJB container.

Then, Web accessors are developed and deployed to provide a Web-based user interface for account management. This Web front end enables bank personnel to manipulate accounts: create new accounts and edit or delete accounts.

Tutorial Solution

A complete solution for this example, which includes models and all other development artifacts, may be found on the Convergent Architecture Web site: www.ConvergentArchitecture.com.

In some places, notational conventions are combined. For example, *project*.**asprj** is used to designate a project file for which the name is specified by the user.

The notational convention for navigating menus is **Menu** → **Submenu** → . . . . Context menus are accessed by clicking the right mouse button.

Business Modeling with C-BOM

This section covers the business modeling and requirements acquisition aspects of the analysis-by-design work flow (see Chapter 6). The tasks of this work flow are supported by the convergent business object modeler (C-BOM) module, which assists in

- Modeling of business object responsibilities and collaborations (static structure of the model)
- Modeling of use-case scenarios (dynamic behavior of the model)

The completed business object model includes the following deliverables:

- Detailed domain requirements in the form of a business object model
- Debugged domain scenarios in the form of visual business use-case scenarios, state transition tables, and run-throughs

SOFTWARE PREREQUISITES

The following software prerequisites must be met for hands-on use of this tutorial:

- ArcStyler version 2.6 or higher.
- Rational Rose 2000e or 2001 or 2001a.
- JBuilder4 or 5. The use of JBuilder (or other Java IDE) is optional because the ANT (command-line) build environment is also explained in this tutorial. The advantages of each were explained in Chapter 7.
- The ArcStyler technology projection cartridge for your target J2EE/EJB container (BEA WLS 5.1 and Borland Application Server 4.5 are used in the example).
- Tomcat servlet engine 3.2 or compatible engine (usually delivered with the application server).
- ArcStyler **iO_JSP_accessors** technology projection cartridge.

NOTATIONAL CONVENTIONS

Table 8.1 lists the notational conventions used in this tutorial.

Table 8.1   Notational Conventions

NOTATION	DESCRIPTION
iBank.asprj	Bold font is used for the names of interfaces, files, and language keywords.
Name	Italics are used for elements that are variable.
Cancel	A sans-serif font is used for the names of GUI widgets, dialogs, menus and their contents, and information you enter into the GUI field.
ENTER	All capital letters designates keys on your keyboard.
`#define`	A fixed-width font is used for code and for information you enter at the command line.

- Descriptions regarding specific design themes such as migration, security, and host-integration
- Model-generated HTML documentation for official business model information and project signoff

This section contains the following subsections:

- Setting up a project
- Modeling CRC cards
- Modeling a business use-case scenario
- Model verification and documentation

Setting Up a Project

Start the ArcStyler from the command line or from your system menu. The ArcStyler commander appears on your desktop.

Before you start modeling, you need to set up an ArcStyler project. An ArcStyler project file is an XML file with the file extension ***.asprj**. It stores the project configuration information. In particular, it contains tags specifying the UML/XML repository file *model*.**asrep** and the Rose model *model*.**mdl** associated with the ArcStyler project.

Figure 8.1 shows the ArcStyler commander after creating the **iBank** project and repository. The repository already contains a default package, **iOCATBase**. This package contains some basic model elements, such as elementary data types. It is imported automatically in each newly created ArcStyler repository.

Modeling CRC Cards

You will now design the static structure of your business model. The business objects of your model are represented by class responsibility collaboration (CRC) cards.

Adding a Package

CRC cards must be modeled within a business model package. Therefore, you must first add such a package to your repository.

Optionally, you may enter the initial textual project or scenario description.

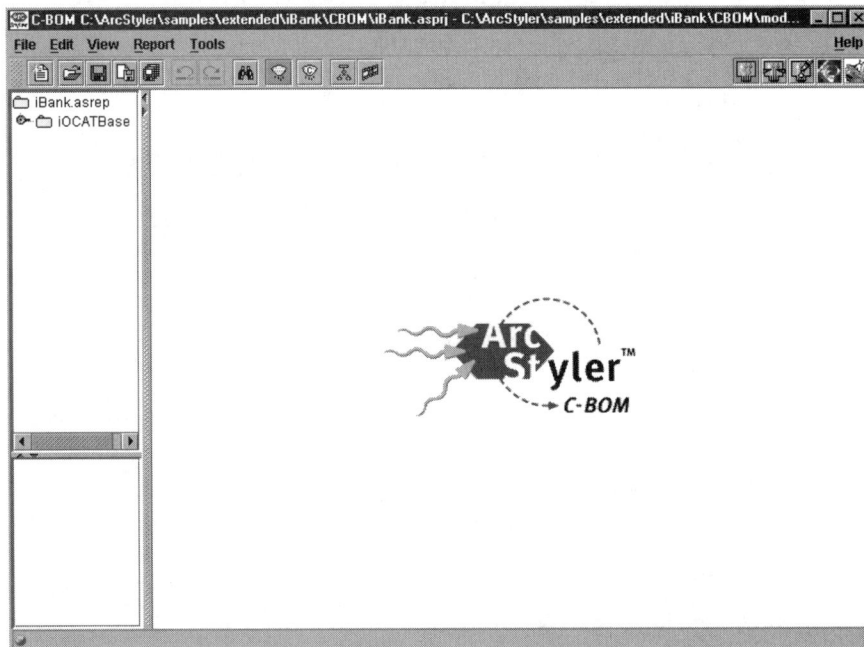

Figure 8.1 The ibank project and repository.

Adding CRC Cards

In this section you design the CRC cards for the **Account** and **Transfer** business objects. Begin with the **Account** object. Proceed as follows:

- Add a new resource CRC card, **Account**, to the **iBank** package.
- Add the responsibilities listed in Table 8.2 in the **Responsibilities** field of the **Account** CRC card.

Model the **Transfer** object as follows:

- Add a new process CRC card, **Transfer**, to the **iBank** package.
- In the **Responsibilities** and **Collaborators** fields of the CRC card, add the responsibilities and collaborators shown in Table 8.3.

Figure 8.2 shows the completed CRC cards.

Modeling a Business Use-Case Scenario

In this section you enter a business use-case scenario for the transfer process. The transfer scenario includes the following steps: Check the balance of the source account, make a withdrawal from the source account, and make a deposit on the destination account. To model this scenario, do the following:

1. Add a new business use-case scenario, **Execute one transfer**, to the **IBank** package.
2. Add three scenario steps.
3. Insert transitions between the following steps:
   - Start point and step 1
   - Step 1 and step 2
   - Step 2 and step 3
   - Step 3 and endpoint
4. Select step 1, and choose **Transfer** as **Client** and **Account** as **Server** from the respective drop-down lists in that part of the workspace. Select the **Know balance** responsibility as the server's **Responsibility**.

Table 8.2 Responsibilities of the Account Business Object

RESPONSIBILITY	KIND	VISIBILITY
Know account number	Knowing	Visible
Know balance	Knowing	Visible
Make deposit	Doing	Visible
Make withdrawal	Doing	Visible

Table 8.3 Responsibilities and Collaborators of the Transfer Business Object

RESPONSIBILITY	KIND	VISIBILITY	COLLABORATOR
Know source account	Knowing	Visible	Account
Know destination account	Knowing	Visible	Account
Know amount to be transferred	Knowing	Visible	
Execute transfer	Doing	Visible	

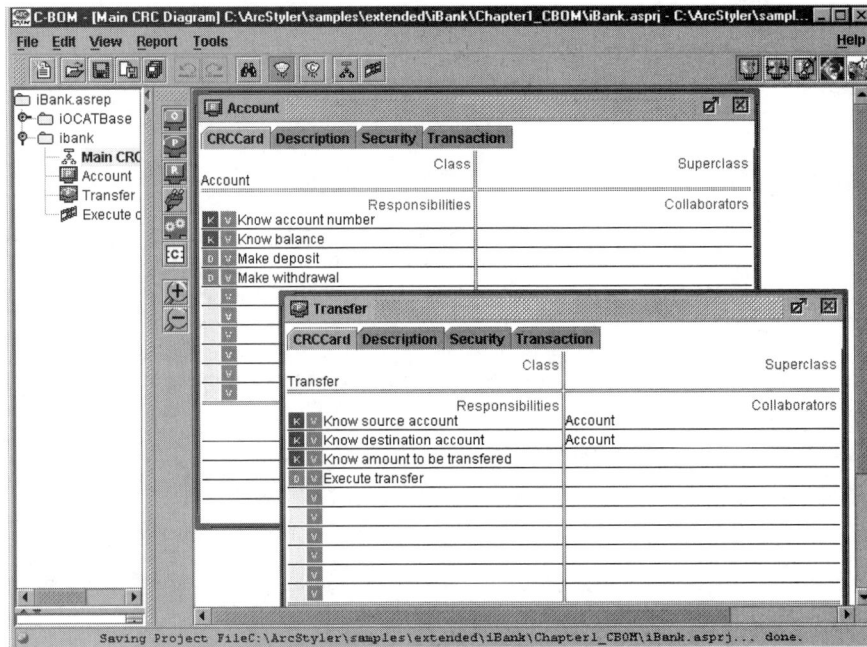

Figure 8.2 CRC cards in the ibank business model.

5. Add the following **Note** to step 1: Check if funds are adequate in source account.

6. Select step 2, and set the same client and server, but select **Make withdrawal** as the server's **Responsibility**.

7. Select step 3, set the same client and server, but select **Make deposit** as the server's **Responsibility**.

8. Add the following **Note** to step 3: **Withdraw and deposit must be an atomic transaction**.

Figure 8.3 shows step 9 of this business use-case scenario modeling procedure.

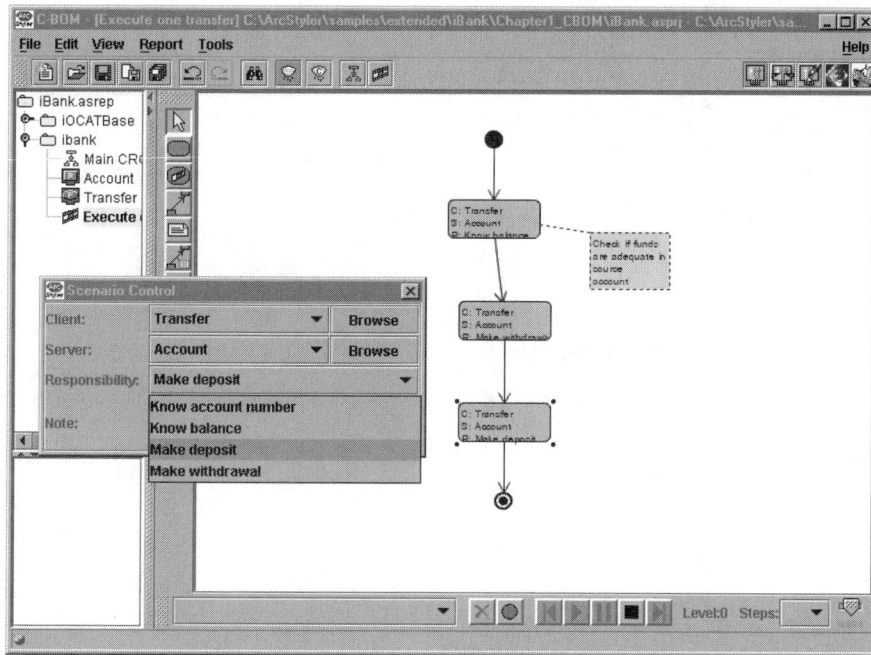

Figure 8.3 Creating the business use-case scenario.

To test the scenario, you now perform a *walk-through,* as described in Chapter 6, the CA process. Once the scenario is verified, the walk-through may be recorded. Playing back the recording constitutes a *run-through,* as described in Chapter 6. Figure 8.4 shows the walk-through recording procedure.

You can now play back (run-through) the scenario by selecting the **Execute one transfer: default case** walk-through from the drop-down menu below the workspace and clicking the **Run Through** button.

Model Verification and Documentation

At this point, the static structure and dynamic behavior of the business model have been modeled. To complete the business-modeling step, you can now verify your model and generate an HTML documentation.

Verification

The C-BOM module provides a configurable model-verification mechanism to verify the structural correctness and completeness of your business model. The following aspects can be validated by default:

- Duplicate class names
- Responsibilities not referenced in a scenario

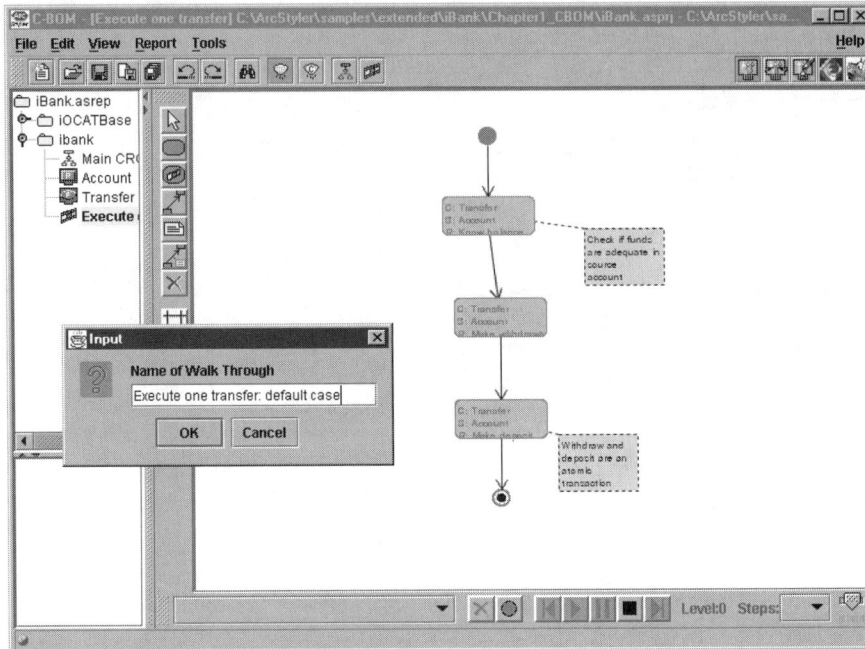

Figure 8.4   Recording a walk-through.

- Business objects not referenced in a scenario
- Cards without responsibilities
- Empty business object documentations
- Business objects not referenced as collaborators

You can verify single model elements or the entire model. The verifier notifies you about the results of the validation. If the validation is not successful, you will get warnings or error messages. In the case of errors, the model must be fixed in order to maintain integrity as defined by the architectural style.

Documentation

Now you can generate the HTML documentation from the model. This report is then used for design review and signoff.

The structured hypertext in this report contains the business-model structure and flows with their descriptions and requirements broken down as follows:

- Model packages and their descriptions
- CRC cards and their descriptions, including the recorded special design themes
- Visual business use-case scenarios
- Walk-throughs and their resulting state transition tables

This document can be placed immediately on the company's intranet or the IT organization's intranet (see Chapter 5) for review.

At this point, you have completed the convergent refinement I (convergent business modeling) activity of the analysis-by-design work flow. Note that this procedure has eliminated the high-risk, high-cost step of translating a domain analysis into a system model.

The initial **iBank** business modeling is now complete. The results have been verified and documented.

Refinement with C-RAS

This section covers the refinement of the business-object model into an initial UML component model. This is the convergent refinement II (convergent UML representation) activity of the analysis-by-design work flow and is supported by the convergent refinement assistant (C-RAS) module.

As detailed in Chapters 6 and 7, the C-RAS bridges the gap between business modeling and UML refinement using convergent mapping patterns and rules as defined by the OPEN Consortium. The result of this refinement step is a convergent design that preserves direct visibility of the business model in the resulting UML-based J2EE/EJB component model. This step increases quality and project transparency by providing bidirectional tracking to the original requirements as well as between rapid-development iterations.

This section contains the following subsections:

- Starting C-RAS
- Refining the account business object
- Refining the transfer business object
- Model verification

Starting C-RAS

Start the ArcStyler, open the project file **iBank.asprj** that you created in the previous section, and click on the C-RAS button in right corner of the ArcStyler tool bar to activate the C-RAS tool.

Figure 8.5 shows the yet unrefined model. The elements visible in the hierarchy browser to the left of the figure are the business objects from the C-BOM, each containing its list of as yet unrefined responsibilities. Each unrefined element is labeled with an exclamation mark (!).

Refining a business object means refining its responsibilities. In general, a responsibility can be refined to one of the following UML model elements within the context of a component interface:

- Attribute
- Operation
- Association

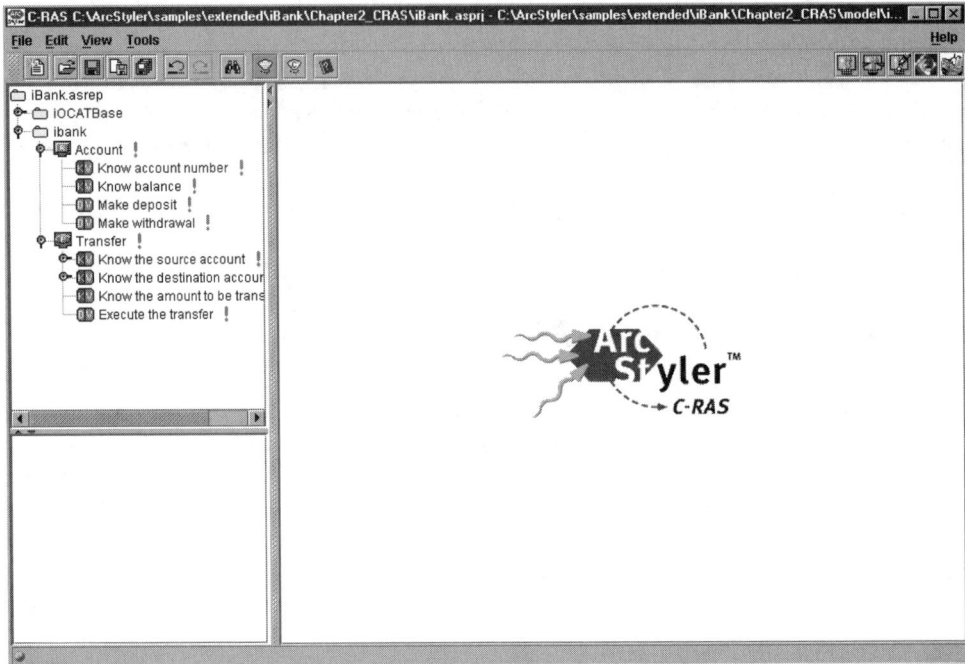

Figure 8.5   The initially unrefined business model.

The refinement patterns suggest that responsibilities for *Knowing* are normally refined to attributes or associations, whereas responsibilities for *Doing* are refined to operations. A responsibility is refined by selecting it in the browser and using its Refine → <RefiningElement> context menu.

Refining the Account Business Object

Refine the responsibilities of the **Account** object as follows:

1. Refine the **Know balance** responsibility with an attribute, **accountNumber**, of type **string**. Figure 8.6 shows the result of this procedure.

2. Similarly, refine the **Know balance** responsibility with an attribute, **balance**, of type **double**. Figure 8.7 shows the result of this procedure.

3. Refine the **Make deposit** responsibility with an operation, **makeDeposit**, with return type <none> and a parameter, **amount**, of type **double** and direction IN. Figure 8.8 shows the result of this procedure.

4. Similarly, refine the **Make withdrawal** responsibility with an operation, **makeWithdrawal**, with return type <none> and a parameter, **amount**, of type **double** and direction IN.

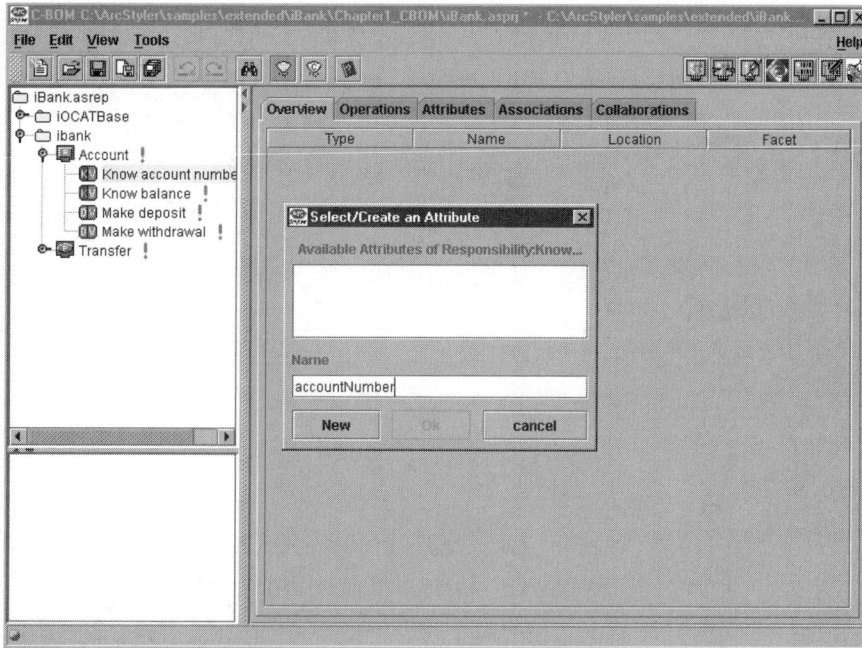

Figure 8.6   Refining the Know account number responsibility.

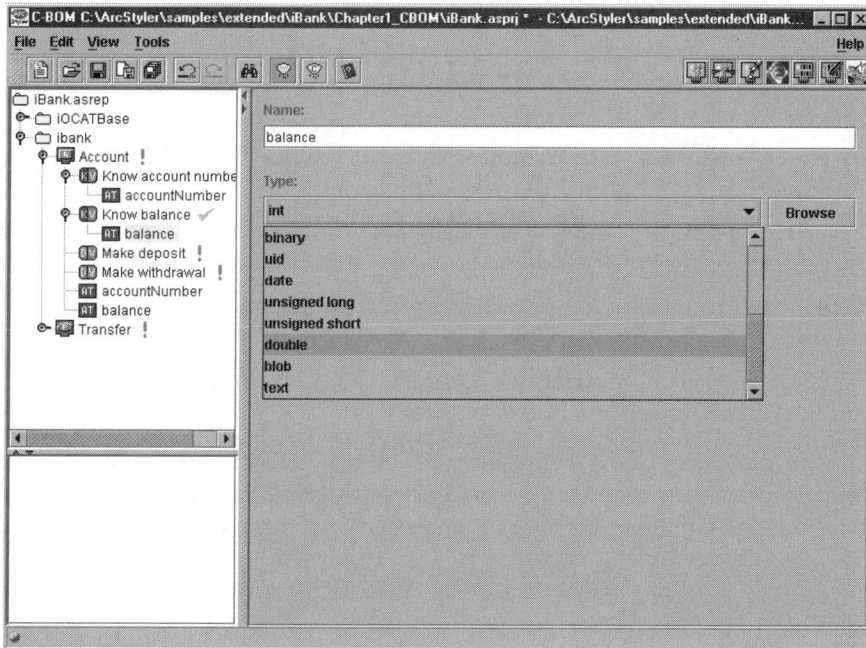

Figure 8.7   Modeling the balance attribute.

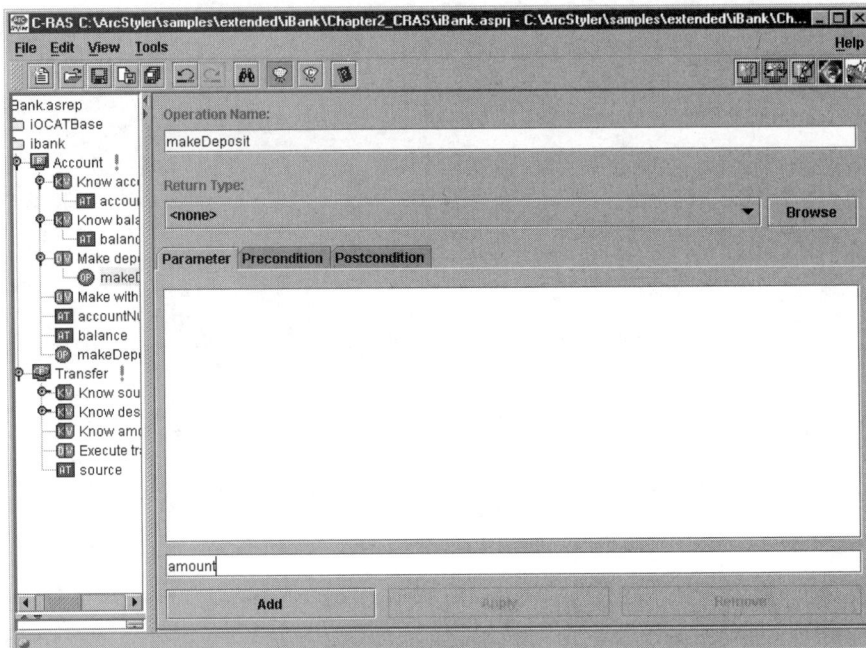

Figure 8.8 Modeling the makeDeposit() operation.

Refining the Transfer Business Object

Now we refine the **Transfer** object.

1. Refine the **Know source account** with an attribute, **source**, of object type **Account**. Figure 8.9 shows this procedure.

2. Similarly, refine the **Know destination account** responsibility with an attribute, **destination**, of type **Account**.

3. Refine the **Know amount to be transferred** responsibility with an attribute, **amount**, of type **double**.

4. Refine the **Execute transfer** responsibility with an operation, **execute**, with return type **<none>** and no parameters.

Now the refinement of the business-model objects to UML convergent components has been completed, as indicated by the checkmark in the Figure 8.10. The checkmark indicates that the refinement of the model element is completed.

Model Verification

The C-RAS module provides a model-verification mechanism to verify the structural correctness and completeness of the UML model. You can verify single model elements or the entire model using the element's **Verify** context menu.

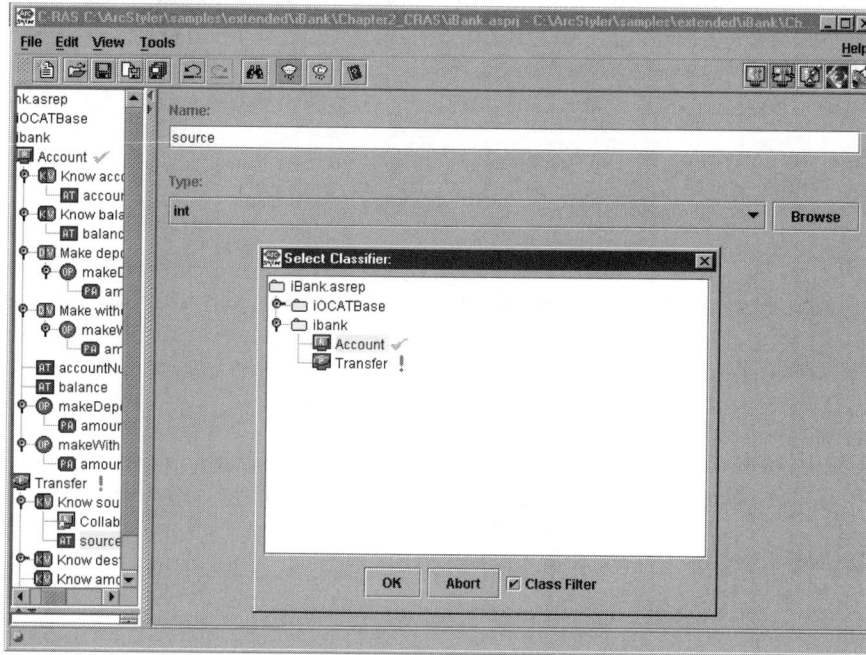

Figure 8.9 Modeling the source attribute.

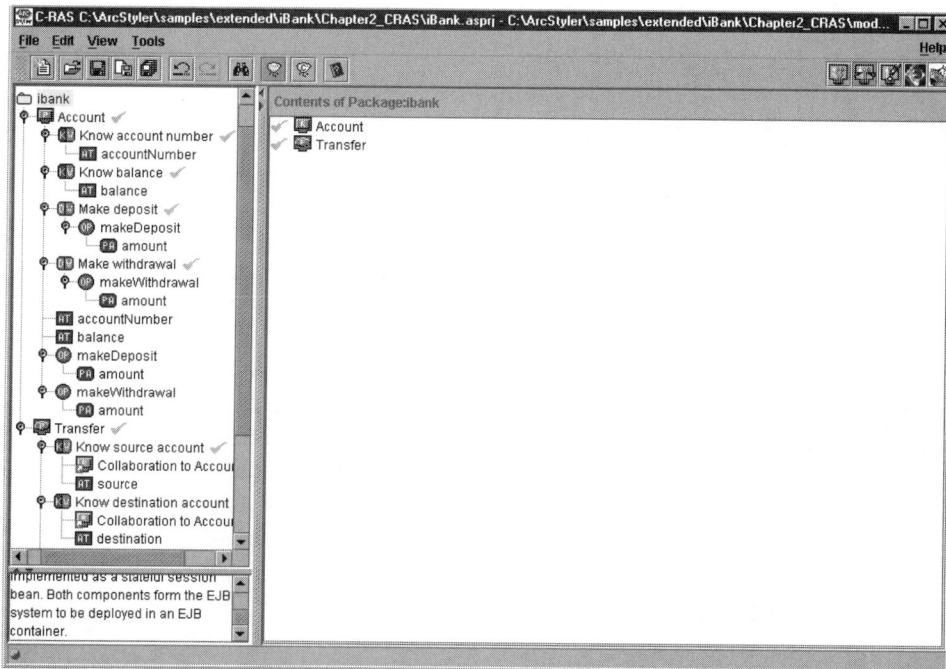

Figure 8.10 Refined to UML components.

The verifier notifies you as to the results of the validation. If the validation is not successful, you will get warnings or error messages. In the case of errors, the model must be fixed in order to maintain integrity as defined by the architectural style.

At this point, the UML convergent component model has been created.

J2EE/EJB Modeling with C-REF/UML

This section covers the technical refinement of the UML component model. This is the convergent refinement III (convergent UML refinement) activity of the analysis-by-design work flow, which is supported by the convergent EJB/UML refiner for Rational Rose (C-REF).

The C-REF module assists you in refining the UML model according to the UML modeling style and technology projection, as described in Chapter 7. The C-REF provides design assistants and defaults to technically refine all components and their relationships. This simplifies modeling while still permitting extensions and adjustments by experts.

This section contains the following subsections:

- Starting the C-REF
- Modeling the account component
- Modeling the transfer component
- Modeling deployable components
- Model verification

Starting the C-REF

The C-REF module operates as an architectural shell around Rational Rose. Performance, compatibility, and ease of use from within the Rose environment are a high priority. To achieve this, the ArcStyler consolidates its open UML/XML repository (C-MOD) with the Rose internal repository. This consolidation is encapsulated properly and, as such, is transparent to all modules of the ArcStyler. The consolidated format is referred to as the *Rose native format*. The conversion between the Rose native format and the ArcStyler UML/XML repository is bidirectional and lossless. Also, it only needs to be carried out when you move back and forth between the C-RAS and C-REF modules. To move from the C-RAS module into the Rose-centric C-REF, you import the external C-MOD repository into its corresponding C-REF/Rose repository in Rose (Rose native format). Once in the C-REF/Rose environment, modeling proceeds using Rose within the ArcStyler shell. All modules use the C-REF/Rose native format. The ArcStyler C-MOD repository can be stored and reloaded in the Rose native format or exported to the external C-MOD at any time.

From C-RAS to C-REF

When you have completed the initial UML refinement in C-RAS, click on the Rose button in the right corner of the ArcStyler tool bar. This saves the current project and

domain configuration, starts Rational Rose, and automatically loads the current Arc-
Styler project file, **iBank.asprj.**

You will be asked to import the model information from the ArcStyler repository,
iBank.asrep, associated with the project. A new Rose model, **iBank.mdl**, will be created as target of the import (or an existing **iBank.mdl** will be loaded as the target).
After the import is completed, save the Rose model using the Rose menu **File** → **Save.**
The new Rose model, **iBank.mdl**, is automatically associated with the ArcStyler project file, **iBank.asprj.**

Once the repository has been imported, this import does not have to be repeated
unless you explicitly move back and make changes in the C-BOM. The repository
information has been automatically stored in Rose, and the project constellation has
been stored in the ArcStyler project file. From now on, a double-click on the
iBank.asprj file will start the C-REF/Rose.

At this point, the C-REF/Rose environment should resemble Figure 8.11.

Modeling the Account Component

In this section you will model or tune the following EJB properties of the **Account** component:

- Entity bean with container-managed persistence (CMP)
- Attribute `accountNumber` as key attribute
- Default `create()` method with empty parameter list
- User-defined `create()` method with parameter `accountNumber`

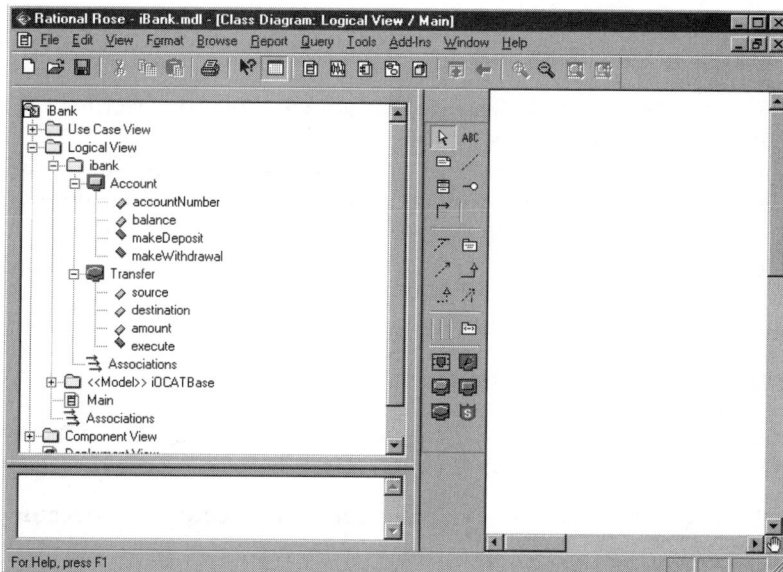

Figure 8.11   The initial C-REF/Rose model.

In the UML model, these properties are managed in the component's ArcStyler property sheets.

EJB Properties

The EJB properties of the **Account** component are specified in the **ArcStylerEJB 1.1** property sheet of component's Rose specification dialog. The following properties are relevant for the **Account** component:

ModelingStyle–Compact. The bean is modeled using the *compact bean* pattern.

Bean Home Name–<empty>. This specifies the JNDI name the container uses to look up the home interface. If nothing is specified, the component name will be used.

BeanType–Entity.

PersistenceManagement–Container. The **Account** component is implemented as entity bean with container-managed persistence.

IsReentrant–False. The entity bean is not reentrant.

TransactionType–Container. The transaction management is handled by the container.

ContainerTransaction–Required. The container invokes the bean with a valid transaction context. See the EJB 1.1 specification.

CommitOption–Cartridge Default. This specifies that the database access during a transaction is defined by the technology projection cartridge.

GenDfltFactories–EmptyParameterList. A default create method with empty parameter list is generated in the bean's home interface.

GenFindAllInstances–True. A `findAllInstances()` method is generated in the bean's home interface.

Figure 8.12 shows the completed **ArcStylerEJB 1.1** property sheet for the **Account** component.

By default, all nonderived attributes of the CMP entity bean are stored persistently. Now you will specify the **accountNumber** attribute of the **Account** component as key attribute. This is done in the **ArcStylerEJB 1.1** property sheet of the attribute's Rose specification dialog by setting the **PartOfPrimaryKey** property to **True**, as shown in Figure 8.13.

User-Defined Factory Method

You will further customize and tune the design by modeling a user-defined factory method that takes the **accountNumber** attribute as parameter. To do so, proceed as follows:

1. Add a new operation, **create**, with the stereotype **create** to the **Account** component.

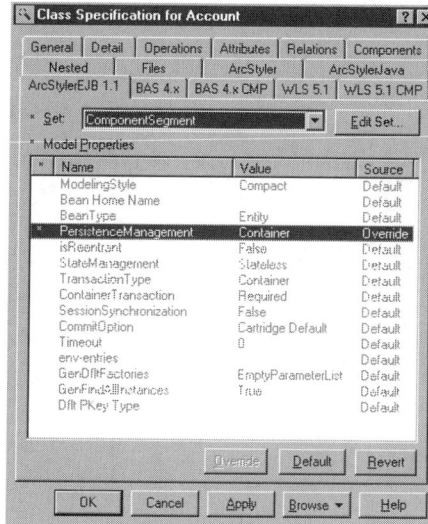

Figure 8.12   EJB properties of the account component.

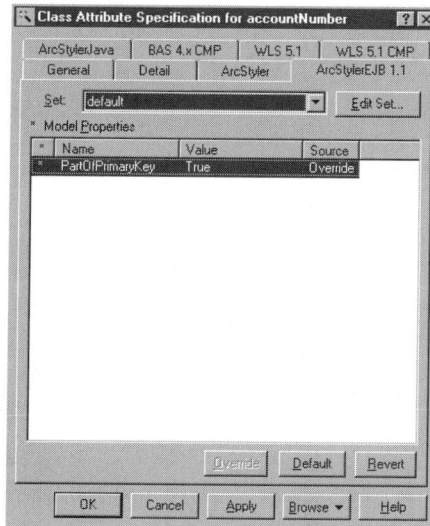

Figure 8.13   EJB properties of the accountNumber attribute.

2. Add a parameter, **accountNumber**, of type **string** to the operation.

The technical refinement of the **Account** component is now complete.

Modeling the Transfer Component

In this section you will model the following EJB properties of the **Transfer** component:

- Stateful session bean
- Default create method with all attributes as parameters

EJB Properties

The EJB properties of the **Transfer** component are specified in the **ArcStylerEJB 1.1** property sheet of the component's Rose specification dialog. The following properties are relevant for the **Transfer** component:

- **ModelingStyle–Compact.**
- **Bean Home Name–**<empty>.
- **BeanType–Session.**
- **StateManagement–Stateful.**   The **Transfer** component is implemented as stateful session bean.
- **TransactionType–Container.**
- **ContainerTransaction–Required.**
- **GenDfltFactories–AllAttributesAsParameters** .   A default create method with all attributes as parameters is generated in the bean's home interface.

Figure 8.14 shows the completed **ArcStylerEJB** 1.1 property sheet for the **Transfer** component.

The technical refinement of the **Transfer** component is now complete.

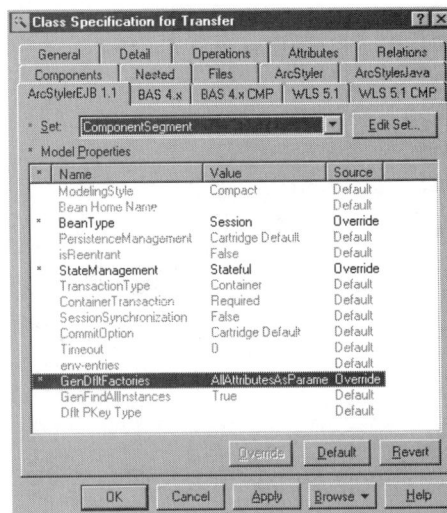

Figure 8.14   EJB properties of the Transfer component.

Modeling Deployable Components

Now you will model the assembly in terms of its individual *deployable components*. At this point, the assembly includes an EJB archive that packages the **Account** and **Transfer** components as well as an EJB client archive needed by the Web accessors. The Web application will be developed later in the tutorial, but we want to first deploy and test the business components in the EJB container.

Deployable components are modeled in a package in the **Component View** of the Rose model. To model an EJB archive, proceed as follows:

1. Add a new package, **libs,** to the **Component View.**
2. Add a new component, **model**, with the stereotype EJBArchive to the **libs** package.
3. Assign the **Account** and **Transfer** components to the EJB archive by dragging the components to the **model** component.
4. Make sure that the Set in the cartridge-specific property sheet of the **model** component (for example, **BAS 4.x, WLS 5.1**) is set to **EJBArchive**, and check the **Test Server Address** and **Test Server Port** properties in this property sheet.

The Web accessors or any other clients will need an EJB client archive component as well, which you also can create now:

1. Add a new component, **stubs**, with the stereotype **EJBClientArchive** to the **libs** package.
2. Drag and drop the **Account** and **Transfer** beans to the client archive.
3. Make sure that the **Set** in the cartridge-specific property sheet of the **stubs** component is set to **EJBClientArchive**, and check the **Test Server Address** and **Test Server Port** properties in this property sheet.

Model Verification

It is now time check the stylistic integrity of the UML model and make sure that it can be projected successfully to the selected infrastructure. The C-REF tool provides a configurable model-verification mechanism (also known as *model validation*) to validate the UML model according to the requirements of the architectural style. The following aspects can be verified:

- Structural correctness
- UML constraints
- Rational Rose constraints
- Technical feasibility (Java constraints, container-specific J2EE/EJB constraints)

You can verify single model elements or the entire model. If problems are found, messages regarding the problems, their causes, and their severities are presented. Warning messages manifest dubious or suboptimal model constellations, and error messages indicate problems that must be fixed in order to remain style-conform.

At this point, you have a refined the UML model of your business components and assembly components to the level where the convergent generator (C-GEN) generator, and technology projection cartridge can take over and generate a deployable infrastructure.

Generating the EJB Components with C-GEN

This section covers the code-generation steps in the architectural IDE that essentially support all the construction-phase work flows in the CA process.

In this step, the C-GEN module and the technology projection cartridge are activated from the C-REF UML model to create major portions of the deployment infrastructure as well as the test and build environment. As explained in Chapter 7, the depth and width of this infrastructure are so extensive that it is referred to as *fan-out*.

The C-GEN is a powerful JPython-based generator engine that uses one or more technology projection cartridges to program and drive the generation process. A cartridge provides the templates, scripts, and optimization rules for a particular runtime environment (for example, an J2EE/EJB container). Moreover, it supplies the model verifiers used by the C-REF module (see preceding section) to verify the technical feasibility of the UML model with respect to the target technology.

This section contains the following subsections:

- Configuring the code generator
- Running the code generator

Configuring the Code Generator

Before you can start with the code generation, you must configure the code generator. In particular, you must specify the following:

- A source code output directory
- A technology projection cartridge for the target runtime environment
- A template path specifying where the templates (and template extensions) are located
- Database configuration information
- Configuration of the tools used by the build process (for example, J2EE/EJB container, Tomcat servlet engine)

The code generator is configured in the **C-GEN** tab of the ArcStyler configuration dialog.

The Generate Panel

In the **Generate** panel of the **C-GEN** tab, you must specify the following:

- **Generated Source Directory.** This specifies the source code output directory.

- **Template Directory.**   This specifies the path where the code generator searches for the templates.
- **Project Name.**   This specifies the name of the project, for example, **IBank Tutorial**.

Figure 8.15 shows the completed configuration of the **Generate** panel.

The Projections Panel

In the **Projections** panel of the **C-GEN** tab, you must specify the following:

- **Chosen Technology Projections.**   This specifies the technology projection cartridges to activate.
- Each cartridge provides cartridge-specific properties that must be configured. To configure these properties, select the *projection*.**tpr** file in the **Chosen Technology Projections** field.

Figure 8.16 shows the **Projections** panel for the BEA Weblogic server cartridge.

The Database Panel

In the **Database** panel of the **C-GEN** tab, you must configure the database used by the container to store entity beans with container-managed persistence. Usually, an EJB container provides a default database. For simplicity, we will use this default database in this tutorial.

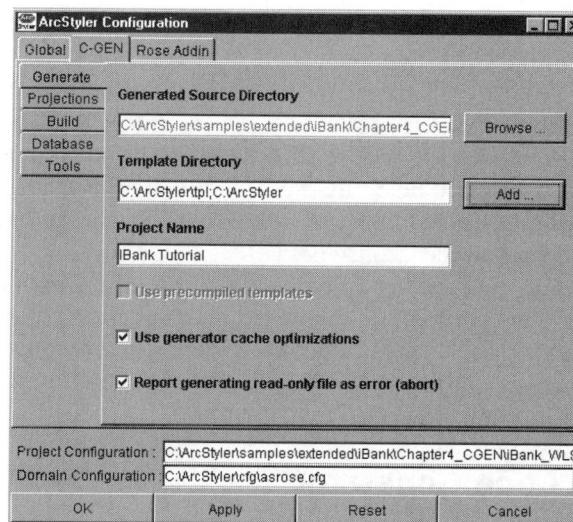

Figure 8.15   The Generate panel.

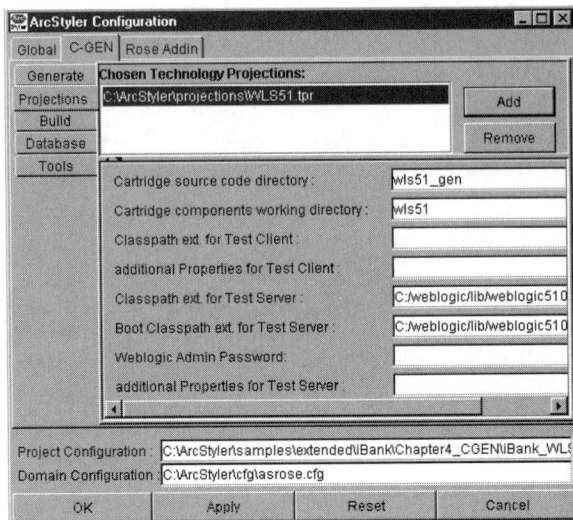

Figure 8.16 The Projections panel.

To do so, choose **Cartridge Default** from the **Database Type** drop-down menu. The default configuration for the container's default database will now be generated automatically into the EJB deployment descriptors.

All other fields can be left empty for the default database.

For details about the database configuration and the default database of a particular EJB container, please refer to the corresponding cartridge documentation.

The Tools Panel

In the **Tools** panel of the **C-GEN** tab, you must configure the tools used by the target technology projection. In particular, you must configure the installation root of your EJB container because this may vary on any given machine.

To do so, select the target tool from the **Choose the tool you want to configure** drop-down menu. In the **Installation** field you must specify the installation path of the tool. Use the **Browse** button to open a directory selector dialog. If required by the tool, you may specify a license key in the **License** field.

For details about the tool configuration needed for your technology projection cartridge, please refer to the appropriate cartridge documentation.

Figure 8.17 shows the **Tools** panel for the BEA Weblogic server container.

Now that you have configured the code generator, save the configuration using the Rose menu **Tools** → **ArcStyler** → **Save Configuration**.

Running the Code Generator

Now run the code generator. In the Rose browser, select the entire **Logical View** package, and use its **ArcStyler** → **Generate** context menu to generate all artifacts. These arti-

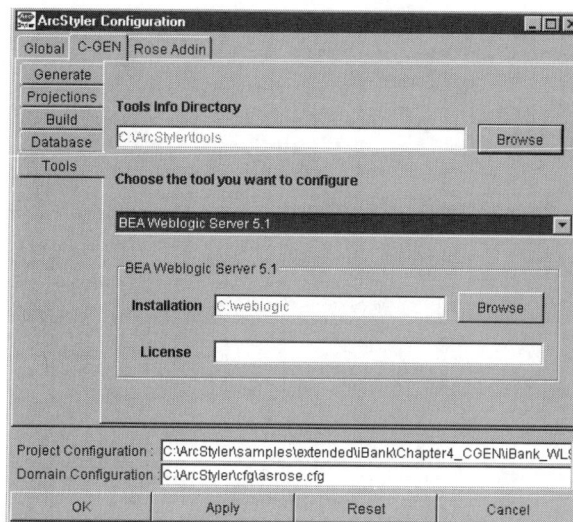

Figure 8.17 The Tools panel.

facts include the following at this point. The JSP and other Web artifacts will be generated in later section using an accessor cartridge.

- Java sources (home interface, remote interface, bean implementation class).
- The Java sources are generated in the **%SRC%/<container_id>_gen/ibank** directory, where **%SRC%** is the source-code output directory you configured in the **Generate** panel.
- Default test client.
- The default test client, **modelTestClient.java**, is generated in the **%SRC%/ components/libs/model** directory.
- Standard deployment descriptor.
- The standard deployment descriptor is generated in the **%SRC%/components/libs/model/META-INF** directory.
- Container-specific deployment descriptors.
- The container-specific deployment descriptors are generated in the **%SRC%/components/libs/model/<container_id>/META-INF** directory.
- Container-specific build support files.
- The container-specific build support files are generated in the **%SRC%/ components/libs/model/<container_id>** directory.

Progress and information pertaining to the code generation are logged to the Rose log window. Figure 8.18 shows an example of the generator output in the log window.

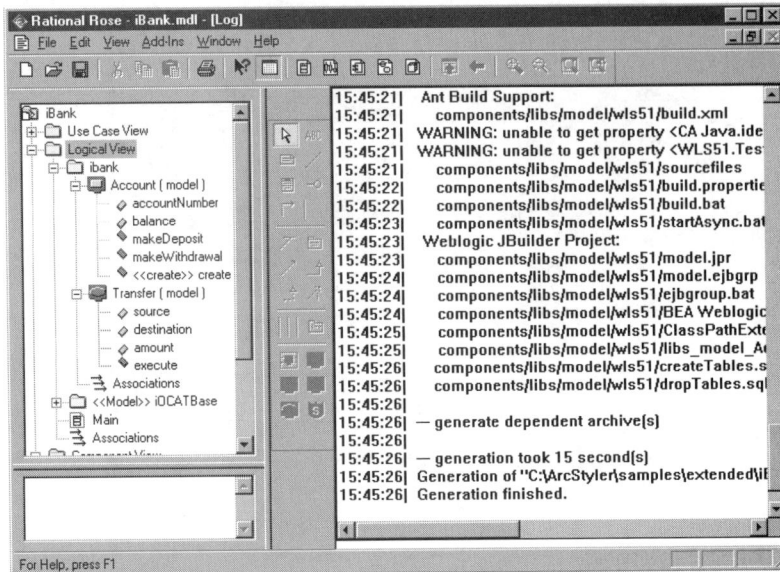

Figure 8.18 Rose log window.

Building, Deploying, and Testing the EJB Components

This section shows how to use one of several build, deploy, and test constellations supported by the architectural IDE. It exhibits support for the implementation cycle work flows, test work flows, and several aspects of the deployment and monitoring work flow.

After the code has been generated, the following tasks are at hand:

- Customize the code.
- Build the EJB JAR file.
- Deploy the EJB JAR file in a test container.
- Test the EJB components using the default test client.

The simple, ANT-based execution of these tasks is covered in the following subsections:

- Code customization
- Build support

Code Customization

In this section, you will implement some custom business logic in the **Account** and **Transfer** beans. Moreover, you will implement custom test code in the default test client.

As explained in Chapter 7, the code generator uses the concept of protected areas to support round-trip development. Protected areas are code segments that are preserved across subsequent runs of the code generator. Custom business logic and other information that cannot be specified in the UML model are entered in these protected areas.

You can use any editor to customize the source code. However, Borland's Java IDE is explicitly supported by the architectural IDE for this purpose. A JBuilder project file, **model.jpr**, was generated in the **%SRC%/components/libs/model/<container_id>** directory. It contains information regarding the Java sources, deployment descriptors, test packages, and other JBuilder information associated with the EJB archive component, **model**, that you created in the previous C-REF section.

The AccountBean.java File

The **AccountBean.java** file was generated into the **%SRC%/<container_id>_gen/ibank** directory. In this file you must implement the following methods:

- `ejbCreate()` for the custom, user-defined factory method you added previously
- `makeDeposit()`
- `makeWithdrawal()`

The following code fragment shows the implementation of the user-defined factory method:

```
    public java.lang.String ejbCreate(java.lang.String accountNumber)
throws CreateException
    {
      /* START OF PROTECTED AREA  <<ejbCreate:string>> */
      // @todo - initialize all key attributes
      // insert custom code here
      // this return value is ignored by the container (EJB 1.1 Spec,
§9.4.2)
      this.accountNumber = accountNumber;
      return null;
      /* END OF PROTECTED AREA 2022d7ea000000b5 */
    }
```

The following code fragment shows the implementation of the `makeDeposit()` method:

```
    public void makeDeposit(double amount)
    {
      /* START OF PROTECTED AREA  <<makeDeposit:double>> */
      // insert custom code here
      setBalance(getBalance()+amount);
      /* END OF PROTECTED AREA 9d700c2d0000002b */
    }
```

The `makeWithdrawal()` method is implemented analogously as follows:

```
public void makeDeposit(double amount)
{
  /* START OF PROTECTED AREA  <<makeDeposit:double>> */
  // insert custom code here
  setBalance(getBalance()-amount);
  /* END OF PROTECTED AREA 9d700c2d0000002b */
}
```

The TransferBean.java File

The **TransferBean.java** file also was generated into the **%SRC%/<container_id>_gen/ ibank** directory. In this file you must implement the `execute()` method. This is done as follows:

```
public void execute()
{
  /* START OF PROTECTED AREA  <<execute>> */
  // insert custom code here
  try
  {
    source.makeWithdrawal(amount);
    destination.makeDeposit(amount);
  }
  catch(Throwable ex)
  {
    ex.printStackTrace(System.err);
  }
  /* END OF PROTECTED AREA 9d700c2d0000002b */
}
```

The modelTestClient.java File

The **modelTestClient.java** file was generated into the **%SRC%/components/libs/ model** directory. In this file you must implement the custom test code. The test code is implemented within the <<main>> protected area. The following code fragment shows an example implementation:

```
/* START OF PROTECTED AREA  <<main>> */
// sample type casting instruction
// SampleHome home = (SampleHome)
javax.rmi.PortableRemoteObject.narrow(ref,SampleHome.class);
// insert your custom code here
System.out.println("Welcome to the IBank Tutorial!");
Object ref = context.lookup("Account");
AccountHome home = (AccountHome)
javax.rmi.PortableRemoteObject.narrow(ref,AccountHome.class);
Account sourceAccount = null;
```

```
        Account destinationAccount = null;
        try {
            // try to lookup source account object
            sourceAccount = home.findByPrimaryKey("00001");
            destinationAccount = home.findByPrimaryKey("00002");
        } catch(FinderException e) {
            // account does nor exist yet so value of sourceAccount
remains null
            System.out.println("Source account not found on server.");
        } catch (RemoteException e)  {
            System.out.println("-> Remote Exception "+e);
            System.exit(1);
        }
        try {
            // create accounts if previous find was unsuccessfull
            if (sourceAccount==null){
                System.out.println("Create source account's remote
interface");
                sourceAccount = (Account) home.create("00001");
                System.out.println("—> AccountBean created");
            }
            if (destinationAccount==null){
                System.out.println("Create destination account's remote
interface");
                destinationAccount = (Account) home.create("00002");
                System.out.println("—> AccountBean created");
            }
            // put money on source account
            System.out.println("Deposit 1000 on account " + "00001");
            sourceAccount.makeDeposit(1000.0);
            // show balance of accounts before transfer
            System.out.println("Balances of accounts before transfer:");
            System.out.println("Balance of account " +
sourceAccount.getAccountNumber()
                                                + " is " +
sourceAccount.getBalance() );
            System.out.println("Balance of account " +
destinationAccount.getAccountNumber()
                                                + " is " +
destinationAccount.getBalance() );
            // create transfer object
            System.out.println("Create transfer remote interface");
            ref = context.lookup("Transfer");
            TransferHome home2 = (TransferHome)
javax.rmi.PortableRemoteObject.narrow(ref,TransferHome.class);
            Transfer transfer = (Transfer)
home2.create(sourceAccount,destinationAccount,300);
            System.out.println("—> TransferBean created");
            // execute transfer
            System.out.println("Making transfer of 300 from account " +
"00001"
```

```
                                                + " to account " +"00002");
        transfer.execute();
        // show balance of accounts after transfer
        System.out.println("Balances of accounts after transfer:");
        System.out.println("Balance of account " +
sourceAccount.getAccountNumber()
                                          + " is " +
sourceAccount.getBalance() );
        System.out.println("Balance of account " +
destinationAccount.getAccountNumber()
                                          + " is " +
destinationAccount.getBalance() );
        java.util.Collection col = home.findAllInstances();
        java.util.Iterator it = col.iterator();
        System.out.println("Found the following accounts:");
        while (it.hasNext()) {
            Account acc = (Account)
javax.rmi.PortableRemoteObject.narrow(it.next(),Account.class);
            System.out.println("Account " + acc.getAccountNumber());
        }
        return;
    } catch (RemoteException e)  {
        System.out.println("-> Remote Exception: "+e);
        e.printStackTrace();
        System.exit(1);
    } catch (Exception e) {
        System.out.println("-> Exception: "+e);
        e.printStackTrace();
        System.exit(1);
    }
    /* END OF PROTECTED AREA 88807f8b000000bb(C) */
```

Moreover, you must implement the <<import>> protected area at the beginning of the file as follows:

```
/* START OF PROTECTED AREA  <<import>> */
// insert your import statements
import ibank.*;
import javax.ejb.*;
import java.rmi.*;
/* END OF PROTECTED AREA d86cd7c700000022(C) */
```

Build Support

In this section you will build the EJB archive, **model.jar**, and the EJB client archive, **stubs.jar**.

The ArcStyler provides extensive support for building, deploying, and testing your EJB component system. This includes both ANT-based command-line build support and Java IDE-based build support.

ANT-Based Build Support

The C-GEN generated ANT scripts for the EJB archive component, **model**, and the EJB client archive component, **stubs**, in the **%SRC%/components/libs/model/<container_id>** and **%SRC%/components/libs/stubs/<container_id>** directories, respectively. The build targets are defined in the ANT build file, **build.xml**. The Java properties needed for the build process are defined in the **build.properties** file. Both files contain protected areas so that you can customize the build process at any time.

To build, deploy, and test the EJB archive, open a command shell and go to the **%SRC%/components/libs/model/<container_id>** directory. Now activate the following build targets. These are the critical-path subset of the available build targets.

- Compile the Java sources and generate the EJB JAR file, **model.jar**, using the following command: `build`. The JAR file is stored in the **%SRC%/components/libs** directory.

- Start the EJB container and deploy the EJB JAR file using the following command: `build runServer`.

- Run the default test client, **modelTestClient**, using the following command: `build runClient`.

- To build the EJB client archive, open a command shell and go to the **%SRC%/components/libs/stubs/<container_id>** directory. The main target to build the EJB client archive is `build`. It compiles the Java sources and generates the EJB client JAR file, **stubs.jar**. The JAR file is stored in the **%SRC%/components/libs** directory.

In general, the build process is highly container-specific. For details, please refer the respective technology projection cartridge documentation. One such cartridge document is presented in the bonus chapter on the Web site, which covers the details of the technology projection component in reference manual form. Other cartridge documentation is also available via the Convergent Architecture Web site.

Figure 8.19 shows the output from the default test client as started from the command line.

IDE-Based Build Support

In the previous steps, build support for Borland's Java IDE JBuilder also was generated automatically. The respective JBuilder project files, libraries, and configurations were generated into the **%SRC%/components/libs/model/<container_id>** and **%SRC%/components/libs/stubs/<container_id>** directories, respectively.

The advantage of Java IDE-based build support is that you can use the IDE for visual debugging and testing.

For details, refer the respective technology projection cartridge documentation. One such cartridge document is presented in the bonus chapter on the Web site, which covers the details of the technology projection component in reference manual form. Other cartridge documentation is also available via the Convergent Architecture Web site.

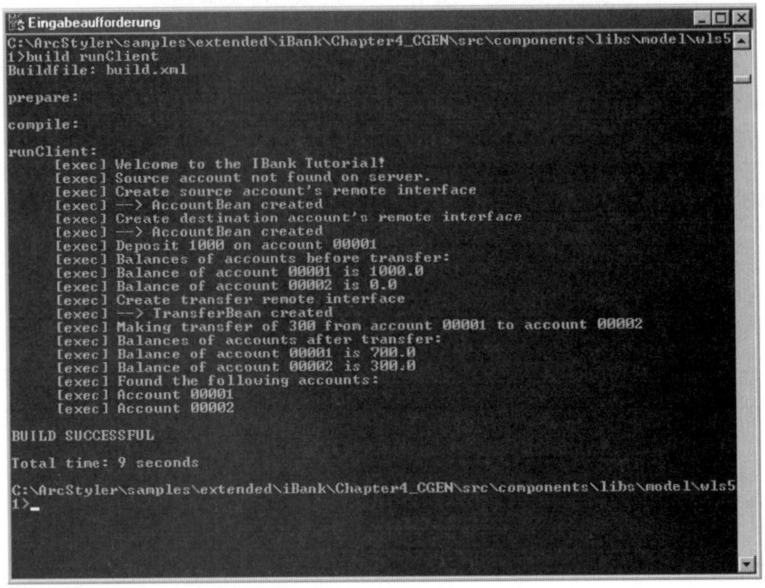

Figure 8.19   Test client output for the iBank tutorial.

Modeling the Web Accessors in C-REF

In the preceding sections you completed development of the business components. The business components are now deployed and ready to do business as EJB components in an application server. In the remainder of this tutorial you will take on the role of accessor developer (see Chapter 5) and develop the accessor components for Web access—a graphic user interface (GUI) that enables clients to interact with the EJB component system. This will be achieved according to the CA process as defined in Chapter 6 with support of the architectural IDE as described in Chapter 7.

You will proceed as follows:

- Create accessor models in UML using the C-REF/Rose module.
- Generate accessor infrastructure for a Web-channel using the JSP accessor cartridge.
- Build, deploy, and test the Web user interfaces.

This section covers the UML modeling steps. It contains the following subsections:

- Generating default accessor models
- Extending the default accessor model
- Modeling the Web application deployment component

Generating Default Accessor Models

The accessor modeling style and its automation support in the architectural IDE enable us to generate default accessor models based on an existing business component model. These default accessors are designed to cover the most common accessor use-case scenarios. The most common scenarios involve the following client interaction with the business component system:

- Show a particular instance of a business component.
- Show all existing instances of a business component.
- Create an instance of a business component.
- Remove a particular instance of a business component.
- Modify a particular instance of a business component.

For details on default accessors and their underlying design, consult the bonus chapter and other information available on the Convergent Architecture Web site.

In this tutorial we will use the default accessor model generator to generate accessors to manipulate **Account** components: create new accounts and edit or delete existing accounts. To do so, proceed as follows:

1. Select the **Account** component in the C-REF/Rose browser and use its **ArcStyler** → **Accessors** → **Create** → **Collection Editor** accessor context menu. This will create a subpackage in the **iBank** package, **DefaultaccessorsPackage**.

2. In order to use brief notations in your model, rename the **DefaultaccessorsPackage** package into **GUI** package.

Figure 8.20 shows the new default accessor package with its new name, **GUI**.
The GUI package contains various accessors, represented by the icon, and representers, symbolized by the icon:

- **Account_CreatorDR.**   Representer representing a GUI that enables the client to enter the account number of the account to be created
- **Account_EditorDA.**   Accessor controlling the edit interaction with an account
- **Account_EditorDR.**   Representer representing a GUI that enables the client to manipulate an account
- **Account_SEditorDA.**   Accessor that controls the manipulation of a collection of accounts
- **Account_SEditorDR.**   Representer representing a GUI to display a collection of accounts and enable clients to trigger activities to manipulate accounts

An accessor component is a UML class with the stereotype **Accessor** (see the bonus chapter on the Web site for detail on modeling style). It represents the flow control of a user interface. Accessors can have attributes to store information processed within the accessor. A representer component, a subunit of an accessor, is also a UML class with the stereotype **Representer**. It is used to display information to the client and to receive

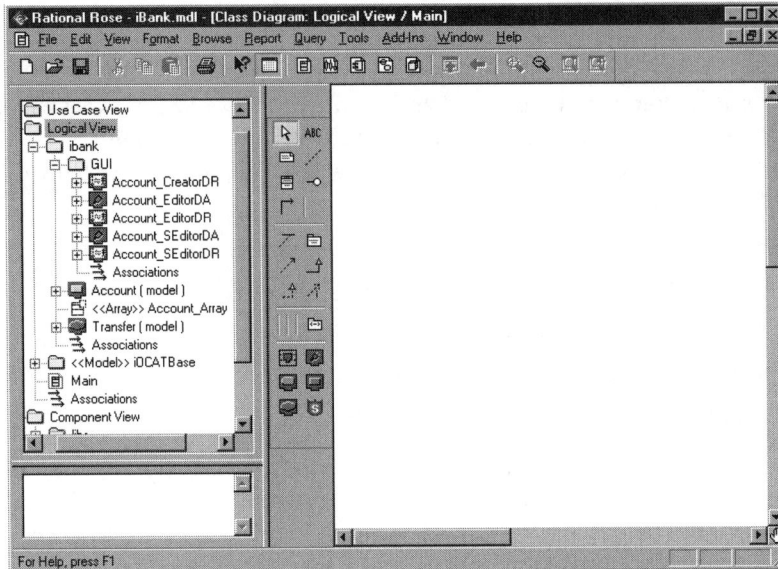

Figure 8.20   The default accessor package.

input from the client. Representers can have attributes to store the information displayed to or received from the client.

The Generated Accessor State Model

Observing the newly generated default accessors, the main accessor is the **Account_SEditorDA**. It controls the entire user interface. The flow control of an accessor is modeled in a state/activity diagram that also has been generated automatically. Figure 8.21 shows the state/activity diagram for the **Account_SEditorDA** accessor.

The central element in the **Account_SEditorDA**'s state/activity diagram is the **EditAccountS** representer state. This state is associated with the **Account_SEditorDR** representer. The **Account_SEditorDR** represents a GUI that displays all existing accounts and provides trigger elements to trigger transitions in the accessor's state model. As indicated in the model, the client can trigger the following transitions:

Create a new account.   The **Account_SEditorDA** accessor transitions to the **createAccount** representer state. This state is associated with the **Account_CreatorDR** representer. The **Account_CreatorDR** represents a GUI that enables the client to input the account number for the new account. From the **createAccount** representer state the accessor either transitions back to the **EditAccountS** representer state, or it transitions to the **add** activity. This activity is responsible for creating a new **Account** component with the account number provided by the client. From the **add** activity the accessor transitions to the **Account_Editor** state.

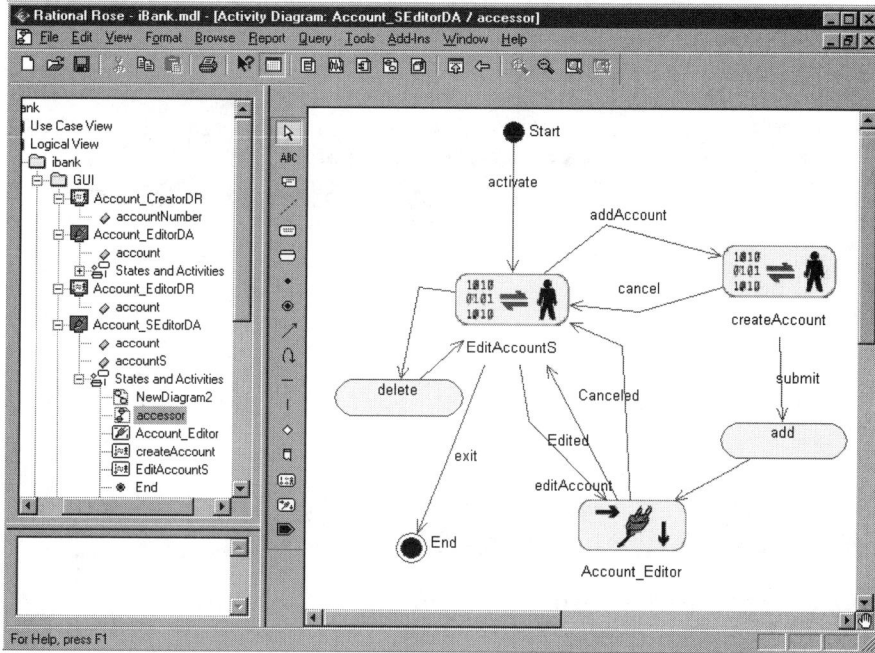

Figure 8.21   State/activity diagram of the Account_SEditorDA accessor.

Edit an account.   The **Account_SEditorDA** accessor transitions to the
Account_Editor state. This is an embedded accessor state associated with the
Account_EditorDA accessor. In this state the main accessor, **Account_SEdi-
torDA**, delegates the control to the embedded accessor, **Account_EditorDA**.
This accessor controls the edit interaction for a single account. It provides a
representer, **Account_EditorDR**, that is a GUI where the client can edit the balance of the selected account. For details, take a look at the corresponding
state/activity diagram of the **Account_EditorDA** accessor component. From the
Account_Editor state the accessor transitions back to the **EditAccountS** representer state. Two transitions are provided: **Cancelled** and **Edited**. Which one is
used depends on the end state of the embedded accessor, **Account_EditorDA**.

Delete an account.   The **Account_SEditorDA** accessor transitions to the **delete**
activity. This activity is responsible for deleting the selected **Account** component. From the **delete** activity the accessor transitions back to the **EditAccountS**
representer state.

A representer state must be associated with a specific representer, and an embedded
accessor state must be associated with an specific accessor. This is done in the **RepresenterState**'s or **EmbeddedAccessorState**'s **ArcStyler** specification dialog. Figure 8.22
shows the dialog for the **EditAccountS** representer state.

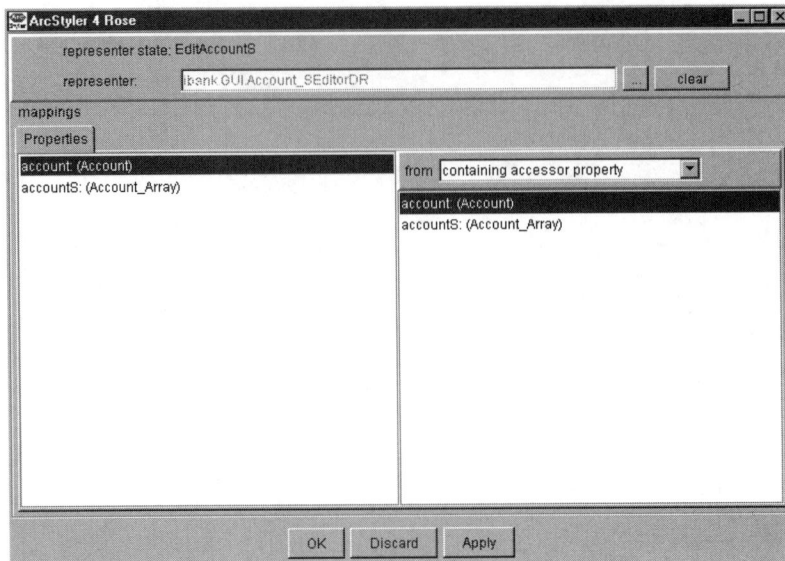

Figure 8.22   State specification dialog.

In the lower part of the state's property sheet you can specify the resource mapping for the state. This maps the attributes of the associated representer or embedded accessor in the left panel, **Properties**, to the respective attributes of the controlling accessor (in our example this is the **Account_SEditorDA** accessor) shown in the right panel.

The resource mapping defines the data flow in the model. A resource mapping causes the attribute of the representer or embedded accessor to be initialized with the current value of the associated attribute of the controlling accessor.

Modeling Representers

Representers are detailed using the representer's ArcStyler specification dialog. Figure 8.23 shows the dialog of the **Account_SEditorDR** representer.

At the top of the dialog you can specify the **Representer type: COLLECTION**, which specifies that the representer will display a collection of instances (for example, the **Account_SEditorDR** representer), or **SLICE**, which means that the representers will display exactly one instance (for example, the **Account_CreatorDR** representer).

In the left panel you can model the **Interaction Attributes** and **Events** provided by the representer. Interaction attributes represent edit fields or text fields in the representer (for example, edit fields in a JSP). Events represent buttons in the user interface that trigger corresponding transitions in the state machine of the controlling accessor.

In the lower right part of the representer's specification dialog you can specify the resource mapping between an interaction attribute and the associated representer

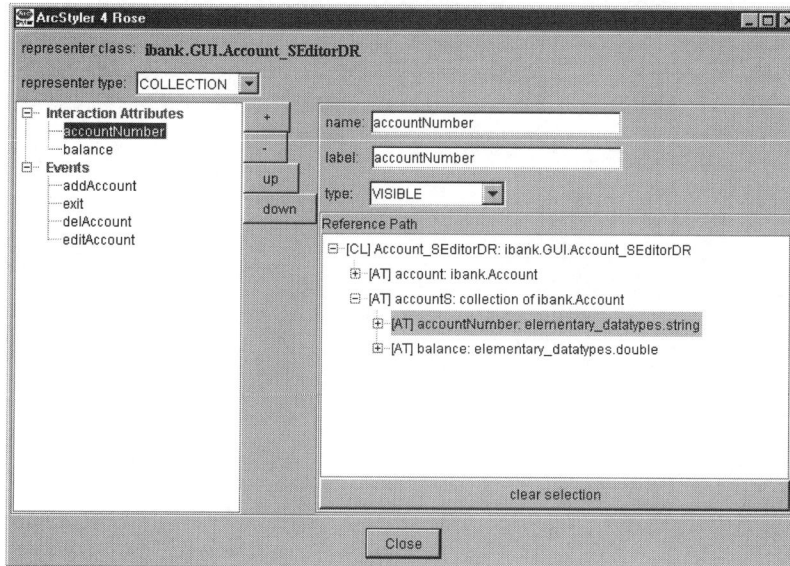

Figure 8.23   Representer specification dialog.

attribute to be displayed in the interaction attribute's text or edit field. Figure 8.23 emphasizes the resource mapping between the **Interaction Attribute**, **accountNumber**, and the **accountNumber** attribute of the representer's **accountS** attribute.

Extending the Default Accessor Model

In this section you will start from default accessor model to create your own customized accessor. You will add an activity, **init**, to the state/activity diagram of the main accessor, **Account_SEditorDA**. This activity will be responsible for finding all existing accounts and initializing the **accountS** attribute of the **Account_SEditorDA** accessor with the found collection of accounts.

Proceed as follows:

1. Add a new activity, **init**.
2. Redirect the **activate** transition from the **Start** state to the **init** activity by dragging the transition arrow.
3. Add a new transition from the **init** activity to the **EditAccountS** representer state.

Figure 8.24 shows the completed diagram for the customized accessor.

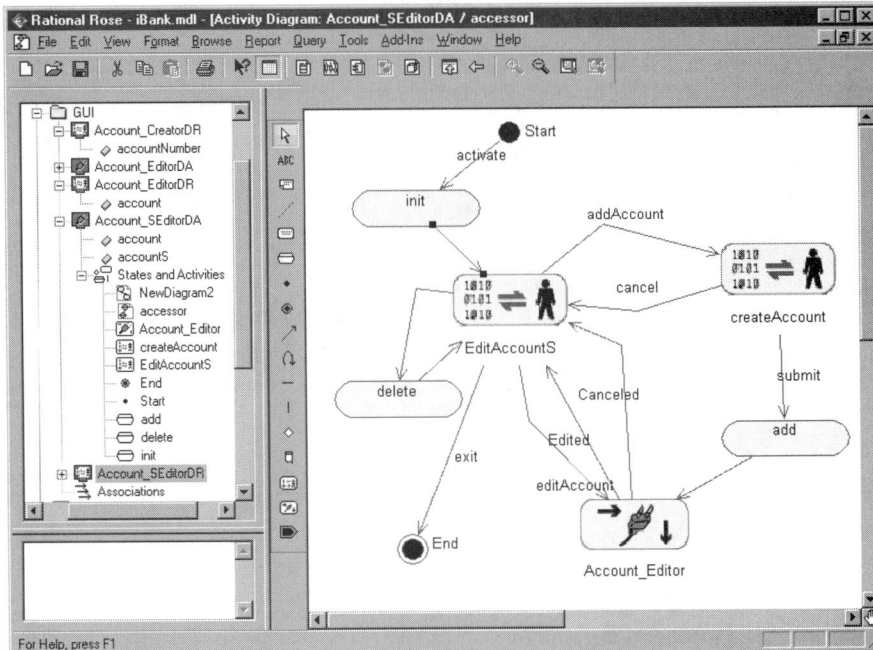

Figure 8.24 Modified state/activity diagram

Modeling the Web App
Deployment Component

Now you will extend the assembly model in terms of the accessor's *deployable compo-nents* for the Web application. You will model the a Web application archive (WAR) that packages the accessor and representer components of the model for automatic deploy-ment into a Web server.

To model the Web application archive, proceed as follows:

1. Add a new component, **webapp**, with the stereotype **Webapplication** to the
   libs package you created earlier for the business components.

2. In the **webapp** component's ArcStyler specification dialog, specify the
   Account_SEditorDA accessor as root accessor that takes the main control.

Figure 8.25 shows the result.

In order to guarantee a complete assembly for the deployed environment, the deployment dependencies between the packaged Web accessor components and the packaged business components is also modeled. In the UML model, this is expressed by adding a dependency relation between the Web application component and the EJB client archive component, **stubs**. To model this dependency, proceed as follows:

1. Add a component diagram, **Dependencies**, to the **libs** package.

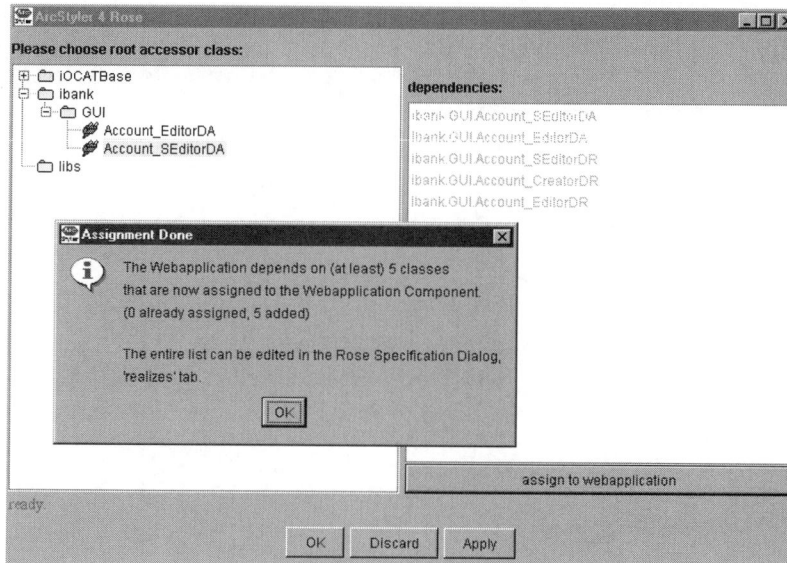

Figure 8.25   Assigning the root accessor.

2. Drag and drop the **stubs** and **webapp** components from the Rose browser into the diagram and insert a dependency from the **webapp** component (client component) to the **stubs** component (server component).

Figure 8.26 shows the **Dependencies** diagram.

At this point, you have a refined the UML model of your accessor components and assembly components to the level where the C-GEN generator and technology projection cartridge can take over and generate a deployable infrastructure.

Generating the Web Application with C-GEN

This section covers the code-generation steps for the Web accessors. The architectural IDE is now used to support these accessor-specific aspects of the CA process work flows.

In this step, the C-GEN module and accessor technology projection cartridge are activated from the C-REF UML model. These are used to generate major portions of the deployment infrastructure as well as the test and build environment for the JSP/servlet-based Web application.

This section contains the following subsections:

- Configuring the code generator
- Running the code generator

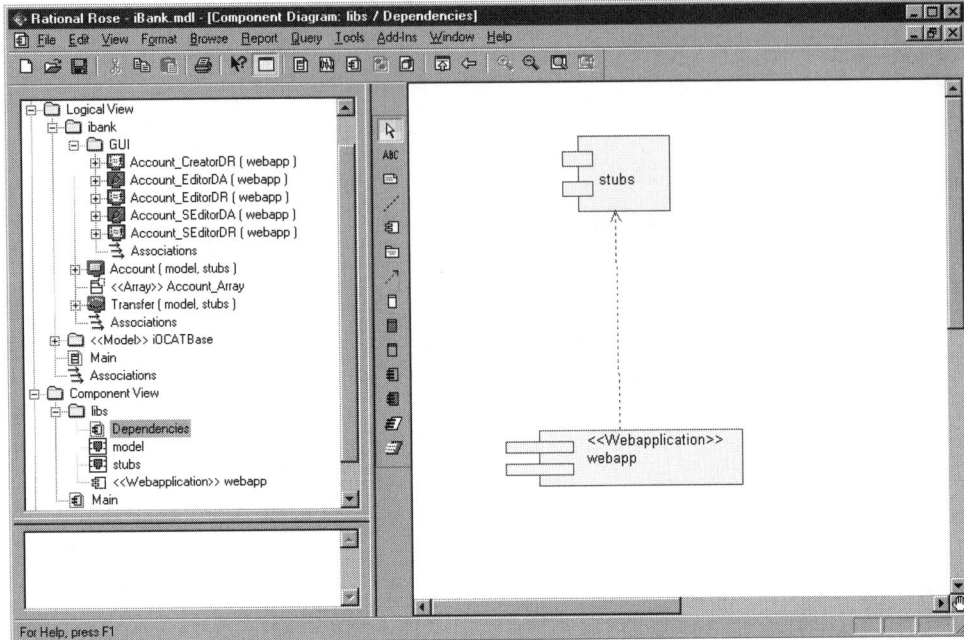

Figure 8.26   The Dependencies diagram.

Configuring the Code Generator

Before you start generating accessor code, you must configure the code generator using the ArcStyler configuration dialog.

The Generate Panel

In the **Generate** panel, you must specify the following:

- **Generated Source Directory.**   This specifies the source-code output directory.
- **Template Directory.**   This specifies the path where the code generator searches for the templates.
- **Project Name.**   This specifies the name of the project, for example, **iBank Tutorial**.

Figure 8.27 shows the completed configuration of the **Generate** panel.

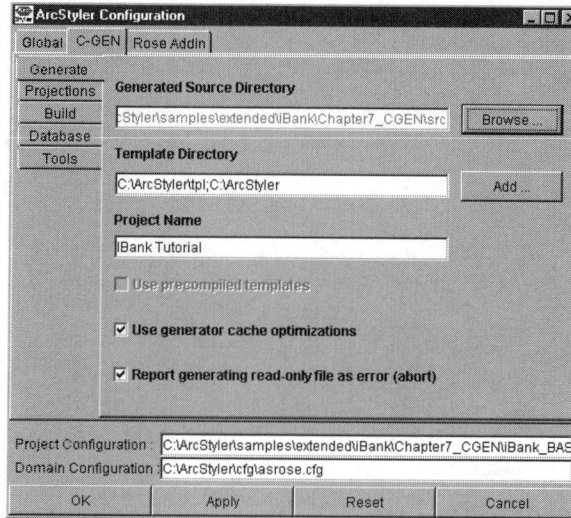

Figure 8.27   The Generate panel.

The Projections Panel

In the **Projections** panel, you must specify the technology projection cartridges needed for accessor code generation. Add the following *projection*.**tpr** files in the **Chosen Technology Projections** field:

- *projection*.**tpr** file corresponding to your target EJB container. You should have done this already in a previous section of the sample.
- **iO_JSP_accessors.tpr** file corresponding to the JSP/servlet cartridge.
- For this cartridge, you also must configure the JBuilder version installed in your local environment.

Figure 8.28 shows the **Projections** panel configured with the accessor cartridge as well as the Borland Application Server cartridge and JBuilder4.

You have now configured the code generator. Save the configuration.

Running the Code Generator

By default, the C-GEN generates code for all technology projections configured in the **Projections** panel. However, because the EJB business components were already generated in previous sections, we only need to generate the code for the Web accessors here. To do so, select the entire **Logical View** package in the C-REF/Rose browser and use its **ArcStyler** → **Configure** Generation context menu. The selector dialog shown in Figure 8.29 pops up where you should select only the JSP/servlet cartridge.

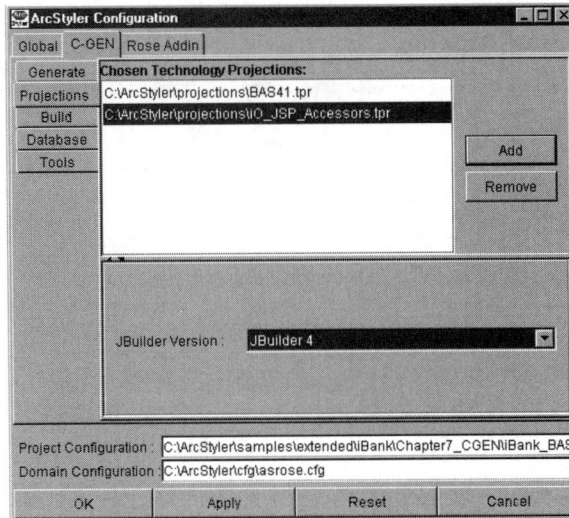

Figure 8.28 The Projections panel.

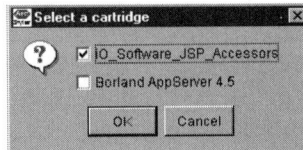

Figure 8.29 The cartridge selector dialog.

Now you can run the code generator. In the C-REF/Rose browser, select the **Logical View**, and use its **ArcStyler** → **Generate** context menu in order to generate all artifacts for the Web accessor infrastructure. In this instance, the generated infrastructure includes the following:

- Java sources for the accessor and representer components.
- The Java sources are generated in the **%SRC%/ui_jsp_gen/java/ibank/GUI** directory, where **%SRC%** is the source-code output directory you configured in the **Generate** panel.
- JSP sources for the representer components .
- The JSP sources are generated in the **%SRC%/ui_jsp_gen/site/ibank/GUI** directory.
- Web application build support files.
- The container-specific build support files are generated in the **%SRC%/ components/libs/webapp/ui_jsp** directory.

Progress and information pertaining to the code generation are logged to the Rose log window, as shown in the Figure 8.30.

Building, Deploying, and Testing the Web Application

This section shows how to use one of several build, deploy, and test constellations for Web accessors. It exhibits the architectural IDE support for accessor aspects of the implementation cycle work flows, test work flows, and deployment and monitoring work flow.

Once the infrastructure has been generated, the following tasks are at hand:

- Customize code.
- Build the Web application WAR file.
- Deploy the WAR file in a Web server.
- Test the Web application in an Internet browser.

This section contains the following subsections:

- Code customization

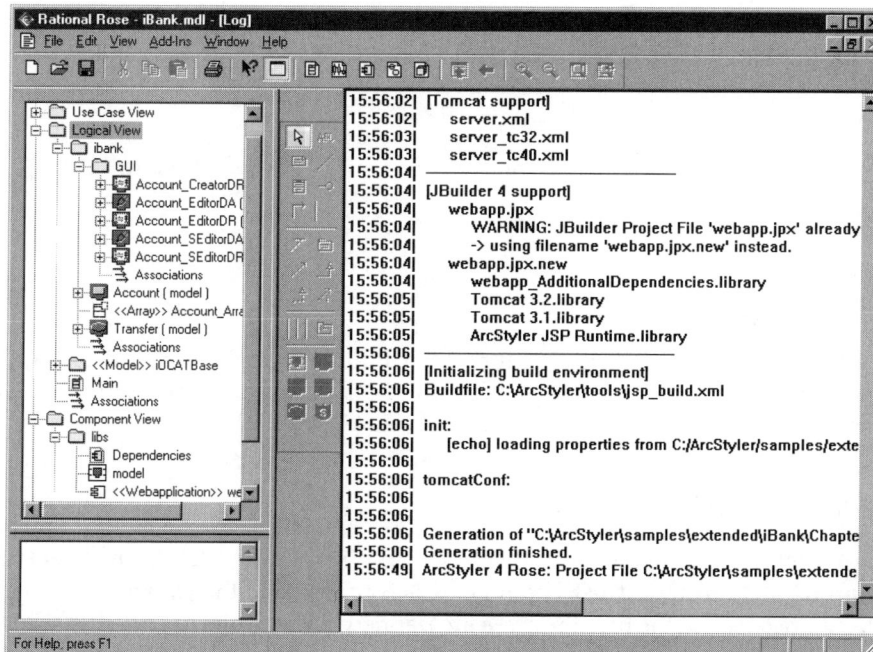

Figure 8.30   Rose log window.

- Build support
- Running the Web application

Code Customization

In this section you will implement the **init** activity methods modeled in the state/activity diagram of the **Account_SEditorDA** accessor. Moreover, you will customize some properties in the **web.xml** file generated for the Web application.

You can use any editor to customize the source code. However, Borland's Java IDE is explicitly supported by the architectural IDE for this purpose. A JBuilder project file, **webapp.jpx**, was generated in the **%SRC%/components/libs/webapp/ui_jsp** directory. It contains the Java sources, the JSP sources, the **web.xml** file, a **launch.html** file to test the Web application in an Internet browser, and other JBuilder-specific configuration information.

The Account_SEditorDA.java File

The **Account_SEditorDA.java** file was generated into the **%SRC%/ui_jsp_gen/java/ ibank/GUI** directory. In this file you must complete the generated doInit() method for the **init** activity.

The following code fragment shows the implementation of the doInit() method:

```
java.util.Collection col = getAccountHome().findAllInstances();
java.util.Iterator it = col.iterator();
m_AccountS = new ibank.Account[col.size()];
int i=0;
while(it.hasNext()) {
    ibank.Account acc = (ibank.Account)
javax.rmi.PortableRemoteObject.narrow(it.next(),ibank.Account.class);
    System.out.println("Account " + acc.getAccountNumber());
    m_AccountS[i++] = acc;
}
```

Build Support

The ArcStyler provides extensive support for building, deploying, and testing Web applications. In this section you will complete these tasks using both ANT-based command-line support and, optionally, the JBuilder Java IDE support.

ANT-Based Build Support

The C-GEN module generates ANT scripts in the **%SRC%/components/libs/ webapp/ui_jsp** directory. The build process is configured in the **jsp.xml** file. The Java properties needed for the build process are defined in the **project.properties** file. Both files contain protected areas so that the build process can be customized at any time.

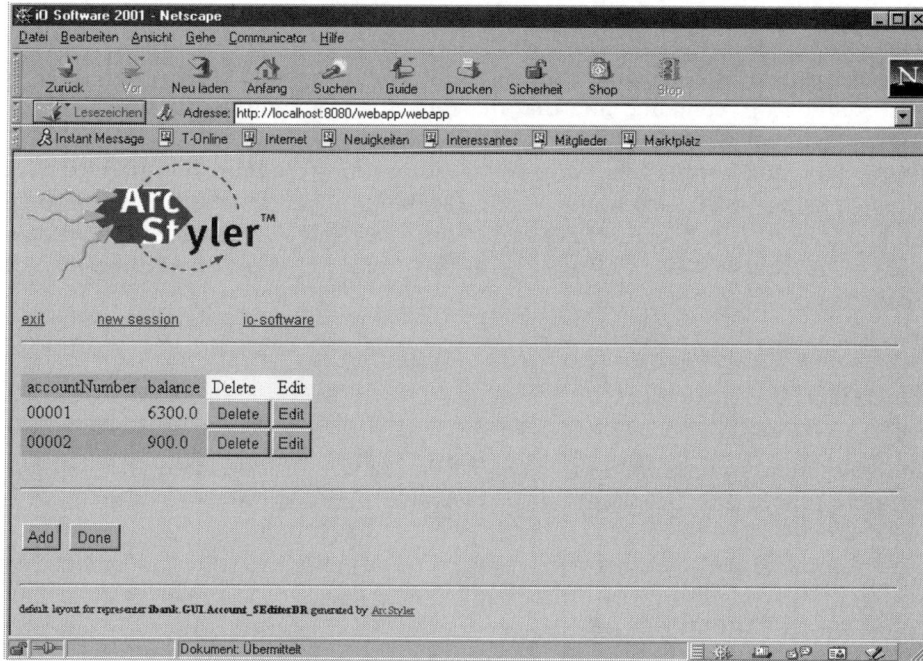

Figure 8.31   The running Web application.

Now activate the following build targets. These are the critical-path subset of the available build targets.

`build`.   This compiles the JSP and Java sources and generates the WAR file, **webapp.war**. The WAR file is stored in the **%SRC%/components/libs** directory.

`build startTomcat`.   This starts the Tomcat servlet engine.

In general, the build process is highly container-specific. For details, please refer the respective accessor cartridge documentation. One such cartridge document is presented in the bonus chapter on the Web site, which covers the details of the technology projection component in reference manual form. Other cartridge documentation are also available via the Convergent Architecture Web site.

IDE-Based Build Support

In the previous steps, build support for Borland's Java IDE JBuilder also was generated automatically. The respective JBuilder project files, libraries, and configurations were generated into the **%SRC%/components/libs/webapp/ui_jsp** directory.

The advantage of Java IDE-based build support is that you can use the IDE for visual debugging and testing.

For details, please refer the respective accessor cartridge documentation.

Running the Web Application

Before you run the Web application, make sure that business components are deployed in the running EJB container and that the Tomcat servlet engine has been started as described previously.

Now start your favorite Internet browser by activating the **launch.html** file that was generated in the **%SRC%/components/libs/webapp/ui_jsp** directory. This will run the Web application. Figure 8.31 shows one of the interrelated accessor GUIs you developed earlier. This accessor GUI was generated from the **Account_SEditorDR** representer.

Summary

The iBank tutorial presented in this chapter has led you sequentially through many central aspects of the CA process and its commensurate support in the architectural IDE.

The tutorial started you off with convergent business modeling and moved you through the stages of convergent UML refinement stages to arrive at an assembly of deployable J2EE/EJB business components. You then learned how to generate and refine Web accessor models and how to generate the entire J2EE/EJB infrastructure from the UML model. Lastly, you saw how to build, deploy, and test both the EJB business component and the Web accessors using the generated infrastructure.

For additional tutorials and samples, refer to the Convergent Architecture Web site: www.ConvergentArchitecture.com.

Bibliography

Books

Alexander, C. 1975. *The Oregon Experiment*. New York: Oxford University Press. ISBN 0-19-501824-9.

Alexander, C., et. al. 1977. *A Pattern Language: Towns, Buildings, Construction*. New York: Oxford University Press. ISBN 0-19-501919-9.

Coplein, J. 1992. *Advanced C++ Programming Styles and Idioms*. Reading, MA: Addison-Wesley. ISBN 0-201-54855-0.

Coplien, J., Schmidt, D., eds. 1995. *Pattern Languages of Program Design*. Reading, MA: Addison-Wesley. ISBN 0-201-60734-4.

Droste, M. 1998. *Bauhaus 1919-1933*. Berlin: Bauhaus-Archiv Museum fuer Gestaltung, Klingelhoeferstr. ISBN 3-8228-7601-1.

D'Souza, D. 1998. *Objects, Components, and Frameworks with UML: The Catalysis Approach*. Reading, MA: Addison-Wesley. ISBN 0-201-31012-0.

Gilb, T. 1988/1999. *Principles of Software Engineering Management*. Reading, MA: Addison-Wesley. EPM99-EPM: Evolutionary Project Management: **www.natural-metrics.freeserve.co.uk/download.htm**.

Graham, I., Henderson-Sellers B., Younessi H. 1997. *The OPEN Process Specification*. Reading, MA: Addison-Wesley Longman. ISBN 0-201-33133-0.

Henderson-Sellers, B., Simons, Y. 1998. *The OPEN Toolbox of Techniques*. Reading, MA: Addison-Wesley. ISBN 0-201-33134-9.

Herrmann, W., ed. 1992. *In What Style Should We Build? The German Debate on Architectural Style*. Santa Monica, CA: Getty Center for the History of Art and the Humanities. ISBN 0-89236-199-9.

Heyer, P. 1993. *Architects on Architecture: New Directions in America*. New York: Van Nostrand Reinhold. ISBN 0-442-01751-0.

Hofstadter, D. 1979. *Goedel Escher Bach*. New York: Vintage Press. ISBN 0-394-75682-7

Kane, G. 1988. *Mips RISC Architecture*. Englewood Cliffs, NJ: Prentice-Hall. ISBN: 0-13-584749-4.

Kruchten, P. 1998. *The Rational Unified Process*. Reading, MA: Addison-Wesley Longman. ISBN 0-201-60459-0.

Taylor, D. A. 1995. *Business Engineering with Object Technology*. New York: John Wiley & Sons. ISBN: 0-471-04521-7.

Taylor, D. A. 1997. *Object Technology: A Managers Guide,* 2d ed. Reading MA: Addison-Wesley. ISBN 0-201-30994-7.

Warmer, J. 1999. *The Object Constraint Language: Precise Modeling with UML*. Reading, MA: Addison-Wesley Longman. ISBN 0-201-37940-6.

Papers and Articles

Aalst, V. 1998. "Formalization and Verification of Event-Driven Process Chains." *Computing Science Reports,* 98/01; citeseer.nj.nec.com/208211.html.

Ambler, S. 1997. "Architecture Driven Modeling: The 'T' Approach." Microsoft MSDN Online; msdn.microsoft.com/library/periodic/period97/Modeling.htm.

Girouard, M. 1963. "Monticello, Virginia, The Home of Thomas Jefferson from 1771 to 1826." *Country Life*, 133 (January 17, 1963): 108.

Iggulden, D., Rees, O., Van der Linden, R. 1994. "Architecture and Frameworks: Advanced Network System Architecture Phase III (ANSA Phase III)." APM.1017.02, October 25, 1994; www.ansa.co.uk.

Kruchten, P. 2000. "Developing Large Scale Systems with the Rational Unified Process." RUP 2000, technical white paper; www.rational.com/products/whitepapers/sis.jsp.

Lewis, T. 1999. "Where the Smart Money Is?" *IEEE Computer,* November 1999: 136; computer.org.

Oberg, R. 2000, "Applying Requirements Management with Use-Cases." RUP 2000, technical white paper TP505; www.rational.com/products/whitepapers/100622.jsp.

Standards (RFCs, ITU Recommendations, etc.)

EJB. 2001. The Enterprise Java Beans specifications may be found at java.sun.com/products/ejb.

IEEE. 2000. "Architectural Description of Software Intensive Systems." *IEEE Standard 1471-2000,* IEEE Computer Society; www.ieee.org.

J2EE Blueprints. 2001. Available from java.sun.com/j2ee/blueprints.

J2EE Patterns. 2001. Available to members of the Java Developer's Connection through developer.java.sun.com/developer/restricted/patterns/J2EEPatterns AtAGlance.html.

J2EE. 2001. The Java 2 Enterprise Environment specifications may be found at java.sun.com/j2ee.

JCP. 2001. The Java Community Process. Available at java.sun.com/about Java/communityprocess.

MDA. 2001. "OMG Model-Driven Architecture Initiative." Available at www.omg.com/mda.

UML. 2000. "The OMG Unified Modeling Language Specification." Version 1.3, March 2000. Available at www.omg.org/cgi-bin/doc?formal/2000-03-01.

Tools

ANT. 2000. The Apache Jakarta Project. Available at jakarta.apache.org/ant/index.html, jakarta.apache.org/ant/manual/index.html.

BEA Systems Corporation. 2001. The WebLogic Server. Available at www.beasys.com.

Borland Corporation. 2001. The Borland Application Server. Available at www.borland.com.

iO GmbH. 2001. Interactive Objects Software GmbH. The ArcStyler Architectural IDE for J2EE/EJB. Available at www.ArcStyler.com, www.io-software.com.

JUnit. 2000. Available at www.junit.org/.

Rational Corporation. 2000. The Rational Unified Process.

Rational Corporation. 2001. Rational Rose 2001 Modeler Edition. Available at www.rational.com.

Notes

Chapter 1

1. Definition from the *American Heritage Dictionary*: "Of or relating to an *architectural style* prevalent in Western Europe from the 12th through the 15th century and characterized by pointed arches, rib vaulting and flying buttresses. Of or relating to an architectural style derived from medieval Gothic."

2. A similar analogy can be made with music.

3. Many aspects of convergence will be discussed in detail in later chapters. Essentially, it means the alignment of business and IT models into one common, synchronized model.

4. This use of the word architecture conforms with many accepted definitions and taxonomies of IT architecture. For a good definition, see IEEE (2000).

5. Marketing-driven designs conceived to create or capitalize on a trend in the marketplace irrelevant of the maturity or long-term contribution of the design. Analogous to many *prêt-à-porter* fashion trends in the clothing industry.

6. The Virginia State Capitol is described as the "first adaptation of a temple for a modern public building not only in America, but in the world" (Girouard 1963).

7. Formal specification languages such as B, Z, and VDM remain the domain of mathematicians. However, progress is being made to improve the formality of widespread modeling techniques.

8. This is in contrast to reverse engineering or implementation-driven approaches.

9. American Heritage Dictionary (1994): "**en·tro·py** n., pl. en·tro·pies. **1.** Symbol S for a closed thermodynamic system, a quantitative measure of the amount of thermal energy not available to do work. **2.** A measure of the disorder or randomness in a closed system. **3.** A measure of the loss of information in a transmitted message. **4.** A hypothetical tendency for all matter and energy in the universe to evolve toward a state of inert uniformity. **5.** Inevitable and steady deterioration of a system or society."

10. This is not the case in most design styles and tools today, where, in every instance, upstream from the compiler, design styles and tools operate in the optimistic bliss of zero constraints only to hit the wall of reality during system implementation.

Chapter 2

1. I am not alone in this point of view. See Lewis (1999), for example.

2. IDE is an acronym for integrated development environment, made popular in the IT field by mainstream programming IDEs. IT-architectural IDE may be abbreviated to architectural IDE when the IT context is clear.

3. Often referred to as business-to-customer (B2C) interaction.

4. Often referred to as enterprise application integration (EAI) and business-to-business (B2B) interaction, respectively.

5. See the Convergent Architecture Web site, www.ConvergentArchitecture.com, for projections to further J2EE/EJB servers as well as to other implementation frameworks.

6. As explained later in this book, I call a person who is effectively fulfilling the role of architect according to the Convergent Architecture a *convergent architect*.

7. Or a J2EE/EJB-type environment, such as a closely related CORBA components server. Mapping alternatives to other server infrastructures are discussed in Chapter 7 and in the Web site chapter.

Chapter 3

1. Epiphenomenon: A term coined by Douglas Hofstadter (Hofstadter 1979) denoting emergent properties (Taylor 1997) of a system that cannot be attributed to a single act or unitary feature within a system, but rather is a cumulative result of complex interactions within a system. Adjectives used to explain software or team behavior, such as *performance, reliability,* and *usability,* are usually epiphenomena.

2. In 1995 I investigated this similarity and am convinced that neither party knew of the other's work at the time.

3. *American Heritage Dictionary* (1994): "**i·so·mor·phism** n. **2.** Mathematics. A one-to-one correspondence between the elements of two sets such that the result of an operation on elements of one set corresponds to the result of the analogous operation on their images in the other set."

4. It is disconcerting to see that this is not usually the case. Most IT consultants, in fact, have never attempted to model their own business domain.

Chapter 4

1. Aspects that we are actively contributing to the Model-Driven Architecture (MDA 2001) initiative at the OMG.

2. See the *Convergent Architecture* Web site, www.ConvergentArchitecture.com, for more information on such resources.

3. In modern Internet terminology, UI-accessors cater to the specific requirements of business-to-customer (B2C) interactions, whereas SI-accessors address the specific requirements of business-to-business (B2B) interactions, B2X, business process integration, and Web services.

4. Although patterns permeate *Convergent Architecture*, this is not a book on patterns. Some of the patterns used are well known, some are recently published, and others are unpublished. They are applied in a matter-of-fact way throughout the architectural style and, in the interest of my focus on architectural style, will not be pointed out explicitly in each instance. Outlining each pattern and describing how it is used and implemented would constitute enough material for an entire book itself. For a good starting point on many of the design patterns used by *Convergent Architecture*, see java.sun.com/j2ee/blueprints/design_patterns.

5. In current OMG/MDA terminology, the TPC constitutes the *core UML models* (UML profiles) and the standard *mappings* plus additional stylistic guidelines and the respective automation levels of the technology projection.

6. Which in theory is always a good idea, but is not always practical.

7. Object orientation adds three powerful modeling tools to traditional procedural representations. One of these tools is *type abstraction,* also known as *inheritance.* The other two are class-level *data abstraction* (encapsulation) and *function abstraction* (polymorphism). See Taylor (1997) for a pragmatic introduction to these concepts.

8. Another well-known style defines driving on the left side of the road as its standard.

9. With respect to current OMG/MDA concepts, the business components begin with a core model at the level of a responsibility-driven design at the CRC business model level and evolve along a structured path, via mapping patterns, into UML along the course of convergent model refinement (see Chapter 6).

Chapter 5

1. Some prefer the term *owner* to *manager* because manager has so many different interpretations. I have chosen to use the term manager to remain in line with the RUP terminology, and then to define what I mean when I use the word manager.

2. A system architect, as defined by the RUP, who is effectively fulfilling this role in the context of *Convergent Architecture* is a convergent architect.

3. This is a style-specific application of the concepts formulated in RUP Technical White Paper TP505, "Applying Requirements Management with Use-Cases" (Oberg 2000).

4. This is a style-specific application of the concepts formulated in the RUP Work Guideline, "Developing Large-Scale Systems with the Rational Unified Process" (Kruchten 2000).

5. Note that an assembly is an organization from a purely IT perspective. It organizes deployable IT resources. It does not represent a core business organization and is assigned this special name to make this distinction clear.

Chapter 6

1. I refer to this as *style-driven assisted modeling*.

2. Defining every detail of software development as an activity is impossible. Trying to achieve this would bloat the process to the point where nobody paid any attention to it. Not only would it be too voluminous, it also would be unrealistically constraining. An effective process must be very selective about what it prescribes and what it leaves up to the well-defined responsibilities of the IT organization.

3. The desirable side effect of this cycle is that the design is always in sync with the implementation, the integrity of the design is immediately verified at the UML level, and the system design is implicitly documented in UML.

4. This is equivalent to applying patterns to generate other customized or more highly specific patterns.

Chapter 7

1. Component inheritance is not defined by the current J2EE/EJB standard; thus any support for component inheritance constitutes a unique, added-value feature of the particular application server. The extent and usability of these features differ greatly between application servers.

2. There are several very good reasons for generating intermediate JPython code from all the interacting parts of the cartridge, for example, to improve reuse, debugging, and generation performance.

3. It is important to note that this constitutes generated code that was automatically derived from a previously generated model, which was derived in an assisted manner from a business model. Not just one automation step, but a whole series of increasingly powerful automation steps are made possible by the architectural style.

Index

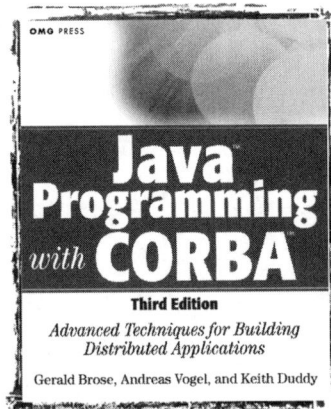